Racial Inequity in Special Education

Racial Inequity

in

Special Education

Edited by
DANIEL J. LOSEN
GARY ORFIELD

Foreword by
SENATOR JAMES M. JEFFORDS

The Civil Rights Project at Harvard University
Harvard Education Press

Library of Congress Control Number 2002107059
ISBN 1-891792-05-9 (cloth)
ISBN 1-891792-04-0 (paper)

Published by Harvard Education Press,
an imprint of the Harvard Education Publishing Group

Harvard Education Press
8 Story Street, 5th Floor
Cambridge, MA 02138

Cover Design: Alyssa Morris
Cover Photo: © Susie Fitzhugh
Editorial Production: Dody Riggs
Typography: Sheila Walsh

The typeface used in this book is Adobe Garamond, a contemporary typeface
based on one created by Claude Garamond in the early 1500s.

To Sammy and Lenny

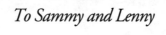

Contents

Foreword

I was a freshman member of Congress in 1975, one of only seventeen Republicans elected to the House of Representatives in the wake of Watergate. As such, I was named the ranking Republican on the Select Education Subcommittee and charged with helping to write what would later become the Individuals with Disabilities Education Act (IDEA).

As you will learn from reading *Racial Inequity in Special Education,* the benefits of special education are not always extended equally to students with disabilities, despite the best intentions of the law. These alarming disparities suggest that we need to do better. We *must* do better.

I commend the authors for taking a hard look at this subject. This book provides important direction, for those of us in Congress and for those in our schools. The authors show us where we need to do better to ensure equal educational opportunities for *all* of our students, whatever their race or socioeconomic status. Where school leadership fails to address those issues that have an adverse impact on children of color and children with disabilities, we must bolster our efforts to protect every child's civil rights.

There is no doubt that successfully addressing the issues raised in this book, particularly as they relate to children of color, will require an infusion of funding for higher quality teaching in both general and special education, early intervention, increased training for school administrators and teachers, and greater access to effective special education supports and services in the least restrictive environment. We must also ensure that even the highest poverty school districts have the means necessary to provide the free appropriate public education that all children with disabilities are entitled to.

I see this as part of a larger issue—to get adequate resources properly targeted for all children who need them. When the initial special education legislation was being drafted in 1975, twenty-six federal court decisions had been consolidated to make the case that children with disabilities had a constitutional right to receive a free and appropriate education. We had to see that this was enforced, and it was not an easy task. As we labored over the details, those of us who worked on the bill agreed that this was a difficult but extremely important step.

We knew it would be costly, and we all believed that since it was a federal constitutional guarantee, the federal government should bear a good portion of the cost. In the end, we agreed that 40 percent of the additional costs of special education would be paid by the federal government.

We have seen much progress since we passed the initial legislation. Children with disabilities are now being educated alongside their peers in unprecedented numbers. We have shown that education helps these children lead more independent and fulfilling lives. We have learned that investing in special education enriches society as a whole.

But we have fallen woefully short on our funding commitment. Today, the federal government pays only 17 percent of special education costs. The chronic underfunding of special education is inexcusable. It was also a major factor in my decision to leave the Republican Party in 2001 and declare myself an independent.

When I went to battle with the Bush administration last year over reaching the 40 percent funding figure, the administration argued against approving any increase until the overidentification of special education children, specifically minorities, was fully studied. I countered that by not fully funding special education we were robbing other vital educational programs, such as early education, which are such a critical part of our system.

The evidence overwhelmingly shows that quality early education dramatically reduces the need for special education placement in later years. Therefore, it could be said that the lack of early educational programs such as Head Start is more likely the reason for high identification of special education needs. My arguments were made to no avail.

States and towns are left to bear the burden of the federal government's failure to live up to its long-ignored promise. In my home state of Vermont, and in the nation, this is a trend that cannot be sustained. If we had met our 40 percent commitment, Vermont's share of special education funding would have been $32.6 million in fiscal year 2002, rather than $13.2 million. I have heard the cries for help, from parents, teachers, local school boards, and legislators. In fact, state legislatures throughout the country have made full funding of IDEA a top priority.

This problem will only grow worse as the number of children enrolled in special education continues to grow. Figures recently released by the U.S. Census Bureau suggest that one out of every twelve children in the United States has a physical or mental disability, a sharp increase from the previous decade. Special education enrollments have spiraled in the past decade, and more children are being diagnosed with multiple disabilities.

The solution is not difficult. I have proposed legislation to boost special education funding by $2.5 billion each year until 2007, at which time Congress will have met its 40 percent commitment. I will continue these efforts for as long as I serve in the U.S. Senate, and I remain hopeful that we will eventually succeed. The gaps in our system are not entirely about money, but fully funding special education would ease the pressures on schools throughout the country.

We have come a long way since 1975, but there is still much work to be done.

SENATOR JAMES M. JEFFORDS
Independent-Vermont

Acknowledgements

The editors are deeply grateful to have worked with the authors who contributed papers to this volume. Their diverse perspectives, work, and insights have made putting this book together an exciting and extremely rewarding experience.

Carolyn Peelle deserves an especially warm thank you. She did a tremendous amount of editing, and her tireless efforts were essential to the successful completion of this volume. Much credit also goes to Dody Riggs of the Harvard Education Press. Without her good-spirited time management, careful edits, and coordination of the publishing process this work would not be possible.

Dennis Hayes, the membership of the NAACP, and numerous other civil rights advocates must be thanked, as it was their inquiries that prompted the Civil Rights Project at Harvard University to explore the racial inequities in special education.

The research presented in these chapters was first introduced during our 2000 conference, "Minority Issues in Special Education," which was made possible by a grant from the Spencer Foundation, to which we are grateful. We are also grateful to the Carnegie Corporation, the Ford Foundation, the John D. and Catherine T. MacArthur Foundation, and the Charles Stewart Mott Foundation for their support of work on K–12 education issues at the Civil Rights Project.

We were extremely fortunate to have the collective wisdom of professors Martha Minow, Christopher Edley, Jr., Tom Hehir, and Beth Harry to guide us in approving paper proposals and helping plan our original conference. We owe special recognition to the American Policy Youth Forum and the National Institute for Urban School Improvement for their important contributions following the conference.

This book is the product of intensive collaboration with experts in the field. The entire staff of the Civil Rights Project has also provided an enormous amount of support for the production of the book in countless ways; our special thanks go to Elizabeth DeBray, Johanna Wald, Marilyn Byrne, John Yun,

Angelo Ancheta, Laurent Heller, Alison Harris, Scott Palmer, and Stelios Koutnatzis.

Dan Losen would also like to acknowledge the love, help, humor, and generosity of his wife Sarah Novogrodsky, and of his parents, Stuart and Joyce Losen, all of whom, as public school educators, have inspired him with their hard work and dedication to improving the education experiences of disadvantaged children and their families.

Dan would also like to express deep gratitude to his mentors in education law and policy, Christopher Edley, Jr., Thomas Mela, and Martha Minow. He has had the good fortune to benefit from their caring, support, acumen, and wisdom. Finally, as this book evolved from research conference concept to book publication, Gary Orfield has been a constant source of encouragement, inspiration, leadership, and levity. The critical insights Dan has gained from working with these mentors has enlightened him in immeasurable ways and enabled him to better serve the goal of racial justice in education.

Gary Orfield expresses his deep admiration for the dedication, care, understanding, and endless hard work of Dan Losen, without whom this important work could never have been accomplished.

Racial Inequity in Special Education

DANIEL J. LOSEN
GARY ORFIELD

Before Congress passed the Education for All Handicapped Children Act—now known as the Individuals with Disabilities Education Act (IDEA)—nearly half of the nation's approximately four million children with disabilities were not receiving a public education.[1] Of the children who were being educated in public schools, many were relegated to a ghetto-like existence in isolated, often run-down classrooms located in the least desirable places within the school building, or sent to entirely separate facilities.[2] Since its passage in 1975, the IDEA has brought tremendous benefits: today, approximately six million children with disabilities enjoy their right to a free appropriate public education.[3] IDEA's substantive rights and procedural protections have produced significant and measurable outcomes for students with disabilities: their graduation rates have increased dramatically, and the number of these students who go on to college has almost tripled since 1978 (though it is still quite low).[4]

Despite these improvements, the benefits of special education have not been equitably distributed. Minority children with disabilities all too often experience inadequate services, low-quality curriculum and instruction, and unnecessary isolation from their nondisabled peers. Moreover, inappropriate practices in both general and special education classrooms have resulted in over-representation, misclassification, and hardship for minority students, particularly black children.

A flood of concerns expressed by community leaders about minority children being misplaced in special education prompted The Civil Rights Project at Harvard University to commission the research for this book. Since the early 1970s, national surveys by the Office for Civil Rights (OCR) of the U.S. Department of Education have revealed persistent overrepresentation of minority children in certain disability categories.[5] The most pronounced disparities then were black[6] children who, while only 16 percent of the total school enrollment, represented 38 percent of the students in classes for the educationally mentally retarded.[7] After more than twenty years, black children constitute 17 percent of the total school enrollment and 33 percent of those labeled mentally retarded— only a marginal improvement.[8] During this same period, however, disproportionality in the area of emotional disturbance (ED) and the rate of identification for both ED and specific learning disabilities (SLD) grew significantly for blacks.[9]

To better understand this persistent overrepresentation trend, as well as growing reports of profound inequities in the quality of special education, The Civil Rights Project set out to find the best research available. In the original call for papers we asked leading scholars from around the country to document and clarify the issues for minority students with regard to special education. As researchers pursued this task and analyzed possible contributing factors, our fears about the persistence of these problems, the complexities of the contributing factors, and the lack of proven solutions were confirmed.

Our primary purpose in presenting this information is to identify and solve the problem, not to assign blame. This research is intended to inform the debate on special education and racial justice and to provide educators, researchers, advocates, and policymakers with a deeper understanding of the issues as they renew their efforts to find workable solutions. Using national-, state-, district-, and school-level data, these studies document the current trends for minority students regarding identification and restrictiveness of placement. They explore some of the most likely causes, dispel some myths and oversimplified explanations, and highlight the complex interplay of variables within the control of educators at all levels of government. Recognizing the critical role that advocacy has played in securing the rights of all children to educational opportunity, this book also provides analysis of the evolving role of the law in stopping inappropriate practices that harm children of color, and in guaranteeing equitable benefits from special education.

The findings in this book point to areas where much improvement is needed and offer an array of ideas for remedies and suggestions for continued research. It is important to recognize that concerns about special education are nested in concerns about inequities in education generally. Special education overrepresentation often mirrors overrepresentation in many undesirable categories—including dropping out, low-track placements, suspensions, and involvement with juvenile justice—and underrepresentation in desirable categories such as gifted and talented (see Figure 1). Because special education inequities are often tied to general education issues, remedies should address shortcomings in both special and general education. The recommendations, which are aimed at improving policy and practice, were developed through ex-

FIGURE 1

Racial Disparities for Special Education Mirror Disparities in
Other Aspects of Schooling

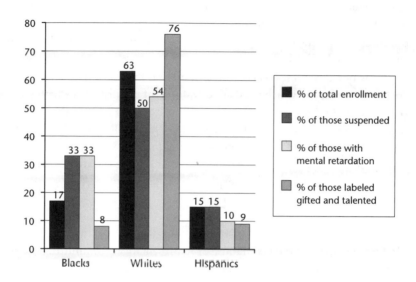

Source: Office for Civil Rights 1998 data (see note 8).

tensive analysis of the efforts and experiences of educators, policymakers, attorneys, and civil rights enforcement agents. We hope the recommendations will help prevent harmful misidentification and inappropriate placements of minority students, and encourage effective and equitable leadership, enforcement, and distribution of resources to ensure that all children who need special education support receive appropriate and high-quality services.

ISSUES EXPLORED AND FINDINGS

Much of the empirical research in this book explores patterns of overrepresentation of minority children by disability category and whether, once identified, they experience relatively less access to the general education classroom than similarly situated white children. The evidence suggests that black overrepresentation is substantial in state after state. The studies reveal wide differences in disability identification between blacks and Hispanics and between black boys and black girls that cannot be explained in terms of social background or measured ability.

Both the statistical and qualitative analyses in this book suggest that these racial, ethnic, and gender differences are due to many complex and interacting factors, including unconscious racial bias on the part of school authorities, large resource inequalities that run along lines of race and class, unjustifiable reliance on IQ and other evaluation tools, educators' inappropriate responses to the pressures of high-stakes testing, and power differentials between minority parents and school officials.

This book examines whether the numerous causes of overrepresentation are likely race linked, which is a distinctly different inquiry from whether intentional racial discrimination is the primary cause. Absent a blatantly discriminatory (i.e., illegal as written) policy or practice, to establish that different treatment is purposeful and racist requires specific proof of intent, which is usually discovered through legal enforcement proceedings. The research in this book is obviously not specific enough to explore questions of intent.[10]

Overidentification

On October 4, 2001, the U.S. House of Representatives Committee on Education and the Workforce convened hearings about the overidentification of minority students in special education. In his testimony, Representative Chaka Fattah concluded with the following story of Billy Hawkins:

> For the first fifteen years of his, life Billy Hawkins was labeled by his teachers as "educable mentally retarded." Billy was backup quarterback for his high school football team. One night he was called off the bench and rallied his team from far behind. In doing so, he ran complicated plays and clearly demonstrated a gift for the game. The school principal, who was in the stands, recognized that the "retarded boy" could play, and soon after had Billy enrolled in regular classes and instructed his teachers to give him extra help. Billy Hawkins went on to complete a Ph.D. and is now Associate Dean at Michigan's Ferris State University.[11]

Students like Billy Hawkins seldom get the "call off the bench" and an opportunity to shine in front of their principal. Instead, they are removed from the mainstream and never realize their talent. Unfortunately, some in Congress responded to findings we released in earlier reports and to stories like Dr. Hawkins' by opposing efforts to guarantee and fully fund special education at the level Congress originally intended,[12] claiming a need to "fix" special education before providing more funds.[13] This book addresses discrete areas of deep racial inequity within a much larger system of special education. It would be wrong to restrict or withhold promised expenditures for all students with disabilities in every state of the nation based on the issues identified in this research.

Of the inequalities in education experienced by minority schoolchildren, those in special education are better documented than most. In 1998, approximately 1.5 million minority children were identified as having mental retardation, emotional disturbance, or a specific learning disability.[14] More than 876,000 of these were black or Native American,[15] and black students were nearly three times as likely as white students to be labeled mentally retarded.[16] Mental retardation diagnoses are relatively rare for all children, and the last twenty years have witnessed a modest decrease in the percentages of students labeled mentally retarded for nearly all racial groups.[17]

Despite this fact, U.S. Department of Education data from 2000–2001 show that in at least thirteen states more than 2.75 percent of all blacks enrolled were labeled mentally retarded. The prevalence of mental retardation for whites nationally was approximately 0.75 percent in 2001, and in no state did the incidence among whites ever rise above 2.32 percent.[18] Moreover, nearly three-quarters of the states with unusually high incidence rates (2.75%–5.41%) for blacks were in the South.[19] This is arguably a continuation of the problem as a southern phenomenon that was first observed in the National Research Council's data from 1979,[20] although both then and now many northern states also exhibit remarkably high rates. One positive sign is that southern states exhibited the largest decreases in sheer percentages since 1979.[21]

The data in these studies are generally analyzed in one of three ways. In one, a given minority group's percentage enrollment in the general population is compared to that group's percentage identification in a given disability category. In the second, the actual risk level for a minority group is calculated by dividing the number of students from a given racial group with a given disability by the total enrollment of that racial group. And in the third way, these risk levels are calculated for each minority group and then compared. These comparisons are described as risk ratios and are usually reported in comparison to white children.[22]

In chapter two, Tom Parrish, a senior research analyst with the American Institutes for Research, calculates risk levels using U.S. Department of Education data based on the number of children eligible for special education reported by each state for children between the ages of six and twenty-one in 1998, and compares that with census estimates of children of the same age for each state for the same year. Parrish then calculates the risk ratios for each minority group by cognitive disability category for every state and for the nation.

He finds that black children are 2.88 times more likely than whites to be labeled mentally retarded and 1.92 times more likely to be labeled emotionally disturbed.

Blacks are the most overrepresented minority group in every category and in nearly every state.[23] The gross racial disparities that exist between many minority groups and whites in terms of mental retardation also exist in other cognitive disability categories, but are less pronounced. Nationwide, blacks and Native Americans are less often overidentified for specific learning disabilities (i.e., black children are more than twice as likely as white children to be found to have a specific learning disability in only nine states).

Parrish also shows the extent of overidentification of other minorities in the ED and SLD categories.[24] In the SLD category, for example, only in Hawaii are Asian Americans/Pacific Islanders identified at nearly twice the rate of whites. On the other hand, Native American children in six states are identified at more than twice the rate of whites.

Latinos and Asian Americans are generally underidentified compared to whites in most states and in most categories, raising the possibility of inadequate attention to their special needs; however, the state-level data may underreport the problem for some groups. According to a 1982 National Research Council (NRC) report, district-level data on Hispanics from 1979 suggested that a wide variety of both over- and underrepresentation tended to cancel each other out in aggregate state-level data.[25] Neither the 2002 NRC report, "Minority Students in Special and Gifted Education," nor the studies in this book conducted a district-level analysis with national data comparable to that contained in the 1982 study of Hispanic identification rates. However, Alfredo Artiles, Robert Rueda, Jesús José Salazar, and Ignacio Higareda, in their analysis of large urban school districts in California, reveal that disproportionate representation in special education is far more likely for (predominantly Latino) English-language learners in secondary school than in elementary school. Thus, the problem may even be hidden when elementary and secondary school data are aggregated at the district level.

Edward Fierros and James Conroy's research in chapter three, which does examine district-level data from throughout Connecticut and from selected U.S. cities, suggests that the state data may miss disturbing trends for minority overrepresentation in a given category or educational setting.[26] Generally speaking, the most serious racial disparities (both under- and overrepresentation) become apparent when data on minority children are disaggregated by race/ethnicity subgroups, cognitive disability category, gender, and placement—at least down to the district level.

Educational Placement

Readers should not forget that students with disabilities are entitled to receive supports and services in a setting best suited to their individual needs, and not to be automatically assigned to a separate place, subjected to low expectations, or excluded from educational opportunities. While substantially separate educational environments are certainly best for some individuals, it is equally well established in research that students with disabilities benefit most when they are educated with their general education peers to the maximum extent appropriate, and this is reflected in the law.[27]

Fierros and Conroy's work demonstrates that, once identified as eligible for special education services, both Latinos and blacks are far less likely than whites to be educated in a fully inclusive general education classroom and far more likely to be educated in a substantially separate setting. The data Fierros and Conroy explore show a consistent trend toward less inclusion for minority children at the national, state, and district levels. The relationship between race and greater exclusion, also not examined in the NRC's 2002 report, suggests that, among students with disabilities, black and Latino children with disabilities may be consistently receiving less desirable treatment than white children. Fierros and Conroy further disaggregate the racial data by disability type for the state of Connecticut and find a lower level of inclusion for blacks and Hispanics compared to whites among each of the three disability types examined (students with mental retardation, emotional disturbance, and specific learning disabilities).

The concern with the overrepresentation of minorities would be mitigated if the evidence suggested that minority children reaped benefits from more frequent identification and isolation. But as government officials acknowledge[28] and as data demonstrate, this does not appear to be the case.[29]

Low-Quality Evaluations, Supports, and Services

In their chapter, David Osher, Darren Woodruff, and Anthony Sims illustrate how the issue is often not as simple as the false identification of a nondisabled minority child. Many minority children do have disabilities but are at risk of receiving inappropriate and inadequate services and unwarranted isolation. Osher et al. point out that, for some children, receiving inappropriate services may be more harmful than receiving none at all. For others, not receiving help early enough may exacerbate learning and behavior problems.

Both problems are reflected in disturbing statistics on outcomes for minority children with disabilities. As Donald Oswald, Martha Coutinho, and Al Best report in the opening lines of the book's first chapter, there are dramatic differences in what happens to minority students with disabilities after high school:

> In the 1998–1999 school year, over 2.2 million children of color in U.S. schools were served by special education (U.S. Department of Education, 2000). Post–high school outcomes for these minority students with disabilities are strikingly inferior. Among high school youth with disabilities, about 75 percent of African American students, as compared to 47 percent of white students, are not employed two years out of school. Slightly more than half (52%) of African Americans, compared to 39 percent of white young adults, are still not employed three to five years out of school. In this same time period, the arrest rate for African Americans with disabilities is 40 percent, as compared to 27 percent for whites (Wagner, D'Amico, Marder, Newman, & Blackorby, 1992).

In addition to these patterns, Osher, Woodruff, and Sims provide new data depicting substantially higher rates of disciplinary action and placement in correctional facilities for minority students with disabilities still in school. Based on their review of the data and other research, they suggest that investments in high-quality special education and early intervention are sorely needed and could reduce the likelihood that minority students with disabilities will develop serious discipline problems or eventually wind up in correctional facilities.

Racial Discrimination and Other Contributing Factors

In a society where race is so strongly related to individual, family, and community conditions, it is extremely difficult to know what part of the inequalities are caused by discrimination within the school. These studies, however, do uncover correlations with race that cannot be explained by factors such as poverty or exposure to environmental hazards alone. While the scope of this research does not attempt to depict a definitive causal link to racial discrimination, the research does suggest that unconscious racial bias, stereotypes, and other race-linked factors have a significant impact on the patterns of identification, placement, and quality of services for minority children, and particularly for African American children.

The researchers recognize that factors such as poverty and environmental influences outside of school contribute to a heightened incidence of disability in significant ways. All analysts who attempt to sort out the causes of inequality in U.S. institutions of course face the dilemma that some of the differences in subtracted control variables are themselves products of other forms of racial discrimination. For example, if a researcher determined that 40 percent of the association between race and shorter life expectancy could be explained by poverty, we have to understand that the poverty in question may be influenced by employment discrimination or be due in part to a second-generational effect of segregated schooling. Therefore, despite the importance of statistical controls, it is well established that many controls will lower the estimates of the effect of race when race is examined as an isolated variable. What happens in school is only a subset of the far more pervasive impact of racial discrimination that affects minority families and their children.

Even when researchers assume that poverty is independent of race and subtract race and other background variables, many of the trends highlighted by this research appear to contradict the theory that poverty is primarily to blame and that race is not a significant factor. Those trends include the following: (a) pronounced and persistent racial disparities in identification between white and black children in the categories of mental retardation and emotional disturbance, compared with far less disparity in the category of specific learning disabilities; (b) a minimal degree of racial disparity in medically diagnosed disabilities as compared with subjective cognitive disabilities; (c) dramatic differences in the incidence of disability from one state to the next; and (d) gross disparities between blacks and Hispanics, and between black boys and girls, in identification rates for the categories of mentally retarded and emotionally disturbed.

The data on disproportionate representation is compatible with the theory that systemic racial discrimination is a contributing factor where disparities are substantial. Moreover, the trends revealed in this book are consistent with the theory that different racial groups, facing different kinds of stereotypes and bias, would experience racial disparities differently. States with a history of racial apartheid under de jure segregation, for example, account for five of the seven states with the highest overrepresentation of African Americans labeled mentally retarded—Mississippi, South Carolina, North Carolina, Florida, and Alabama.[30] This trend suggests that the "soft bigotry of low expectations" may have replaced the undeniable intentional racial discrimination in education against blacks that once pervaded the South.[31] In contrast, *no* southern state was among the top seven states where Hispanic children deemed mentally retarded were most heavily overrepresented.[32]

The effects of poverty cannot satisfactorily explain racial disparities in identification for mental retardation or emotional disturbance. Regression analysis suggests that race, gender, and poverty are all significant factors. Oswald, Coutinho, and Best specifically asked whether, "taking into account the effects of social, demographic, and school-related variables, gender and ethnicity are significantly associated with the risk of being identified for special education."[33] Their examination of each factor at the district level (based on all of the districts surveyed in OCR's database combined with the National Center for Education

Statistics, Common Core of Data) finds that, although disability incidence often increases with poverty, when poverty- and wealth-linked factors are controlled for, ethnicity and gender remain significant predictors of cognitive disability identification by schools.[34] Specifically, wealth-linked factors included per pupil expenditure, median housing value, median income for households with children, percentage of children in households below the poverty level, and percentage of adults in the community who have a twelfth-grade education or less and no diploma.

Most disturbing was that in wealthier districts, contrary to the expected trend, black children, especially males, were *more likely to be labeled* mentally retarded.[35] Moreover, the sharp gender differences in identification within racial groups, also described in the 2002 NRC report,[36] are not explained by the poverty theory.

Large demographic differences among minority groups are also discussed by Parrish and by Fierros and Conroy, and each confirms that the influence of race and ethnicity is significant, and apparently distinct from that of poverty. For example, Parrish reviews the data for each racial group across all fifty states and finds that, in comparison to whites, each minority group is at greater risk of being labeled mentally retarded as their percentage of the total enrolled population increases.[37]

That poverty does account for some of the observed racial disproportions in disability identification comes as no surprise. Certain minority groups are disproportionately poor. Logically, one would expect poverty to cause a higher incidence of "hard" disabilities (e.g., blindness and deafness) among members of low-wealth minority groups, due to the impact of poor nutrition and inadequate prenatal care.[38] But the most recent research shows that blacks in any given state are substantially less likely to be overrepresented in these hard categories.[39]

Finally, the theory that poverty and socioeconomic factors can explain all or most of the observed racial disparities fails to account for the *extreme* differences between black overrepresentation and Hispanic underrepresentation, differences that are even more significant in many states than disparities between blacks and whites.[40] For example, blacks in Alabama and Arkansas are more than seven to nine times as likely as Hispanics to be labeled mentally retarded.[41] Moreover, nationally and in many other states,[42] the disparity in identification rates for mental retardation and emotional disturbance between blacks and Hispanics is greater than the disparity between blacks and whites. Yet Hispanics, like blacks, are at far greater risk than whites for poverty,[43] exposure to environmental toxins in impoverished neighborhoods,[44] and low-level academic achievement in reading and math.[45] Thus, the high variation in identification rates among minority groups with similar levels of poverty and academic failure casts serious doubt on assertions by some researchers that it is primarily poverty and not bias that creates these deep racial disparities.[46]

Multiple Contributing Factors

Most students with disabilities enter school undiagnosed and are referred by regular classroom teachers for evaluations that may lead to special education identification and placement. Therefore, the cause of the observed racial disparity is rooted not only in the system of special education itself, but also in the system of regular education as it encompasses special education.[47] Most students referred for evaluation for special education are deemed in need of services.[48] If differential referral is a key element, then the perceptions and decisions of classroom teachers, as well as school-level policies and practices that have an impact on students in regular classrooms, are, likewise, key elements.

Based on years of research, Beth Harry, Janette Klingner, Keith Sturges, and Robert Moore conclude in their chapter that "[t]he point at which differences [in measured performance and ability] result in one child being labeled disabled and another not are totally matters of social decisionmaking."[49] Special education evaluations are often presented to parents as a set of discrete decisions based on scientific analysis and assessment,[50] but even test-driven decisions are inescapably subjective in nature.[51] The existence of some bias in test *content* is not the primary concern. Harry et al.'s research, for example, describes how subjective decisions creep into all elements of the evaluation *process,* including whom to test, what test to use, when to use alternative tests, how to interpret student responses, and what weight to give results from specific tests. All of these alter the outcomes.[52] As Harry et al. point out, "a penstroke of the American Association on Mental Retardation (AAMR)" lowered the IQ score cutoff point for mental retardation from 85 to 70, "swiftly curing thousands of previously disabled children."[53]

School politics, power relationships between school authorities and minority parents, the quality of regular education, and the classroom management skills of the referring teacher also introduce important elements of subjectivity that often go unrecognized.[54] Other race-linked forces at work include poorly trained teachers who are disproportionately employed in minority schools (some of whom use special education as a disciplinary tool),[55] other resource inequalities correlated to race,[56] beliefs in African American and Latino inferiority and the low expectations that accompany these beliefs,[57] cultural insensitivity,[58] praise differentials,[59] fear and misunderstanding of black males,[60] and overcrowded schools and classrooms that are disproportionately located in school districts with high percentages of minority students.[61] Add to these forces the general phenomenon of white parents' activism, efficaciousness, and high social capital exercised on behalf of their children[62] compared to the relative lack of parent power among minority parents,[63] and one can understand how the combination of regular education problems and the special education identification process has had a disparate impact on students of different races and ethnicities.

Sweeping reforms may also trigger harmful outcomes. For example, Artiles et al.'s preliminary examination of the "Unz Initiative," which eliminated bilingual education in California, suggests that English-language learners whose access to language supports is limited are more likely to be placed in restrictive special education settings. And as Jay Heubert describes in detail in his chapter, over the last ten years the use of high-stakes testing may have disproportionately punished poor and minority students, students with disabilities, and English-language learners:[64] "There is evidence that states with high minority enrollments in special education are also likely to have high-stakes testing policies."[65] Heubert goes on to cite evidence that "promotion testing is . . . likely to increase, perhaps significantly, the numbers of students with disabilities and minority students who suffer the serious consequences of dropping out."[66] He points out that the National Research Council has described simple retention in grade as "an ineffective intervention."[67] The aspirational benefits of raising standards aside, Heubert concludes that minority students with disabilities are at "great risk . . . especially in states that administer high-stakes promotion and graduation tests. . . ."[68]

The Status of the Law and Enforcement Policy

Beginning with *Brown v. Board of Education,* litigation and enforcement under civil rights law has been essential to improving racial equity in education. Title VI of the Civil Rights Act of 1964 provided an important lever for racial justice in education that was especially effective when the federal government made enforcement a high priority.[69] Critically important was that, under the Title VI regulations, plaintiffs could use statistical evidence to prove that even a policy that was race neutral on its face had an adverse and unjustifiably disparate impact on children of color in violation of the law. As Daniel Losen and Kevin Welner describe in their chapter, the legal landscape shifted dramatically following the U.S. Supreme Court's 2001 ruling in *Alexander v. Sandoval,* which declared that there is no implied private right of action to bring legal challenges under "disparate-impact" theory. Therefore, court challenges that would rely on serious statistical disparities to prove allegations of discrimination are nearly extinguished today.[70] Although the government and individuals filing complaints with government agencies may still use the Title VI regulations to redress the racially disparate impact of neutral policies, enforcement of disparate impact regulations is more vulnerable to an administration's enforcement policy preferences than ever before.

Untouched by *Sandoval* is the potential to challenge policies or practices where the racial disparities in special education identification or placement arise in the context of hearings on school desegregation. For example, in Alabama in 2000, a court review of consent decrees in that state resulted in a settlement yielding comprehensive state- and district-level remedies for overidentification of minorities.

Losen and Welner point out that disability law is becoming a relatively stronger basis for leveraging remedies from states and school districts where overidentification, underservicing, or unnecessarily restrictive placements are an issue. They explain further how systemic legal actions are better suited for seeking effective comprehensive remedies that could address contributing factors in both regular and special education. In her chapter, Theresa Glennon closely examines and evaluates the Office for Civil Rights' enforcement efforts where disability law and Title VI converge. Glennon's recommendations include better coordinated investigations and interagency information sharing, clearer guidance for schools, and more comprehensive compliance reviews by well-trained investigators.

Sharon Soltman and Donald Moore provide an extensive analysis of how to fashion a remedy through litigation in a case known as *Corey H.* Their thorough chapter combines many years of research on effective practices with models of school improvement. They set forth a roadmap for school district reform to ensure that children with disabilities in Illinois be educated in the least restrictive environment as required by law. The multitiered *Corey H.* remedy entails a ten-year process for change, in one set of schools each year. The plaintiffs also won a large infusion of state funding to make implementing the *Corey H.* requirements a fully funded mandate. Further research on the efficacy of the court-ordered remedy should prove extremely useful to policymakers and others seeking to guarantee that minority children with disabilities have appropriate educational opportunities.

The only study in this volume that explores restricting federal funds as a remedy does so in the context of analyzing the viability of the Department of Education's Office for Special Education Programs' (OSEP) enforcement mechanisms for redressing racial disproportionality. In that study, Thomas Hehir argues forcefully for more frequent exercise of partial withholding by enforcement agents that is narrowly targeted to leverage compliance by specific states or districts in certain areas. As Hehir points out, partial withholding would allow OSEP to ratchet up its enforcement efforts without wholesale withdrawal of federal funds, which would heighten the risk of political backlash and have a negative impact on students in properly run programs. Likewise, federal policymakers should improve IDEA implementation and civil rights enforcement without imposing wholesale limitations on federal special education funding, which would have a negative impact on children with disabilities nationwide. Of course, there may be extreme cases in noncompliant districts where the only way to end serious violations is to cut off general funds, which proved very effective in spurring the desegregation of southern schools.[71]

Moreover, Tom Parrish's research suggests that some state funding formulas are contributing to problems of overidentification. Some of these formulas fail to follow the federal model, which relies on U.S. Census data to determine allocations. The most problematic state formulas instead channel funds by disability identification and/or program and are suspected of creating incentives for overidentification.

RECOMMENDATIONS

These studies and the NRC's 2002 report both suggest that special education issues faced by minority children often begin with shortcomings in the realm of general education well before teachers or parents seek an evaluation for special education eligibility.[72] Therefore, policy solutions that fail to consider the connection with general education classrooms will unlikely bring about significant change.[73]

A New Federal Initiative with Implications for State Accountability

Our nation's education policy is at a crossroads. Leaders demand an end to the "soft bigotry of low expectations" and our government has promised to improve the achievement of all children in 2002 through the new education reform act, known as the No Child Left Behind Act. Racial equity is rooted in the commitment to teach all children well, with particular attention to meeting the needs of minority children.

To tackle racial disparities in achievement and graduation rates, the president and Congress embraced three reform approaches: public reporting, accountability at all levels (school, district, and state), and mandatory enforcement. These three reform approaches could be used to address the gross racial disparities in special education identification, restrictiveness of placement, and quality of services.

For policymakers, there is no need to pinpoint a specific cause or allege race discrimination in order to achieve racial equity. Scholars report that many schools today still operate under a deficit model, where school authorities regard students with disabilities as the embodiments of their particular disability and ask only *what the special educators are required to do in order to accommodate the student's problem.*[74] A universal commitment to equity in special education would help erode this deficit model by shifting the focus to *what all public educators should do to improve educational opportunities and outcomes for all children.*

There is bipartisan acknowledgement that special education issues faced by minority children need a federal legislative response. This apparent consensus holds promise for effective federal reform. Reform attempts in the recent past can be improved upon. In 1997 the IDEA was amended to require states to collect and review data on racial disproportionality in both identification and placement and to intervene where disproportionality is significant.[75] Before that, in 1995, the Office for Civil Rights made racial disproportionality in special education a top priority. The persistence of this problem suggests that states' legal obligations under IDEA and our civil rights enforcement priorities have not been met.

OCR was once a major force in the effort to desegregate our nation's schools, suggesting that the agency's efficacy is related to political will as much as it is to resources. It is apparent that there is a glaring need for stepped-up enforcement and oversight by both federal and state agencies. These actions must be geared toward encouraging the active participation of educators at all levels if there is to be any hope of meaningful and lasting improvement. Most important, aggressive efforts to remedy these issues are only the starting point. The efficacy of enforcement interventions and attempted reforms must be evaluated in terms of the outcomes for minority children.

Both general and special education teachers and administrators need better training to deliver effective instruction in the least restrictive, most inclusive environment appropriate. Meeting this need, along with the need for better data collection on racial and ethnic disparities and enhanced civil rights enforcement, would require an infusion of special education funds, which could be expected to result in net gains in education outcomes and savings in juvenile justice expenditures in the long term. By increasing federal oversight and by encouraging states to intervene where appropriate, the federal government could help improve the quality of instruction, supports, and services received by minority students in both regular and special education.

Although OCR still does not collect national data to determine racial disparities in the educational environment,[76] the 1997 IDEA amendments obligate the states to collect sampled data.[77] If the government required every state and school district to collect disaggregated data by race with disability category and educational setting (all three together), research on overrepresentation would benefit tremendously.

Moreover, much general education reform law is predicated on the concept that public pressure at the local level from parents and community stakeholders will stimulate meaningful improvements. To generate local reform pressure, the Bush education program requires public reporting of test achievement by a number of student subgroups, including disability status and major racial and ethnic subgroups. Policymakers could likewise stimulate meaningful improvements in special education by amending the IDEA to require public reporting of racial disparities in special education identification and placement.

IDEA should also require states to intervene under specified circumstances (they now have complete discretion) and to provide technical assistance to effect reforms. Such required intervention and assistance would likely foster greater self-reflection and improvement at the district level. While adopting mandatory interventions would be helpful, given the context of shrinking state education budgets, an emphasis on rewards and continued supports to foster successful efforts must be an integral part of any new enforcement efforts.

Finally, new mechanisms for minority children to exercise their rights under IDEA, including legal services support, would help considerably.

Toward Comprehensive Solutions to Systemic Problems at the District Level

The research and analysis presented in this volume are intended to serve educators, advocates, and policymakers alike. In addition to raising awareness of the issues, suggesting changes in legislation, and improving the enforcement of existing requirements, much can be accomplished with greater determination by school leadership.

For communities of color, disproportionate representation in special education is just one facet of the denial of access to educational opportunity. Denial begins in the regular education setting with school segregation, low tracking, test-based diploma denial and retention, overly harsh discipline, less access to programs for the gifted, and resource inequalities that have a distinctly racial dimension.

Education leaders who suspect a problem at their school can accomplish a great deal by clearly stating that this problem is one that they and their staff can do something about, and that it has a racial dimension. By squarely shouldering responsibility and resolving to improve outcomes for all children as they tackle the racial disparities, school leaders can also reduce racial tensions among staff and in their school community and recover lives and talents that would otherwise be wasted. Tackling these issues should be a shared responsibility, not the duty of the principal or special education administrator alone. Furthermore, technical assistance can be sought from state and federal agencies, including OCR and OSEP, without triggering legal action.

School leaders concerned with the issues raised above can also renew their efforts to involve parents and community in innovative ways. Some suggested methods include entering into partnerships with community organizations in order to boost minority parent involvement, and engaging school-based councils that would share decisionmaking power, working more closely with social service agencies to ensure that at-risk students receive high-quality services and that social workers and teachers are collaborating effectively, and increasing direct outreach to families.[78]

Moreover, teachers need support to change their practice and improve classroom outcomes. In many cases regular classroom teachers have received little or no training in working with students from diverse backgrounds or with special education students, or have had little practicum experience in inclusive classrooms.[79] Similarly, many special education teachers have not had the degree of training in the core curriculum or on how to work in a full-inclusion setting.[80] Without both academic and multicultural training and time for special education and regular education teachers to collaborate, it is unrealistic to expect significant improvement.

Protecting the civil rights of all students benefits society at large. Obviously, it is much better if this problem is solved within the school than through external enforcement. Strong leadership at all levels could make an important difference. There is a great deal of work that can and should be done by schools, by districts, by states, and by federal lawmakers and enforcement agents that would improve educational opportunities for minority children in general, and make tremendous progress in solving the specific problems highlighted in this book.

There are no quick fixes. The problems explored in the pages that follow have many roots, and creating better outcomes requires difficult changes at many levels. Far more research is needed on the practices that produce inequality and the reforms that can successfully correct them. We need to reach the point at which every child is treated as if he or she were our own child, with the same tirelessly defended and protected life possibilities. In schools where we can predict the racial makeup of a special education class before we open the door, we must have leadership, if possible, and enforcement, if necessary, to ensure that each child receives the quality academic support and special services he or she truly needs without diminishing any of the opportunities that are any child's right in American society. We hope this book will contribute to that dream.

NOTES

1. Pub. L. No. 105-17, Sec. 601(c)(2)(B) and (C) (1997) (codified as amended at 20 U.S.C. § 1400 (c)(2)(B) and (C) (1994 & Supp. V. 1999).

2. NATIONAL COUNCIL ON DISABILITY, BACK TO SCHOOL ON CIVIL RIGHTS: ADVANCING THE FEDERAL COMMITMENT TO LEAVE NO CHILD BEHIND (2000) [hereinafter NCD 2000].

3. *Id.* at 6.

4. *Id.*

5. COMMITTEE ON MINORITY REPRESENTATION IN SPECIAL EDUCATION, NATIONAL RESEARCH COUNCIL, MINORITY STUDENTS IN SPECIAL AND GIFTED EDUCATION (M. Suzanne Donovan and Christopher T. Cross eds., forthcoming 2002)[hereinafter NRC 2002], *available at* www.nap.edu/books/0309074398/html (last visited July 22, 2002).

6. Where the data was collected using the term *black,* we use that term to describe the group otherwise referred to as African American.

7. PANEL ON SELECTION AND PLACEMENT OF STUDENTS IN PROGRAMS FOR THE MENTALLY RE-TARDED, NATIONAL RESEARCH COUNCIL, PLACING CHILDREN IN SPECIAL EDUCATION: A STRATEGY FOR EQUITY (Kirby A. Heller et al. eds., 1982) [hereinafter NRC 1982].

8. OFFICE FOR CIVIL RIGHTS, U.S. DEPARTMENT OF EDUCATION, ELEMENTARY AND SECONDARY SCHOOL CIVIL RIGHTS COMPLIANCE REPORTS (2000) [hereinafter OCR 1998 data], *available at* www.ed.gov/offices/OCR/data.html (Although issued in 2000, 1998 data are reported throughout).

9. NRC 2002, *supra* note 5, at 2-9, 2-10.

10. The National Research Council (NRC) describes eight separate studies over a span of twelve years that suggest that teachers made negative judgments of students due to race or ethnicity bias; see NRC 2002, *supra* note 5, at 5-10. However, based on other research, NRC states that the evidence is insufficient to draw a conclusion regarding the impact of racial discrimination. *Id.* at 2-21.

11. Testimony of Representative Chaka Fattah, *available at* http://www.house.gov/apps/list/press/pa02_fattah/misident.html (last visited, July 22, 2002). The story of Billy Hawkins was originally reported in *U.S. News & World Report* on December 13, 1993.

12. For a general description of the federal funding scheme under IDEA, see 147 CONG. REC. S1889 (2001) (statement of Sen. Jeffords); *see also* 143 CONG. REC. S4401 (1997) (statement of Sen. Gregg) (emphasizing that "the Federal Government has failed to live up to its obligation to fund 40 percent of the cost of special education.").

13. Representative John Boehner, Chairman of the House Education and the Workforce Committee, *IDEA Must Be Fully Funded—But First It Must Be Fixed* (fact sheet, April 16, 2002), *available at* http://edworkforce.house.gov/issues/107th/education/idea/fact.htm (last visited, July 22, 2002).

14. OCR data 1998, *supra* note 8.

15. OCR data 1998, *supra* note 8.

16. *See* Parrish, this volume.

17. NRC 2002, *supra* note 5, at Table 2-2.

18. The states were Alabama, Arkansas, Florida, Georgia, Indiana, Iowa, Kentucky, Montana, Nebraska, Ohio, North Carolina, South Carolina, and West Virginia. During that school year (2000-2001), the national average for blacks was 2.06 and Hispanics 0.51; see U.S. DEP'T OF EDUCATION, OFFICE OF SPECIAL EDUCATION PROGRAMS, DATA ANALYSIS SYS-

TEM (DANS), Table AA17, *available at* http://www.ideadata.org/tables24th\ar_aa17. htm (last visited July 22, 2002) [hereinafter OSEP 2001 Report].

19. Id.

20. NRC 1982, *supra* note 7.

21. JEREMY FINN, PATTERNS IN SPECIAL EDUCATION PLACEMENT AS REVEALED BY THE OCR SUR-VEYS, *in* NRC 1982, *supra* note 7, at 365.

22. Artiles et al., in this volume, perform the well-established statistical risk comparison called odds ratios, which calculates the actual odds of being identified with a particular disability for each racial group and then compares them. *See, e.g.,* SCOTT MENARD, AP-PLIED LOGISTIC REGRESSION ANALYSIS 12-13 (1995).

23. Parrish, Table 2, this volume.

24. Hispanics are significantly overrepresented in the category of emotional disturbance in New York, Connecticut, and Pennsylvania. Native Americans are identified at nearly five times the rate of whites in Nebraska, and between two and five times the rate in nine states. *Id.*

25. *See* Finn, *supra* note 21, at 374.

26. These districts themselves have such a high degree of racial isolation (e.g., a 90% minor-ity district) that they often lack the comparison group necessary to discuss inter-district racial disparities.

27. *See, e.g.,* Losen and Welner, this volume.

28. According to Assistant Secretary of Education Judy Heumann, Director of the Office for Special Education and Rehabilitative Services under President Clinton, the system of both regular and private education is racially discriminatory because "[m]inority chil-dren are more likely not to receive the kinds of services they need in the regular ed[ucation] system and the special ed. system. . . . And special education is used as a place to move kids from a regular classroom out into a separate setting." *The Merrow Re-port: What's So Special About Special Education?* (PBS television broadcast, May 10, 1996) [hereinafter *The Merrow Report*], *transcript available at* http://www.pbs.org/ merrow/tv/transcripts/index.html (last visited July 8, 2002).

29. *See* Oswald, Coutinho, and Best, this volume; James M. Patton, *The Disproportionate Representation of African Americans in Special Education: Looking Behind the Curtain for Understanding and Solutions,* 32 J. SPECIAL EDUC. 25-31 (1998).

30. *See* Parrish, Table 2, and Fierros and Conroy, Table 1, in this volume.

31. The 1982 study of national data by Jeremy Finn also found the highest levels of over-representation of African American children in "mental retardation" in the southern states. *See* Finn, *supra* note 21, at 364-66; *see also* John U. Ogbu, *Castelike Stratification as a Risk Factor for Mental Retardation in the United States, in* RISK IN INTELLECTUAL AND PSYCHOSOCIAL DEVELOPMENT 8-85 (Dale C. Farran and James D. McKinney eds., 1986).

32. Parrish, this volume, Table 2.

33. *See* Oswald et al., this volume.

34. *See* Oswald et al., this volume. Further, the impact of sociodemographic factors was dif-ferent for each of the various gender/ethnicity groups. *See id.*

35. *See id.*

36. *See* NRC Report 2002, *supra* note 5 (Figure 2-11 depicts the largest gender gaps among blacks with MR at nearly a full percent (.97), where in all other groups the difference was always less than a third of a percent and ranged from .15 to .3.).

37. Parrish, Table 2, this volume.
38. "Hard" categories include physical disabilities that are generally discernable through a medical examination and are rarely disputed. *See* Parrish, this volume.
39. Parrish uses the benchmark of twice the rate of whites to define extensive overrepresentation. Parrish, this volume, Table 1. Table 1 shows that blacks are substantially overidentified (more than twice as likely as whites) for mental retardation and emotional disturbance in thirty-eight and twenty-nine states, respectively, yet overrepresented to a similar degree in hearing impairments and orthopedic impairments in only five and four states, respectively. *Id.*
40. Parrish, Table 2, this volume.
41. *Id.*
42. In twenty-four states the odds for blacks compared to Hispanics for mental retardation, and in thirty-six states the black to Hispanic odds for emotional disturbance, are larger than for blacks compared to whites. Parrish, this volume.
43. NRC Report 2002, *supra* note 5.
44. *Id.*
45. *See, e.g.,* P. L. DONAHUE ET AL., THE NATION'S REPORT CARD: FOURTH-GRADE READING 2000, at Figure 2.3 (April 2001), *available at* http://nces.ed.gov/pubsearch/pubsinfo.asp?pubid=2001499 (last visited, July 22, 2002). The NRC Report implies a connection between high lead levels and minority overrepresentation, yet fails to explore any data specifically linking overrepresentation in MR and risk of lead exposure. In fact, a recent study of exposure to lead paint commissioned by the Office of Lead Hazard Control, U.S. Department of Housing and Urban Development (April 18, 2001) shows that the risk is highest in the northeastern states and lowest in the south. ROBERT P. CLIKNER ET AL., NATIONAL SURVEY OF LEAD AND ALLERGENS IN HOUSING, VOLUME I: ANALYSIS OF LEAD HAZARDS, 3-2, 3-10, 4-4 (2001). It is important to note that for blacks, the incidence of MR is extraordinarily high in the majority of southern states and below the national average in northeastern states. *See* OSEP 2001 Report, *supra* note 18. These divergent demographics suggest that risk for lead exposure does not track closely the risk for MR identification experienced by black children.
46. *See, e.g.,* Donald MacMillan and Daniel J. Reschly, *Overrepresentation of Minority Students: The Case for Greater Specificity or Reconsideration of the Variables Examined,* 32 J. SPECIAL EDUC. 15 (1998); Loretta A. Serna et al., *Intervention Versus Affirmation: Proposed Solutions to the Problem of Disproportionate Minority Representation in Special Education,* 32 J. SPECIAL EDUC. 48, 48 (1998) (suggesting that we do not have enough information to conclude that bias is a major cause of disproportionate representation). The Eighteenth Annual Report to Congress discusses research suggesting that poverty, and not race or ethnicity, is the most important factor influencing the disproportionality. *See* U.S. DEPARTMENT OF EDUCATION, EIGHTEENTH ANNUAL REPORT TO CONGRESS ON THE IMPLEMENTATION OF THE INDIVIDUALS WITH DISABILITIES EDUCATION ACT 86 (1996), *available at* http://www.ed.gov/pubs/OSEP96AnlRpt (last visited, July 22, 2002) (citing MARY WAGNER, THE CONTRIBUTIONS OF POVERTY AND ETHNIC BACKGROUND TO THE PARTICIPATION OF SECONDARY SCHOOL STUDENTS IN SPECIAL EDUCATION (1995)). The report to Congress concedes that Wagner formed this conclusion despite the fact that her own study also found that when income is accounted for, statistically significant disproportionate representation remains in three categories, including mental retardation. *Id. See also* Daniel J. Reschly and John L. Hosp, *Predictors of Restrictiveness for African-American*

and Caucasian Students, 68 EXCEPTIONAL CHILDREN 225-38 (2001). This study was developed for use by expert testimony on behalf of the defense of a school district charged with discrimination in *Coalition to Save Our Children v. State Board of Education of Delaware,* 901 F. Supp. 784, 821 (D. Del. 1995); 90 F.3rd 752, 763 n. 13 (3d Cir. 1996)). Dr. Reschly opined that "with better measures of poverty the [racial] gap would be further reduced if not eliminated."

47. Jim Ysseldyke, for example, discusses the importance of considering the opportunities to learn available to the student rather than simply focusing on a deficit that lies within the student when students' cognitive abilities are assessed, the clear implication being that what we assess as a cognitive disability may actually be a failure to provide a student with an adequate opportunity to learn. *See* Jim Ysseldyke, *Reflections on a Research Career: Generalizations from 25 Years of Research on Assessment and Instructional Decision Making,* 67 EXCEPTIONAL CHILDREN 295, 304 (2001).

48. *Id.* at 303 (describing among other things how, "[o]nce a classroom teacher or parent refers a student [for an evaluation] it is likely that the student will be found eligible for special education services. . . . We have demonstrated repeatedly that teachers refer students who bother them.").

49. *See* Harry et al., this volume.

50. *See id.*

51. *See id.*

52. *Id.; see generally* Ysseldyke, *supra* note 46.

53. Beth Harry and M. Anderson, *African American Males in Special Education: A Critique of the Process,* 63 J. NEGRO EDUC. 602, 607 (1994).

54. *See generally* Ysseldyke, *supra* note 47, at 304 (stating "there are no reliable psychometric differences between those labeled learning disabled (LD) and low-achieving students . . . but most have chosen simply to ignore [these findings]"); Harry et al., this volume.

55. For a review of the research about teacher quality and service of minority students, see the work of Linda Darling-Hammond, in particular Linda Darling-Hammond, *Teacher Quality and Student Achievement: A Review of State Policy Evidence,* 8 EDUCATIONAL POLICY ANALYSIS ARCHIVES, No. 1 (2000); *see also* Richard M. Ingersoll, *The Problem of Underqualified Teachers in American Secondary Schools,* 28 EDUCATIONAL RESEARCHER 26 (1999); Deborah L. Voltz, *Challenges and Choices in Urban Teaching: The Perspectives of General and Special Educators, in* MULTIPLE VOICES FOR ETHNICALLY DIVERSE EXCEPTIONAL LEARNERS 41-53 (2001). For a discussion of the use of special education placement to racially segregate children, see KENNETH J. MEIER ET AL., RACE, CLASS, AND EDUCATION: THE POLITICS OF SECOND-GENERATION DISCRIMINATION (1989). For a discussion of its use as a disciplinary tool, see Osher et al., this volume.

56. These other resources include textbooks, library books, science laboratories, the schools' physical plant quality, class size, field trips, enriched courses, college counseling, and computer equipment. *See* Richard Rothstein, *Equalizing Educational Resources on Behalf of Disadvantaged Children, in* A NATION AT RISK: PRESERVING PUBLIC EDUCATION AS AN ENGINE FOR SOCIAL MOBILITY 31-92 (Richard Kahlenburg ed., 2000).

57. *See* PAULINE LIPMAN, RACE, CLASS AND POWER IN SCHOOL RESTRUCTURING (1998); *see also* MICHELLE FINE, FRAMING DROPOUTS: NOTES ON THE POLITICS OF AN URBAN PUBLIC HIGH SCHOOL (1991).

58. FINE, *supra* note 57; *see also* JEAN ANYON, GHETTO SCHOOLING: A POLITICAL ECONOMY OF URBAN EDUCATIONAL REFORM (1997).

59. For example, in the American Association of University Women's *How Schools Short-change Girls*, research is cited on student teacher interaction on the basis of gender, race, ethnicity and or social class. The studies indicate that white males receive more attention than males from various racial and ethnic minority groups; that black males are perceived less favorably by their teachers and seen as less able than other students; that black females receive less reinforcement from teachers than do other students. THE AAUW REPORT, HOW SCHOOLS SHORTCHANGE GIRLS 122-23 (1992); *see also* Harry and Anderson, *supra* note 51, at 610.

60. See Brenda L. Townsend, *Disproportionate Discipline of African American Children and Youth: Culturally Responsive Strategies for Reducing School Suspensions and Expulsions*, 66 EXCEPTIONAL CHILDREN 381 (2000); James F. Gregory, *Three Strikes and They're Out: African American Boys and American Schools' Responses to Misbehavior*, 7 INT'L J. OF ADOLESCENCE & YOUTH 25 (1997); James F. Gregory, *The Crime of Punishment: Racial and Gender Disparities in the Use of Corporal Punishment in the U.S. Public Schools*, 64 J. NEGRO EDUC. 454 (1996); Maurice C. Taylor and Gerald A. Foster, *Bad Boys and School Suspensions: Public Policy Implications for Black Males*, 56 SOCIOLOGICAL INQUIRY 498 (1986).

61. *See* Campaign for Fiscal Equity v. New York, 187 Misc. 2d 1 (2001); *see also* JONATHAN KOZOL, SAVAGE INEQUALITIES: CHILDREN IN AMERICA'S SCHOOLS (1991).

62. A parallel phenomenon occurs with regard to tracking and gifted placements. *See* Amy S. Wells and Irene Serna, *The Politics of Culture: Understanding Local Political Resistance to Detracking in Racially Mixed Schools*, 66 HARV. EDUC. REV. 93 (1996); Daniel J. Losen, Note, *Silent Segregation in Our Nation's Schools*, 34 HARV. C.R.-C.L. L. REV. 517, 525 (1999); for a discussion of social capital, see Pierre Bourdieu, *The Forms of Capital, in* HANDBOOK OF THEORY AND RESEARCH FOR THE SOCIOLOGY OF EDUCATION (John G. Richardson ed., 1985).

63. Voltz, *supra* note 55; Harry and Anderson, *supra* note 53, at 612.

64. *See* ALFIE KOHN, THE CASE AGAINST STANDARDIZED TESTS: RAISING THE SCORES, RUINING THE SCHOOLS 35-41 (2000); Walt Haney, *The Myth of the Texas Miracle in Education*, 8 EDUC. POL'Y ANALYSIS ARCHIVES, 1 pt. 4 (2000), *available at* http://epaa.asu.edu/epaa/v8n41 (last visited, July 22, 2002); Linda McNeil and Angela Valenzuela, *The Harmful Impact of the TAAS System of Testing in Texas: Beneath the Accountability Rhetoric* (2000), *available at* http://www.law.harvard.edu/groups/civilrights/conferences/testing 98/drafts/mcneil_valenzuela.html (last visited, July 22, 2002). *See also* NOE MEDINA & MONTY NEILL, FALLOUT FROM THE TESTING EXPLOSION: HOW 100 MILLION STANDARDIZED EXAMS UNDERMINE EQUITY AND EXCELLENCE IN AMERICA'S PUBLIC SCHOOLS (3rd ed. 1990); Jay Heubert, *High Stakes Testing: Opportunities and Risks for Students of Color, English-Language Learners, and Students with Disabilities, in* THE CONTINUING CHALLENGE: MOVING THE YOUTH AGENDA FORWARD (M. Pines ed., forthcoming) (manuscript at 5, on file with authors).

65. Heubert, this volume.

66. *Id.*

67. *Id.*

68. *Id.*

69. GARY ORFIELD, THE RECONSTRUCTION OF SOUTHERN EDUCATION: THE SCHOOLS AND THE 1964 CIVIL RIGHTS ACT (1969).

70. *See* Losen and Welner, this volume.

71. *See* Orfield, *supra* note 69.

72. NRC 2002 Report, *supra* note 5, at 10-1.

73. Of course in certain states or districts changing a particular special education policy or practice, i.e., the heavy reliance on IQ tests, that evidence suggests is a primary factor, could have a significant impact.

74. *See, e.g.,* MARTHA MINOW, MAKING ALL THE DIFFERENCE 82-84 (1990).

75. 20 U.S.C. § 1400(c)(8)(A).

76. *See* Glennon, this volume

77. 20 U.S.C. § 1400(c)(8)(A).

78. Some of these suggestions come from Vincent L. Ferrandino, *Challenges for 21st–Century Elementary Principals,* 2001 PHI DELTA KAPPAN 440.

79. *See* Harry, this volume.

80. NRC Report 2002, *supra* note 5, at 5-32, 5-33.

CHAPTER ONE

Community and School Predictors of Overrepresentation of Minority Children in Special Education[1]

DONALD P. OSWALD

MARTHA J. COUTINHO

AL M. BEST

THE CRISIS IN MINORITY STUDENT EDUCATION

In the 1998–1999 school year, over 2.2 million children of color in U.S. schools were served by special education (U.S. Department of Education, 2000). Post–high school outcomes for these minority students with disabilities are strikingly inferior. Among high school youth with disabilities, about 75 percent of African American students, as compared to 47 percent of white students, are not employed two years out of school. Slightly more than half (52%) of African Americans, compared to 39 percent of white young adults, are still not employed three to five years out of school. In this same time period, the arrest rate for African Americans with disabilities is 40 percent, as compared to 27 percent for whites (Wagner, D'Amico, Marder, Newman, & Blackorby, 1992).

In the face of such bleak outcomes, it is essential to better understand the overrepresentation of minority students in special education. This chapter addresses the question of the relationship between the overrepresentation of minority children in special education and a set of demographic, fiscal, and school-related variables. The intent of the study was to determine to what extent this overrepresentation can be explained by these predictor variables. The research was based on a conceptual framework of alternative hypotheses regarding overrepresentation. Hypothesis 1 proposes that ethnic groups are differentially susceptible to disability, while Hypothesis 2 proposes that overrepresentation is the result of special education referral, assessment, and eligibility

1

processes and instruments that are culturally and linguistically loaded and that measure and interpret the ability, achievement, and behavior of students differently across ethnic groups. We investigated these hypotheses using a national sample of school districts to examine the relationship between special education identification rates and predictor variables.

If overrepresentation is a function of genuinely higher disability rates among students of color, national and local responses must address the social conditions that are risk factors for disability. If, on the other hand, the problem arises from systemic bias and discrimination within the public education system, aggressive efforts are required to correct attitudes and behavior associated with the special education identification of minority children.

Our analysis of special education data suggests that both hypotheses may be important in understanding overrepresentation. Statistical models of these data indicate that social, demographic, and school-related variables are significantly associated with special education identification. In some cases, these relationships support the conclusion that toxic social conditions may be producing disproportionately higher rates of disability among children of color. Other findings indicate that a significant portion of the overrepresentation problem may be a function of inappropriate interpretation of ethnic and cultural differences as disabilities.

CURRENT POLICY AND PRACTICES:
AN INEFFECTIVE RESPONSE

Advocacy groups, the research community, and policymakers have investigated, debated, and litigated the problems of equity and overrepresentation of minority students in special education for over thirty years (*Larry P. v. Riles*, 1979, 1984, 1986; *Marshall et al. v. Georgia*, 1984, 1985). There is widespread agreement that schools have failed to implement effective responses to disproportionate representation; that is, responses that lead to better educational experiences and acceptable outcomes for minority children (Harry & Anderson, 1994).

The U.S. Department of Education Office for Civil Rights (OCR) monitors and enforces U.S. statutes barring discrimination against minority students in education. However, for a number of important reasons listed below, this strategy has been insufficient and ineffective:

- Policy responses to overrepresentation of minority students in a particular disability category (e.g., mental retardation) may lead to reduced disproportionality in that category, but increased disproportional representation in another category (Oswald & Coutinho, 2001). In California, for example, between 1980 and 1994, overrepresentation of African Americans among students with mild mental retardation essentially disappeared; during the same time period, however, African American students experienced substantially increased disproportionality among students with learning disabilities (U.S. Department of Education, 1994).

- Keeping minority students who are already performing poorly in the general education systems that failed them (or inappropriately returning them there from special education) perpetuates inferior educational outcomes for these students (Macmillan & Balow, 1991).

- Accurate estimates of disproportionate representation are rarely available to inform policy responses. Statements characterizing overrepresentation are often based on nonrepresentative samples or unclear definitions of disproportionality, and findings are often selectively reported to support a particular viewpoint, creating an impression that either exaggerates the scope of the problem or inappropriately minimizes and dismisses it (Coutinho & Oswald, 1999, 2000).

- Educators and policymakers lack sound, empirically based information about the influence of community, fiscal, and school-related factors on minority disability identification rates. Monitoring approaches do not take into account the likelihood that demographic, school-related, fiscal, and community factors influence identification rates and that minority children are disproportionately exposed to the potentially toxic effects of such factors.

IMPROVING THE SPECIAL EDUCATION PROCESS AND OUTCOMES FOR MINORITY STUDENTS

A critical gap exists between what is now known and the knowledge that is needed to improve the experience of minority students. Sound, conceptually based empirical research is essential to provide policymakers and educators with information that can lead to significantly improved results. Such research must (a) consider alternative hypotheses regarding overrepresentation in order to improve our understanding of how community, school-related, and fiscal factors influence special education identification; and (b) systematically investigate the options available for improving the minority student experience. Considerable attention has been given to the hypothesis that disproportionality is the result of biased special education referral, assessment, and eligibility processes. Substantial research has also been devoted to questions of instruments that are culturally and linguistically loaded, which measure and interpret the ability, achievement, and behavior of students differently across ethnic groups (Gottlieb, Gottlieb, & Trongue, 1991; Harry & Anderson, 1994).

An alternative hypothesis is that ethnic groups are differentially susceptible to educational disability; that is, that the underlying distribution of educational disability varies across ethnic groups, which in turn influences rates of referral and identification as disabled. Environmental, demographic, health, economic, community, and educational factors may differentially affect the susceptibility of different ethnic groups to educational disability (Coutinho & Oswald, 1999, 2000). An exploratory study by Oswald, Coutinho, Best, and Singh (1998) found that a set of community- and school-related variables accounted for a significant proportion of the variability in the rate of identification of mental retardation and emotional disturbance for African American students as compared to other students.

In sum, there is evidence to support both hypotheses, and each influences disproportionate minority representation. Technically sound analyses at the community level are needed to indicate how ethnicity influences identification for special education, once the effects of other relevant community variables are accounted for. Such research is required in order to guide policy changes that assure that (a) only children who are disabled are identified as such, and (b) proactive interventions occur at the community level to achieve equity and improved outcomes for students of color.

PURPOSE OF THE STUDY

This chapter has three purposes. First, we present the results of a conceptually based empirical study of how a set of demographic, fiscal, and school-related factors are associated with the disproportionate representation of minority children in special education in the United States. Second, we provide specific recommendations for additional research needed to better understand how demographic, fiscal, and school-related variables influence disproportionality at the community level. Finally, we discuss policy recommendations as to how communities might respond to disproportionality within the context of community characteristics (e.g., demographic profile) and school resources.

METHOD

Data Sources

Every two years, the Office for Civil Rights (OCR) collects information on a nationally representative sample of school districts. The data are used to compile the Elementary and Secondary School Civil Rights Compliance Report, the chief source of data on the status of civil rights in the nation's schools (U.S. Department of Education, 1998).[2] For this report, we considered only the information on enrollment and disability categories from the school year 1994–1995, the most recent survey data available at the time we conducted the study.

The National Center for Educational Statistics Common Core of Data CD-ROM (NCES-CCD93 Disc) has information on all school districts in the country. The information in this data set was matched with the OCR data so that only those districts that participated in the 1994 OCR survey were included. Nine sociodemographic variables from the National Center for Educational Statistics Common Core of Data were chosen as predictor variables. The variables were selected on the basis of several criteria: (a) the variable had been examined in earlier work in the literature and possessed demonstrable conceptual links to disability identification; (b) the variable operationalized a construct about which specific predictions could be generated, based on the alternative hypotheses being tested; (c) the variable was included in the NCES-CCD data set; and (d) the variable had few missing values in the NCES data set. In addition, the variables included some community characteristics that could be altered through political intervention (e.g., per pupil expenditure, student-teacher ratio) and some that are relatively fixed (e.g., percent nonwhite).

Variables selected from the Common Core of Data as predictor variables were: student-teacher ratio (STR), per pupil expenditure (PPE), percentage of children enrolled who are "at risk" (At Risk), percentage of enrolled students who are nonwhite (Nonwhite), percentage of enrolled students who are Limited English Proficient (LEP), median housing value in $10,000 units (Housing), median income for households with children in $100,000 units (Income), percentage of children in households below the poverty level (Poverty), and percentage of adults in the community with a twelfth-grade education or less and no diploma (No Diploma).

Analysis Methods

We examined the effects of gender, ethnicity, and sociodemographic factors on the students in a school district who are identified with Mental Retardation (MR), Serious Emotional Disturbance (SED), or Learning Disability (LD). The fourth disability category in this study, "None," included students with lower incidence disability conditions (e.g., Other Health Impaired, Autism), as well as all regular education students. Our study endeavored to answer the question, "Are these district-level and child-level variables significantly associated with the likelihood of being identified as a child with MR, SED, or LD?" More specifically, the analyses reported here addressed questions such as, "Does

TABLE 1
Identification Odds Ratios for Gender/Ethnicity Group
Compared to White Females

Gender	Ethnicity	MR Odds Ratio	LD Odds Ratio	SED Odds Ratio
M	American Indian	1.66	2.903	5.024
M	Asian Amer./Pac. Islander	0.50	0.783	0.915
M	Black	3.26	2.343	5.527
M	Hispanic	0.95	2.104	2.354
M	White	1.36	2.279	3.810
F	American Indian	1.21	1.339	1.374
F	Asian Amer./Pac. Islander	0.40	0.350	0.229
F	Black	2.02	0.978	1.376
F	Hispanic	0.70	1.021	0.588
F	White	1.00	1.000	1.000

the level of poverty in the community significantly affect the chances that a student will be identified as mentally retarded?" "Does being an African American male significantly affect the chances that a student will be identified as SED?" and, most important, "Taking into account the effects of poverty, housing, per pupil expenditure, etc., do ethnicity and gender *still* significantly affect the likelihood of being identified for special education?"

RESULTS

A simple analysis of the data showed that, without taking into account the effects of social, demographic, and school-related factors, gender and ethnicity are significantly associated with the risk of being identified for special education. To clarify this finding, using white females as the comparison group, we compared the likelihood of being identified as MR, SED, or LD for students in each of the gender/ethnicity groups. Thus, for example, white males were 3.8 times as likely as white females to be identified as a student with SED (i.e., odds ratio = 3.8), while black males were 5.5 times as likely (see Table 1). These data starkly represent the extent of the problem of disproportionality across gender and ethnic groups.

We also found that the sociodemographic conditions of a school district are strongly associated with the proportion of students identified; that is, without taking into account students' gender and ethnicity, some portion of the variation in districts' identification rates can be explained by this combination of predictor variables.

We next sought to determine whether both individual student characteristics and districts' sociodemographic characteristics would continue to be significantly associated with identification in a combined model and whether the relationships between the predictor variables and identification rates were the same for each gender/ethnicity group. A model that included the nine sociodemographic variables, gender, and race was found to be significantly better than both the model with only the sociodemographic predictors and the model with only student gender and ethnicity characteristics. There were also significant predictor interactions between gender/ethnicity and sociodemographic characteristics. These findings indicate that, even after accounting for the effects of district sociodemographic characteristics, students' gender and ethnicity are important in determining the likelihood of identification. In addition, the model demonstrates that the impact of sociodemographic factors is different for each of the various gender/ethnicity groups.

Predictor Variables and Identification Rates

To illustrate the implications of the findings with respect to public policy and best practice, we examine in greater detail the relationship between three of the sociodemographic variables and identification rates. For the purpose of illustration, we selected Poverty, Nonwhite, and Per Pupil Expenditure (PPE) because they have implicit interest with respect to the alternative hypotheses regarding disproportionate representation, that is, differential susceptibility versus systemic bias.

Poverty   The general consensus among advocates and researchers is that increased poverty is associated with increased risk for disability. Thus, if ethnic groups were differentially susceptible to disability, we would expect susceptibility to be positively related to poverty. Ethnic groups that experience more poverty should display increased risk for disability, and communities with more poverty should have higher rates of special education identification. Further, across the distribution of poverty, disproportionality may be driven in part by the fact that children belonging to minority ethnic groups are more likely to be found living in poverty than white children.

On the basis of the OCR data, the logistic model estimates identification rates for each gender/ethnicity group at every possible value of the sociodemographic predictors. Figure 1 shows the predicted values for MR identification across the full range of Poverty, while holding each of the other predictor variables at the median. Thus, the figure illustrates the relationship between MR identification and Poverty, when the effects of all other predictor variables are statistically removed (i.e., held constant).

The data revealed some unexpected findings. For example, predicted values for MR identification among black students declined substantially as Poverty increased. Further, among the communities with the lowest Poverty rates, the identification rate for black males was substantially higher than even the most liberal prevalence estimates. Finally, disproportionality among Native American students, and even more strikingly among black students, was most pronounced in the relatively low-Poverty communities (for additional detail, see Oswald, Coutinho, Best, & Nguyen, 2001).

For SED and LD, the relationship between identification rate and Poverty was in the expected direction for black and Hispanic students; that is, as Poverty increased, so did identification. For white and Native American students, the trends for LD identification were less pronounced but generally in the opposite direction; communities with more Poverty tended to identify somewhat fewer students as LD (for additional detail, see Coutinho, Oswald, Best, & Forness, 2002).

The Poverty data can be viewed as supporting differential susceptibility for SED and LD among black and Hispanic students. The MR data, however, appear to support a hypothesis of systemic bias. Some portion of the disproportionality in low-Poverty communities may be due to white students with MR being given another disability classification, thus artificially depressing the white rate. Nonetheless, the absolute levels of MR identification among black students (especially black males) in low-Poverty communities suggest that a substantial number are being labeled MR inappropriately. The situation in high-Poverty communities is more difficult to interpret. However, the data suggest that, in these communities, the system may be breaking down entirely so that many students with MR go unidentified or are given another disability classification. For example, segregated, high-Poverty schools and districts may have less capacity to provide for students' needs.

Percentage of Enrolled Children Who Are Nonwhite   With respect to Nonwhite, the expected relationship with disability identification is null. There is no apparent rational reason to hypothesize that living in a community that includes greater (or smaller) numbers of ethnic minorities should represent a risk factor for disability for students of any ethnicity. If such a relationship is observed, and particularly if the relationship is different for the various gender/ethnicity groups, one has little choice but to suspect systemic bias or discrimination.

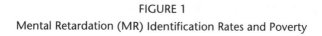

FIGURE 1

Mental Retardation (MR) Identification Rates and Poverty

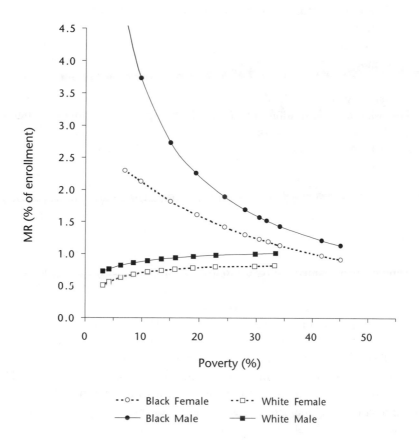

For MR and SED, white student identification rates are generally consistent with rational expectations; living in communities with greater or smaller numbers of ethnic minorities appears to have relatively little effect on identification. As communities become increasingly Nonwhite, however, white students are substantially less likely to be identified as LD. For black students, particularly black male students, living in a community with few Nonwhite students is a substantial risk factor for MR and SED identification, leading to marked disproportionality at that end of the distribution. Conversely, Native American students living in high-Nonwhite communities have substantially higher identification rates, particularly for SED. Figure 2 illustrates the relationship between Nonwhite and SED identification.

In sum, disability identification and Nonwhite proportion are related. The findings indicate a need to carefully scrutinize SED and MR identification in low-Nonwhite communities with an eye toward detecting inappropriate identification that is based more on difference than on disability. High-Nonwhite communities require some careful consideration with respect to SED identification among Native American students.

Per Pupil Expenditure   Per Pupil Expenditure might be expected to have some relationship to identification in that schools that spend more money per pupil should be more likely to identify appropriate numbers of students with disabilities and less likely to sustain special education eligibility processes that are systematically biased.

The observed relationships between identification rates and PPE, however, are complex. For students with SED, the trends match expectations reasonably well; systems that spend more also identify more students with SED. Disproportionality does not vary dramatically across the distribution except for Hispanic and Native American males, where increased PPE substantially increases disproportionality for these two groups. Disproportionality among students with MR also tends to increase across the distribution for black females and Hispanic students. At the low end of the Per Pupil Expenditure distribution (< $5,000), disproportionality is higher for black and Hispanic students with LD.

In sum, Per Pupil Expenditure appears to have a modest relationship to identification. Communities that spend less money have somewhat more disproportionate identification of Hispanic and African American students as LD. However, for black females and Hispanic students with respect to MR, communities that spend more for education show greater disproportionality. While increased overall education expenditure may result from identifying more children for special education, there is no clear, rational explanation as to why it should be associated with increased disproportionality.

IMPLICATIONS AND RECOMMENDATIONS

The findings reported above demonstrate the complexity of factors that influence special education identification. Sociodemographic factors are clearly associated with identification rates and with disproportionate representation across gender and ethnic groups. Further, the effects of these factors are often different for the various gender/ethnicity groups and are sometimes counterintuitive. However, this work may help to identify the profiles of sociodemographic conditions that are associated with significant disproportionate identification.

FIGURE 2

Serious Emotional Disablity (SED) Identification Rates and Percent Nonwhite

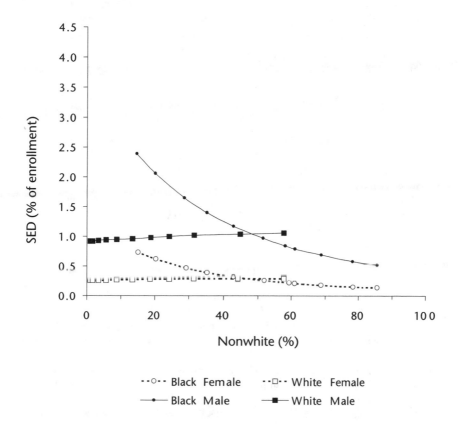

In spite of the importance of sociodemographic factors, however, child gender and ethnicity also contribute to the likelihood of identification in important ways. This finding, along with the patterns observed in some of the sociodemographic variables, lend indirect support to the systemic bias hypothesis. Further study of the effects of sociodemographic variables may contribute to exploration of bias by highlighting the community characteristics associated with suspect patterns of identification.

Policymakers and educators need access to information that provides a profile of how community and school resources and other sociodemographic factors may contribute to the disproportionate representation of minority students in special education. Toward that end, a conceptually and empirically guided research agenda is needed to disentangle effects related to differential susceptibility from those related to systemic biases in the special and regular education systems. Such research is needed at the community level to provide knowledge regarding the significance of disproportionality and recommendations regarding how to reform educational practices in a manner that yields equitable and effective educational experiences and improved education outcomes for all students.

NOTES

1. Preparation of this manuscript was supported in part by the Field-Initiated Studies Program of the National Institute on Educational Governance, Finance, Policymaking, and Management, Office of Educational Research and Improvement, U.S. Department of Education (Grant No. R308FG70020).
2. Additional details regarding the datasets and methods used for this report may be obtained by contacting Donald Oswald, Ph.D., Virginia Commonwealth University, Box 980489, Richmond, VA 23298-0489.

REFERENCES

Coutinho, M. J., & Oswald, D. P. (1999). Ethnicity and special education research: Identifying questions and methods. *Behavioral Disorders, 24,* 66–73.

Coutinho, M. J., & Oswald, D. P. (2000). Disproportionate representation in special education: A synthesis and recommendations. *Journal of Child and Family Studies, 9,* 135–156.

Coutinho, M. J., Oswald, D. P., Best, A. M., & Forness, S. R. (2002). Gender and sociodemographic factors and the disproportionate identification of minority students as emotionally disturbed. *Behavior Disorders, 27,* 109–125.

Gottlieb, J., Gottlieb, B. W., & Trongue, S. (1991). Parent and teacher referrals for a psychoeducational evaluation. *Journal of Special Education, 25,* 155–167.

Harry, B., & Anderson, M. G. (1994). The disproportionate placement of African American males in special education programs: A critique of the process. *Journal of Negro Education, 63,* 602–619.

Larry P. v. Wilson Riles. 343 F. Supp. 1306 (N.D. Cal. 1972) (preliminary injunction). Aff'd 502 F. 2d 963 (9th cir. 1974); 495F. Supp. 926 (N.D. Cal. 1979) (decision on merits). Aff'd (9th cir. No. 80-427 Jan. 23, 2984). Order modifying judgment, C-71-2270 RFP, Sept. 25, 1986.

Macmillan, D. L., & Balow, I. H. (1991). Impact of *Larry P.* on educational programs and assessment practices in California. *Diagnostique, 17,* 57–69.

Marshall et al. v. Georgia. U.S. District Court for the Southern District of Georgia, CV482-233, June 28, 1984.

Oswald, D. P., & Coutinho, M. J. (2001). Trends in disproportionate representation in special education: Implications for multicultural education policies. In C. A. Utley & F. E. Obiakor (Eds.), *Special education, multicultural education, and school reform: Components of a quality education for students with mild disabilities* (pp. 53–73). Springfield, IL: Charles C. Thomas.

Oswald, D. P., Coutinho, M. J., Best, A. M., & Nguyen, N. (2001). The impact of socio-demographic characteristics on the identification rates of minority students as mentally retarded. *Mental Retardation, 39,* 351–367.

Oswald, D., Coutinho, M., Best, A., & Singh, N. (1998). Ethnicity in special education and relationships with school related economic and educational variables. *Journal of Special Education, 32,* 194–206.

U.S. Department of Education. (1994). *Office for Civil Rights E&S time series data: 1968–1994.* Washington, DC: Author.

U.S. Department of Education. (1998). *Office for Civil Rights—fiscal year 1998: Annual report to Congress.* Washington, DC: Author.

U.S. Department of Education. (2000). *Twenty-second annual report to Congress.* Washington, DC: Author.

Wagner, M., D'Amico, R., Marder, C., Newman, L., & Blackorby, J. (1992). *What happens next? Trends in postschool outcomes of youth with disabilities. The second comprehensive report for the National Longitudinal Transition Study of Special Education Students.* Menlo Park, CA: SRI International.

CHAPTER TWO

Racial Disparities in the Identification, Funding, and Provision of Special Education

THOMAS PARRISH

This chapter examines the extent to which some minority students are over-represented among students receiving special education, while some also may be underserved. Not only is this an issue of civil rights and equity, but it also has economic significance: annual special education expenditures are estimated to exceed $50 billion in 1999–2000, or about 14 percent of total public education spending (Chambers, Parrish, & Harr, 2002).

In at least forty-five states, black children in special education are exten-sively overrepresented in some categories. Extensive overrepresentation is also found for American Indian children. Underrepresentation appears widespread for Asian American/Pacific Islander children in most categories, with Hispanic children being overidentified in some states and underidentified in others.

The category of disability where overrepresentation is most likely is mental retardation (MR). Each racial minority group shows overrepresentation in this category in at least one state. Blacks are the minority group for which MR overrepresentation is the greatest. Only twelve states do not overrepresent blacks to an extensive degree in the MR disability category. Furthermore, given the seeming variability in classifying students across the "soft" disability catego-ries of MR, emotional disturbance (ED), and specific learning disability (LD), overrepresentation of black students appears even worse than the count of thirty-eight overidentifying states in the category of MR would suggest.[1] Of the twelve states that do not overrepresent black students in the category of MR, six overrepresent them in one of the other soft categories.[2]

It may be expected that certain racial groups would exhibit higher percent-ages of students with disabilities due to socioeconomic factors. For example, black children in this country are known to have relatively higher rates of child poverty and malnutrition. However, the data analyzed for this study indicate that the high degree of racial disproportionality in special education cannot be attributed solely to the effects of poverty. Despite the anticipated positive relationship between poverty and health conditions as anticipated precursors to placement in special education (U.S. Department of Education, 1997), prior examination of this issue shows no significant relationship between identification for special education and poverty (McLaughlin & Owings, 1993).

It is well established that blacks, for example, are disproportionately poor, which could be expected to correspond with higher levels of special education identification due to related factors such as poor health, inferior schools, and family stress. However, comparisons of identification levels have shown that the degree of racial disparity in rates of identification for black children with "hard" disabilities that are easy to diagnose medically, such as visual or hearing impairment, is significantly smaller than the degree of racial disparity in rates of identification for the soft, subjective categories.

This chapter also examines the extent to which these patterns of over- and underrepresentation relate to the allocation of special education resources. Special education formulas that vary funding based on category of disability appear to show a troubling link with overidentifying and underfunding minority students. These funding formulas may over-emphasize disability at the expense of more important considerations, such as accurate identification, equitable funding, and the provision of appropriate services. Neutral funding formulas, such as those required for distribution of federal funds under the Individuals with Disabilities Education Act (IDEA), seem to be less associated with minority overrepresentation and are more likely to provide equitable special education funding for high-minority districts. These neutral formulas, along with enhanced monitoring and enforcement, are needed to ensure appropriate identification and labeling.

To decrease reliance on special education services for underachieving minority children, policymakers should address more directly the academic needs of students who are struggling to meet these new standards. For example, the current Bush administration calls for improving reading instruction in the early grades. Others have called for more extensive prereferral interventions in the general education setting. For example, efforts can be made to better tailor instructional methods and behavioral responses of teachers to an individual student's learning and emotional needs. The idea is that teachers should attempt a variety of educational strategies to reach students who are struggling academically or socially before referring them for special education evaluation (Hartman & Fay, 1996; Parrish, 2001.

Even when supplemental resources follow higher rates of special education representation for minority students, troubling questions remain about the identification criteria for such disability categories as MR or ED and how they are applied. More disturbing, however, are findings that even where certain groups of students are overrepresented as MR, the supplementary resources and services that are assumed necessary for these students often do not follow. Are minority students being under-funded and underserved in special education at the same time they are being overidentified?

This chapter provides an overview of special education finance across the nation, followed by a description of the data sources and methods used in this analysis. Findings on special education funding in relation to over- and under-representation, the placements received, and the services provided by race are presented. The chapter concludes with a section on the implications for reform.

FUNDING SPECIAL EDUCATION

Over 12 percent of all public school–age children receive special education services. Special education has risen as a percentage of total enrolment every year since the passage of IDEA in 1975. The most current study of special education spending (Chambers et al., 2002) estimated total spending for the average special education student to be 1.9 times that of a non–special education student. The growth of special education enrollments, and consequently in special education spending, has become an increasingly contentious issue over the past several years (Parrish, 2000). Concern has also been expressed about the degree to which special education spending is taking resources from general education programs (Rothstein, 1997).

Special education is funded through a mix of local, state, and federal funds, with the latter contributing about 9 percent of the total cost (Parrish & Anthony, 2002), while the remaining percentage of support comes from state and local contributions, with the relative shares varying considerably from state to state. For example, Oklahoma reported that 3 percent of the state's special education programs were supported through state revenues, while Wyoming reported 90 percent state support (Parrish & Anthony, 2002). For all states, special education spending that is not offset by federal revenues must be supported through state and local funds.

The limited data available on national special education spending suggest that the local share of special education spending has been growing over the past few years. This has contributed to concerns that special education funds are increasing at the cost of other local education programming (Parrish & Anthony, 2002).

The allocation formula governing special education funding at the federal level has changed considerably over the past few years. Since the passage of the IDEA, federal special education funds have been allocated on the basis of a fixed dollar amount per student identified for special education. A new federal funding system, passed as a part of the IDEA reauthorization in 1997, allocates federal aid primarily on a state's total school-age population (70%) with an adjustment for poverty (30%) (Parrish & Anthony, 2002). Under this new system, the amounts of money allocated to states and to school districts are the same regardless of the mix of services provided or disability category assigned. Two districts with the same total enrollment would be eligible to receive the same federal funding even though one may have much higher proportions of students in more severe categories of disability, such as autism.

Allocation rules also vary considerably across the states. For example, while Wyoming now reimburses districts for 100 percent of all special education costs, most other states have more generic systems providing funding based on the number of students receiving special education services or on general enrollment. For the purposes of this paper, state special education funding systems are divided into three basic approaches:

1. *Unlinked:* Districts with high rates of student identification for special education do not generate more funds than districts with lower identification rates.
2. *Service Linked:* The amount of money received is a direct function of how many students are identified for services overall, but the amount of funding is not linked to students' category of disability.
3. *Service and Category Linked:* Funding differentials are directly linked to higher-cost categories of disability or placement.

The analysis of these three approaches to funding yields a somewhat surprising answer to the question of whether additional special education funding is likely to accompany patterns of overrepresentation. This research shows that states that vary funding by category of disability are more likely to overrepresent *and* underfund minority students. For example, one might expect that students with what have generally been found to be higher-cost categories of disability would get the most financial assistance in states that use formulas that differentiate funding by type of disability. Conversely, one might predict that when supplemental funding does not follow a higher-cost designation, for example, MR, that the services MR children need may be less likely to be provided. Therefore, the findings that category-linked formulas correlate with both overrepresentation and underservice are counterintuitive, potentially disturbing, and require further investigation. This type of pattern also further intensifies concerns of overrepresentation; that is, classification into more severe categories of disability than are warranted without the receipt of appropriate supplemental services.

DATA SOURCES AND METHODS

An extensive analysis of spending on special education programs across the nation has recently been completed (Chambers et al., 2002). In addition to this national study, individual expenditure analyses were completed for eleven states during 2002.[3] However, other than the data resulting from these eleven state studies, the national study does not include special education expenditure information by individual state. Further, the last time all fifty states were asked to report special education spending (Parrish & Anthony, 2002), only thirteen states said they could do so with a high degree of confidence.

Information on the amount of categorical funds made available by the state and the federal government for special education is generally more available.[4] District-level analyses are required to understand the relationship between overidentification in high-minority districts and the amount of categorical funds these students generate. Because federal funding is generally a fixed amount per special education student, federal special education funding at the district level can be fairly easily estimated based on a district's special education enrollment.

In addition, the amount of federal and state special education funds that every district receives are data elements on the Annual Survey of Local Government Finances conducted by the U.S. Bureau of the Census. These data are collected for every school district in the nation in odd fiscal years (FY). The most current year for which these data are available is FY 1997, or the 1997–1998 school year. These data can be matched to the Common Core of School District Data produced by the U.S. Department of Education's National Center for Education Statistics (NCES), which contains a variable "number of students with Individualized Education Programs (IEPs)." This dataset also provides breakouts of district enrollments by race and ethnicity.

By combining these data, it is possible to compare federal and state special education funding per special education student for districts of varying degrees of percent minority enrollment by state. Although all of the districts in the United States are included in this database, under scrutiny the data elements most relevant to this analysis are not available for all states. States were eliminated from this analysis if state and federal special education funding was missing for large numbers of districts, or if the aggregate count of special education students listed by districts for a state did not reasonably approximate the official statewide count of special education students submitted to the U.S. Department of Education. (Although the latter count of special education students is considered much more reliable than the NCES count, it is not reported by district.)

Other sources of data used for this analysis are counts of special education students by race, by disability, by state, and the total count of school-age children by race and state for students ages six to twenty-one provided by the Washington, DC, research firm Westat. Westat collects these data from the states for the U.S. Department of Education, Office of Special Education Programs. Although these data also are not reported at the district level, they allow analyses of the identification of students by race into categories of disability, in relation to the racial composition of the state's overall student population (according to Census data for ages 6–21). This allows state-level comparisons of identification practices that can be compared with funding practices. Where information on state special education funding was lacking from the NCES data, state-level information was filled in to the extent available from data provided by the states through a survey recently administered by the National Association of State Directors of Special Education (NASDSE). Last, analyses of the services received by students, by disability, and by racial category within California were conducted using the student-level special education database maintained by the California State Department of Education.[5]

To measure and compare identification patterns by race, by category of disability, and by state, "risk ratios" were calculated. Based on special education and overall population counts by race as used in this paper, this ratio compares the risk of a child in a particular minority group being labeled as having a certain disability to the risk of a white child. Any racial group can be compared to any other using this procedure, but as white children are in the majority in forty-four states, this seemed to be the most logical comparison group. When the ratio is greater than 1 for a given racial group in a category of disability, the risk that a child of this race will be labeled as having the identified disability is greater than the risk of a white child being so labeled. The higher the ratio, the greater the likelihood of a minority child being labeled as having a certain disability as compared with a white child.[6]

Given that the purpose of this paper is to explore possible relationships between funding formulas and over- and underrepresentation of minority students, a relatively conservative standard has been adopted. Overrepresentation is defined as twice the risk of identification in relation to that for white students, with underrepresentation defined as one-half the risk. However, it should not be inferred that these standards, which rely on extensive levels of over- and underrepresentation, should apply to general determinations of over-

and underrepresentation, for which tests of statistical significance or other criteria are better suited.

In addition, differing identification rates are only shown when statistically significant at a .01 level of confidence. These are differences of sufficient magnitude that there is less than a 1 percent likelihood (.01) of their occurring by chance.

IDENTIFICATION RATE COMPARISONS

Using the risk ratios described above, counts of students by category of disability and race were compared to those for white children by state. Table 1 shows the patterns that exist across racial groups and the disability categories of mental retardation, emotional disturbance, and specific learning disabilities. For each state, risk ratios are shown by race for identification for each of the three primary disability categories, MR, ED, and LD. Together, these three cognitive disability categories account for the largest number of children. They are also the categories for which over- and underrepresentation seem most likely to occur.

Using this high standard for disproportionate identification, the number of states in which black students were overrepresented in the disability categories of mental retardation and emotional disturbance is shown, as well as the degree of racial disparity. For example, black children are overrepresented for mental retardation in thirty-eight states. Moreover, the risk of a black child being labeled mentally retarded are more than four times greater than for a white child in the states of Connecticut, Mississippi, North Carolina, Nebraska, and South Carolina. Conversely, the risk of an Asian American/Pacific Islander child being designated as emotionally disturbed are less than one-fourth the chance of a white student being so designated in over one-half the states.

It should be noted that the state-level comparisons present aggregated information by state. Dramatic variations between individual districts and regions within a state might exist that are not revealed in the state-level aggregates. Therefore, the under- or overrepresentation shown for a state does not necessarily depict what is occurring in individual districts.

An interesting observation is the greater likelihood of children in the various minority groups being placed in the category most prone to overrepresentation (MR) when the minority group constitutes a relatively large proportion of the state's population. Examples include Asian American/Pacific Islander in Hawaii, with a risk ratio of 3.48 for MR, compared to their national average of .54. Asian American/Pacific Islander children constitute nearly 59 percent of all school-age children in Hawaii, much higher than that found in any other state. Similarly, in Alaska, where American Indian children comprise

TABLE 1 Risk Ratios for Mental Retardation, Emotional Disturbance, and Specific Learning Disabilites by Race and Ethnicity[a]

	Mental Retardation				Emotional Disturbance				Specific Learning Disabilities			
	American Indian	Asian/ Pacific	Black	Hispanic	American Indian	Asian/ Pacific	Black	Hispanic	American Indian	Asian/ Pacific	Black	Hispanic
United States	1.31*	0.54*	2.88*	0.77*	1.24*	0.29*	1.92*	0.74*	1.50*	0.39*	1.32*	1.17*
Alaska	2.43*	1.49	2.07	1.21	1.54	0.15	2.12	0.36	1.74*	0.69	2.01*	0.86
Alabama	1.13	0.38	3.89*	0.43*	0.76	0.17	1.27*	0.24	2.09*	0.22*	0.97	0.46*
Arkansas	1.12	0.97	3.00*	0.44*	0.00	0.93	1.12	0.25	0.66	0.44*	1.10	0.63*
Arizona	1.50*	0.70	2.97*	1.65*	0.59*	0.23*	1.67*	0.43*	1.43*	0.29*	1.59*	1.20*
California	1.45	0.89	1.89*	1.28*	1.30	0.17*	2.58*	0.38*	1.78*	0.32*	2.05*	1.10*
Colorado	1.89	0.98	3.48*	1.89*	1.75	0.61	2.05*	0.84	1.91*	0.40*	1.69*	1.25*
Connecticut	3.27	0.66	4.76*	3.25*	2.88*	0.23*	2.62*	1.92*	1.72	0.22*	1.49*	1.38*
Delaware	0.00	0.68	3.61*	2.01*	1.34	0.41	2.45*	0.45	1.11	0.16*	2.55*	1.43*
Florida	2.13*	0.65*	3.91*	1.19*	2.61*	0.13*	2.14*	0.63*	1.96*	0.26*	1.20*	0.93*
Georgia	0.31	0.43*	3.09*	0.82	0.60	0.25*	1.38*	0.28*	0.62	0.24*	0.71*	0.61*
Hawaii	1.60	3.48*	1.43	0.67	1.90	1.16	0.91	0.38*	1.28	1.82*	0.83	0.51*
Iowa	1.69	0.54*	2.62*	0.90	1.99	0.32*	4.31*	0.83	1.77*	0.39*	1.87*	0.92
Idaho	2.11	0.77	1.34	1.77*	1.10	0.27	0.65	0.39	1.97*	0.23*	1.49	1.13
Illinois	0.59	0.58*	3.09*	1.05	0.61	0.19*	2.16*	0.61*	0.59	0.22*	1.21*	0.94*
Indiana	0.90	0.43*	3.31*	0.83	0.58	0.19*	1.78*	0.35*	0.73	0.14*	0.96	0.51*
Kansas	1.47	0.53	2.93*	1.26	1.40	0.16*	2.20*	0.71	1.23	0.35*	1.41*	0.93
Kentucky	0.17	0.22*	1.60*	0.36*	0.17	0.22	3.87*	0.43	0.42	0.28*	1.52*	0.54*
Louisiana	1.35	0.49	3.31*	0.39*	1.24	0.07	2.90*	0.41	2.21*	0.19*	1.86*	0.36*
Massachusetts	0.89	0.29*	1.41*	1.13	0.87	0.29*	1.41*	1.13	0.88	0.28*	1.45*	1.14*
Maryland	2.74	0.73	3.29*	0.66	1.96	0.22*	2.13*	0.52*	1.42	0.20*	1.31*	0.80*
Maine	0.44	0.52	1.53	0.79	0.12	0.42	1.69	1.14	0.66	0.38*	1.40	0.74
Michigan	1.39	0.93	2.34*	0.82	1.52	0.69	1.09	0.58*	1.41*	0.84*	1.04	0.92
Minnesota	1.76*	0.82	2.48*	1.39	3.33*	0.27*	3.29*	1.01	1.95*	0.71*	2.72*	1.38*
Missouri	0.58	0.41*	2.75*	0.53*	0.67	0.21*	2.45*	0.53*	0.54*	0.20*	1.52*	0.54*
Mississippi	0.46	0.63	4.31*	0.20	NA**	NA**	0.94	0.22	0.45	0.25*	1.72*	0.33*

	Mental Retardation				Emotional Disturbance				Specific Learning Disabilities			
	American Indian	Asian/ Pacific	Black	Hispanic	American Indian	Asian/ Pacific	Black	Hispanic	American Indian	Asian/ Pacific	Black	Hispanic
Montana	**2.00***	0.77	**3.18**	0.54	1.31	0.81	**3.75**	0.60	**2.19***	0.67	**5.44***	0.29*
North Carolina	**2.97***	0.55*	**4.08***	0.94	0.68	0.18*	**2.76***	0.46*	0.96	0.34*	**1.10***	0.70*
North Dakota	1.45	1.28	1.36	0.74	1.24	0.37	**2.61**	1.62	1.32	0.38	1.19	0.92
Nebraska	**2.31***	0.29	**4.08***	1.45*	**4.83***	0.31	**6.06***	0.56	**2.94***	0.38*	**1.69***	1.04
New Hampshire	0.41	0.23	0.95	0.45	0.91	0.24	1.14	0.39	0.22	0.13*	0.39	0.32*
New Jersey	2.28	1.01	**3.60***	2.39*	0.20	0.19*	**2.40***	1.02	0.76	0.25*	**1.28***	0.87*
New Mexico	1.47	1.12	**2.18***	1.66*	0.71	0.14	**1.88***	0.87	1.09	0.47*	**1.93***	1.27*
Nevada	1.72	1.26	**3.13***	1.20	0.55	0.32	**1.74***	0.24*	1.69*	0.43*	**2.09***	0.92
New York	1.80	0.66*	**2.32***	1.72*	**2.57***	0.27*	**2.56***	2.33*	1.39*	0.36*	**1.64***	1.22*
Ohio	0.67	0.27*	**2.59***	0.93	1.21	0.15*	**2.64***	0.92	0.76	0.28*	0.87*	0.73*
Oklahoma	1.76*	0.34*	**3.44***	0.94	1.02	0.29	**1.90***	0.39*	1.74*	0.27*	**1.58***	0.87
Oregon	1.57	0.57	**2.48***	0.85	1.71	0.20*	**2.85***	0.36*	1.43*	0.26*	1.08	0.78*
Pennsylvania	1.28	0.41*	**1.86***	1.55*	**2.28***	0.21*	**2.38***	1.54*	1.24	0.28*	**1.29***	1.43*
Rhode Island	0.78	0.91	**2.58***	1.98*	1.05	0.26	**1.89***	0.84	0.70	0.28*	**1.26***	1.16
South Carolina	1.41	0.32	**4.30***	0.47*	0.93	0.20	**2.04***	0.46	0.53	0.18*	**1.26***	0.48*
South Dakota	1.25	0.71	2.49	0.64	**2.30***	0.29	2.36	1.55	1.33*	0.69	**2.00***	0.74
Tennessee	0.41	0.35*	**3.46***	0.38*	0.28	0.18	1.47	0.31	0.40*	0.21*	1.09*	0.40*
Texas	1.33	0.70*	**3.21***	1.42*	1.09	0.13*	**1.45***	0.66*	1.21	0.23*	**1.54***	1.23*
Utah	1.28	0.76	1.75	1.30	1.44	0.66	**3.73***	1.06	**2.34***	0.65*	**2.25***	1.36*
Virginia	0.47	0.72	**3.02***	1.43*	1.09	0.27*	**1.61***	1.08	0.84	0.41*	1.14*	1.37*
Vermont	1.50	0.37	0.91	0.00	1.92	0.41	1.61	0.25	0.50	0.29	1.36	0.33
Washington	**2.89***	0.81	**2.75***	1.68*	**2.24***	0.24*	**2.89***	0.52*	**2.25***	0.55*	**2.10***	1.31*
Wisconsin	1.44	1.16	**3.16***	1.25	**2.63***	0.21*	**1.99***	0.75	**1.58***	0.67*	**1.41***	0.97
West Virginia	0.80	0.28	**1.52***	0.15	1.39	0.17	**2.77***	0.66	0.67	0.14*	1.14	0.52
Wyoming	1.01	1.78	**2.04**	1.04	1.39	0.37	2.35	0.73	1.50	0.23	1.84	1.03

ᵃ The data underlying this table are from the U.S. Department of Education (1998).

Boldface indicates double the rate of whites. Asian/Pacific indicates Asian American/Pacific Islander.

* Indicates statistical significance at the .01 level

** NA, not applicable, is shown for Mississippi because no American Indian or Asian/Pacific students were identified for Emotional Disturbance in that state for the 1998–1999 school year.

TABLE 2
Mental Retardation Risk Ratios in High- and Low-Percentage
Minority States by Race[a]

Percent Minority	American Indian		Asian/Pacific		Black		Hispanic	
	Risk of MR compared to whites	% of total enrollment that are Am. Ind.[b]	Risk of MR compared to whites	% of total enrollment that are Asian/Pac.	Risk of MR compared to whites	% of total enrollment that are black	Risk of MR compared to whites	% of total enrollment that are Hispanic
Lowest Ten States	1.07	0.2%	0.66	0.7%	1.77	0.8%	0.42	1.2%
Highest Ten States	1.75	8.4%	1.14	10.8%	3.59	31.6%	1.55	25.6%

a The data underlying this table are from the U.S. Department of Education (1998).

b "Total enrollment" refers to special education and general education combined.

over 21 percent of student enrollment, the risk for American Indian children being identified as mentally retarded are considerably larger than the national average (2.43 vs. 1.31).

For the disability category of mental retardation, this trend holds across all minority groups (see Table 2). For black children, the risk of being designated mentally retarded (in comparison to white children) range from 3.59 in the ten states in which the proportion is the highest to 1.77 in the ten states where the proportion is the lowest. Thus, the ratio is about twice as high for blacks in states where they are more heavily concentrated.

For Hispanic children, the odds are more than three times as great in the ten states with the highest percentage of Hispanic students (1.55 vs. 0.42) as in the states with the lowest percentage of Hispanics. Many of the highest-percentage minority states are southern and southwestern states with histories of segregation.

Identification Disparities in Soft versus Hard Categories of Disability

One approach to attempting to isolate the effect of poverty as opposed to race on the disproportionate identification of black students for special education is to compare the identification patterns observed for black students in soft versus hard categories of disability. This division into soft and hard categories is somewhat of an artificial distinction, as all categories of disability contain some form of medical determination in their definition. However, the categories of disability called specific learning disability, mental retardation, and emotional disturbance are sometimes referred to as soft categories because they are more subjec-

TABLE 3

Comparison of Risk Ratios between Blacks and Whites in Hard and Soft Disability
Categories in the United States and in Selected States[a]

	Soft Disabilities			Hard Disabilities[b]
	MR	ED	SLD	
Connecticut	4.76	2.62	1.49	1.49
Mississippi	4.31	0.94	1.72	1.07
South Carolina	4.30	2.04	1.26	1.30
North Carolina	4.08	2.76	1.10	1.03
Nebraska	4.08	6.06	1.69	1.50
Florida	3.91	2.14	1.20	1.09
Alabama	3.89	1.27	0.97	1.11
Delaware	3.61	2.45	2.55	1.30
New Jersey	3.60	2.40	1.28	2.18
Colorado	3.48	2.05	1.69	1.34
United States	2.88	1.92	1.32	1.18

Blacks were most overrepresented for mental retardation (MR) in the ten states selected.

[a] All data are from 1998 U.S. Department of Education Office of Special Education Programs. See Table 1 for indications on statistical significance.

[b] The hard disabilities category includes hearing impairments, visual impairments, orthopedic impairments, deaf-blindness, multiple disabilities, and traumatic brain injury.

tively and less medically determined than categories such as deafness or blindness, which are deemed hard because they are less prone to subjectivity and are readily diagnosed medically. Arguably, if the effects of poverty, including diminished nutrition and limited access to preventive health care, cause more black students to be identified for the soft category of mental retardation, then these factors should have a similar effect on the incidence of the hard categories of deafness and blindness.

However, the data show substantial incongruence between the level of overrepresentation for hard and soft categories. Nationwide, blacks are almost exactly as likely as white students to be identified for the hard disability categories, while they are nearly three times (2.88) more likely than whites to be identified as mentally retarded and nearly twice as likely to be identified as ED (1.92). Furthermore, as Table 3 shows, we found substantially less racial disproportionality for hard categories in the ten states that were highest for overrepresenting black students as MR. These data suggest that something more than the effects of poverty are causing black students to be disproportionately identified for some categories of disability.

TABLE 4

Placement and Service Characteristics by Race for California

	Percent in General Education with Related Services (a)	Percent in Resource Room (b)	Percent in Private School (c)	Percent in Special Education Self-Contained (d)	Percent Requiring Intensive Services (e)
American Indian	21%	48%	2%	29%	20%
Asian American/ Pacific Islander	32%	32%	1%	35%	27%
Black	17%	41%	4%	37%	29%
Hispanic	22%	44%	1%	33%	25%
White	27%	46%	2%	24%	23%

Source: California Special Education Management System (CASEMIS).

PLACEMENTS AND SERVICES BY RACE

A more extensive, detailed view of the mix of special education services received by individual students can be found in the California Special Education Management Information System (CASEMIS). This file contains a broad range of information about the more than 600,000 children who receive special education services in California. Because California is so populous, these data provide a detailed snapshot of approximately one-eighth of the nation's students.

Table 4 shows the types of placements and services that result from these patterns of identification by race and by disability. Column (e) shows that black students are more likely than white students to be designated as requiring intensive services (29% vs. 23%) and more likely to be placed in such restrictive settings as self-contained special education classrooms (37% vs. 24%) and private special education schools (4% vs. 2%). Also, the gap between restrictive settings and the need for intensive services is most pronounced for minorities. While this gap [the difference between columns (d) and (e)] equals 8–9 percent for minority students, it equals 1 percent for white students. This suggests that whites are generally only placed in more restrictive self-contained classes when they need intensive services. Minority students, however, may be more likely to be placed in the restrictive setting whether they require intensive services or not.

Another view of the placements and services received by California students by race is presented in Table 5. It compares breakouts of total student enrollment, special education enrollment, special education private school enroll-

TABLE 5

Distribution by Race of California Students Overall,
in Special Education, and in the California Youth Authority

	White	Hispanic	Black	Asian	Other	Total
All Students	40%	41%	9%	9%	1%	100%
Special Education	43%	37%	14%	3%	3%	100%
Private Special Education Schools	48%	19%	30%	1%	2%	100%
Residential Private Special Education	58%	15%	21%	3%	3%	100%
California Youth Authority	15%	47%	29%	7%	2%	100%

Source: California Special Education Management System (CASEMIS).

ments, and students under the jurisdiction of the California Youth Authority. While the distribution of special education by race is reasonably reflective of all students, this picture changes dramatically in the case of private special education schools, and particularly in the case of residential private special education schools. As these placements rise in cost, peaking at the very costly private special education residential placements, white participation increases dramatically in relation to the percentage of white children in the population (from 40% to 58%). Black enrollments also rise in relation to their percentage of the population (from 9% to 30% in private special education schools) until the most costly placement of special education residential schools, where black students drop to 21 percent representation. Hispanic students show a dramatic reverse pattern, with their representation dropping from 41 percent of all students to 15 percent of residential private special education schools.

Most students (63%) in private special education schools in California are identified as having an emotional disturbance. Many of these children find themselves in these schools because they have demonstrated some form of anti-social behavior. Children exhibiting such behaviors sometimes end up in residential private special education placements, where they are likely to receive intensive treatment, while in other cases they may be placed with the California Youth Authority, a placement that is more punishing than remedial.

Black children are overrepresented in these three types of settings in relation to their percentage of the population (9% vs. 21% vs. 29%). Very different placement patterns are seen for Hispanic and white children. Although nearly equally divided in the population (41% vs. 40%), Hispanics represent 47 percent of the children under the jurisdiction of the California Youth Authority, compared to 15 percent for white children. These figures are close to being reversed in private special education school settings, where Hispanic children constitute 15 percent of the population, compared to 58 percent for white children.[7]

SPECIAL EDUCATION FUNDING IN RELATION TO OVER- AND UNDERREPRESENTATION

What is the relationship between special education identification rates for minority students and special education funding? In the case of overrepresentation of minority students in more severe and generally higher-cost disability categories, it might be expected that added special education funding would follow these higher rates of designation. But this was not the case. The following analysis presents a complex pattern that suggests a possible link between identification rates and certain types of funding formulas.

For the purpose of these analyses, state formulas are divided into three categories: those directly linked to the overall number of students identified for special education and/or the services provided; the subset of these linked formulas in which the funding amounts vary by category of disability; and formulas that are not linked to any measure of special education incidence or service.

Table 6a separates the states by the three approaches to special education funding described above [column (b)].[8] It also lists the state's risk ratio for minority children as mentally retarded relative to that of white children [column (c)]. Table 6a also shows the percentage difference in special education funding received by the highest and the lowest quartiles of districts in the state in terms of minority enrollment [column (d)]. For example, the amount shown for South Carolina indicates that the average amount of state special education funding per special education student in the highest-percentage-minority districts was 3.8 percent more than in the lowest-percentage-minority districts. In New Jersey, however, the opposite trend was observed, with the state's highest-minority districts receiving 33.2 percent less in average state funding per special education student than the lowest-minority districts.

Is additional special education funding found in high-minority districts in states where minority students are overrepresented for mental retardation? Do racial disproportion and funding patterns vary by type of special education funding formula?

Further funding comparisons were conducted to find out whether high-minority districts in states with high rates of overrepresentation for MR received additional special education funding. Although there was no uniform

TABLE 6a

Comparison of Special Education Funding Formula with Minority Risk Ratios and with Special Education Per Pupil Expenditures in High- and Low-Minority Districts

States Ranked by Minority Risk Compared to White (a)	Formula Type (b)	Risk Ratio for Mental Retardation (c)	Special Education Funding Differential per Student in High- versus Low-Minority Districts[b] (d)
South Carolina	Service and Category Linked	4.06	3.8%
Connecticut	Service Linked	3.65	85.8%
North Carolina	Service Linked	3.61	5.5%
Delaware	Service and Category Linked	3.15	−2.2%
Louisiana	Service Linked	3.03	−2.1%
Maryland	Unlinked	2.74	99.9%
New Jersey	Service and Category Linked	2.71	−33.2%
Arkansas	Service Linked	2.65	45.3%
Florida	Service and Category Linked	2.62	31.8%
Indiana	Service and Category Linked	2.55	−7.7%
Virginia	Service Linked	2.52	0.6%
Nebraska	Service Linked	2.36	−3.7%
Missouri	Service Linked	2.31	41.9%
Wisconsin	Service Linked	2.26	25.0%
Ohio	Service and Category Linked	2.23	−18.9%
Colorado	Unlinked	2.10	10.4%
Illinois	Service Linked	2.07	−38.1%
Mississippi	Service Linked	1.98	3.2%
Kansas	Service Linked	1.88	77.3%
Texas	Service Linked	1.84	−0.1%
Nevada	Service Linked	1.71	−9.2%
Pennsylvania	Unlinked	1.64	−12.8%
North Dakota	Service Linked	1.33	41.1%
California	Service Linked	1.29	23.7%
Utah	Unlinked	1.23	13.3%
South Dakota	Service Linked	1.23	55.8%
Wyoming	Service Linked	1.16	−2.0%
Vermont	Service Linked	0.46	−1.6%

[a] All data are from 1998 U.S. Department of Education Office of Special Education Programs. See Table 1 for indications on statistical significance.

[b] Annual Survey of Local Government Finances conducted by the U.S. Bureau of the Census and the Common Core of School District Data produced by the U.S. Department of Education's National Center for Education Statistics (NCES) for the 1997–1998 school year.

Service Linked: All students identified for special education and/or the services provided.

Service and Category Linked: Subset of these linked formulas in which the funding amounts vary by category of disability.

Unlinked: Formulas that are not linked to any measure of special education incidence or service (e.g., national averages).

TABLE 6b
Summary of Spending Differentials and MR Risk Ratios
in High- versus Low-Minority Districts

Comparison Group (a)	Number of States (b)	Risk Ratio for Mental Retardation (c)	Special Education Funding Differential, High- versus Low-Minority Districts (d)
By Degree of Overrepresentation of Minority Students			
Highest	14	2.87	20.8%
Lowest	14	1.58	10.2%
By Formula Type			
Service and Category Linked	6	2.89	−4.4%
Service Linked	18	2.07	19.4%
Unlinked	4	1.93	27.7%

Source: 1998 U.S. Department of Education Office of Special Education Programs.

pattern, the evidence generally suggests that some fiscal premium for high-minority districts appears to be associated with high rates of overrepresentation.

Specifically, of the twenty states with sufficient financial data, sixteen showed a positive relationship between the percentage minority enrollment in a district and district special education funding per pupil. However, twelve states showed a negative relationship. Moreover, a comparison of the half of these states with the largest risk ratios to the half with the lowest risk ratios shows a 20.8 percent funding differential favoring high-minority districts among the states with the highest risk ratios. This compares with a 10.2 percent differential for high-minority districts in states showing the lowest risk ratios. Thus, some fiscal premium for high-minority districts appears to be associated with higher degrees of overrepresentation.[9]

The clearest pattern of funding differentials between high- and low- percentage-minority districts appears to be by type of funding formula. Interestingly, the six states with funding formulas that specifically place higher premiums on higher-cost disabilities, such as MR (Service and Category Linked), are much more likely to have minority students overrepresented for mental retardation. At the same time, four of the six show negative special education funding differentials disfavoring high-minority districts.

When the degree of minority overrepresentation is compared by formula type, the largest average risk ratio (2.89) is shown for the six states with formulas that differentiate funding by category of disability partially or totally. This suggests that state formulas that place revenue premiums on more severe categories of disability, such as MR, may somehow affect the overidentification of minority students.

Interestingly, of the twenty-eight states, the four that have funding systems with no relationship to any measure of special education provision show the highest degree of resource targeting to high-minority districts (with a 27.7% differential). The eighteen states with funding systems linked to special education provision, but not specifically to category of disability, show special education funding favoring high-minority districts by 19.4 percent. Only the states basing funding on disability category show a negative relationship between special education funding and percentage of minority students, with an average of –4.4 percent. Two of the three states with the greatest disparity in special education funding for high- and low-minority districts, Ohio and New Jersey, have funding systems that vary by category of disability.

It may not be wise to overspeculate about this rather counter-intuitive relationship, especially when based on six states that show considerable variation in overidentifying and underfunding minority students. On the other hand, when taken as a whole, these states look substantially different from their counterparts, which do not have systems that fund differently by category of disability.

For example, although minority students in New Jersey are overrepresented in the mental retardation disability category, they are generally underrepresented in special education overall. Thus, overidentification for MR does not lead to higher special education funding flowing to high-minority districts. In Ohio, although black students are overdesignated for mental retardation, all four categories of minority students are underrepresented in what is by far the largest special education category, learning disability.

The policy implications of these findings in relation to disability-based formulas are not clear, but they challenge the assumption of equity associated with differentiating special education funding by category of disability. The strongest rationale underlying this type of funding system is that, by having higher dollar allocations associated with more severe categories of disability, special education funding will flow to where they are most needed. Based on the findings above, this assumption must be questioned unless it can be argued that, even though minority students are more likely to be designated mentally retarded, their overall special education needs are less than those of their white counterparts.

IMPLICATIONS FOR POLICY REFORM

Clear patterns of overrepresentation of minority children are found, which vary dramatically by state, by category of disability, and by race. Across all disabilities and states, Hispanic children are represented in special education at about the same rate as white students. However, at least one study that looked at district-level disparities suggest that Hispanic children may be substantially overrepresented in some districts and underrepresented in others (Finn, 1982). Black and American Indian children are overrepresented, while Asian American/Pacific Islander children are underrepresented. Overrepresentation in the mental retardation disability category is shown for each of the minority categories in at least one state. The likelihood of overrepresentation in this category of disability for a minority group seems to be greater in states where the minority group is the largest. For example, Asian American/Pacific Islander students show overrepresentation for mental retardation in Hawaii, where they comprise a large portion of the population, as compared to underrepresentation for Asian American/Pacific Islander children nationally.

What policy interventions do these troubling findings suggest? One is that these kinds of data should be tracked on an ongoing basis, incorporated into the monitoring processes of state and federal agencies administering special education programs, and reported to policymakers, advocates, and the public at large. Can Connecticut, Mississippi, North Carolina, Nebraska, and South Carolina be in compliance with special education and civil rights law when black students are over four times more likely than white students to be designated mentally retarded?

One would expect that, where higher concentrations of disabilities do exist, supplemental funds and services should also be found. However, special education formulas that differentiate funding by category of disability appear not to be working that way. A concern long associated with formulas that place funding premiums on certain categories of disability is that such categories may create fiscal incentives to overidentify students into these disability groups. Why would these incentives be more likely to pertain to minority students? Perhaps they have fewer advocates to protect them from these economic incentives.

Poverty does not appear to explain the patterns of overrepresentation revealed in this chapter. For example, using data from the years 1976, 1980, and 1983, McLaughlin and Owings (1993) found a significant negative relationship between the percentage of school-age children living in poverty and identification rates for learning-disabled students for two of these three years. These authors also found a significant negative relationship between poverty and identification rates for emotionally disturbed students in one of these three years. No significant relationship between poverty and overall special education identification rates was shown for any of the three years (Parrish & Verstegen, 1994).

Parrish and Hikido (1998) examined the relationship between the percentage of children living in poverty, the percentage of minority students, and overall allocations of state special education funding across the nation's school districts. Their analysis suggests a much stronger relationship between special education and race than between special education and poverty. State special education funding was 17 percent more in the quartile of districts across the nation with the highest percentage of students in poverty than in the quartile of districts with the fewest students in poverty.[10] However, special education funding was 41 percent higher in districts with the highest percentages of minority students.

In addition, the wide variations in over- and underrepresentation shown in this chapter suggest subjective identification and inconsistency in the identification process despite IDEA's clear guidelines. IDEA, Part B, states: "The term 'children with learning disabilities'. . . does not include children who have learning problems which are primarily the result of . . . environmental, cultural, or economic disadvantage." However, research has demonstrated that identification decisions for students with mild disabilities, who make up the vast majority of the special education student population, are based on some combination of objective criteria, subjective criteria, and local state and federal policies (Ysseldyke, Algozzine, Richey, & Graden, 1982; Ysseldyke, Algozzine, Shinn, & McGue, 1982). For these reasons, links shown to exist between at-risk conditions related to poverty and incidence levels of disabling conditions may not translate into a positive relationship between poverty and special education identification (Parrish & Verstegen, 1994).

A majority of the states allocate more education resources and more special education resources to high-minority districts. However, this pattern seems only weakly linked to patterns of overrepresentation.

Variation in the type of special education funding system suggests that funding systems based on category of disability are particularly prone to troubling patterns of minority overrepresentation and resource distribution. These systems appear much more likely to show over-representation of minority students into the disability category mental retardation, while at the same time providing greater special education funding to districts enrolling the lowest percentages of minority students.

Finally, in addition to special education funds not tracking well to the overidentification of minority students, data from California suggest that black students are more likely to be found in restrictive settings than their white counterparts, including the juvenile justice system. Hispanic students, who are generally underrepresented in special education in California, are also overrepresented in the state's juvenile corrections system.

Finance systems that differentiate funding by the student's category of disability are based on the assumption of a strong link between category of disability and cost. Numerous finance studies (e.g., Moore et al., 1988), however, have shown this connection to be much more tenuous than was commonly thought, with as much variation in cost found within categories of disability as across them.

High-minority districts are much more reliant on categorical funding sources, such as special education, than low-minority districts (Parrish & Hikido, 1998). While base funding is 10 percent lower per student in high-minority districts, categorical funding is twice as high. Until we achieve greater equity in base funds across districts, high-minority districts are likely to continue to look to categorical programs such as special education for remedial education support.

A more fundamental concern associated with these formulas is that they tend to emphasize the wrong thing. They may be placing too much emphasis on category of disability at the expense of more appropriate foci for funding formulas, such as the equitable distribution of funds, accurate identification and labeling of students, and the delivery of appropriate services.

Census-based funding systems, which have no link to variations in the identification of special education students or the provision of services, are predicated on an opposite notion of funding than those adjusted by category of disability. Census-based systems assume comparable distributions of disability across jurisdictions. Some variations of this model, such as the system recently adopted by the federal government, skew these Census-based distributions in favor of higher-poverty states and districts. This may be the best way to ensure that special education funds are allocated where they are most needed without creating incentives for overidentification. Perhaps this is why the states with census-type systems, designated in Table 4 as "Unlinked," were the least likely to overidentify minority students and the most likely to distribute more special education funds to high-minority districts.

In addition to removing fiscal incentives for identifying special education students, and especially for identifying them into certain disability categories, other policy interventions are also likely to mediate the overidentification of minority children. One is equity in base funding for education. The more that base funds for education are inadequate in high-minority districts, the greater the pull of fiscal incentives to seek supplemental categorical funds such as special education (Parrish & Hikido, 1998). Another strategy is creating alternatives to special education. If special education is the only place where students with learning difficulties can receive supplemental help, the greater the attraction of this program will be.

Pressure to place more and more students in special education may also be increased by the recent emphasis on education accountability. If high-minority districts are held to higher standards of performance without the supplemental resources needed to achieve them, minority children may increasingly be found to need remediation. Without alternatives, it may become even more likely in the future that these services will be provided through special education. This is unlikely to be the best way to assist many of these children and appears likely to further exacerbate minority overidentification.

Although there may be agreement in principle that special education should be implemented, administered, and funded in a color-blind fashion, this does not seem to be the case. Clearer guidelines for identification, stricter monitoring and enforcement, equitable base funding, the creation of remediation alternatives, and neutral funding formulas may not fully resolve the situation, but they seem likely to help and to be reasonable objectives for policymakers to pursue.

NOTES

1. "Soft" disability categories are those that are more subjectively and less medically determined than "hard" disabilities, which are readily diagnosed medically.
2. LD is the category that is least likely to reflect overidentification. However, in states like California where the *Larry P. v. Riles,* 793 F.2d 969 (9th Cir. 1984) case greatly restricted the placement of black students in MR, we do see black overidentification in LD (as well as in ED). A possible reason why black overrepresentation in LD is generally less common, however, may be that white and middle-class parents whose children are eligible for services may be in a position to more actively contest the more stigmatizing labels of MR and ED in favor of LD.
3. Special education expenditure studies were completed by the Center for Special Education Finance at the American Institutes for Research for the states of New York, New Jersey, Rhode Island, Delaware, Alabama, Maryland, Ohio, Indiana, Kansas, Missouri, and Wyoming.
4. Funding differs from spending. That is, while the amount of money made available to districts from state and federal sources is generally known, what is not known is how much comes from local sources to meet the full cost of providing special education programs and services.
5. This database, the California Special Education Management Information System (CASEMIS), is updated for every special education student in California every year.
6. For a complete description of risk ratios, see Bohrnstedt and Knoke (1994, pp. 178–181).
7. It is important to keep in mind that Alfredo Artiles' work (see Artiles et al., this volume) suggests that when these data are broken down by age, older Hispanic students are overidentified and younger students are underidentified.
8. As discussed, good data were only available for twenty-eight states.

9. Although this pattern generally holds, it is not uniform. Maryland, with a strong positive relationship favoring special education funding in high-poverty districts, and New Jersey, with a strong negative relationship, overidentify minority students at about the same rate (2.74 vs. 2.71). Conversely, South Dakota shows relatively little overidentification (1.23), but shows special education revenue allocations strongly favoring high-minority districts (by 55.8%).

10. However, special education funding was 41 percent higher in districts with the highest percentages of minority students. The data suggest that race is a much stronger predictor for special education than poverty.

REFERENCES

Bohrnstedt, G. W., & Knoke, D. (1994). *Statistics for social science data analysis* (3rd ed.). Itasca, IL: F. E. Peacock.

Chambers, J. G. (1998). *Development of a national geographic cost of education index (GCEI) for public schools.* Palo Alto, CA: American Institutes for Research.

Chambers, J., Parrish, T., & Harr, J. (2002). *What are we spending on special education services in the United States?* Palo Alto, CA: American Institutes for Research, Center for Special Education Finance.

Finn, J. D. (1982). Patterns in special education placement as revealed by the OCR surveys. In K. A. Heller, W. H. Holtzman, & S. Messick (Eds.), *Placing children in special education: A strategy for equity.* Washington, DC: National Academy Press.

Hartman, W. T., & Fay, T. A. (1996). *Cost-effectiveness of instructional support teams in Pennsylvania.* Palo Alto, CA: American Institutes for Research, Center for Special Education Finance.

McLaughlin, M. J., & Owings, M. (1993). Relationships among states' fiscal and demographic data and the implementation of PL 94-142. *Exceptional Children, 59,* 247–261.

Moore, M. T., Strang, E. W., Schwartz, M., & Braddock, M. (1988). *Patterns in special education service delivery and cost.* Washington, DC: Decisions Resources.

Parrish, T. B. (2000). Special education: At what cost to general education? In *CSEF Resource* (winter 1999–2000). Palo Alto, CA: American Institutes for Research, Center for Special Education Finance.

Parrish, T. (2001). Who's paying the rising cost of special education? *Journal of Special Education Leadership, 14*(1), 4–12.

Parrish, T., & Anthony, J. J. (2002). *State special education finance systems and expenditures, 1999–00.* Palo Alto, CA: American Institutes for Research, Center for Special Education Finance.

Parrish, T. B., & Hikido, C. (1998). *Inequalities in public school district revenues* (NCES 98-210). Washington, DC: U.S. Department of Education, National Center for Education Statistics.

Parrish, T. B., & Verstegen, D. (1994). *Fiscal provisions of the Individuals with Disabilities Act: Policy issues and alternatives.* Palo Alto, CA: American Institutes for Research, Center for Special Education Finance.

Rothstein, R. (1997). *Where's the money going?* Washington, DC: Economic Policy Institute.

U.S. Department of Education. (1997). *Nineteenth annual report to Congress to assure the free appropriate public education of all children with disabilities.* Washington, DC: Author.

Ysseldyke, J., Algozzine, B., Richey, L., & Graden, J. (1982). Declaring students eligible for learning disability services: Why bother with the data? *Learning Disability Quarterly, 5,* 37–44.

Ysseldyke, J., Algozzine, B., Shinn, M., & McGue, M. (1982). Similarities and differences between low achievers and students classified learning disabled. *Journal of Special Education, 16*(1), 73–85.

CHAPTER THREE

Double Jeopardy:
An Exploration of Restrictiveness and
Race in Special Education

EDWARD GARCIA FIERROS

JAMES W. CONROY

SPECIAL EDUCATION:
SUPPORT AND SERVICES, NOT A PLACE

Following the 1954 U.S. Supreme Court decision in *Brown v. Board of Education,* segregated school districts often sought ways to circumvent school desegregation. As the National Research Council suggested in 1982, "One device to screen out minority students, which relied heavily on intelligence tests, may have been special education, especially classes for mildly mentally retarded students. For example, the repeal of the law in California excluding Mexican-Americans from white schools coincided with the legislative creation of programs for EMR [the educationally mentally retarded] students" (National Research Council [NRC], 1982, p. 33). In 1975, Congress passed the Education for All Handicapped Children Act partly as a response to the fact that public schools often treated students with disabilities as second-class students, placing them in separate classrooms where they were unnecessarily isolated from the general education classroom.

The Education for All Handicapped Act (PL 94-142), now the Individuals with Disabilities Education Act (IDEA), sought to remedy the denial of access to schools and the unjustified segregation of students with disabilities. The law has consistently required that schools provide a continuum of educational settings and services so that students with disabilities can be educated with their nondisabled peers in the least restrictive environment to the maximum extent appropriate. The term *restrictive* describes the extent to which students with disabilities are educated outside of regular classrooms and isolated from their nondisabled peers. Restrictiveness is measured by the percentage of the typical school day that a student spends in a regular or "general" education classroom.[1] "Fully inclusive" and 100 percent outside the general classroom are opposite ends of the spectrum.[2]

This research reveals that special education students from minority racial groups are more likely than whites to be placed in restrictive educational settings. This disproportionate level of restrictiveness is most pronounced for African Americans and Hispanics. In addition to concerns about the segregative effect of such placements, research has documented that students with disabilities generally benefit more from inclusion, although it also confirms that some students with disabilities make greater progress when they are educated in a separate setting for all or part of the school day when their individual academic and/or behavioral needs call for it. In every state, however, once identified for special education services, minority students are more likely to be restricted than whites, suggesting a disturbing lack of effective mainstreaming programs and unwarranted isolation.

Under IDEA, identifying a student as being eligible for special education services must be entirely separate from deciding the proper level of inclusion/restrictiveness. At the heart of IDEA is the principle that each student will receive individualized services. Decisions to place any student in a given educational setting must be individually tailored to best meet the needs of the student, and not dictated by the administrative convenience of a school, district, or existing program of special education. The issue of placement is often confused with that of identification for special education services. Part of this confusion stems from the frequent and incorrect notion that special education is a place, rather than a system of supports and services.

Disturbing patterns of isolation in special education—most pronounced for African American children—point to a large and complex set of issues. As this research shows, this isolation phenomenon is not uncommon in urban schools, including those with predominantly minority populations. It is certainly possible that the increased isolation of minority students disproportionately labeled for special education in some schools may be a product of racial bias. At the same time, racially isolated, high-poverty urban schools may be using special education as triage because they lack supports for inclusive educational placements. As a recent National Research Council report points out, some poorly prepared or supported teachers may refer students for special education evaluation as a way to deal with discipline problems and insufficient resources (NRC, 2002).

Special education teachers may be ill trained or supported when it comes to providing high-quality inclusion for students. Furthermore, special education programs in urban schools generally suffer from the same resource shortfalls, inexperienced and highly mobile teacher corps, and poor administrative supports that plague their general education counterparts (NRC, 2002). Thus, inadequacies within special education may be compounded by the difficulties involved with providing services in poorly functioning general education settings.

This chapter seeks to add a fuller description to the growing body of research on minority overrepresentation in special education. To seek a remedy, we first need to identify the extent of the pattern and then explore its complex mechanisms. In earlier studies, the categories mental retardation (MR), emotional disturbance (ED), previously called severe emotional disturbance (SED), and specific learning disability (SLD) have been found to include a disproportionate number of black students compared to their percentage in the overall student population—with the greatest levels of overrepresentation in the area of MR (Artiles & Trent, 1994; Conroy, 1999; Coutinho & Oswald, 2000; Finn, 1982; Stainback & Stainback, 1996). The variation in the disproportionality of black MR student placement has been attributed to teachers' perceptions and attitudes in identifying characteristics of special needs students (Grossman, 1995; Harry, 1992; Utley & Mortweet, 1999), high-stakes assessments (Grossman, 1995; Harry, 1992), differing state-level special needs education funding formulas (Parrish, this volume), and differences among states in data collection procedures and terminology (Danielson & Bellamy, 1989).

The research presented here describes restrictiveness and its relationship to overidentification, but it does not explore the possible causes or solutions. This research does indicate that, nationwide, the percentage of black students who receive their special education supports and services in restrictive educational settings is substantially higher than the percentage of similarly situated white students. At the time of this study there was no national dataset that described levels of restrictiveness by disability category with race/ethnicity. However, there are two prevalent trends in the data: 1) once identified, minority students from every major racial group are more likely than white students with disabilities to be removed from the general education classroom for all or part of their school day; and 2) black students are most often overidentified in the disability categories that have the highest correlation with isolation from the general education setting, mental retardation and emotional disturbance.

Two additional levels of analysis further substantiate the national- and state-level findings: first, a survey of selected urban districts, and second, an in-depth analysis of comprehensive data from Connecticut that directly shows restrictiveness according to disability category by race/ethnicity. The examination of ten large urban school districts generally found rates of restrictiveness that were much higher than their home state's levels of restrictiveness in all three categories. Most striking, the Connecticut study directly showed substantially higher rates of restrictiveness for every minority group within each category studied, along with extremely wide variations in labeling and placement rates for minority students across school districts. Viewed together, this national-, state-, and district-level research suggests not only widespread violations of IDEA's least restrictive environment requirements, but also that minority students within a given state are disproportionately subjected to possibly unlawful treatment.

RESTRICTIVENESS FROM THE REGULAR EDUCATION CLASSROOM SETTING[3]

The regular classroom setting has been described as an essential part of a full educational experience for all students (Coutinho & Rupp, 1999; Crockett & Kauffman, 1999; U.S. Department of Education, 1999). Research has shown that "social interactions between students with and without disabilities are enhanced when students with disabilities are served in regular classes—and are beneficial for many students without disabilities" (U.S. Department of Education, 1999, p. 6). Rea, McLaughlin, and Walther-Thomas (2002) have found that students with specific learning disabilities served in inclusive classrooms earned higher grades, achieved higher or comparable scores on standardized tests, committed no more behavioral infractions, and attended more days of school than students served in the pullout program. The three most common instructional settings for students with disabilities are Inclusive, Resource Room, and Substantially Separate (see Figure 1).

Although the national data have only become available recently, many prior studies concluded that minorities have continued to be disproportionately overrepresented relative to their white counterparts in resource rooms, separate classrooms, and separate school facilities (Harry, 1992; Grossman, 1995). These restrictive placements mean that minority special education students' educational experiences are likely to be delivered in unequal and separate classroom environments (Crockett & Kauffman, 1999; Grossman, 1995). For example, Coutinho and Repp (1999) reported that, for the 1992–1993 school year, nearly 60 percent of students with disabilities ages three to twenty-one were taught outside the regular classroom. In addition, Lipsky and Gartner (1997) stated that "the negative consequences of the separate special education system are greater for students from racial minorities" (p. 33).

FIGURE 1
Most Common Instructional Settings for Students with Disabilities

---

Inclusive:

Regular class includes students who receive the majority of their instruction in a regular classroom and receive special education and related services outside the classroom for less than 21 percent of the school day.

Resource Room:

Resource room includes students who receive special education and related services outside the general classroom for at least 21 percent but not more than 60 percent of the school day. This may include students placed in resource rooms with part-time instruction in a regular class.

Substantially Separate:

Separate class, separate school, and residential facilities includes students who receive special education and related services outside the general classroom for greater than 60 percent of the school day. The term *separate class* generally refers to placements in self-contained special classrooms with part-time instruction in general classes or placed in self-contained classes full time on a general education school campus. (United States Department of Education, 1996; U.S. Department of Education, 2000a)

DATA SOURCES AND METHODOLOGY

This research examines restrictiveness rates and racial/ethnic proportionality for students deemed eligible for special education placements and identified as having mental retardation, emotional disturbance, and specific learning disability. First, national special education placement data from the Office of Special Education Programs (OSEP) will be examined to determine the potential risk for black and Hispanic students with disabilities to be restricted from the regular education classroom. Second, to achieve a basic understanding of the ramifications of overrepresentation in each disability category (i.e., MR, ED, and SLD), national U.S. Office of Civil Rights (OCR) data will be explored to look at restrictiveness rates. Specifically, the restrictiveness rate of each state by three cognitive disability categories was paired with an analysis of state-level identification rates for blacks and Hispanics. Third, a selection of urban, mostly high-minority school districts will be examined to learn how these urban districts' rates of restrictiveness align with that of their state. Finally, data from Connecticut, where racial disproportionality in identification is high for most minority groups, is examined in depth to see whether inferences drawn from the national database are borne out by more complete data from a separate database.

The data for this study were drawn from three sources: the *2002 Office of Special Education Programs, Data Analysis System* (U.S. Department of Education, 2001a); the *Fall 1998 Elementary and Secondary School Civil Rights Compliance Report* (U.S. Department of Education, 2000); and the Connecticut Integrated Special Student Information System (ISSIS), which was produced as part of the discovery process for examination by Dr. James Conroy, who testified as an expert for the plaintiffs in *C.A.R.C. v. State of Connecticut Board of Education,* a class action lawsuit that reached settlement in 2001 (Conroy, 1997; Conroy, Nerney, & Bowen, 1998; Nerney, Conroy, & Bowen, 1997).[4]

Fall 1998 Elementary and Secondary School Civil Rights Compliance Report

Since 1968, the OCR has conducted a biannual compliance report to help enforce students' civil rights in public schools. Using a stratified random sample of 5,898 school districts, the 1998 dataset for the first time included all those districts under court orders initiated by the U.S. Justice Department (U.S. Department of Education, 2000). The reported results in the dataset are national and state projections based on a probability sample of public school districts and schools. The data used in the analysis for this study were national-, state-, and district-level projections of membership, mental retardation, emotional disturbance, and specific learning disability.

OSEP Data

The IDEA requires that the Office of Special Education Programs Data Analysis System (DANS) collect race data from all states as posted on its website (IDEAdata.org). OSEP data were collected for race for all states in the 1998–1999 and 1999–2000 school years (U.S. Dept. of Education, 2001b). The OSEP data differs from the OCR data in that all the OCR data are projections based on sampling, whereas the OSEP data are from nearly every district and based on an actual child count, not primarily on projections. The OSEP data were reported in separate tables as numbers of students with disabilities in each educational setting disaggregated by race. The percentages for the OSEP data as reported here were calculated on the basis of the total for all three educational settings so that approximately 100 percent of students with disabilities for each racial group were represented.

The data available nationally allowed for two types of analysis. First, it was possible to determine the educational placement percentages for all students with disabilities disaggregated by race using the data provided by OSEP. This permitted a comparison of the level of restrictiveness for black, Hispanic, and

FIGURE 2

National Racial Disparities in Inclusion for Blacks, Hispanics, and Whites

Among students with disabilities, blacks and Hispanics are each more likely than whites to be educated in a substantially separate educational setting and denied access to inclusive educational settings.

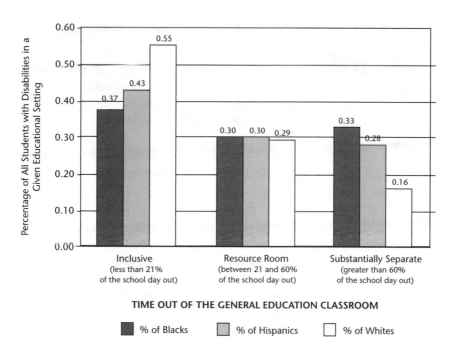

Source: U.S. Department of Education, Office of Special Education Programs, Data Analysis System (2002).

white students with disabilities. Second, OCR data from 1998 enabled us to show the level of restrictiveness by disability category but not race. The OCR data also enabled us to calculate the risk that black or Hispanic students would be labeled for a given disability category compared to the risk for white students. From the OCR data we determined the risk ratio for blacks being labeled mentally retarded and the likelihood that students with mental retardation would be included in the general classroom. However, neither of the national datasets allowed for a comprehensive disaggregated picture of race with disability with educational setting. For example, at the national level we could not determine the risk that blacks with mental retardation would be included in the general classroom compared to the risk for whites with mental retardation. This level of analysis, however, was achieved with data collected by the state of Connecticut described at the end of this chapter.

RESTRICTIVENESS IN SPECIAL EDUCATION BY RACE

Risk indexes for levels of inclusion were calculated for blacks, Hispanics, and whites in order to compare their respective rates of representation in the *fully inclusive* setting (less than 21% time outside the regular classroom), *resource room* (21% to 60% time outside the regular classroom), and *substantially separate* placements (greater than 60% time outside the regular classroom). The risk level is calculated by dividing the number of students with special needs for each racial group within each placement category by the total number of students deemed eligible for special needs. Risk indexes were calculated for all minority groups, but are only presented for blacks, whites, and Hispanics because of their greater aggregate numbers.

NATIONAL DATA ANALYSIS

Blacks and Hispanics are much less likely to be educated in an inclusive setting and more likely to be substantially separate from their white counterparts (Figure 2). In short, inclusion in the regular classroom may be a benefit that black and Hispanic students with disabilities enjoy less often than whites once they are part of the special education system.

RESTRICTIVENESS COMPARED WITH MINORITY
OVERREPRESENTATION BY DISABILITY TYPE

To compare overrepresentation with restrictiveness, we used OCR data to examine placement rates for minority students who are deemed eligible for special education based on the labels of mental retardation, emotional disturbance, and specific learning disability. Although OCR data allowed further analysis by designating three subgroups of mental retardation (i.e., mild MR, moderate MR, and severe MR), we aggregated these in a single category named MR.[5] In a large majority of the states in the OCR dataset, the number of students designated as having mild MR represented the largest MR subgroup, while those students with moderate and severe MR accounted for a much smaller proportion of the MR group (U.S. Department of Education, 2000).

The national- and state-level results and comparisons include data for all major minority groups in racial categories used by the OCR.[6] However, further

TABLE A

National Special Education Percentages by Race and Ethnicity

	American Indian/ Alaska Native	Asian Amer./ Pacific Islander	Hispanic	Black (non-Hispanic)	White (non-Hispanic)	Percentage of All Students
Percentage* of students deemed eligible for three specific disability categories**						
Mental Retardation (MR)	1.28	0.64	0.92	2.64	1.18	1.37
Emotional Disturbance (ED)	1.03	0.26	0.55	1.45	0.91	0.93
Specific Learning Disability (SLD)	7.45	2.23	6.44	6.49	6.02	6.02

Source: Department of Education, Office for Civil Rights, Fall 1998 Elementary and Secondary School Civil Rights Compliance Report: Projected Values for the Nation and Individual States (2002).

* Percentages are based on weighted projections to national totals from 1998 OCR survey data.

** MR, ED, and SLD were the special education categories used in the 1998 OCR survey data—the special education groups in this study do not include all students receiving special education.

analyses were limited to blacks and Hispanics because of their relatively larger numbers in the general population and their dominance in large urban school systems. Blacks and Hispanics are the two largest minority groups in the United States, together accounting for 32 percent of the 1998 U.S. student population.

The percentage of students in a given racial group with a specific type of disability is calculated on the basis of each group's representation in the overall student population. The percentages in Table A are based on the number of students from a particular ethnic group with a given disability divided by their total enrollment. As shown in Table A, these percentages help reveal the patterns of overrepresentation of minorities relative to whites, given their representation in the overall student population. For example, 2.64 percent of all enrolled blacks were labeled MR in 1998, compared to only 1.18 percent of enrolled whites. To determine the likelihood for blacks compared to whites for being identified as having MR is a simple matter of comparing the percentage of each race that is labeled MR. As this study indicates, this comparison consistently shows that blacks are at substantially greater risk than whites of being labeled MR nationally. But, as important, the risks vary dramatically from one state to the next. The findings that blacks are substantially overrepresented relative to their white counterparts in MR and ED are numerically very similar to those found by Parrish in this volume.

Table A lists the percentage of students deemed eligible for three specific disability types within five ethnic groups, including whites for comparison. For example, Hispanics made up 15.01 percent of the overall student population and were identified for specific learning disabilities at a rate of 6.44 percent. In contrast, white students accounted for 62.66 percent of the overall population and had a lower rate of SLD identification (6.02%).[7]

To simplify the comparison between overrepresentation and restrictiveness, the rates of restrictiveness were narrowed from the three placement categories in the OCR database to two. OCR survey respondents were asked to provide data based on the three restrictiveness categories described earlier in Figure 1: less than 21 percent (one day or less per week), 21–60 percent (one to three days per week), or greater than 60 percent (three days or more). For this research, the second and third levels were combined into one category, greater than 21 percent, and expressed as a percentage of the school day. The collapsing of the two highest levels is similar to the procedure employed by the U.S. Department of Education's Office of Special Education and Rehabilitative Services in differentiating fully inclusive special education from pullout services (U.S. Department of Education, 2001b). The decision was also based in part on the uncertainty of the amount of time students spend outside the regular education classroom in the middle category. The finding that placement patterns for a large majority of states heavily favored either the first (less than 21%) or the third (greater than 60%) restrictiveness categories also factored into the decision to focus on two rather than three levels of restrictiveness.

The data on educational setting disaggregated by disability type show that restrictiveness levels (greater than 21% of the day outside the regular education classroom) for the 1997–1998 school year were highest for the MR and ED categories, and that students with MR were rarely educated in inclusive settings. As Figure 3 shows, 82 percent of their placements fit the more restrictive descriptions of resource room or substantially separate. Students with ED were slightly less likely to be educated in such non-inclusive settings (70%). Students with SLD were the least likely to be removed from general classrooms, with just 56 percent not in fully inclusive educational settings (see Figure 3). According to recent data collected by OSEP for the 2000–2001 academic year, these OCR calculations based on data from the 1997–1998 school year may *underestimate* the degree of restrictiveness. The more recent figures from OSEP are: 86 percent for students with MR, 74.22 percent for students with ED, and 55 percent for students with SLD (U.S. Department of Education, 2001a). Please note that the datasets from OCR and OSEP are based on different questionnaires and responses. They are nonetheless consistent in depicting very high rates of restrictiveness.

FIGURE 3

MR, ED, and SLD Levels of Restrictiveness

Greater than 21 percent time spent outside the regular education classroom
(1997–1998 school year)

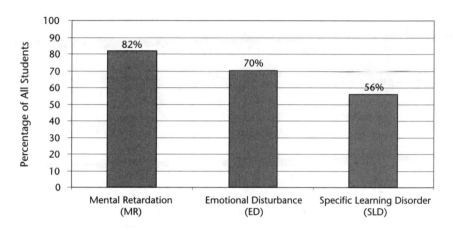

Source: U.S. Department of Education (2000).

This level of restrictiveness is of serious concern in light of both the requirement that students be educated in the least restrictive environment to the maximum extent appropriate and the overrepresentation of blacks in these categories.

Another way to think about under- and overrepresentation is to compare a racial group's representation in the total enrollment to their enrollment in a given disability category. For example, Table B shows that black students constituted 17.14 percent of the enrolled students but 33.04 percent of all students with mental retardation. Conversely, Hispanic students constituted 15.01 percent of the enrolled students but only 10.04 percent of the students with mental retardation. Table B suggests that on a national scale black students are overrepresented for MR and ED, while Hispanic students are underrepresented in these two categories.

Particularly problematic is the high level of restrictiveness (82%) in MR, a disability category in which blacks are substantially overrepresented compared to their overall enrollment (Table B), or when blacks' risk for mental retardation is compared to the risk rate of whites (Table A). This latter analysis allows for direct comparisons of risk rates described in Table A. The OCR data show that blacks are nearly two and one-quarter times as likely to be so labeled.

TABLE B

Representation by Race within Selected Disability Categories

	American Indian/ Alaska Native	Asian Amer./ Pacific Islander	Hispanic	Black (non-Hispanic)	White (non-Hispanic)
Percent of Overall Enrollment	1.11	4.08	15.01	17.14	62.66
Percent of Students with Mental Retardation (MR)	1.04	1.90	10.04	33.04	53.97
Percent of Students with Emotional Disturbance (ED)	1.23	1.16	8.87	26.92	61.82
Percent of Students with Specific Learning Disability (SLD)	1.38	1.51	16.04	18.48	62.60

Source: Department of Education, Office for Civil Rights, Fall 1998 Elementary and Secondary School Civil Rights Compliance Report: Projected Values for the Nation and Individual States (2002).

Percentages are based on weighted projections to national totals from 1998 OCR survey data.

MR, ED, and SLD were the special education categories used in the 1998 OCR survey data—the special education groups in this study do not include all students receiving special education.

In the next layer of analysis we compared risk indexes of minority students with white students for specific special education categories in every state (Fleiss, 1973). This comparison, sometimes referred to as odds ratios (NRC, 2002), is expressed as follows: a ratio of greater than 1.0 shows that the risk of designation are larger than for the comparison group; a ratio of 1 indicates that there is no difference between the two groups; and a ratio of less than one indicates the comparison group (i.e., white students) has a greater likelihood of designation.

ANALYSES OF STATE LEVEL OF RESTRICTIVENESS AND OVERREPRESENTATION

The national trends in rates of restrictiveness and rates of disproportionality often mask more problematic state-level statistics. An examination of state-level MR, ED, and SLD restrictiveness and disproportionality rates as reported in OCR survey data help to identify those states that are serving more of their students in regular education classrooms and identifying special education students at a rate that is roughly proportional to their representation in the general population, compared to those that are not. This examination also helps identify potential relationships between demographic variables and MR, ED, and SLD placement patterns for students in general and disproportionality rates for minority subgroups. To illuminate this relationship, Table 1 also includes an indicator or disproportionality index of those states with disproportionality rates greater than 1.5 and below 3.0 denoted by a ✓, and greater than 3.0 denoted by ✓✚.

Although the range of restrictiveness for MR students is very wide for the fifty states, from a low of 46 percent in Utah to a high of 92 percent in Georgia, thirty-one states show restrictiveness levels for over 80 percent of their MR students; only two states restrict less than 60 percent of their MR students. The practical significance of these levels of restrictiveness is that vast numbers of special education students have their educational experiences outside the general education settings.

Issues of racial discrimination aside, the rates of restrictiveness for students with MR in states across the country are troubling. Specifically, these indices suggest noncompliance with the IDEA requirement for placing students in the Least Restrictive Environment (LRE). The concern is even more troubling when you consider the concurrent high levels of restrictiveness and disproportionality that minority MR students face. For example, in thirty-eight states that provided information to OCR, black students are more than one and one-half times as likely as their white counterparts to be deemed eligible for MR (and more than three times as likely in seven states; see Table 1). In nineteen states both black and Native American students are disproportionately represented for MR. Hispanic students with MR experience disproportionate rates in six states. The Asian American and Pacific Islander MR students experience the smallest occurrence of disproportionality, in four states. The inequitable rates of disproportionality between minority groups once again find blacks with the greatest level of disproportionality relative to whites. The segregative effect of the disproportionality means less time in the regular class, less time with peers, and likely reduced access to the general curriculum.

For students designated as having an emotional disorder, the national level of restrictiveness is over 70 percent (see Table 2). Although the national ED restrictiveness rate is not as high as for MR, some troubling and familiar patterns persist. The restrictiveness rates range from a low of 36.45 in New Hampshire to a high of 89.06 in Delaware. Forty-three states place more than half of their ED students out of the regular education setting more than 21 percent of the school day.

Not surprisingly, the rates of disproportionality for minority ED students were not as prevalent as for the MR students. Other research studies found in-

TABLE 1

National and State Levels of Restrictiveness for Students Deemed Eligible for
Mental Retardation (MR) Designation with Minority Disproportionality Indices

State	Percentage of Students Restricted from Regular Classroom More Than 20% of Time	Black	Hispanic	Asian Amer./ Pacific Islander	American Indian/ Alaska Native
United States	81.95	✓			
Georgia	92.15	✓			
Maine	91.41				✓
Missouri	90.93	✓	✓		✓
Maryland	90.57	✓			✓
Nevada	90.49	✓			✓
Wisconsin	89.91	✓			
Delaware	89.57	✓			
New Jersey	89.53	✓	✓	✓	
West Virginia	88.89				
Wyoming	88.80	✓		✓	✓
Arizona	88.41				
Pennsylvania	87.92				
Michigan	87.79	✓			
New York	87.69				
New Mexico	87.49			✓	
Illinois	87.11	✓			
Hawaii	86.14	✓	✓	✓	
Alaska	85.32	✓			✓
Virginia	84.62	✓			
Arkansas	84.40				
Indiana	84.10	✓			
California	83.74	✓			✓
Oklahoma	83.71	✓			✓
Washington	83.71	✓			
Mississippi	82.82	✓ +			
Louisiana	81.93	✓			
Connecticut	81.89	✓ +	✓ +		✓
North Carolina	81.55	✓ +			
Alabama	81.51	✓ +			✓
Minnesota	80.20	✓			✓

State	Percentage of Students Restricted from Regular Classroom More Than 20% of Time	Black	Hispanic	Asian Amer./ Pacific Islander	American Indian/ Alaska Native
Montana	80.16	✓			✓
Ohio	79.72				
Tennessee	79.52	✓			
Kentucky	78.54				
South Carolina	77.62	✓ +			✓
Colorado	76.85	✓			✓
Kansas	75.40				
North Dakota	73.84	✓			✓
Nebraska	72.39	✓			✓
South Dakota	71.73	✓			
Florida	69.81	✓ +			
Oregon	67.86	✓			
Rhode Island	67.23	✓			✓
Iowa	64.81	✓			
Massachusetts	64.26	✓ +		✓ +	✓
Idaho	64.01	✓			✓
New Hampshire	63.13	✓	✓ +		
Vermont	52.86				
Utah	45.84	✓			
Texas*	0.00	✓			

Source: Department of Education, Office for Civil Rights, Fall 1998 Elementary and Secondary School Civil Rights Compliance Report: Projected Values for the Nation and Individual States (2002).

A "✓+" designates a risk ratio greater than 3, where the subgroup was three or more times as likely as whites to be labeled MR; A "✓" designates a risk ratio greater than 1.5 but less than 3. Blank spaces are those states where the risk ratio was less than 1.5.

*Texas did not provide information on restrictiveness.

consistent placement patterns by race and by special need designation. Some studies suggest that the increased time spent in the regular education classroom is largely attributable to a special needs student's race (Conroy, 1999; Harry, 1992).

The national average level of restrictiveness for students identified with a specific learning disability was 56.03, which means that more than half the SLD students spend at least 21 percent of their time in school outside the regu-

TABLE 2

National and State Levels of Restrictiveness for Students Deemed Eligible for
Emotional Disturbance (ED) Designation with Minority Disproportionality Indices

State	Percentage of Students Restricted from Regular Classroom More Than 20% of Time	Black	Hispanic	Asian Amer./ Pacific Islander	American Indian/ Alaska Native
United States	70.30	✓			
Delaware	89.06	✓			✓
Michigan	82.25				✓
New Mexico	82.25	✓			
Kentucky	79.68	✓ ✢			
Illinois	79.63				
Massachusetts	78.93	✓			
Iowa	78.93	✓ ✢			
New York	78.70	✓			✓
Louisiana	78.23				
California	78.11	✓			
Pennsylvania	77.91	✓			
Arkansas	77.23				
New Jersey	74.89	✓			
Missouri	74.89	✓			
Alaska	74.70	✓			
Georgia	74.50				
Virginia	73.64				
Mississippi	72.21				
North Carolina	71.48	✓			✓
Oklahoma	71.03				
Tennessee	70.05				
Wyoming	69.71	✓			✓
Indiana	69.43	✓			
Ohio	69.35	✓			
Montana	68.06	✓ ✢			
Wisconsin	67.99	✓			✓
Maine	67.89				
Nevada	67.40				
West Virginia	65.64	✓			
Connecticut	64.85	✓	✓		

State	Percentage of Students Restricted from Regular Classroom More Than 20% of Time	Black	Hispanic	Asian Amer./ Pacific Islander	American Indian/ Alaska Native
Maryland	64.58				
South Carolina	62.80	✓			
Kansas	62.11				
Arizona	62.07				
Washington	61.11	✓			✓
South Dakota	60.26				✓
Utah	59.85	✓ +			
Nebraska	59.76	✓ +			✓
Hawaii	58.78				
Rhode Island	56.03	✓			✓
Florida	56.02	✓			
Alaska	55.77				
Colorado	50.34				
Oregon	48.07	✓			
Minnesota	47.51	✓			✓ +
Idaho	47.39	✓			
North Dakota	40.17	✓			✓
New Hampshire	36.65	✓			
Vermont	0.00	✓			✓
Texas*	*0.00*				

Source: Department of Education, Office for Civil Rights, Fall 1998 Elementary and Secondary School Civil Rights Compliance Report: Projected Values for the Nation and Individual States (2002).

A "✓+" designates a risk ratio greater than 3, where the subgroup was three or more times as likely as whites to be labeled ED; A "✓" designates a risk ratio greater than 1.5 but less than 3. Blank spaces are those states where the risk ratio was less than 1.5.

*Texas did not provide information on restrictiveness.

lar classroom setting (see Table 3). Once again, wide discrepancies in state-level restrictiveness rates were found, with Delaware (75.35%) on the high end and North Dakota (13.75%) on the low end. In twenty-four states, more than half of the SLD students spend at least 21 percent of their schooling outside the regular education classroom setting. Interestingly, in only four states are more than three-quarters of students with SLD included in the regular education setting for at least 79 percent of the school day. The higher inclusion rate for SLD stu-

TABLE 3

National and State Levels of Restrictiveness for Students Deemed Eligible for
Specific Learning Disability (SLD) Designation with Minority Disproportionality Indices

State	Percentage of Students Restricted from Regular Classroom More Than 20% of Time	Black	Hispanic	Asian Amer./ Pacific Islander	American Indian/ Alaska Native
United States	56.03	✓			
Delaware	75.35	✓			
Pennsylvania	68.60				
Illinois	67.98				
New Mexico	65.25	✓		✓	
Mississippi	65.04				✓
California	62.00	✓			
Kentucky	61.46				
Georgia	61.30				
Michigan	61.01				
Louisiana	60.42				
Wisconsin	60.18				
Arkansas	59.36				
New Jersey	59.03				
Ohio	58.01				
Maryland	56.98				
Nevada	56.96	✓			✓
West Virginia	56.70				
Hawaii	54.56		✓		
Arizona	54.31				
Florida	54.11				
Utah	53.32	✓			✓
Alabama	52.19				
Indiana	51.89				
South Carolina	51.37				
Tennessee	49.40				
Missouri	49.02				
Wyoming	47.85	✓			✓
Kansas	46.27				
Washington	46.16	✓			✓
New York	46.11				

State	Percentage of Students Restricted from Regular Classroom More Than 20% of Time	Black	Hispanic	Asian Amer./ Pacific Islander	American Indian/ Alaska Native
Maine	45.17				
Alaska	43.82				
Oklahoma	42.56				✓
Iowa	41.31				
Virginia	40.98		✓		✓ +
Montana	39.67	✓			✓
Connecticut	37.98				
Nebraska	37.29				✓
Rhode Island	33.59				✓
Massachusetts	33.37				
Colorado	33.31				
North Carolina	32.99				
Minnesota	29.81	✓			✓
South Dakota	29.27				✓
Idaho	26.11				✓
New Hampshire	21.85				
Oregon	21.81				
Vermont	16.37				
North Dakota	13.75				✓
Texas*	0.00				

Source: Department of Education, Office for Civil Rights, Fall 1998 Elementary and Secondary School Civil Rights Compliance Report: Projected Values for the Nation and Individual States (2002).

A "✓+" designates a risk ratio greater than 3, where the subgroup was three or more times as likely as whites to be labeled SLD; A "✓" designates a risk ratio greater than 1.5 but less than 3. Blank spaces are those states where the risk ratio was less than 1.5.

*Texas did not provide information on restrictiveness.

dents is concurrent with much of the research that shows that SLD students are less likely than MR and ED students to be restricted from the regular education classroom setting (Grossman, 1995; Lipsky & Gartner, 1997; U.S. Department of Education, 1999).

Many states separate students with MR, ED, and SLD from their non-disabled peers at alarmingly high rates (Tables 1–3). But the high rate of variability among states suggests that there might also be wide ranges of restrictiveness and disproportionality within each state. If this is true, then even states showing relatively low degrees of restrictiveness and disproportionality in aggregated data may nonetheless have individual school districts with rates that are disturbingly high. The next section explores this possibility in detail.

DISTRICT-LEVEL ANALYSES OF ENROLLMENT, RESTRICTIVENESS RATES, AND DISPROPORTIONALITY

The examination of district-level data in ten urban school districts with high black or Hispanic populations found *levels of* restrictiveness that were greatly masked in the national- and state-level analyses. Findings regarding rates of restrictiveness for students overall are presented for large urban school districts in Atlanta, Baltimore, Detroit, Los Angeles, New Haven, Omaha, Philadelphia, San Diego, and Birmingham, Alabama. The district-level results also include the percentage of black and Hispanic enrollment relative to the overall student enrollment, and the percentages of blacks and Hispanics among MR, SLD, and ED designees. Of this list, only two of these cities were below the U.S. average.

The most important pattern revealed by the district data is that minority students attending these high-minority school districts, if found eligible for special education, were also at very high risk of being placed in a restrictive educational setting. In many high-minority districts the level of restrictiveness was substantially higher than average restrictiveness for the district's state and for the nation. Furthermore, the general findings of disproportionality in the district-level analysis are consistent with those reported by Parrish in this volume.[8]

In these high-minority urban districts, the percentage of students with MR who spent more than 21 percent of their school days outside the regular education classroom ranged from 71.33 percent in Birmingham to 99.21 in Atlanta public schools (Table 4). Eight of the ten U.S. school districts identified in this study have rates of restrictiveness that are higher than the district's home state. For example, in Detroit, only 1.71 percent of students with MR were removed for less than 21 percent of their school day or more in the regular education setting. In contrast, for Michigan as a whole, a far larger percentage of students, 12.81, experienced inclusion. Table 4 reveals that in all ten urban school districts black students designated as MR make up a greater proportion of the cognitive disability group than would be expected. For example, in Atlanta, where 99.21 percent of students with MR are excluded from the regular education classroom more than 21 percent of the time, blacks represent 90.13 percent of the district's enrollment, yet they make up nearly all of Atlanta's MR population (96.98%).

TABLE 4

Mental Retardation—Overall Level of Restrictiveness*, Percentage** of
Overall Enrollment, and Percentage MR Designation in Ten U.S. School Districts
Compared to Black and Hispanic Enrollment

District	Percentage Students Spending More Than 21% Time Outside Regular Classroom	Percentage Black of Overall Enrollment**	Percentage of Blacks Among MR Designees	Percentage Hispanic of Overall Enrollment**	Percentage of Hispanics Among MR Designees
United States	81.95	17.14	—	15.01	—
Atlanta	99.21	90.13	96.98	2.22	1.18
Philadelphia	98.69	64.55	71.27	12.17	13.09
Detroit	98.29	91.35	93.03	3.26	1.47
Omaha	97.86	31.17	50.66	9.90	5.19
Baltimore	96.63	29.23	38.30	1.32	0.53
New Haven	93.07	57.67	68.65	27.27	22.82
New Orleans	85.68	90.31	95.00	1.44	0.75
Los Angeles	84.03	14.03	17.81	68.75	66.82
San Diego	78.33	16.58	20.38	36.22	38.33
Birmingham	71.33	95.40	97.89	0.29	0.07

Source: Department of Education, Office for Civil Rights, Fall 1998 Elementary and Secondary School Civil Rights Compliance Report: Projected Values for the Nation and Individual States (2002).

* Restrictiveness of student placement is determined by the number of hours or the extent to which students with disabilities are restricted from placement in a regular education classroom.

** Percentages are based on weighted projections to national and state totals from 1998 OCR survey data.

The percentages of Hispanic students eligible for MR relative to their overall enrollment numbers are opposite from the results for black students eligible for MR (Table 4). Eight of ten districts have fewer Hispanic students with MR than would be expected, given their home district's overall Hispanic enrollment.

The rates of restrictiveness for students designated as having emotional disturbance ranged from 69.10 percent in Birmingham to 95.94 percent in Philadelphia (see Table 5). In the ED category, all the selected urban school districts rates of restrictiveness were greater than the rate for their respective states. For nine of ten districts, more than 80 percent of students with the ED designation were restricted from the regular classroom. In effect, students with ED in all of

TABLE 5

Emotional Disorder—Overall Level of Restrictiveness*, Percentage** of Overall
Enrollment, and Percentage ED Designation in Ten U.S. School Districts
Compared to Black and Hispanic Enrollment

District	Percentage Students Spending More Than 21% Time Outside Regular Classroom	Percentage Black of Overall Enrollment**	Percentage of Blacks Among ED Designees	Percentage Hispanic of Overall Enrollment**	Percentage of Hispanics Among ED Designees
United States	70.30	17.14	—	15.01	—
Philadelphia	95.94	64.55	67.32	12.17	13.96
Detroit	94.97	91.35	89.93	3.26	2.97
Omaha	94.83	31.17	50.88	9.90	2.45
Atlanta	91.00	90.13	87.72	2.22	0.69
San Diego	87.29	16.58	34.80	36.22	16.52
New Orleans	86.76	90.31	97.14	1.44	0.00
Los Angeles	84.03	14.03	42.09	68.75	14.36
Baltimore	83.28	29.23	38.10	1.32	1.23
New Haven	80.98	57.67	66.18	27.27	20.77
Birmingham	69.10	95.40	89.45	0.29	0.00

Source: Department of Education, Office for Civil Rights, Fall 1998 Elementary and Secondary School Civil Rights Compliance Report: Projected Values for the Nation and Individual States (2002).

* Restrictiveness of student placement is determined by the number of hours or the extent to which students with disabilities are restricted from placement in a regular education classroom

** Percentages are based on weighted projections to national and state totals from 1998 OCR survey data.

these districts spent much of their time in resource rooms or separate classes, not in the regular classroom. Moreover, the percentage of black students with the ED designation was disproportionate in seven of the ten school districts.

Hispanic students labeled ED were underrepresented in nine of the ten districts (see Table 5). The underrepresentation was most notable in those cities with the greatest numbers of Hispanic students (i.e., Los Angeles, San Diego, and Chicago). This finding raises the concern of a lack of needed services for Hispanic students, due to their underidentification for eligibility from the special needs designation.

TABLE 6

Specific Learning Disability—Overall Level of Restrictiveness*, Percentage**
of Overall Enrollment, and Percentage SLD Designation in
Ten US School Districts Compared to Black and Hispanic Enrollment

District	Percentage Students Spending More Than 21% Time Outside Regular Classroom	Percentage Black of Overall Enrollment**	Percentage of Blacks Among SLD Designees	Percentage Hispanic of Overall Enrollment**	Percentage of Hispanics Among SLD Designees
United States	56.03	17.14	—	15.01	—
Philadelphia	93.21	64.55	58.63	12.17	16.25
New Orleans	90.58	90.31	94.45	1.44	0.94
Los Angeles	88.35	14.03	40.15	68.75	37.63
San Diego	87.29	16.58	25.78	36.22	34.89
Detroit	83.46	91.35	91.41	3.26	2.73
Atlanta	79.38	90.13	89.12	2.22	2.68
Omaha	70.33	31.17	37.73	9.90	6.98
Birmingham	59.35	95.40	93.58	0.29	0.18
New Haven	58.40	57.67	60.55	27.27	27.83
Baltimore	55.10	29.23	33.29	1.32	1.12

Source: Department of Education, Office for Civil Rights, Fall 1998 Elementary and Secondary School Civil Rights Compliance Report: Projected Values for the Nation and Individual States (2002).

* Restrictiveness of student placement is determined by the number of hours or the extent to which students with disabilities are restricted from placement in a regular education classroom.

** Percentages are based on weighted projections to national and state totals from 1998 OCR survey data.

The level of restrictiveness for students with the specific learning disability in the selected districts is unusually high—nine of them were considerably higher than the state average (see Table 6). The rates of restrictiveness ranged from 55.10 percent in Baltimore to 93.21 percent in Philadelphia. Although the percentage of black students with SLD was much closer to the expected number in the general population in all but two districts (San Diego and Los Angeles), the findings are disturbing for all students, given the high rates of exclusion from the regular classroom and the large numbers of students with the SLD label.

The percentage of Hispanic students with SLD was fairly close to the expected average in nine of the ten districts (see Table 6). Los Angeles, the district with the largest Hispanic population, reveals a large underrepresentation of Hispanic SLD students relative to their percentage of enrollment in the school district.

ANALYSES OF INCLUSION BY RACE AND GENDER IN CONNECTICUT

As mentioned in the introduction, no readily available dataset shows educational placement disaggregated by race with disability type. However, IDEA requires states to report this information. Working for plaintiffs in a lawsuit, Jim Conroy obtained access to Connecticut's data through legal discovery proceedings. Connecticut was notably high in its overrepresentation of both blacks and Hispanics for special education. Specifically, blacks in Connecticut are four times as likely as whites to be identified as mentally retarded (Parrish, this volume). But the Connecticut database, Connecticut Integrated Special Student Information System (ISSIS),[9] did allow the complete analysis of placement disaggregated by race with disability category.

The Connecticut state database contains one basic record for each student involved in special education. The data were collected on forms that contain information about students' age, grade, gender, primary and secondary special education identification, placement type, and a variety of other demographic and programmatic information (Conroy, 1999). According to the 1998–1999 Connecticut data, 95,442 children were assigned to special education programs. For the purposes of this study, students labeled as uncategorized infant, gifted, art talented, or regular education were excluded, resulting in a sample of 69,549 children between the ages of six and twenty-one with a disability level.

For the state- and district-level analyses of Connecticut, 1998–1999 school year student-level data were examined for district variation in the mental retardation designation, ethnic variations in MR labeling, and restrictiveness rates for MR students by race.

Mental Retardation

The *P.J., et al. v. State of Connecticut, Board of Education, et al.* lawsuit settlement on May 18, 2001, ended eight years of litigation over least restrictive environment.[10] The improvement in the rates of inclusion for Connecticut minorities found in Figure 4 may reflect the impact of the litigation (filed in 1993) and/or the change in the federal law in 1997—or some combination of the two. Moreover, the results suggest that improvement is possible.

FIGURE 4

Mental Retardation (MR) Inclusion Rates by Race and Gender, Connecticut
(1995–1996 and 1998–1999 School Years)

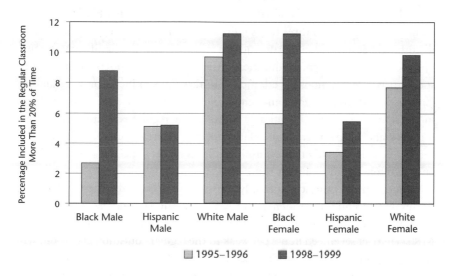

Source: Conroy (1999).

For both the 1995–1996 and 1998–1999 school years, black and Hispanic male students with MR in Connecticut were less likely to be educated in an inclusive setting than their white male counterparts (Figure 4). The finding for Hispanic females with MR is also troubling, as they spend less time in the regular classroom setting than do their white female counterparts. Although the finding for black male MR students is consistent with the national and state findings presented in this study, the Connecticut data revealed that, although often underrepresented nationally for MR, Hispanics in Connecticut were both overrepresented for MR and overrepresented in more restrictive settings compared to whites in each of the three cognitive disability areas examined. Also unexpected was that the rate of inclusion for black female MR students in Connecticut (11.2%) was equal to that of white males (11.2%).

An investigation of Connecticut's practices in special education has found extremely wide variations in labeling and placement practices across school districts. The OCR data found that mental retardation identification rates varied from less than 1 percent of the overall student population to more than 20 percent. For example, the high-minority districts of Bridgeport and New Haven had MR identification rates above 20 percent, while several dozen school districts label fewer than 5 percent (Conroy, 1999). Interestingly, Hartford labels only 3.8 percent of their special education students as MR. These variations in districts serving high percentages of minority students raise questions about the labeling differences in Connecticut's larger urban school districts.

The inconsistent levels of MR inclusion and the fact that blacks and Hispanics are nearly two to three times more likely than whites to be labeled MR is disturbing, because Connecticut students with MR spend a significant amount of time outside the regular education setting relative to students in the other special needs designations. In addition, the variations in inclusion rates among Connecticut districts suggest an inequitable distribution of services to students in the state. Finally, the inequitable access to the regular education classroom for black and Hispanic students relative to their white counterparts becomes a form of double jeopardy that punishes students twice—once for their MR label and once for the color of their skin.

Inclusion rates vary considerably across these selected districts (Table 7).[11] For example, Stamford students with MR spent an average of 5.64 hours per week in the regular education setting, while Naugatuck students eligible for MR spent over seventeen hours per week in the regular education classroom setting. The statewide data for Connecticut shows that white males and females enjoyed twice as much time in the regular classroom as black and Hispanic males and females (Conroy, 1995).

These extraordinary variations were found across ethnicity and inclusion variables, and as a result have important policy implications. The Connecticut study found that:

- placement and inclusion are strongly related to a student's classification
- labels vary sharply by ethnic group
- placement and integration are strongly affected by ethnicity
- MR students are far less integrated than other students with special needs
- the disproportionate labeling of minorities with MR combines with discriminatory placement and integration practices to place minority students in double jeopardy
- the general patterns indicative of ethnic bias and exclusionary effects did not change greatly from the 1986–1987 to 1995–1996 school years, but showed some improvement in 1998–1999. (Conroy, 1999)

Emotional Disturbance

As in the examination of mental retardation labeling, black and Hispanic students (both male and female) were more likely to be labeled with the emotional disturbance label. White ED students spend a significantly greater amount of

TABLE 7

Variations in Mental Retardation Student Inclusion Rates for
Selected Connecticut Districts (1998–1999)

Town	Average Hours per Week in Regular Education Classroom	Number of Students
Stamford	5.64	135
New Britain	5.85	162
Hartford	7.04	252
West Haven	7.33	137
New Haven	7.50	675
Enfield	7.85	66
Danbury	8.22	94
Bridgeport	8.44	609
East Hartford	8.48	51
Waterbury	8.63	253
Norwich	8.68	84
Hamden	8.96	65
New London	9.69	93
West Hartford	10.00	54
Meriden	10.22	162
Norwalk	10.57	130
Middletown	11.47	50
Manchester	12.34	59
Stratford	12.89	59
Naugatuck	17.46	93

Source: The 1998–1999 School Year, Connecticut Integrated Special Services Student Information System (ISSIS) student-based information system by which the Connecticut School Districts accounts to the State Department of Education for students identified or served under the provisions of Public Law 89-313. The School District annually submits on the specified dates Form ED 331, Special Education Census, and Form ED 332, Funding Eligibility, for each student eligible for special education and/or related services.

time than blacks and Hispanics in the regular education classroom (Figure 5). Other data revealed that the labeling rates for black students deemed eligible for ED are similar to those at national and state levels, but for Hispanics, the rates are higher than would be expected. An average of 37 percent of white ED students spend their day in the regular classrooms, while only an average of 25 percent of black and Hispanic ED students were able to share a regular education classroom (Conroy, 1999).

FIGURE 5

Emotional Disturbance (ED) Inclusion Rates by Race and Gender, Connecticut
(1998–1999 School Year)

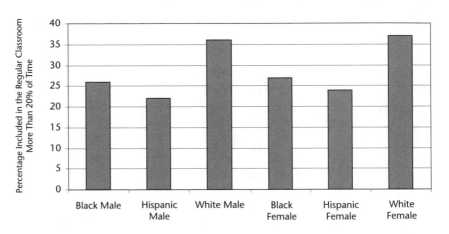

Source: Conroy (1999).

Specific Learning Disability

The inclusion rates for white students with SLD averaged 68 percent, while the inclusion rates averaged 45 percent for black and Hispanic students eligible for SLD (Figure 6). Once again, black and Hispanic students spend less time in the regular education classroom than white students with similar special needs designations.

The inclusion rate disparities in Connecticut between black and Hispanic special education students and their white counterparts is problematic. The federal definition of regular classroom is being educated with nondisabled peers at least 80 percent of the time. Many black and Hispanic students in Connecticut are being doubly segregated, both from their own peers, and from school districts rich in resources (Conroy, 1999). The double jeopardy problem applies to both black and Hispanic special needs students in Connecticut because they are first disproportionately identified for special education and then segregated to a much greater extent than their white counterparts. The data in Tables 1, 2, and 3 suggest that this phenomenon may exist in many states, especially for black children.

FIGURE 6

Specific Learning Disablity (SLD) Inclusion Rates by Race and Gender,
Connecticut (1998–1999 School Year)

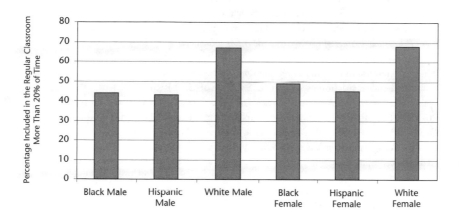

Source: Conroy (1999).

SUMMARY

Disproportionality, especially for African American males in both identification *and placement*, is extremely high in some states and school districts, and of substantial and significant magnitude in the majority of states and school districts analyzed. Given that the Individual with Disabilities Education Act, as amended in 1997, requires states to intervene where racial disproportionality in either identification or placement is significant, this research suggests that many, if not most, states should now be engaged with many school districts in attempting to remedy these problems.

But it is unlikely that advocates and policymakers have ready access to the kind of information examined here. As noted, the data from Connecticut were made available only through the process of legal discovery in a class action lawsuit. Therefore, state and federal departments of education should be required to report both identification rates and restrictiveness by race and disability category together. Most important, this level of detail must be available to the public and community advocates. Without public reporting, it is unlikely that state education administrators will feel sufficient pressure to meet their legal duty to act as required by federal law.

NOTES

1. Although the law states "regular," we use the term *general* as a substitute wherever appropriate.
2. Further levels of restrictiveness, such as receiving services in a hospital or residential program, all fall within 100 percent outside the regular classroom.
3. Time spent outside the regular education setting is greater than 20 percent of the time.
4. *P.J., et al. v. State of Connecticut, Board of Education, et al.* May 18, 2001—Settlement Agreement.
5. Mild retardation, moderate retardation, and severe retardation are definitions of degrees of mental retardation used by the U.S. Office of Civil Rights.
6. American Indian/Alaskan Native, Asian/Pacific Islander, Blacks, and Hispanics
7. The SLD figure is based on the sampled membership of Hispanics in the 1997–1998 OCR dataset (i.e., 6,904,713) and the number of Hispanic students considered eligible for SLD designation (i.e., 444,436).
8. For example, Hispanics, although generally underrepresented for MR, ED, and SLD, did exhibit a pronounced increase in identification rate and some instances of overrepresentation in those districts where they constituted relatively larger percentage of the overall population (Harry, 1994; Parrish, this volume).
9. The Integrated Special Student Information System (ISSIS) is a student-based information system by which the Connecticut School District accounts to the State Department of Education for students identified or served under the provisions of Public Law 89-313. The School District shall submit annually on the specified dates Form ED 331, Special Education Census, and Form ED 332, Funding Eligibility, for each student eligible for special education and/or related services.
10. 1993 *C.A.R.C. v. State of Connecticut Board of Education* class action lawsuit.
11. Only districts with a minimum of fifty students were included to ensure stability.

REFERENCES

Artiles, A., & Trent, S. (1994). Overrepresentation of minority students in special education: A continuing debate. *Journal of Special Education, 27*, 410–437.

Conroy, J. (1997). Labeling and placement practices in Connecticut's special education system: Analyses of the ISSIS data base. Unpublished manuscript submitted to Shaw and Laski, attorneys in *CARC v. Tirozzi.*

Conroy, J. W. (1999). *Connecticut's special education labeling and placement practices: Analyses of the ISSIS data base.* Unpublished report, Center for Outcome Analysis, Rosemont, PA.

Conroy, J., Nerney, T., & Bowen, J. (1998). *Connecticut's special education labeling and placement practices: Patterns of out of district placement.* Rosemont, PA: Center for Outcome Analysis.

Coutinho, M., & Oswald, D. (2000). Disproportionate representation in special education: A synthesis and recommendations. *Journal of Child and Family Studies, 2,* 135–156.

Coutinho, M., & Repp, A. C. (1999). *Inclusion: The integration of students with disabilities.* Belmont, CA: Wadsworth.

Crockett, J. B., & Kauffman, J. M. (1999). *The least restrictive environment: Its origins and interpretations in special education.* Mahwah, NJ: Lawrence Erlbaum.

Danielson, L. C., & Bellamy, G. T. (1989). State variation in placement of children in segregated environments. *Exceptional Children, 55,* 448–455.

Finn, J. D. (1982). Patterns in special education placement as revealed by the OCR survey. In K. A. Heller, W. H. Holtzman, & S. Messick (Eds.), *Placing children in special education: A strategy for equity* (pp. 322–381). Washington, DC: National Academy Press.

Fleiss, J. L. (1973). *Statistical methods for rates and proportions.* New York: John Wiley & Sons.

Grossman, H. (1995). *Special education in a diverse society.* Needham Heights, MA: Allyn & Bacon.

Harry, B. (1992). *Cultural diversity, families, and the special education system: communication and empowerment.* New York: Teachers College Press. (ERIC Document Reproduction Service No. ED 343 967)

Harry, B. (1994). *The disproportionate representation of minority students in special education: Theories and recommendations* (Project Forum, Final Report). Alexandria, VA: National Association of State Directors of Special Education. (ERIC Document Reproduction Service No. ED 374 637)

Lipsky, D. K., & Gartner, A. (1997). *Inclusion and school reform: Transforming America's classrooms.* Baltimore: Brookes.

National Research Council. (1982). *Placing children in special education: A strategy for equity* (K. Heller, W. Holtzman, & S. Messick, Eds.). Washington, DC: National Academy Press.

National Research Council. (2002). *Minority students in special and gifted education* (M. Donovan & C. Crass, Eds.). Washington, DC: National Academy Press.

Nerney, T., Conroy, J., & Bowen, J. (1997). *Connecticut's special education labeling and placement practices: The role of gender and ethnicity.* Danbury: Western Connecticut Association for Human Rights.

P.J., et al. v. State of Connecticut, Board of Education, et al. May 18, 2001—Settlement Agreement.

Rea, P., McLaughlin, V., & Walther-Thomas, C. (2002). Outcomes for students with learning disabilities in inclusive and pullout programs. *Exceptional Children, 68,* 203–223.

Stainback, W., & Stainback, S. (1996). *Controversial issues confronting special education: Divergent perspectives* (2nd ed.). Needham Heights, MA: Allyn & Bacon.

U.S. Department of Education. (1996). *Eighteenth annual report to Congress on the implementation of the Individuals with Disabilities Education Act.* Washington, DC: U.S. Government Printing Office.

U.S. Department of Education. (1999). *Twenty-first annual report to Congress on the implementation of the Individuals with Disabilities Education Act.* Washington, DC: U.S. Government Printing Office.

U.S. Department of Education. (2000). *Elementary and secondary school civil rights compliance report: Projected values for the nation and individual states—1998.* Washington, DC: U.S. Government Printing Office.

U.S. Department of Education. (2001a). *Office of Special Education Programs: Data programs, March 2000.* Available on-line at http://www.ideadata.org/documents.html

U.S. Department of Education. (2001b). *Twenty-third annual report to Congress on the implementation of the Individuals with Disabilities Education Act.* Washington, DC: U.S. Government Printing Office.

Utley, C. A., & Mortweet, S. L. (1999). The challenge of diversity. In M. Coutinho & A. C. Repp (Eds.), *Inclusion: The integration of students with disabilities* (pp. 59–90). Belmont, CA: Wadsworth.

CHAPTER FOUR

Of Rocks and Soft Places: Using Qualitative Methods to Investigate Disproportionality

BETH HARRY

JANETTE K. KLINGNER

KEITH M. STURGES

ROBERT F. MOORE

Disproportionality in special education placements occurs through a process of social construction by which decisions about disability and its appropriate treatments are negotiated according to official and unofficial beliefs and practices. The idea that disabilities are socially constructed is not new (Bogdan & Knoll, 1988; Mehan, Hartwick, & Meihls, 1986), nor is it difficult to demonstrate. One need only recall the 1969 decision of the American Association on Mental Retardation (AAMR) to change the cutoff point for mental retardation from an IQ score of 85 to 70. As has frequently been observed, that decision effected a swift "cure" for thousands of individuals labeled mentally retarded (Mercer, 1973). Equally vulnerable to change is the construct of learning disability, whose definition has relied on a discrepancy between students' scores on an IQ test and their scores on a measure of academic performance (Artiles, Trent, & Kuan, 1997). The longstanding debate over the validity of this criterion (Fletcher et al., 1998; Fletcher & Morris, 1986; Stanovich, 1991), as well as researchers' observations of variable implementation of eligibility criteria (MacMillan, Gresham, & Bocian, 1998), suggest that it may not be long before the conceptualization and operationalization of this disability also undergo radical revision. The category of emotional disorders, which is equally controversial, continues to defy efforts at standardization. The reliance on checklists and anecdotal information from teachers, as well as the notorious unreliability of projective testing (Gresham, 1993; Knoff, 1993; Motta, Little, & Tobin, 1993), demonstrate the social-construction process at work.

To say that disabilities are socially constructed is not to say that differences in performance and ability do not exist among students. It does say, however, that we do not always know if measured performance reflects ability, and that the point at which differences result in one child being labeled disabled and another not are matters of social decisionmaking. This is the main reason that the disproportionate designation of minorities as disabled is problematic. The second reason is that there continues to be doubt that placement in special education programs results in beneficial outcomes for many students (Kavale, 1990). If the process is a matter of social decisionmaking that leads to questionable outcomes, then there is clearly a problem.

GAPS IN OUR UNDERSTANDING OF DISPROPORTIONALITY

To discover what lies behind disproportionality, then, research must use methods that can document the social processes that lead to it. Statistical analysis can be used to provide a powerful teasing out of the variables that are associated with disproportionality, as can be seen in the research of Oswald, Coutinho, Best, and Singh (1999). That research displays the complex interplay among numerous key variables, such as size of group in a district and various aspects of socioeconomic status. What we still need to learn is why these patterns occur: What is the chain of events that sets students from certain kinds of backgrounds, in certain kinds of school districts, on the road to special education placement? What is the thinking of those making the decisions that lead to these patterns? What are the students actually like? Why are these students referred while others are not? What is the role of parents in the process, and how do they perceive it?

Equally important are the kinds of questions that can lead to solutions rather than only to identifying problems: What policies and practices protect students from inappropriate referral? What kinds of information assist professionals in making decisions that truly individualize the process, rather than merely ensuring compliance with district guidelines? How do thoughtful teachers distinguish between children they can help and those with needs truly beyond the capacity of the typical general education classroom? How do caring professionals ensure that even the most denigrated parent is treated with respect when he or she comes to a referral or placement conference?

Ethnographic research is particularly well suited to address these questions. Despite its focus on the controversial and potentially divisive issue of overrepresentation, the overall goal of this study is to identify exemplary processes that can counteract whatever negative circumstances and practices contribute to inappropriate placements in special education. Our work is based on a combination of three data collection strategies: the extensive use of open-ended interviews that elicit the perspectives of insiders to the process; observations of insiders' actions; and the examination of relevant school documents. This triangulation of methods is complemented by triangulation of data sources, which include school and school district personnel, family members, and the students themselves. The conceptual basis for understanding disproportionality derives from the work of Heller, Holtzman, and Messick (1982), who argue that disproportionality is a problem if any aspect of the process that leads to it is biased against the group of concern. Thus, our data collection attends to all phases of the placement process—the classroom ecologies from which students are referred to special education, the reasons for referral, the decisionmaking process that leads to assessment, the actual assessment, and the resulting placement.

We designed the research process following Strauss and Corbin's conditional matrix (1998), by which conditions surrounding an event are conceptualized as a series of concentric circles, from the most proximal to the most distal. Thus we envisioned the research as a funnel, through which we began by studying the most distal elements—that is, nationwide, statewide, and districtwide patterns of ethnic distribution of students in special education. We then proceeded to study the official policies for placement in the school district and the rates of special education placement in various regions of the district, and then at particular schools.

After selecting twelve schools that offered a variety of demographic features, we then developed a broad picture of those schools through interviews with school personnel, observations of all K–3 regular education classrooms, and observations of a sample of support and/or placement conferences. The research funnel narrowed further as we selected two classrooms in each school to observe intensively, focusing on those children about whom teachers were concerned and who might be referred to the special education process. We observed these children in various school settings, and observed support and/or placement conferences and psychological evaluations wherever possible. We followed students into their post-evaluation placements, whether in general or special education, and also observed in all of the special education classrooms in their schools. In this chapter we focus on one key aspect of the decisionmaking process: the issue of the reliance on psychometric testing for eligibility for special education services. We chose this issue because, after years of debate on its appropriateness, psychological evaluation continues to be the centerpiece of the special education placement process.

PSYCHOLOGICAL ASSESSMENT AS THE CENTERPIECE
OF SPECIAL EDUCATION PLACEMENT

In the context of overrepresentation, the debate around evaluation has focused on whether or not psychological tests are racially and/or culturally biased. The traditional approach to evaluating the presence of bias in psychological assessment has been to analyze the tests themselves for validity. While many scholars (e.g., Jensen, 1974; Sandoval, 1979) have argued that statistical analyses can and do prove nonbias in testing, others (e.g., Figueroa, 1983; Travers, 1982) have countered this argument. Further, some scholars (e.g., Dent, 1976; Hilliard, 1977) have submitted that bias is self-evident in that the tests inevitably reflect the cultural knowledge base and cognitive and linguistic orientations of their creators. Another aspect of the debate on validity is represented by the notion of "consequential validity" (Popham, 1997; Shepard, 1997), which means that the evaluation of test validity must include the uses to which the test is put. Specifically, proponents of this view argue that the outcomes should promote social justice for the individuals tested. Snow (1995), in a comprehensive and balanced review of the arguments around validity, called for continued research on the contextual aspects of learning and testing, on racial and cultural bias in testing, and on the improvement of special education programs. He concluded that "students should not be classified into separate programs without good evidence that such separate treatment indeed results in educational advantages over what would have been expected for each student without such classification" (p. 36).

In the case of our research, while the presence and influence of bias are central to our concerns, our focus is not on whether racial or cultural bias is built into the tests themselves. Rather, we are focused on how school personnel handle the presence of biases of various types, the extent to which such biases are allowed to infiltrate the assessment process, and how biases can be minimized.

Further, we must note that the construct of race as traditionally understood in the United States is greatly modified in the context of a multicultural, multilingual setting where white Americans are in the minority.[1] In this context, race cannot be used as a monolithic construct that carries connotations of specific circumstances, cultures, or ethnicities. Rather, it can only refer to the apparent physiognomy of individuals. Indeed, one cannot consider racial bias in this setting without simultaneously considering attitudes toward culture, language, national origin, and socioeconomic status. For example, in this setting students who appear to be black may be U.S. born, or may be from the English-speaking Caribbean, or from Haiti, the Dominican Republic, or a number of other countries. This means that these black students may speak a variety of languages and/or dialects, including American Standard English, African American Vernacular English, Caribbean Standard English, English- or French-based Creoles, French, Spanish, and varieties of Spanish. It also means that the cultural practices of these students' families may be very different from those of mainstream America, and equally different from one another. The same variety is also true of their socioeconomic status; for example, tremendous disparities are found among groups designated as Hispanic. Further, these Hispanic and black groups are perceived among themselves, and by the local community, as holding differing places on the social ladder. The biases of school personnel, therefore, come from many sources and go in many directions, and within-group bias is as likely to exist as intergroup bias.

We frame our question this way: To what extent is the actual assessment a discrete and objectively conducted event? Is it separable from everything that has led up to it, or to what extent is it influenced by prior events, external pressures, and personal beliefs and biases? To what extent is this interrelatedness positive or negative in its impact on children? By the time the case gets to the point of psychological assessment, to what extent do prior events and impressions infiltrate and influence the assessment? We are not the first to raise this question. Mehan, Hartwick, and Meihls (1986), in a five-year ethnographic study, focused on how team decisions were made and concluded that "placement outcomes were more ratifications of actions that had taken place at previous stages of the decisionmaking process than decisions reached in formal meetings" (p. 164). Thus, although the assessment is at the center of the referral and placement process, it is not a discrete occurrence. In fact, Reschly (2000) argues that the psychological evaluation should not be seen as the chief event in special education placement, since children who get to the psychologist's table are there by virtue of a history of failure in the regular education classroom.

There are many steps between observing a child's low performance and the decision to evaluate. It is the response of teachers and administrators to the child's poor performance that moves the process forward. The assessment process, on paper a rigorous scientific method, in reality comprises a series of human interactions, at the center of which is a person of considerable skill who must respond to numerous pressures. These include the needs of the child, the needs of the teachers and administrators, the demands of parents, and a set of external pressures such as high-stakes testing, the school's reputation in the district, and the demand for timely resolution of the presenting problems. These challenges reflect the real life of urban schools.

Despite ongoing debate, psychological assessment continues to be interpreted by most practitioners as a rigorous, scientific method that serves as the gateway to special education—one might say the "rock" that ensures that a child is truly eligible for the costly and specialized services of special education. Indeed, our interviews with teachers, administrators, related service personnel, and family members revealed little expression of doubt regarding the adequacy and validity of psychological assessment. With only a few exceptions, interviewees expressed confidence in the criteria established for eligibility and in the ability of the assessment process to discern who truly meets the criteria and who does not. Children ostensibly either qualify or don't qualify for services.

In the field as a whole there have been many attempts to acknowledge the limitations of psychological assessment. For example, the Individuals with Disabilities Education Act (IDEA) seeks to avoid diagnosis, so in many school districts, including the locale of this study, the psychologist does not actually diagnose a disability. Rather, he or she determines for which special education services a child is eligible. This approach is an attempt to counter the reification of the concept of disability by focusing on placement and services, rather than within-child deficits. In reality, however, the usual procedure is to determine eligibility using the same criteria commonly used as indicators of disability. Thus, the determination of eligibility continues to rely almost totally on the child's IQ score, academic achievement level, and behavioral features. Another attempt to make the assessment as relevant as possible is the inclusion of the psychologist in much of the prereferral process, so that all members of the multidisciplinary team can gain mutual benefit from one another's skills and share differing perspectives on the child. Thus, the psychologist often becomes a key member of the child-support team, whose purpose is to decide what prereferral interventions should be tried and whether or not the child should be evaluated further. Indeed, the preeminent role of the psychologist has been well documented by Mehan et al. (1986).

FROM ROCKS TO MUDDY WATERS: DETERMINING ELIGIBILITY FOR SERVICES

Bronfenbrenner (1979), in his seminal conceptualization of the importance of ecological validity in research, observed that researchers tend to get caught "between a rock and a soft place, the rock being rigor and the soft place being relevance" (p. 513). With regard to the assessment of children thought to have high-incidence disabilities, we would go further, arguing that the conception of rigor itself *can only* make sense if it includes the "soft places" of assessment. Assessment of intelligence and of emotional functioning at the mild end of the spectrum is unquestionably a "soft" science. As Bronfenbrenner pointed out, then, research that seeks to understand the assessment process must be capable of accessing those soft places—the assumptions, beliefs, personal judgments, and socially negotiated decisions—that go into assessment. Indeed, to corrupt the metaphor even further, we would say that effective research on this topic must recognize that *there is no rock.* Rather, research must be able to navigate the muddy waters of the assessment process.

The Soft Places of Assessment

As we argued in the beginning, the definitions of the high-incidence disabilities and the criteria by which we try to operationalize them, represent social decisions not factual phenomena. Thus, what is conceived of as the discrete event of psychological assessment is really the culminating capstone of a series of social processes. In the following discussion, we will address questions regarding six aspects of the process. We believe these questions are important because they will lead to better understanding of the limitations and potential strengths of psychological assessment. The first question is essential to understanding a child's difficulties; the next three relate to influences that feed into the assessment; and the final two concern factors that are inherent in the actual assessment.

1. What roles do teachers' informal diagnoses play in the assessment?
2. What roles do school personnel's preconceptions about the child's family circumstances play in the assessment?
3. To what extent is the assessment affected by external pressures for identification and placement?
4. What role does the classroom ecology play in the learning or behavioral difficulties exhibited by the child?
5. How is the assessment affected by the way disability categories are defined and operationalized?
6. What factors influence psychologists' selection of instruments and conduct of the assessment?

In this section, we outline the role of these factors and illustrate the power of qualitative research methods to explore and explain them.

Teachers' Informal Diagnoses of Children's Problems   The central role of the referring teacher has been documented by a long line of research. In 1984, Gerber and Semmel published a piece called "Teacher as Imperfect Test: Reconceptualizing the Referral Process." Their argument was that teachers' perceptions of the reasons for children's learning difficulties were a very good predictor of what would be found by the psychological assessment, and that teachers' judgments could be as reliable as those of psychologists. Other researchers have corroborated this idea (e.g., Gresham, Reschly, & Carey, 1987; Shinn, Tindal,

& Spira, 1987). The latter study, however, offered the caveat that teacher judgments did display gender and ethnicity biases. Certainly, it is well known that 90 percent of referred students will be identified as having a disability (Algozzine, Christenson, & Ysseldyke, 1982), and several scholars have pointed to the teacher's decision to refer as the key to the entire process (e.g., Pugach, 1985). Our observations and interviews suggest that we should extend this line of thinking to ask, To what extent do teachers' informal explanations of the causes of children's difficulties actually influence the assessment process and subsequent decisions about placement?

As mentioned above, in this school district the psychologist is typically a part of the team (i.e., Child Study Team) that is charged with deciding whether a child's referral should move forward to evaluation or be returned to the regular classroom teacher to implement alternative instructional strategies. Our data show a range of approaches taken by psychologists in these conferences. Some tend to play the role of the specialist without inviting much input from teachers, while others are more inclusive of team members' views. For example, one psychologist would often ask the referring teacher a question such as, "Do you think the difficulties are just a reaction to the home situation, or do you think there's an intrinsic problem here?" Their intention is to get the view of someone who knows the child well. This psychologist seems to acknowledge the limitations of the discrete test that she will give the child; by the same token, it seems likely that the teacher's diagnosis will affect the psychologist's view.

In another school, a teacher expressed dismay after a team conference because he felt that the psychologist had expected him to agree with her recommendation that a child be placed on medication for hyperactivity. The teacher felt that the psychologist had been pushing her own agenda and had not validated his efforts to work with the child in the classroom. The varying relationships between the psychologist and the school-based team are evident in these interactions. The psychologist who plays more of a specialist role is visibly less interactive and personal with the school personnel. Informal conversations before conferences also reveal considerable interplay of opinion between teachers and psychologists.

The Influence of School Personnel's Impressions of the Family   The foregoing issue, school personnel's impressions of children, is usually related to their impressions of the family. Our interviews and observations document school personnel's unabashed expression of negative opinions about the families of children referred. In our interviews, general statements about the role of dysfunctional families in children's disabilities are so pervasive as to indicate a powerful predisposition to blame families for children's learning and behavioral difficulties. These comments are generally tied to implicit or explicit references to ethnicity, culture, and/or socioeconomic status of the families. Such views are particularly evident in conferences for children who have been referred for behavior problems. Indeed, the tone of the conversation about parents is often of a nature that would never take place were the parent present. When the parent is present, the negative expectations are more subtle but still evident. Despite this widespread pattern, there are individuals who present a much more positive view of families, and the difference in their attitudes is clearly visible in the respectful tone of their interactions with family members.

An example of such a negative mindset was evident in the following situation. The day before a placement conference, there was some discussion between an administrator and a teacher regarding whether or not the mother was expected to attend the conference. One person thought she had written to say that she would not come, while the other said she had told him she would come. The concluding comment to the discussion was that her word may not be too reliable since she "has nine kids; some of them are with her and the others are farmed out somewhere else." (The reality of this family situation is that the four younger children live with the mother while the five older ones live with their father's family in a nearby state.) When the conference began the next day and the mother was not yet present, one member responded by commenting explicitly that the mother's lack of attendance clearly showed that she does not care about her child. In reality, the parent was actually in the school building for the meeting (and had arrived early), but had been detained momentarily in the office on another matter. As the meeting progressed after the mother arrived, the team's condescending behavior toward her diminished as she proved herself to be well prepared and well informed on all matters pertaining to her child.

In a conference at another school, a different psychologist commented to the researcher prior to beginning the assessment that the child came from a dysfunctional family. Her reason for this conclusion was that the mother was incarcerated and there seemed to be "a lot of people living in the house." This information had been gleaned from the teacher and from the child's social history. The child performed well on the Wechsler Intelligence Scale for Children (3rd ed., WISC III), with a combined score of 108. However, she became steadily less responsive to the projective testing, especially after the psychologist asked specific questions about her mother. When the psychologist came to do the House Tree Person test with this child, the child drew a picture with about nine people, who she said were her family. However, on being asked to identify them, the child specified about three or four of the figures and then shrugged her shoulders and became silent. The psychologist told the researcher afterward that this was indicative of the dysfunctionality in the home. Visits to the child's home revealed that, although her mother was incarcerated, this child lived in an apparently stable extended family headed by a grandmother, two aunts, and six children, all cousins. The prominent display in the living room of trophies and awards earned by the child and others in the home indicated the value placed on these children and their accomplishments.

There are several competing explanations for the child's reluctance to participate in the projective testing. For one, this intelligent child could easily have sensed that the psychologist's questions about her mother reflected some negative judgment. Without opportunity to establish a trusting relationship with this adult, why should the child reveal potentially damaging information? Second, the child may well have been instructed by her family not to tell strangers details of their family life. Third, the child herself may have been experiencing some embarrassment about her mother's absence. Indeed, in the subsequent placement conference, attended by the child's grandmother and aunt, the grandmother expressed the opinion that "There's nothing wrong with my granddaughter. She just wants her mother." The child was subsequently placed in a self-contained class for behavior disorders, and the receiving teacher commented within two weeks of the placement that she could not understand why the child was placed in the program since her behavior was fine from her first day in the class.

Our data also indicate examples where the teacher's diagnosis is not corroborated by the psychological evaluation. However, in these cases the psychologist may have social consequences to meet as a result of his/her determination. For example, one psychologist found that a child referred for emotional disturbance did not qualify for services under that disability. The school staff involved were irate when they heard that this was the outcome of the assessment and they went to the conference ready to do battle with the psychologist. However, the psychologist solved the problem by classifying the child as eligible for services under the category "Other Health Impaired, with ADHD" (Attention Deficit Hyperactivity Disorder).

At another school, a teacher who had been complaining for several months about a child's behavior came to the point of deciding whether to refer. In discussing the child, she commented that his mother was in a mental institution, so she speculated as to whether that was part of the problem. She described the child's tendency to gaze around the room and be inattentive, and wondered whether he might be hearing voices. However, when the teacher was asked to write detailed anecdotal records of the child's behavioral problems, the list included only items such as writing on his desk, gazing around, and playing with his pencil. The psychologist tested this child, including projective testing, and concluded that there was no indication whatever of emotional disturbance or any kind of behavioral disorder. Nevertheless, the psychologist's sense that there was pressure from the administration to place this child seems to have affected the outcome. We detail this in the following section.

External Pressures for Identification and Placement   Beyond teachers' perspectives, psychologists are also influenced in their choices by the pressure they feel to identify children for special education. In the foregoing case, there was considerable pressure in the school for the referral of failing children in order to get them the special education services they were perceived to need, and also to protect the school's scores in statewide testing. As we noted above, the psychologist did not find the child eligible for emotional disturbance, which was the main reason for referral. She did conclude, however, that although the child did not really have a learning disability (LD), he could be qualified for this program because of low math scores. The child's reading was on or close to grade level. The psychologist commented that the placement would be good for the child because he would be placed with a very nurturing teacher and would benefit from the individualized attention. Reflecting on this, it is not possible to tease out whether it was the psychologist's concern for the child that swayed her decision or whether she was trying to meet the expectations of the school personnel. Whichever is the best explanation, the fact remains that the decision to place this child was based on factors related to personal concerns or social relationships, not on a rigorous gatekeeping process.

Another psychologist spoke quite openly about the pressure from administrators and teachers and indicated that she does her best to meet these needs by choosing instruments that will be likely to "find" the disability suspected by school personnel. When a student is found to qualify for special education services based on the psychologist's assessment, this is considered validation for the referring teacher. The school district keeps track of how many students are referred and placed in each school, and those teachers and schools that have a high percentage of referred students qualifying are praised, since their referrals are seen as having been appropriate.

The Exclusion of Information on Classroom Ecology   The foregoing sections point to several beliefs and perspectives that influence the assessment. Yet there is one obvious factor that is generally ignored—the ecology of the classroom from which the child has come. Keogh has repeatedly called for research on the contextual elements that may contribute to children's failure to learn (Keogh, 1998; Keogh & Speece, 1996). On the issue of behavior, Kellam, Ling, Merisca, Brown, and Ialongo (1998) demonstrated that the experience of a disorderly classroom atmosphere in the first grade predicted a trajectory of increasingly aggressive behavior for boys who were initially resistant to school discipline. Classroom ecology is certainly a key issue, yet our numerous observations of conferences show few examples of this information being taken into account in the decisionmaking process. Interestingly, the only cases where we observed this involved a strong teacher who readily acknowledged that perhaps a child would do better with a different teacher; this solution was tried and with good success. We have seen classrooms characterized by weak or nonexistent instruction and behavior management, and have never heard the question raised as to whether a child might learn more or behave better in a different classroom. Clearly, the staff members present in a conference must continue to work together after the conference, so if the issue is the teacher rather than the child, it is difficult to get this information on the table. It appears from informal conversations with teachers that it is well known among them who are perceived to be strong and weak teachers, but colleagues are reluctant to jeopardize their relationships with one another. The psychologist, on the other hand, has probably been in only a handful of classrooms in the school and typically does not observe in the rooms of children referred to the support team. Our research has several examples of children referred for potential behavior disorders who are coming from classrooms where disorderly behavior is the norm because of the teacher's lack of skills.

The Effects of Operational Definitions on Choice of Assessment Instruments and Placement Decisions   The actual event of psychological assessment is the capstone event of a long process. As we mentioned earlier, changing the terminology from *handicap* to *services* usually does not alter what is done to determine eligibility. The testing is still designed to find or not find a disability. With regard to intellectual disabilities, the discrepancy and exclusionary criteria and the IQ score as a proxy for intelligence are at the heart of the muddy waters of assessment. The history of overrepresentation in the mental retardation category and the greater stigma associated with that category have led to a preference for the learning disability label. Both categories rely on the use of an IQ measure, a criterion that can be interpreted as working both for and against minorities. It works for minorities in that it may protect them from inappropriate placement in the learning disability category, yet it may deny them that placement even when it is appropriate. Further, it may work against them in that it may relegate them to the more stigmatizing category of mental retardation. Let us explain briefly.

First, it is now generally understood among experts that an IQ test is essentially an achievement test, based on exposure to certain beliefs and information to which the children of educated and middle-class families are more likely to have had access (Garcia & Pearson, 1994; Goodnow, 1976; Mercer, 1973; Williams, 1974). Thus, the poor and/or minority child is less likely to display a discrepancy, since his or her score is likely to be lower to begin with. Second, as Collins and Camblin (1983) pointed out almost two decades ago, the exclusionary criterion, by which the child's deficits should not be attributable to environmental circumstances, further decreases the likelihood that the poor and/or minority child will be designated LD. The field is looking for intrinsic deficit, not environmentally induced low achievement. The discrepancy criterion, however, specifies that this deficit has an element of surprise, because the child's intelligence is, overall, normal. If being intelligent is to be measured by an IQ score, then it is harder for the poor or minority child to meet this definition, since some minorities are known to score lower on these measures. Thus the learning disability category has *not* traditionally been one in which minorities are overrepresented. Recently, however, the figures in certain states and school districts show an increase in the assignment of minorities to this category (U.S. Department of Education, Office for Civil Rights, 1999), and the reasons for this have been well described by Gottleib, Gottleib, and Wishner (1994).

If the discrepancy is not achieved, then the child whose IQ score is low enough will qualify for mental retardation, while the child whose IQ surpasses the cutoff score for that category will not qualify for special education services. This child presumably will fall between the cracks. Our data indicate that psychologists who, for various reasons outlined in the rest of this paper, believe that the child should be placed may then make decisions that will allow them to manipulate the child's classification in a way to receive special education services. Thus, they may choose an IQ instrument on which the child can score higher in order to show a 15-point discrepancy between IQ and achievement. Another option is to choose an instrument known to be less verbally loaded, so as to give the minority child an opportunity to be assessed more on nonverbal than on language performance. At one placement conference, the psychologist and other participants discussed a third-grade nonreader who was now at a high intermediate level of English-language proficiency. The psychologist reported that the student's IQ score, according to the Kaufman Assessment Battery for Children (KABC) IQ test, was 74, which the psychologist at first described as being in the low average range. Later in the meeting, however, she referred to the student's IQ as average. The team found that the student qualified as LD, with a discrepancy between his IQ of 74 and his reading achievement of 38, and recommended placement in an LD program.

A similar phenomenon occurs with regard to the interaction of LD and emotional handicap or behavioral disorder (EH/BD). In some cases it appears that students are pushed toward these latter categories (as we described earlier) and in other cases are protected from them. One six-year-old Cuban American first grader had been referred by his teachers primarily for concerns about his emotional and behavioral functioning. He was a native Spanish speaker classified as ESOL (English for Speakers of Other Languages) Level 4, meaning that he had very good but not fully proficient English-language skills, according to the district's criteria. During the child's staffing the psychologist explained that she had noticed indications of depression and low self-concept. She recommended that the parent take the boy to see a psychiatrist to see why he was depressed and easily distracted, and to find out about medicine to treat his hyperactivity. However, she later told the researcher that although she thought the child was clinically depressed, she had not written this in her report because she had not wanted his case "to go EH" (i.e., did not want him placed in a program for children with emotional handicaps). She preferred the LD category and said, "Sometimes emotional problems are caused by a learning disability. You know, the child gets frustrated because he doesn't know how to do it, and he doesn't know how to handle it." Even though he was working on grade level and his achievement test scores (e.g., WIAT Reading = 98, Numerical Operations = 97, Spelling = 101) were *higher* than his WISC III scores (Verbal = 83, Performance = 90, Composite = 85), she said that he qualified for LD "because he needed individualized attention" and "because of processing deficits" (he was slow in auditory processing and needed to hear directions multiple times). She later explained, "The procedures manual says that if a child is below seven years old, he doesn't have to have the 15-point discrepancy, which is one standard deviation. The procedures manual just states that the child has to be doing poorly academically, because the norms at that age are sometimes deflated. So, he got lucky because he got everything done before he was seven years old." Clearly this psychologist was trying to help the child.

Factors That Influence Psychologists' Selection of Instruments and Conducting of the Assessment   Different training, different beliefs about the efficacy of certain instruments for different populations, and the host of external influences described above result in considerable variation in psychologists' choice and administration of instruments. Our data show this in relation to both IQ and projective testing.

Presently, the area of greatest concern regarding the overrepresentation of African Americans is the Serious Emotional Disorder (SED) category. The determination of eligibility for this category relies heavily on projective testing. Yet the validity of these tests continues to be the subject of serious debate and controversy. Certainly, if the challengers of these tests are correct (Gresham,

1993; Knoff, 1993; Motta, Little, & Tobin, 1993), it is difficult for a psychologist to interpret children's responses without being influenced by the kinds of prior information discussed earlier—teachers' informal diagnoses and negative perceptions about family circumstances. Further, the concept of consequential validity is particularly relevant when children who qualify for SED services are placed in extremely restrictive settings. In the case of projective testing, our discussions with psychologists reveal that, although these tests are commonly used, there are different approaches to them. For example, those who use the Thematic Apperception Test report using it in different ways, such as using all items in the test or only a few selected items. Similarly, some psychologists routinely complete a battery of four or five tests, while others use only a couple if the child seems to be scoring well—that is, not showing signs of emotional disturbance.

Psychologists may make their selection of instruments on the basis of their own philosophies of the applicability of certain tests to certain populations. For example, some psychologists choose the WISC while others use the KABC. Although all are testing children from low-socioeconomic black and Hispanic families, those who use the KABC explain that it is "less verbally loaded" and is therefore more appropriate for children from diverse cultural and linguistic backgrounds. One psychologist offered the opinion that the IQ tests do measure "inborn intelligence."

The tremendous heterogeneity of this school district leads some psychologists to conclude that the IQ test is simply incapable of explaining low performance in the case of children whose cultural experiences are very different from those of their American peers. Children from countries where education is minimally available, such as Haiti or some Central American countries, are particularly challenging to evaluate. For example, in our research, school personnel who have intimate knowledge of Haiti explain that the U.S. method of relying on chronological age for grade placement results in many children being placed in grades two or three years above the level they were at in Haiti. This discontinuity in instructional level is a clear recipe for failure, which, for many students, ultimately results in their being assigned a label of disability. Psychologists who are concerned about this must negotiate the challenge of providing services while finding a way to give the child the greatest benefit of the doubt about his or her potential. This concern sometimes results in children being found to be eligible for an LD program despite the conviction of other team members that the children should really "qualify" for an Educable Mental Retardation (EMR) or EH program (as in the example provided in the previous section). In such cases, school personnel express the opinion that the psychologist has redone the testing with an easier test so as to get a higher IQ score to allow for the LD placement. The psychologist, however, argues that he or she used a battery of appropriate tests to get a true picture of the child's abilities. In such cases, the psychologist may have to withstand considerable disapproval from his or her colleagues.

Psychologists are also influenced by their opinions about the effectiveness of special education. One psychologist expressed a strong belief that she often puts children in special education "to save their lives." Even though she may not think the program is excellent, she believes that the smaller class size and a potentially individualized program serve as a protection for the child. Another psychologist expressed the opposite opinion, that it is much better to deliver services in the mainstream, especially in view of what she saw as the overly restrictive nature of the typical classroom for students designated emotionally handicapped. This psychologist also emphasized the relative nature of both the mental retardation and emotional disturbance categories and the dangers inherent in their application. In the case of the former, she said that is very easy to "make an error" with children from low-socioeconomic and minority backgrounds, and for the latter category she emphasized that standards vary from school to school according to the expectations of the neighborhood. Psychologists also expressed the view that there is greater stigma attached to the EH, BD, or SED classifications than the LD category.

IMPLICATIONS

What are the implications of this picture of a variable, even unpredictable, process of psychological assessment? Certainly one implication is that the process is subjective, if not capricious. This is not to say that well-informed subjectivity is out of place in the assessment process. On the contrary, we believe that it is appropriate for qualified professionals to make informed educational decisions. However, we believe that it is crucial for educators to acknowledge that the placement process is neither scientific nor a true assessment of children's learning potential. Rather, psychological assessment as currently practiced seeks to maintain its status as the rock of special education evaluation by clinging to a mythology that causes practitioners to engage in a series of juggling acts. As experts, they must balance their views against those of colleagues who really know the children. On the other hand, engaging the knowledge of others may either enhance or contaminate the process. They must also decide whether to juggle their tools to fit the demands of bureaucrats as well as the demands of children and families from enormously varying backgrounds. As the gatekeepers to special education, they must uphold the belief that they practice science.

Why are we concerned about the methods used to examine these questions? Only close-up observation of social processes can reveal the power of "soft places"—of unofficial, undocumented aspects of professional practice—to influence that which is considered to be scientific and objective. Qualitative research investigates human processes and enables us to document the complexities and disparities of the assessment process. Qualitative research does not claim to be generalizable, since its samples are small and not representative. However, rigorously conducted ethnographic techniques will produce findings that, under similar circumstances with similar populations, are likely to recur. We do not seek to establish statistical probability but to present rich, convincing portraits that can lead us to anticipate how and why individuals act in real-life social situations. Research that documents the social nature of the trajectory of children referred to special education underscores the need for change in assessment procedures. If the referral, evaluation, and placement process is of questionable validity yet results in the stigma of disability, and in some cases significant segregation from the mainstream, it needs to be revamped. We do not really need to know for certain that it will, in terms of probability, lead to overidentification, but that it can, and why. Well-documented and convincing accounts of how individuals respond to everyday situations demonstrate the social nature of educational decisionmaking.

RECOMMENDATIONS

The field is not short of suggestions for revamping the system, many of which offer a combination of careful qualitative observation of children's learning and systematic measurement of the real variable of concern—the child's actual academic achievement. For example, Reschly, Tilly, and Grimes (1999) and others (Fuchs & Fuchs, 1998) have offered systematic performance-based procedures for identifying which children should receive special education services without putting them through the current expensive and suspect assessment process. These approaches focus on developing a cycle in which assessment of academic performance prescribes instructional interventions, whose effectiveness is then systematically assessed. Several alternative procedures have been recommended as having potential for conducting linguistically and culturally sensitive assessments, such as portfolios and authentic assessment procedures, dynamic assessment, evaluation of the zone of proximal or potential development, and assessment via assisted learning and transfer (Brown, Campione, Webber, & McGilly, 1992; Dent, Mendocal, Pierce, & West, 1991; Figueroa, 1983; Gonzalez, Brusca-Vega, & Yawkey, 1997; Haywood, 1988; Rueda, 1997). Moll

(1990) makes yet a different point; he recommends a search for strengths rather than deficits by identifying and building on the cultural, linguistic, and social funds of knowledge that students and their families bring to the school setting. In a similar vein, our own research points to the potential strengths of school-wide models of parent and community participation, such as the Comer model, full-service schools, and effective Title I services. When properly implemented, all of the above approaches provide a network of support for children, rather than a set of practices based on the assumption that poor academic performance indicates a need for assessment of presumed intellectual potential.

With regard to the ecology of general education classrooms, the quality of the instruction and the classroom management of the referring teacher must be considered crucial variables. Further, and regardless of referral, classroom ecology should be the concern of every teacher and school administrator. The variable quality of instruction and management in our research settings suggests that school administrators have considerable power in determining what kind of classroom practice will be accepted and what will not. Some principals exercise this power so effectively that there is a reasonably uniform level of effective teacher performance throughout the school; others seem to tolerate classroom situations that any casual observer would recognize as conducive to minimal learning and unacceptable behavior. Principals' interventions to ensure high-quality classrooms include high visibility of the principal throughout the school building, special supports for teachers who are struggling, and deliberate decisionmaking regarding the provision of in-service training that meets teachers' needs.

Finally, it is important to note that federal and state guidelines stipulate that (a) multiple data sources should be considered when making eligibility decisions, (b) exclusionary criteria should be applied, and (c) alternative procedures should be used when assessing culturally and linguistically diverse students for whom standardized tests are not deemed appropriate (California Department of Education, 1999; National Joint Committee on Learning Disabilities, 1998; PL 105-17, 1997). Despite these guidelines, however, our data indicate that the placement process continues to be dominated by a rigid approach to the use of traditional psychological assessment as the gatekeeper, and that this is all the more dangerous because of *a failure to recognize the role of unofficial practices and influences.* We believe that the main reason for this pattern is that psychological assessment has been conceptualized as the rock of special education—the proof of disability and, therefore, eligibility for services. We submit that this failure to acknowledge the "soft places" of the assessment process has compounded the problem of overrepresentation. Detailed, qualitative documentation of the social processes that really constitute assessment can dislodge psychological testing from its pedestal and lead to a more useful, less expensive, and less stigmatizing way of helping children with learning and behavioral difficulties.

NOTE

1. This study took place in a southern Florida urban community that is an important international center of Hispanic migration for the middle class and the poor, creating great economic division within that subgroup. It also has a multinational black and African American community with many Caribbean immigrants. Therefore, its racial and ethnic stratification is unlike other U.S. cities in, for example, the Northeast or Midwest. The patterns that are discussed in this chapter obviously are not simply about race; however, race plays into these processes in many complicated ways in a community in which race and ethnicity matter in terms of power and stereotypes.

REFERENCES

Algozzine, B., Christenson, S., & Ysseldyke, J. (1982). Probabilities associated with the referral to placement process. *Teacher Education and Special Education, 5*, 19–23.

Artiles, A. J., Trent, S. C., & Kuan, L. A. (1997). Learning disabilities research on ethnic minority students: An analysis of 22 years of studies published in selected refereed journals. *Learning Disabilities Research and Practice, 12*, 82–91.

Bogdan, R., & Knoll, J. (1988). The sociology of disability. In E. L. Meyen & T. M. Skrtic (Eds.), *Exceptional children and youth: An introduction* (3rd ed., pp. 449–478). Denver: Love.

Bronfenbrenner, U. (1979). *The ecology of human development: Experiments by nature and design*. Cambridge, MA: Harvard University Press.

Brown, A. L., Campione, J. C., Webber, L. S., & McGilly, K. (1992). Interactive learning environments: A new look at assessment and instruction. In B. R. Gifford & M. C. O'Connor (Eds.), *Changing assessments: Alternative views of aptitude, achievement, and instruction* (pp. 121–211). Boston: Kluwer.

California Department of Education. (1999). *California's education code*. Sacramento: Author.

Cole, M., & Bruner, J. (1971). Cultural differences and inferences about psychological processes. *American Psychologist, 26*, 867–876.

Collins, R., & Camblin, L. D. (1983). The politics and science of learning disability classification: Implications for black children. *Contemporary Education, 54*, 113–118.

Dent, H. (1976). Assessing black children for mainstream placement. In R. L. Jones (Ed.), *Mainstreaming and the minority child* (pp. 72–92). Minneapolis: Leadership Training Institute.

Dent, H., Mendocal, A., Pierce, W., & West, G. (1991). The San Francisco public schools experience with IQ testing: A model for non-biased assessment. In A. G. Hilliard (Ed.), *Testing African American students: Special re-issue of* The Negro Educational Review (pp. 146–162). Morristown, NJ: Aaron Press.

Figueroa, R. A. (1983). Test bias and Hispanic children. *Journal of Special Education, 17,* 431–440.

Fletcher, J. M., Francis, D. J., Shaywitz, S. E., Lyon, G. R., Foorman, B. R., Stuebing, K. K., & Shaywitz, B. A. (1998). Intelligent testing and the discrepancy model for children with learning disabilities. *Learning Disabilities Research and Practice, 13,* 186–203.

Fletcher, J. M., & Morris, R. D. (1986). Classification of disabled learners: Beyond exclusionary definitions. In S. J. Ceci (Ed.), *Handbook of cognitive, social, and neuropsychological reports of learning disabilities* (pp. 55–80). Hillsdale, NJ: Lawrence Erlbaum.

Fuchs, L. S., & Fuchs, D. (1998). Treatment validity: A unifying concept for reconceptualizing the identification of learning disabilities. *Learning Disabilities Research and Practice, 13,* 204–219.

Garcia, G. E., & Pearson, P. D. (1994). Assessment and diversity, *Review of Research in Education, 20,* 337–391. Washington, DC: American Educational Research Association.

Gerber, M., & Semmel, M. (1984). Teacher as imperfect test: Reconceptualizing the referral process. *Educational Psychologist, 19,* 137–148.

Gonzalez, V., Brusca-Vega, R., & Yawkey, T. (1997). *Assessment and instruction of culturally and linguistically diverse students.* Needham Heights, MA: Allyn & Bacon.

Goodnow, J. J. (1976). The nature of intelligent behavior: Questions raised by cross-cultural studies. In L. B. Resnick (Ed.), *The nature of intelligence.* Hillsdale, NJ: Erlbaum.

Gottlieb, J., Alter, M., Gottlieb, B., & Wishner, J. (1994). Special education in urban America: It's not justifiable for the many. *Journal of Special Education, 27,* 453–465.

Gresham, F. M. (1993). "What's wrong with this picture?" Response to Motta et al.'s review of human figure drawings. *School Psychology Quarterly, 8,* 182–186.

Gresham, F. M., Reschly, D. J., & Carey, M. P. (1987). Teachers as "tests": Classification accuracy and concurrent validation in the identification of learning disabled children. *School Psychology Review, 16,* 543–553.

Harry, B. (1992). *Cultural diversity, families, and the special education system.* New York: Teachers College Press.

Harry, B., Allen, N., & McLaughlin, M. (1995). Communication or compliance: African American families in the special education system. *Exceptional Children, 61,* 364–377.

Haywood, H. C. (1988). Dynamic assessment: The Learning Potential Assessment Device. In R. L. Jones (Ed.), *The psychoeducational assessment of minority group children: A casebook* (pp. 39–64). Berkeley, CA: Cobb and Henry.

Heller, K. A., Holtzman, W. H., Messick, S. (Eds.). (1982). *Placing children in special education: A strategy for equity.* Washington, DC: National Academy Press.

Hilliard, A. G. (1977). The predictive validity of norm-referenced standardized tests: Piaget or Binet? *Negro Educational Review, 25,* 189–201.

Jensen, A. R. (1974). How biased are culture-loaded tests? *Genetic Psychology Monographs, 90,* 185–244.

Kaufman, A. S., & Kaufman, N. L. (1983). *Kaufman Assessment Battery for Children.* Circle Pines, MN: American Guidance Service.

Kavale, K. (1990). The effectiveness of special education. In T. B. Gutkin & C. R. Reynolds (Eds.), *The handbook of school psychology* (2nd ed., pp. 868–898). New York: Wiley.

Kellam, S. G., Ling, X., Merisca, R., Brown, C. H., & Ialongo, N. (1998). The effect of the level of aggression in the first grade classroom on the course and malleability of aggressive behavior into middle school. *Development and Psychopathology, 10,* 165–185.

Keogh, B. (1998). Classrooms as well as students deserve study. *Remedial and Special Education, 19,* 313–314.

Keogh, B., & Speece, D. L. (1996). Learning disabilities within the context of schooling. In D. L. Speece & B. K. Keogh (Eds.), *Research on classroom ecologies: Implications for inclusion of children with learning disabilities* (pp. 1–14). Mahwah, NJ: Lawrence Erlbaum.

Knoff, H. M. (1993). The utility of human figure drawings in personality and intellectual assessment: Why ask why? *School Psychology Quarterly, 8,* 191–196.

Laosa, L. M. (1977). Nonbiased assessment of children's abilities: Historical antecedents and current issues. In T. Oakland (Ed.), *Psychological and educational assessment of minority children* (pp. 1–20). New York: Brunner/Mazel.

MacMillan, D. L., Gresham, F. M., & Bocian, K. M. (1998). Discrepancy between definitions of learning disabilities and school policies: An empirical investigation. *Journal of Learning Disabilities, 31,* 314–326.

Mehan, H., Hartwick, A., & Meihls, J. L. (1986). *Handicapping the handicapped: Decision-making in students' educational careers.* Stanford, CA: Stanford University Press.

Mercer, J. (1973). *Labeling the mentally retarded.* Berkeley: University of California Press.

Moll, L. C. (Ed.). (1990). Vygotsky and education: Instructional implications and applications of socio-historical psychology. Cambridge, Eng.: Cambridge University Press.

Motta, R., Little, S. G., & Tobin, M. I. (1993). The use and abuse of human figure drawings. *School Psychology Quarterly, 8,* 162–169.

National Joint Committee on Learning Disabilities (NJCLD). (1998). Operationalizing the NJCLD definition of learning disabilities for ongoing assessment in schools. *Learning Disability Quarterly, 21,* 186–193.

Oswald, D. P., Coutinho, M. J., Best, A. M., & Singh, N. (1999). Ethnic representation in special education: The influence of school-related economic and demographic variables. *Journal of Special Education, 32,* 194–206.

Popham, W. J. (1997). Consequential validity: Right concern—wrong concept. *Educational Measurements: Issues and Practice, 16*(2), 9–18.

Pugach, M. C. (1985). The limitations of federal special education policy: The role of classroom teachers in determining who is handicapped. *Journal of Special Education, 19,* 123–137.

Reschly, D. J. (2000). *IQ and special education: History, current status, and alternatives.* Unpublished paper, National Academy of Sciences, National Research Council, Washington, DC.

Reschly, D., Tilly, W. D., & Grimes, J. T. (Eds.). (1999). *Special education in transition: Functional assessment and non-categorical programming.* Longmont, CO: Sopris West.

Rueda, R. (1997). Changing the context of assessment: The move to portfolios and authentic assessment. In A. J. Artiles & G. Zamora-Duran (Eds.), *Reducing the disproportionate representation of culturally diverse students in special and gifted education* (pp. 7–25). Reston, VA: Council for Exceptional Children.

Sandoval, J. (1979). The WISC-R and internal evidence of test bias with minority groups. *Journal of Consulting and Clinical Psychology, 47,* 919–926.

Shepard, L. A. (1997). The centrality of test use and consequences for test validity. *Educational Measurement: Issues and Practice, 16*(2), 5–8.

Shinn, M. R., Tindal, R. A., & Spira, D. A. (1987). Special education referrals as an index of teacher tolerance: Are teachers imperfect tests? *Exceptional Children, 54*(1), 32–40.

Snow, R. E. (1995). *Validity of IQ as a measure of cognitive ability.* Paper presented to National Academy of Sciences, National Research Council, San Diego, CA.

Stanovich, K. (1991). Discrepancy definition of reading disability. Has intelligence led us astray? *Reading Research Quarterly, 26,* 7–29.

Strauss, A., & Corbin, J. (1998). *Basics of qualitative research: Techniques and procedures for developing grounded theory.* Thousand Oaks, CA: Sage.

Travers, J. R. (1982). Testing in educational placement: Issues and evidence. In K. A. Heller, W. H. Holtzman, & S. Messick (Eds.*), Placing children in special education: A strategy for equity* (230–261). Washington, DC: U.S. Department of Education.

U.S. Department of Education. (1997). The Individuals with Disabilities Education Act Amendments of 1997 Public Law 105-17. Available at http://www.ideapractices. org/lawandregs.htm/

U.S. Department of Education, Office for Civil Rights. (1999). *1997 elementary and secondary school civil rights survey: National summaries.* Washington, DC: DBS Corporation.

Williams, R. L. (1974). The problem of match and mismatch in testing black children. In L. P. Miller (Ed.), *The testing of black students: A symposium* (pp. 17–30). Englewood Cliffs, NJ: Prentice-Hall.

CHAPTER FIVE

Schools Make a Difference:
The Overrepresentation of African American
Youth in Special Education and the
Juvenile Justice System

DAVID OSHER

DARREN WOODRUFF

ANTHONY E. SIMS

INTRODUCTION

The percentage of African American children and youth identified as having emotional and behavioral disorders (EBD) who are suspended, expelled, or otherwise removed from local school settings, and who ultimately end up in the juvenile and/or adult correctional system, is far greater than comparable percentages for white youth. For example, while African American children represent only 15 percent of the U.S. school population (age 6–21), they comprise over 20 percent of students referred into special education and over 26 percent of youth identified by schools as emotionally and behaviorally disturbed (U.S. Department of Education, 2000). Nationally, black students are identified as emotionally disturbed at over one and one-half times the rate of white students (National Research Council [NRC], 2002). According to data presented elsewhere in this book, twenty-nine states have EBD identification rates for black students that are more than twice the rates for white students (see Parrish, this volume); furthermore, black males are over five times as likely as white females to be identified as emotionally disturbed (see Oswald, Coutinho, & Best, this volume).

In schools across the United States, African American students (independent of their identification for EBD) are more likely to be suspended and expelled and tend to receive harsher penalties for behavioral offenses than their white peers (Skiba, Michael, Nardo, & Peterson, 2000). While academic outcomes are poor for all youth with EBD, they are particularly dismal for African Americans. For example, the graduation rate for African American youth with EBD is 27.5 percent, compared to 48 percent for white youth with EBD (Osher & Osher, 1996).

In addition to their disproportionate identification for behavioral disorders and removal from school through suspension and expulsion, African American children also constitute 26 percent of school-age youth who are arrested, 30 percent of the cases in juvenile courts, 45 percent of youth in juvenile detention, and 46 percent of cases waived into the adult criminal courts. After leaving high school (Snyder & Sickmund, 1999), African American youth with disabilities are arrested at a 40 percent rate, compared to a 27 percent rate for whites (Oswald et al., this volume). The causes of these negative academic and behavioral outcomes include misinformed judgments and inappropriate and ineffective interventions by education, mental health, and juvenile justice professionals, which reflect the impact of race, class, and culture in both school and the larger community (Johnson, 1994; Nettles, Mucherah, & Jones, 2000).

This chapter uses a variety of data to explore the links between environmental risk factors, overidentification of African American students for special education, and the overrepresentation of African American children and youth in the juvenile justice system. The first primary risk factor is poverty, which disproportionately affects African American children and their psychological, emotional, and social development. Poverty predisposes a disproportionate number of African American children to a high risk for behavioral problems at school entry (e.g., NRC, 2002; NRC & Institute of Medicine, 2000). The second primary risk factor involves the interaction of African American children with the schools that they attend, which disproportionately lack the capacity to address students' needs though universal, early, and intensive behavioral supports and interventions (NRC, 2002). The third primary risk factor relates to the interaction of African American children and youth with community agencies (e.g., the juvenile justice system), which are less likely to address black students' mental health needs proactively and instead are more likely to arrest, adjudicate, and incarcerate these students (Isaacs, 1992; U.S. Public Health Service, 2000a, 2001).

This exploratory study addresses issues of under- and overidentification for special education services, as well as the impact of effective and ineffective school-based interventions. Our findings are consistent with the National Research Council's (2002) examination of racial disproportionality in special education, which suggests that "minority children are disproportionately poor, and poverty is associated with . . . child care environments that are less supportive of early cognitive and emotional development" (p. ES3), and that "minority children are less likely to have experienced well-trained teachers [and] high-quality instruction that carefully puts the prerequisites for learning in place, combined with effective classroom management that minimizes chaos" (p. ES4). Our findings are also consistent with reports from the U.S. surgeon general that delineate the importance of prevention and culturally competent interventions, and of resources for school-based mental health (U.S. Public Health Service, 1999, 2000a, 2001).

THE IMPACT OF SCHOOLS ON OUTCOMES OF CHILDREN WITH EBD

The disproportionate identification of African American children as emotionally and behaviorally disturbed, their disproportionate removal from school through suspension and expulsion, and their systemic adjudication into the juvenile justice system can be analyzed within a life course/social field framework (Kellam & Rebok, 1992). The life course/social field theory is based on the hypothesis that people face specific task demands in various social contexts across major periods of their life span (Kellam & Rebok, 1992). The social tasks that we encounter in life are monitored by "natural raters" who perform policing and gatekeeping functions. For example, parents function as "natural raters" within the family, peers within the peer group, teachers in the classroom, principals in schools, supervisors in the workplace, and police officers and judges in the community (Kellam, 1990; Kellam & Ensminger, 1980). How well children handle the task demands made by natural raters influences their early opportunities for success, which in turn affects how well they meet task demands in future social arenas—for example, whether they can succeed in a career and live successfully in the larger community. The life course/social field framework employs longitudinal study to map an individual's developmental progress, including the antecedents, mediators, and consequences of developmental experiences and behaviors. The school environment plays a critical role in the life course and social development of children.

The Promise of Supportive Schooling: Fostering Resilience and Academic Success

At their best, schools can provide a positive, supportive environmental context that fosters resilience (Blum, McNeely, & Rinehart, 2002; Fox et al., 1999). Schools can (and should) be places where students experience success and receive appropriate support services when needed (e.g., counseling, mentoring, and tutoring) in a nonstigmatizing manner. From a public health perspective, schools can be a setting where necessary interventions can reach the largest number of children and youth at the lowest cost to society (Woodruff et al., 1999). In addition, by developing positive relations with families (Cartledge, Kea, & Simmons-Reed, 2002; Kea, 1997), schools can play an important role in linking the home and community with the goals of the school (Harry, 1992).

Use of the life course/social field framework helps to illuminate relationships between school-based factors and the reduction or exacerbation of negative behavioral, academic, and social outcomes for African American children and youth. For example, analysis of data from the Baltimore Prevention Study (Kellam, Merisca, Brown, & Ialongo, 1998) helps specify how environmental factors can mediate the ability of children to meet the task demands of school. A group of 1,100 students was randomly assigned to classes across nineteen elementary schools in five poor to middle-class Baltimore neighborhoods (65% of the first graders were African American). Students who were highly aggressive in first grade and placed into poorly managed classrooms were 2.5 times more likely to still be highly aggressive six years later than similarly aggressive first graders who were placed into well-managed first-grade classrooms.

The School's Contribution to Negative Developmental Outcomes

Researchers have identified a variety of school-based risk factors that contribute to negative developmental outcomes. These "mine fields" (Reid & Eddy, 1997, p. 344) can contribute to existing risk factors and further increase the risk of poor social outcomes (Caspi & Moffit, 1995). For example, poorly managed schools can be risk-prone contexts where children with behavioral problems frequently generate hostile and punitive reactions from teachers and peers and where early antisocial behavior is reinforced by inappropriate school responses (Reid & Eddy, 1997). Schools can also be a place where students at risk for behavioral problems get caught up in a self-sustaining cycle of classroom disruption and negative consequences (Dumas, Prinz, Smith, & Laughlin, 1999). This cycle includes academic failure, as teachers ignore or are unable to address the academic needs of students with behavioral problems, and forced segregation with antisocial peers, which often reinforces problem behavior (Dishion, McCord, & Poulin, 1999). Finally, schools can frequently be settings for public humiliation as children and youth experience academic failure, peer rejection, and adult sarcasm.

Compared with their white counterparts, black students are more likely to attend schools that have less social and material capital, fewer funds for curriculum and staff development, more inexperienced teachers, and poor teacher morale (Metz, 1997; Skiba, Knesting, & Bush, 2002). Black students are also more likely to attend schools characterized by practices that contribute to the development or escalation of antisocial behavior (Sprague, 2002), such as:

- ineffective instruction
- inconsistent and punitive schoolwide, classroom, and individual behavior-management practices
- lack of opportunity to learn and practice prosocial interpersonal and self-management skills
- unclear rules and expectations regarding appropriate behavior
- failure to correct rule violations and reward adherence to them
- failure to assist students from backgrounds that place them at risk for not bonding with the schooling process

During the 1999–2000 school year, African American students with disabilities were more than three times as likely as whites to be given short-term suspensions. Similarly, they were 2.6 times more likely than whites to be removed from school for more than ten days. Further, African American students with disabilities (as well as Latino and Native American children with disabilities) were 67 percent more likely than whites to be removed on grounds of dangerousness by a hearing officer. When these data are examined on a state-by-state basis, the challenges posed by disproportionate identification practices appear to be even more stark. The risk of black and white students with disabilities being removed from school across all fifty states ranged as high as 25.9 percent for black students to a low of 7.02 percent for white students (Office of Special EducationPrograms, 2000).

AFRICAN AMERICAN CHILDREN AND YOUTH WITH EBD

The statistics on exposure of African American youth to the juvenile justice and adult correctional systems (see Table 1) are closely aligned with national outcome data for African American students identified with EBD. According to the most current longitudinal survey of students in special education (Valdes, Williamson, & Wagner, 1990), 66 percent of African American students identified for EBD received failing grades, compared to 38 percent of white students with EBD. Furthermore, twice as many African American students identified for EBD exited school as a result of dropping out (58.2%) as opposed to graduating (27.5%); this is a significant problem, because 73 percent of all students with EBD who drop out are arrested within three to five years of leaving school (U.S. Department of Education, 1994).

Students with EBD are over thirteen times more likely than other students with disabilities to be arrested while in school (Doren, Bullis, & Benz, 1996),

TABLE 1

Risk of Correctional Placement: Black Students Compared to White Students

25 States with Highest Risk Level	
State	*Risk Comparison*
New Jersey	16.19
Rhode Island	15.19
New Hampshire	13.82
Ohio	12.00
Connecticut	10.66
New York	9.12
Wisconsin	8.38
Illinois	7.80
Alabama	6.49
Minnesota	6.29
Pennsylvania	5.87
South Dakota	5.27
Maryland	5.26
Missouri	5.03
California	5.01
Iowa	4.99
Louisiana	4.84
Kansas	4.52
Idaho	4.39
New Mexico	4.35
Oregon	4.35
Kentucky	4.30
North Carolina	4.23
Virginia	4.06
Michigan	4.05
United States	4.05

An odds comparison of 1.0 translates to equal risk for black students compared to white students. A higher number translates to higher relative risk.

Source: www.idea.org, Table AA14, Students Served under IDEA by Race/Ethnicity, Part B, 1999–2000 School Year, and Table AB11, Students Served in Correctional Facilities under IDEA, by Race/Ethnicity, Part B, 1999–2000 school year.

and more likely than other students with disabilities to be arrested after they leave school (Wagner, 1995). Once arrested, youth with EBD (and with cognitive disabilities) are more likely than their peers to be adjudicated, placed in restrictive settings, and spend more time in such settings than their peers (Osher, Rouse, Woodruff, Kendziora, & Quinn, 2002). Not surprisingly, a disproportionate number of incarcerated youth have behavioral and/or cognitive disabilities.[1] Among these youth, those with EBD are at the greatest risk of incarceration: while they represented less than 10 percent of students with disabilities nationally in 1996, they constituted 42 percent of students with disabilities who were in correctional facilities (U.S. Department of Education, 1999b). Because schools only identify 1 percent rather than the 3 to 6 percent of students who may have such needs (NRC, 2002; U.S. Department of Education, 1999b), the actual percentage may be higher (Costello et al., 1996; Cuffe, 2000; Leone, 1991; Roberts, Attkisson, & Rosenblatt, 1998). For example, when the Diagnostic Interview Schedule for Children was administered to a randomly selected stratified sample, which included 1,005 African American youth age 10–18 who were detained in Cook County, Illinois, researchers found that nearly two-thirds of the males and nearly three-quarters of the females met the diagnostic criteria for one or more psychiatric disorders. Moreover, when conduct disorder was excluded, nearly 60 percent of the males and two-thirds of the females still met diagnostic criteria for one or more psychiatric disorders (Teplin, 2001).

Emotional and behavioral problems are produced and exacerbated by the interaction between individual characteristics and the social environment (Boyce et al., 1998). Though often treated as having a single disorder, many students with EBD have additional emotional, behavioral, and cognitive challenges, such as learning disabilities, attention deficit disorder, anxiety, depression, and conduct disorder (Caron & Rutter, 1991; Fessler, Rosenberg, & Rosenberg, 1991), which in turn place them at risk for substance abuse and delinquent behavior (Loeber, Farrington, Stouthamer-Loeber, & Van Kammen, 1998). Students with EBD often experience aversive school environments marked by lowered academic expectations and support, academic frustration and failure, consistently negative responses from teachers, disciplinary referrals, segregation into settings with antisocial peers, suspension, and high dropout rates (Gunter & Denny, 1998; Wehby, Symons, Canale, & Go, 1998).

Students with EBD are frequently subjected to curricula that emphasize control and behavioral management and fail to provide them with the academic supports necessary to address scattered academic skills, attention problems, and organizational and learning deficits (Nelson, Jordan, & Rodrigues-Walling, 2002; Osher & Hanley, 1996). They rarely have the opportunity to succeed academically and to develop a positive identity as learners.

Addressing EBD effectively often requires both mental health and educational interventions. The failure to provide these interventions in the school setting contributes to the high number of youth with EBD who are involved with the juvenile justice or adult correctional systems. A study that compared mental health needs among a random sample of youth (n = 473) within the juvenile justice system found that 45.9 percent of youth on probation, 67.5 percent of youth who were incarcerated, and 88 percent of youth who were adjudicated to residential treatment centers had EBD (Lyons et al., 2001). Similarly, a study of 95 public and private juvenile facilities reported that 73 percent of the children in these facilities reported mental health problems during their screening (Abt Associates, 1994).

Problems in the School Setting: Over- and Underidentification

Data on the overrepresentation of African American youth in EBD programs are consistent with a general concern regarding the disproportionate representation of African Americans in disability categories (Sims, 1996). Although initial concerns focused primarily on disproportionate representation in mental retardation and learning disabled categories, issues related to the educational experiences of African American students identified with EBD are also now at the forefront.

Several factors are hypothesized to be an influence on racial disproportionality in special education placements:

The Referral Process   Studies of the relationship between initial teacher referral and subsequent special education classifications suggest that subjective judgment by classroom teachers is a highly significant variable in identification (Foster, 1990). Teacher perceptions, gender, race, and socioeconomic status have also been identified as interactive variables in the referral process (Lomotey, 1990).

Assessment Bias   The debate on issues of cultural bias centers on item selection and norming (Hilliard, 1991). Accuracy in the predictive validity of results based on culturally and socially biased instruments has been called into question (Reynolds, Lowe, & Saenz, 1999), with researchers noting the existence of biases that favor the experiences of the dominant culture (Figueroa, 1983).

Cultural Discontinuity   Within classroom learning environments, cultural discontinuity has been identified as a significant factor in the educational problems experienced by minority students (Gay, 2000). Boykin's (1983) work on behavioral and perceptual learning styles among African American and white students suggests that, while similarities exist, so do culturally relevant distinctions, which may help explain student differences.

Systemic Factors   Some proponents of reform argue that special education distorts the problem of school failure by focusing on student deficits rather than on problems in the delivery of general education (Comer, 1997; Edmonds, 1986; Skrtic, 1991). In addition, a number of researchers have pointed to the importance of systemic, schoolwide initiatives in improving outcomes for students with or at risk for EBD (Dwyer & Osher, 2000; Walker, Colvin, & Ramsey, 1995).

Disproportionality in EBD programs raises complex issues. Although schools are more likely to identify African American students as having EBD, schools also fail to identify between one-half and two-thirds of all students who could be identified early in their academic development as needing support services (U.S. Department of Education, 1999a). Therefore, it is possible that, although African American students are overidentified in comparison to white students, they may still be underidentified in terms of need and access to preventive and early behavioral supports in the general education setting.

Underidentification also has significant implications. For example, students who are not identified for services under the Individuals with Disabilities Education Act have fewer due process rights in regard to educational planning, placement change, and school removal than those who are identified. In addition, because students with EBD are at greater risk for delinquent conduct than their peers, unidentified African American students with EBD may not receive the services and supports necessary for staying in school and out of the juvenile justice system (Morrison et al., 2001). For example, research on African American adolescents with mental health problems in juvenile justice facilities suggests that they are less likely than their white peers to have previously received mental health services (Marsteller, Brogan, & Smith, 1997). Furthermore, when they do receive services, African American youth tend to be diagnosed with more severe disorders (Isaacs, 1992) and are provided services in more restrictive and punitive settings (Sheppard & Benjamin-Coleman, 2001).

Although there are problems of underservicing African American students with EBD, given the shortcomings of interventions for students with EBD, overidentification of minorities is a major concern. While educational problems are a reality for all students with EBD, they are an even greater problem for African American students and other children of color who are more likely than white students with EBD to attend low-income schools, be placed in more segregated settings, and receive fewer vocational, counseling and therapy services (Valdes et al., 1990). In other words, African American students with EBD are deprived of opportunities to develop the social, intellectual, emotional, and vocational skills that will help them succeed outside of school.

Problems in the School Setting: Inappropriate Curriculum and Support Services

Once identified for special education, African American students face more significant problems regarding the curriculum they are exposed to and the quality of support services provided than do white students. This view is consistent with data from the most comprehensive analysis of postschool outcomes for children with disabilities, The National Longitudinal Transition Study of Special Education Students (NLTS) (Valdes et al., 1990). Results from this study are based on the experiences of approximately eight thousand youth between the ages of thirteen and twenty-one, from over three hundred districts across the United States. The NLTS data show wide disparities across race in terms of quality of instruction and related services provided to African American (and Hispanic) students identified for EBD when compared to white students with EBD.

According to the NLTS data, African American students with EBD were less likely than their white counterparts (73.6% and 82.8%, respectively) to attend secondary schools offering a comprehensive academic curriculum. African American students were more often enrolled in alternative schools, vocational programs, or other types of restricted settings (e.g., residential/hospital). Vocational and school-to-work services are critical if students in noncomprehensive schools are to have any chance of making a successful transition into postschool life (Rylance, 1997). An increasingly negative picture of the learning environment emerges when the *types* of services available for African American students identified for EBD are factored into students' general overparticipation in noncomprehensive school settings.

Although more often placed in noncomprehensive school settings, African American students identified for EBD were less frequently (40.8%) enrolled in vocational classes than were white students identified for EBD (53.5%). Additionally, the enrollment of white students in occupationally oriented vocational classes (41.5%) exceeded that of African American students (29.4%). Among students enrolled in occupational classes, white students averaged twice as many hours (2.6) per week as African American students (1.3). Among those enrolled in noncomprehensive schools, white students participated in more general education classes (49%) than did African American students (35%), who averaged more time in special education courses. This finding suggests that African American students identified for EBD most frequently receive educational services that neither prepare them for postsecondary education (e.g., college) nor provide them with opportunities to acquire important occupational skills.

Similar disparities emerge when we examine the types of vocational services received by students receiving special education services. For example, a higher percentage of white students (64.1%) than of African American students (55.9%) attend vocational classes specifically designed for disabled students. Furthermore, when these students do participate in general vocational education, white students receive more accommodations (e.g., physical adaptations, increased teacher contact, access to aides, simplified instruction) than do African American students. Racial comparisons across the types of services received by youth with EBD indicate that white youth receive more supportive services in terms of job training, personal counseling, and occupational therapy/life skills training.

Overall, white students sampled in the NLTS study received counseling and therapy services more often than did African American students (77.6% and 64%, respectively). Moreover, significantly more parents of African American students (45.7%) than of white students (29.8%) reported that their children *never* received counseling and therapy services. These racial disparities for counseling and therapy services merit particular concern, since the nature of the EBD disability renders these services integral to meeting the student's educational needs.

Other data highlight these inequalities. Compared to their white counterparts, black youth are less likely to be referred to treatment centers and more likely to be referred to juvenile justice settings (Marsteller et al., 1997; Woodruff et al., 1999). For example, one state study found that "blacks were three times as likely as whites to have detention center placements rather than hospitalization although there was little difference in prevalence of presenting problems by race" (Sheppard & Benjamin-Coleman, 2001, p. 61). Similarly, a study by the San Diego County Department of Mental Health Services of 3,962 children and adolescents who received outpatient mental health services during 1996–1997 (714 were African American) found that, compared to non-Hispanic white youth, African American children and adolescents were more likely to be referred for services from juvenile justice and child welfare agencies and less likely to be referred by their schools. In addition, black adolescents were less likely to receive a special education–linked mental health assessment (Yeh et al., 2002).

ADDRESSING PROBLEMS IN THE SCHOOL SETTING: A WORKING MODEL

Sufficient data exist to develop a working model of the school-based risk factors that African American students with emotional and behavioral problems confront, including 1) the dearth of schoolwide programs and strategies for preventing development of emotional and behavioral disorders; 2) the underidentification of many children in need of behavioral supports; 3) the late EBD identification of other students; and 4) the failure to provide appropriate supports and services to students identified as having EBD.

First, effective universal, schoolwide interventions that can prevent the development or exacerbation of EBD in children do exist (Dwyer & Osher, 2000; Osher, Dwyer, & Jackson, in press), but these interventions are rarely implemented on a scale that can effectively reduce the incidence of emotional and behavioral disorders. Furthermore, the school environment interacts with other risk factors to influence outcomes for African American children (Comer, 1997; Lomotey, 1990). One particular risk factor—inappropriate behavior as measured by natural raters (e.g., the teacher)—leads to referrals and removal from mainstream classrooms. Students identified by teachers and other school staff as exhibiting behavioral problems in and out of the classroom are typically male, come from low-income families, and are disproportionately members of cultural and ethnic minority groups (Friedman, Kutash, & Duchnowski, 1996). Decisions made by these natural raters lead to the removal of many African American students from mainstream classrooms and schools through pull-out programs, disciplinary referrals, placement changes, suspensions, and drop-outs (Larson, 1995; Lee & Burkam, 2001).

Second, while the Individuals with Disabilities Education Act requires school districts to identify all children with a disability, the success of most districts at properly identifying children with special needs is limited at best. School personnel not only fail to identify students with disabilities but also fail to diagnose and address disabilities correctly with surprising frequency. Black students with a learning disability are often misidentified as having EBD or mental retardation (Zabel & Nigro, 1999). While epidemiological estimates suggest a prevalence rate for EBD of between 2 percent and 5 percent (Costello et al., 1996; Roberts et al., 1998; U.S. Department of Education, 1999a), schools have historically identified a little less than 1 percent of students as eligible for services. State identification rates have ranged from .05 percent (Mississippi) to 1.56 percent (Minnesota) (U.S. Department of Education, 1999b).

Third, children with EBD are identified as being eligible for services at a later age than are other students with disabilities (U.S. Department of Education, 1999a). Because of a lack of appropriate and timely intervention, many of these children fall behind academically and have increased behavioral problems. These problems contribute to the tendency to view many African American youth as being socially maladjusted rather than as having a disability. This view of students, along with the failure to provide them with appropriate academic and behavioral supports, contributes to underidentification for services and to disproportionate suspension and expulsion rates (Noguera, 1997), as administrators may not want to provide expensive services or due process protections to these children.[2]

Finally, even if the child is identified as being eligible for special education supports, there is great local variety in the quality and location of services. For example, in the 1996–1997 school year, 50.48 percent of Minnesota students with EBD were served in regular classes, compared to only 9.55 percent of Mississippi's students with EBD (U.S. Department of Education, 1999b).

PROVIDING EFFECTIVE SUPPORTS TO AFRICAN AMERICAN STUDENTS WITH EMOTIONAL AND BEHAVIORAL DISORDERS

Failure to provide effective supports to African American students with and at risk of EBD appears to be directly related to poor academic and social outcomes, including poor grades, disciplinary referrals, suspension, dropping out, and expulsion. Fortunately, alternative approaches are available that can improve supports for these students (and others) (U.S. Department of Education, 1994). Effective approaches should combine three levels of intervention: schoolwide prevention strategies for all students; early intervention strategies for those students found to be at risk for behavioral problems; and targeted, individualized interventions for students with severe behavioral problems.

Providing Support for All Students

It is estimated that children in the United States spend approximately 15,000 hours in school between the first and twelfth grades (Koppish & Kirst, 1993). These hours can be spent in positive or negative social and academic activities, with adult role models who either support children in a positive fashion or subject them to aversive experiences (Metz, 1997). Similarly, time spent in school can involve positive peer interactions that can reinforce positive self-concepts and prosocial behaviors, or involve negative experiences that contribute to negative self-concepts and reinforce antisocial behaviors (Campbell-Whatley & Comer, 2000). Children's early developmental experiences are critical in helping to shape their self-concept, sense of personal efficacy, and motivation for learning, as well as their understanding of the larger world around them and their beliefs about their roles and status in school and society. Therefore, it is important to create learning environments that are supportive of children's total social, cognitive, physical, ethical, and emotional development, and that are responsive to their needs as individuals. With this said, students with or at risk for EBD can benefit from an effective foundation (Dwyer & Osher, 2000) that provides them with the emotional, behavioral, and academic supports that they need. This support should include a caring school community (Battistich, Solomon, Kim, Watson, & Schaps, 1995), effective teaching (Good & Brophy, 1986), an engaging and effective curricular program, and an environment that teaches all students the behavioral skills and provides the supports that are needed to succeed in the school environment (Osher et al., in press).

A second component of schoolwide efforts is employing effective instructional strategies in learning environments that have been demonstrated to help African American students and other children of color. These strategies should be known to have positive benefits for children of color in developing both their academic and critical thinking skills (Gay, 2000)—skills that will be important when students are in school and also in their transition to adulthood. Examples of such strategies include Success for All (Slavin et al., 1996) and Class-Wide Peer Tutoring (Delquadri, Greenwood, Whorton, Carta, & Hall, 1986).

A third important component of schoolwide preventive support is social skills instruction. In order to prevent the development and escalation of violent and aggressive behaviors in children, prosocial skills initiatives have been implemented in schools in such communities as East Baltimore, Maryland (Woodruff et al., 1999), Polk and Hillsborough counties in Florida (Quinn, Osher, Hoffman, & Hanley, 1998), and New York City (Lantieri & Patti, 1996). The purpose of prosocial skills training for students is to increase school- and classroom-appropriate behaviors through the use of prevention, intervention, and skills-training curricula. Prosocial skills-training interventions focus primarily on teaching new skills and strengthening existing skills in students who exhibit or are at risk of developing violent or aggressive behaviors. The prosocial curriculum utilized in East Baltimore teaches many skills, including anger control, empathy, and appropriate ways to seek and receive help. The curriculum is taught to small groups of children three times a week by clinicians, trained teachers, and other school personnel. Based on a prepared behavior management plan, both teachers and students receive support in developing the skills needed to meet the expectations of the school setting. When teachers rated the East Baltimore program after one year, their overall response was positive. Teachers observed students' significant behavioral improvement in the classroom, and parents of participating students also reported improvements in their children's behavior at home.

Cultural competence is a fourth critical component of effective school support. Many educators have limited awareness of and skills for understanding the multiple environmental contexts in which children of color function (Bondy & Ross, 1998; Boykin, 1986). Cultural discontinuity within classroom learning environments has been identified as a significant contributing factor in the overclassification of children of color as disabled (Ford, 1992; Ogbu, 1994). Such limitations result in a tendency to attribute poor school performance to deficient ability levels within the child or to problematic home environments. Culturally competent, family inclusive approaches to instruction permit educators to draw on the interrelations across cognitive, motivational, and value-belief systems of children of color in order to enhance their ongoing learning and development (Cartledge & Milburn, 1996; Osher, Sandler, & Nelson, 2002).

Targeted Early Interventions

While schoolwide interventions can provide a structured school environment that helps to decrease the frequency and intensity of academic and behavior problems, this support will not always be sufficient to eliminate the problems of all students with or at risk for EBD. Research and clinical experience suggest that approximately 5 percent to 35 percent of students in a school may need more intense interventions to help them decrease high-risk behaviors (Colvin, Sugai, & Kameenui, 1993; Osher, Poduska, & Porter, 2001). While not eliminating every risk factor, schools can link to resources within their communities to provide an effective network of resources supporting the cognitive, behavioral, and social emotional development of children (Nettles et al., 2000). Early intervention programs are designed to provide support for students whose behaviors suggest that they may be at risk for more chronic discipline problems. By identifying early signs of behavior problems, schools can begin to address problems before they become more pronounced. By addressing the needs of high-risk students, schools can also provide the necessary supports for success in school and in the larger community. These efforts should build on the schoolwide foundation of support. For example, in East Baltimore, teachers also receive training to identify and assist students who are at risk of or who exhibit early signs of aggressive behavior, thereby helping to prevent these children from developing more chronic and intractable patterns of antisocial behavior (Woodruff et al., 1999).

Intensive Individualized Interventions

African American students with severe emotional and behavioral problems and disorders are frequently removed from mainstream environments through suspension, expulsion, and placement into segregated classes and alternative schools, where they end up spending even more time with antisocial peers—often in environments marked by minimal academic expectations and punitive behavior management philosophies. Segregated placements of students with high levels of behavioral needs can be reduced by providing individualized interventions and supports that build on students' strengths and proactively address their needs. In many cases these supports can be provided in mainstream classrooms. Research suggests that the number of students requiring this level of intervention within a healthy school environment should be no more than 3 percent to 5 percent of the student body (Osher & Hanley, 2001; U.S. Department of Education, 2001). For example, student support centers and individualized services for students with EBD can utilize the skills of both regular and special educators, and individualized services can also be provided in the mainstream classroom (Eber & Nelson, 1997). In Westerly, Rhode Island, public schools have established planning centers where students can receive emotional and behavioral support, resolve conflicts, get assistance with homework, and have a quiet place to relax, and also receive social services (Dodge, Keenan, & Lattanzi, 2002). On the rare occasions when students need to be placed in a separate school environment, it is important that these settings avoid negative, custodial environments and instead provide effective academic and behavioral instruction and support, as well as collaborate with regular schools to facilitate successful reintegration into the regular education setting (Dwyer & Osher, 2000).

CONCLUSIONS

Many African American children go through school with learning and/or behavioral problems and disabilities that are unacknowledged, not addressed, or inappropriately identified. The behavior of these children is often responded to by teachers and other school staff in inappropriate and potentially harmful ways. The net result is that the educational system is allowing children with or at risk for EBD to be funneled into delinquency placements rather than supporting their educational needs through the development and maintenance of appropriate placements and services, including schoolwide interventions that can effectively reduce the need for special education services. Many African American children with or at risk for EBD progress from a system of inadequate school-based supports to suspension to expulsion or dropping out, and finally to placement in the juvenile justice system.

This chapter suggests that the overrepresentation of African American children in the correctional system represents, in part, the outcome of a flawed system of student support across two primary levels. The first systemic flaw stems from the generally inappropriate application of regular education support services to students of color. The second stems from the ineffective application of services to students of color once they are referred into the special education system.

Obviously, schools are not the only setting that can exacerbate the odds that children of color will experience school failure, negative behaviors, or exposure to the juvenile justice system (Rutter, Giller, & Hagell, 1998). Family and community structures also play critical roles in preventing school failure and promoting positive child and youth development, but as the work of Kellam et al. (1998), Reid and Eddy (1997), and others suggests, schools can and should perform a central role in the positive development of children and youth, along with implementing a sound, research-based strategy for reducing and eliminating behavioral risk factors for all students.

The success or failure of schools in supporting positive outcomes for all students depends on their structure, organizational culture, cultural competence, and capacity to provide every student, regardless of background, with the academic, behavioral, and emotional supports to build on their strengths and fully address their needs. Schools can address risk factors and build protective supports for students by comprehensively implementing a three-level approach: 1) building a protective schoolwide foundation through universal interventions; 2) preventing the onset or exacerbation of learning and behavioral problems through selective and targeted early intervention; and 3) addressing more intensive needs through individualized interventions for students with the greatest level of need.

While this approach appears simple, implementing it successfully is not easy in a society marked by racial intolerance and a general stigma against mental health problems. As the late Ron Edmonds (1979) stated:

> We can, whenever and wherever we choose to, successfully teach all children whose schooling is of interest to us. We already know more than we need to do that. Whether or not we do it must finally depend on how we feel about the fact that we haven't so far. (p. 24)

NOTES

1. The precise number is not clear. While a Department of Justice study suggests that 70 percent of incarcerated youth have educational disabilities (Burrell & Warboys, 2000) and some clinically trained juvenile justice staff members report even higher numbers of youth with mental health needs, other survey data report significantly lower percentages. For the best overview of this variation, see Rutherford, Bullis, Anderson, & Griller-Clark (2002). This variation in findings reflects five factors. First, there are false positives and negatives in identifying students as having EBD. Second, some correctional facilities do not have access to special education records, particularly for youth who have dropped out of school. Third, some correctional facilities lack diagnostic capabilities or have little interest in identifying youth for services that they are not staffed to provide. Fourth, there is a great variability in state identification rates (Osher & Hanley, 1995). In the case of EBD, the variability ranges from less than .03 percent of all students to more than 2 percent (U.S. Department of Education, 1999b). Fifth, the

surveys reflect youth in different types of settings (Lyons, Baerger, Quigley, Erlich, & Griffin, 2001).

2. While the social maladjustment clause of the Individuals with Disabilites Education Act only excludes students who are not otherwise eligible for services, schools frequently exclude students who have conduct disorder from services, instead defining them as socially maladjusted, although there are no valid theoretical or empirical grounds for differentiating between conduct disorders and other emotional and behavioral disorders (Cohen, 1994; Nelson, 1992; Nelson & Rutherford, 1988; Skiba & Grizzle, 1992; Stein & Merrell, 1992).

REFERENCES

Abt Associates. (1994). *Conditions of confinement: Juvenile detention and corrections facilities.* Washington, DC: U.S. Department of Justice, Office of Justice Programs, Office of Juvenile Justice and Delinquency Prevention.

Battistich, V., Solomon, D., Kim, D., Watson, M., & Schaps, E. (1995). Schools as communities, poverty levels of student populations, and students' attitudes, motives, and performance: A multilevel analysis. *American Educational Research Journal, 32,* 627–658.

Blum, R. W., McNeely, C. A., & Rinehart, P. M. (2002). *Improving the odds: The untapped power of schools to improve the health of teens.* Minneapolis: University of Minnesota, Center for Adolescent Health and Development.

Bondy, E., & Ross, D. D. (1998). Confronting myths about teaching black children: A challenge for teacher educators. *Teacher Education and Special Education, 21,* 241–254.

Boyce, W. T., Frank, E., Jensen, P. S., Kessler, R. C., Nelson, C. A., Steinberg, L., & MacArthur Foundation Research Network on Psychopathology and Development. (1998). Social context in developmental psychopathology: Recommendations for future research from the MacArthur Foundation Research Network on Psychopathology and Development. *Development and Psychopathology, 10,* 143–164.

Boykin, A. W. (1983). The academic achievement performance of Afro-American children. In J. Spence (Ed.), *Achievement and achievement motives* (pp. 321–374). San Francisco: W. Freeman.

Boykin, A. W. (1986). The triple quandary and the schooling of Afro-American children. In U. Neisser (Ed.), *The school achievement of minority children* (pp. 57–92). Hillsdale, NJ: Lawrence Erlbaum Associates.

Burrell, S., & Warboys, L. (2000). *Special education and the juvenile justice system.* Washington, DC: U.S. Department of Justice, Office of Justice Programs, Office of Juvenile Justice and Delinquency Prevention.

Campbell-Whatley, G. D., & Comer, J. (2000). Self-concept and African-American student achievement: Related issues of ethics, power and privilege. *Teacher Education and Special Education, 23,* 19–31.

Caron, C., & Rutter, M. (1991). Comorbidity in child psychopathology: Concepts, issues, and research strategies. *Journal of Child Psychopathology and Psychiatry, 32,* 1063–1080.

Cartledge, G., Kea, C., & Simmons-Reed, E. (2002). Serving culturally diverse children with serious emotional disturbance and their families. *Journal of Child and Family Studies, 11,* 113–126.

Cartledge, G., & Milburn, J. F. (1996). *Cultural diversity and social skills instruction: Understanding ethnic and gender differences.* Champaign, IL: Research Press.

Caspi, A., & Moffit, T. E. (1995). The continuity of maladaptive behavior: From description to understanding in the study of antisocial behavior. In D. Chicchetti & D. Cohen (Eds.), *Developmental psychopathology: Vol. 2. Risk, disorder, adaptation* (pp. 472–511). New York: Wiley.

Cohen, M. K. (1994). *Children on the boundary: The challenge posed by children with conduct disorders.* Alexandria, VA: National Association of State Directors of Special Education, Project FORUM.

Colvin, G., Sugai, G., & Kameenui, E. (1993). *Proactive school-wide discipline implementation manual.* Eugene: University of Oregon, Behavioral Research and Teaching, College of Education, Project PREPARE.

Comer, J. P. (1997). *Waiting for a miracle: Why schools can't solve our problems—and how we can.* New York: Dutton.

Costello, E. J., Angold, A., Burns, B. J., Erkanli, A., Stangl, D. K., & Tweed, D. L. (1996). The Great Smokey Mountains study of youth: Functional impairment and serious emotional disturbance. *Archives of General Psychiatry, 53,* 1137–1143.

Cuffe, S. P. (2000, October). *Missouri's approach to the collaboration between mental health and juvenile justice systems.* Paper presented at the annual meeting of the American Academy of Child and Adolescent Psychiatry, New York City.

Dishion, T. J., McCord, J., & Poulin, F. (1999). When interventions harm: Peer groups and problem behavior. *American Psychologist, 54,* 755–764.

Delquadri, J., Greenwood, C., Whorton, D., Carta, J., & Hall, R. V. (1986). Classwide peer turoring. *Exceptional Children, 52,* 535–542.

Dodge, N., Keenan, S., & Lattanzi, T. (2002). Strengthening the capacity of schools and communities to serve students with serious emotional disturbance. *Journal of Child and Family Studies, 11,* 23–34.

Doren, B., Bullis, M., & Benz, M. (1996). Predicting arrest status of adolescents with disabilities in transition. *Journal of Special Education, 29,* 363–380.

Dumas, J. E., Prinz, R. J., Smith, E. P., & Laughlin, J. (1999). The Early Alliance prevention trial: An integrated set of interventions to promote competence and reduce risk for conduct disorder, substance abuse, and school failure. *Clinical Child and Family Psychology Review, 2,* 37–53.

Dwyer, K., & Osher, D. (2000). *Safeguarding our children: An action guide.* Washington, DC: U.S. Department of Education.

Eber, L., & Nelson, C. M. (1997). School-based wraparound planning: Integrating services for students with emotional and behavioral needs. *American Journal of Orthopsychiatry, 67,* 385–395.

Edmonds, R. (1979). Effective schools for the urban poor. *Educational Leadership, 37*(10), 15–24.

Edmonds, R. (1986). Characteristics of effective schools. In U. Neisser (Ed.), *The school achievement of minority children* (pp. 93–104). Hillsdale, NJ: Erlbaum.

Fessler, M. A., Rosenberg, M. S., & Rosenberg, L. A. (1991). Concomitant learning disabilities and learning problems among students with behavioral/emotional disorders. *Behavioral Disorders, 16*(2), 97–106.

Figueroa, R. A. (1983). Test bias and Hispanic children. *Journal of Special Education, 17*, 431–440.

Ford, B. (1992). Multicultural education training for special educators working with African American youth. *Exceptional Children, 59*, 107–114.

Foster, H. (1990). Ethnocentrism and racism: The disproportionate representation of minorities and poor in special education programs for the emotionally disturbed. *Perceptions, 25*(2), 16–19.

Fox, N., Leone, P., Rubin, K., Oppenheim, J., Miller, M., & Friedman, K. (1999). *Final report on the linkages to learning program and evaluation at Broad Acres Elementary School.* College Park: University of Maryland.

Friedman, R. M., Kutash, K., & Duchnowski, A. J. (1996). The population of concern: Defining the issues. In B. Stroul (Ed.), *Children's mental health: Creating systems of care in a changing society* (pp. 69–96). Baltimore: Paul H. Brookes.

Gay, G. (2000). *Culturally responsive teaching: Theory, research and practice.* New York: Teachers College Press.

Good, T. L., & Brophy, J. (1986). School effects. In M. C. Wittrock, *Handbook of research on teaching* (2nd ed., pp. 570–602), New York: MacMillan.

Gunter, P. L., & Denny, R. K. (1998). Trends and issues in research regarding academic instruction of students with emotional and behavioral disorders. *Behavioral Disorders, 24*(1), 44–50.

Harry, B. (1992). Restructuring the participation of African American parents in special education. *Exceptional Children, 59*, 123–131.

Hilliard, A. G. (Ed.). (1991). *Testing African American students: Special re-issue* of The Negro Educational Review. Morristown, NJ: Aaron Press.

Isaacs, M. (1992). Assessing the mental health needs of children and adolescents of color in the juvenile justice system: Overcoming institutionalized perceptions and barriers. In J. Cocozza (Ed.), *Responding to the mental health needs of youth in the juvenile justice system* (pp. 141–164). Seattle: National Coalition for the Mentally Ill in the Criminal Justice System.

Johnson, G. (1994). An ecological framework for conceptualizing educational risk. *Urban Education, 29*, 34–49.

Kea, C. (1997). Reconnecting with African-American families. *Reaching Today's Youth, 2*(1), 57–61.

Kellam, S. G. (1990). Developmental epidemiological framework for family research on depression and aggression. In G. E. Patterson (Ed.), *Depression and aggression: Two facets of family interactions* (pp. 11–48). Hillsdale, NJ: Lawrence Erlbaum Associates.

Kellam, S. G., & Ensminger, M. E. (1980). Theory and method in child psychiatric epidemiology. In F. Earls (Ed.), *Studying children epidemiologically* (pp. 145–180) [International Monograph Series in Psychosocial Epidemiology: Vol. 1]. New York: Neale Watson Academic.

Kellam, S. G., Ling, X., Merisca, R., Brown, C. H., & Ialongo, N. (1998). The effect of the level of aggression in the first grade classroom on the course and malleability of aggressive behavior into middle school. *Development and Psychopathology, 10*, 165–185.

Kellam, S. G., & Rebok, G. W. (1992). Building developmental and etiological theory through epidemiologically based preventive intervention trials. In J. McCord & R. E. Tremblay (Eds.), *Preventing antisocial behavior: Interventions from birth through adolescence* (pp. 162–195). New York: Guilford Press.

Koppish, J. E., & Kirst, M. W. (1993). Editor's introduction. *Education and Urban Society, 25*, 123–128.

Lantieri, L., & Patti, J. (1996). *Waging peace in our schools.* Boston: Beacon Press.

Larson, K. (1995, April). *Redefining troublemakers: Creating an ethic of care and inclusion to improve outcomes for adolescents with disabilities and other highest risk adolescents.* Paper presented at annual Leadership Conference, Washington, DC.

Lee, V. L., & Burkam, D. T. (2001, January). *Dropping out of high school: The role of school organization and structure.* Paper prepared for the conference Dropouts in America, Harvard Graduate School of Education, Cambridge, MA.

Leone, P. E. (1991). *Alcohol and other drug use by adolescents with disabilities.* Reston, VA: Council for Exceptional Children. (ERIC Document Reproduction Service No. ED 340 150)

Loeber, R., Farrington, D., Stouthamer-Loeber, M., & Van Kammen, W. (1998). Multiple risk factors for multiproblem boys: Co-occurrence of delinquency, substance use, attention deficit, conduct problems, physical aggression, covert behavior, depressed mood, and shy/withdrawn behavior. In R. Jessor (Ed.), *New perspectives on adolescent risk behavior* (pp. 90–149). Cambridge, Eng.: Cambridge University Press.

Lomotey, K. (1990). An interview with Booker Peek. In K. Lomotey (Ed.), *Going to school: The African American experience* (pp. 14–29). Albany: State University of New York Press.

Lyons, J. S., Baerger, D. R., Quigley, P., Erlich, J., & Griffin, E. (2001). Mental health service needs of juvenile offenders: A comparison of detention, incarceration, and treatment settings. *Children's Services: Social Policy, Research, and Practice, 4*(2), 69–85.

Marsteller, F., Brogan, D., & Smith, I. (1997). *The prevalence of substance use disorders among juveniles admitted to regional youth detention centers operated by the Georgia Department of Children and Youth Services.* Washington, DC: U.S. Department of Health and Human Services, Center for Substance Abuse Treatment.

Metz, M. H. (1997, April). *Keeping students in, gangs out, scores up alienation down, and the copy machine in working order: Pressures that make urban schools in poverty different.* Paper presented at the annual meeting of the American Educational Research Association, Chicago, IL, March, 1997.

Morrison, G. M., Anthony, S., Storino, M. H., Cheng, J. J., Furlong, M. J., & Morrison, R. L. (2001). School expulsion as a process and an event: Before and after effects on children at risk for school discipline. *New Directions for Youth Development, 92*, 45–72.

National Research Council. (2002). *Minority students in special and gifted education.* Washington, DC: National Academy Press.

National Research Council & Institute of Medicine. (2000). *From neurons to neighborhoods: The science of early childhood development.* Washington, DC: Author.

Nelson, C. M. (1992). Searching for the meaning in the behavior of antisocial pupils, public school educators, and lawmakers. *School Psychology Review, 21*(1), 35–39.

Nelson, C. M., Jordan, D., & Rodrigues-Walling, M. (2002). Expand positive learning opportunities and results. *Journal of Child and Family Studies, 11*(1), 13–22.

Nelson, C. M., & Rutherford, R. B., Jr. (1988). Behavioral interventions with behaviorally disordered students. In M. C. Wang, M. C. Reynolds, & H. J. Walberg (Eds.), *Handbook of special education: Research and practice: Vol. 2. Mildly handicapped conditions* (pp. 125–153). New York: Pergamon.

Nettles, S. M., Mucherah, W., & Jones, D. S. (2000). Understanding resilience: The role of social resources. *Journal of Education for Students Placed at Risk, 5*(1, 2), 47–60.

Noguera, P. (1997). Race, class, and the politics of discipline. *Motion Magazine* [On-line serial]. Available: http://www.inmotionmagazine.com/pedro31.html

Office of Special Education Programs. (2000). Unpublished data. Available at www.ideadata. org

Ogbu, J. U. (1994). Understanding cultural diversity and learning. *Journal for the Education of the Gifted, 17,* 355–383.

Osher, D., Dwyer, K., & Jackson, S. (in press). *Safe, supportive, and successful schools step by step.* Rockville, MD: U.S. Department of Health and Human Services, Substance Abuse and Mental Health Services Administration, Center for Mental Health Services.

Osher, D., & Osher, T. (1996). The national agenda for children and youth with serious emotional disturbances. In M. Nelson, R. Rutherford, & B. Wolford (Eds.), *Comprehensive collaborative systems that work for troubled youth: A national agenda* (pp. 149–164). Richmond, KY: National Coalition for Juvenile Justice Services.

Osher, D., & Hanley, T. (1995). The national agenda: Identifying promising practices. *SED Quarterly, 2*(1), 3–6.

Osher, D., & Hanley, T. V. (1996). Implications of the national agenda to improve results for children and youth with or at risk of serious emotional disturbance. In R. J. Illback & C. M. Nelson (Eds.), *Emerging school-based approaches for children with emotional and behavioral problems: Research and practice in service integration* (pp. 7–36). Binghamton, NY: Haworth Press.

Osher, D., & Hanley, T. V. (2001). Implementing the SED national agenda: Promising programs and policies for children and youth with emotional and behavioral problems. *Education and Treatment of Children, 24,* 374–403.

Osher, D., Poduska, J., & Porter, G. (2001). *Multiple risk factors and the need for early intervention among Baltimore children and youth.* Unpublished research memorandum, American Institutes for Research.

Osher, D., Rouse, J., Woodruff, D., Kendziora, K., & Quinn, M. (2002). *Addressing invisible barriers: Improving outcomes for youth with disabilities in the juvenile justice system.* Washington, DC: U.S. Department of Education.

Osher, D., Sandler, S., & Nelson, C. (2002). The best approach to safety is to fix schools and support children and staff. *New Directions in Youth Development, 92,* 127–154.

Quinn, M., Osher, D., Hoffman, C., & Hanley, T. (1998). *Safe, drug-free, and effective schools for ALL students: What works!* Washington, DC: American Institutes for Research, Center for Effective Collaboration and Practice.

Reid, J. B., & Eddy, J. M. (1997). The prevention of antisocial behavior: Some considerations in the search for effective interventions. In D. M. Stoff, J. Breiling, & J. D. Maser (Eds.), *The handbook of antisocial behavior* (pp. 343–356). New York: John Wiley.

Reynolds, C. R., Lowe, P. A., & Saenz, A. L. (1999). The problem of bias in psychological assessment. In C. R. Reynolds & T. B. Gutkin (Eds.), *The handbook of school psychology* (3rd ed., pp. 549–595). New York: John Wiley.

Roberts, R. E., Attkisson, C. C., & Rosenblatt, A. (1998). Prevalence of psychopathology among children and adolescents. *American Journal of Psychiatry, 155,* 715–725.

Rutherford, R. B., Bullis, M., Anderson, C. W., & Griller-Clark, H. M. (2002). *Youth with disabilities in the corrections system: Prevalence rates and identification issues.* Washington, DC: U.S. Department of Education, Office of Special Education Programs.

Rutter, M., Giller, H., & Hagell, A. (1998). *Antisocial behavior by young people.* New York: Cambridge University Press.

Rylance, B. J. (1997). Predictors of high school graduation or dropping out for youths with severe emotional disturbances. *Behavioral Disorders, 23*(1), 5–17.

Sheppard, V. B., & Benjamin-Coleman, R. (2001). Determinants of service placement patterns for youth with serious emotional and behavioral disturbances. *Community Mental Health Journal, 37*(1), 53–65.

Sims, A. (1996). *Individual and group characteristics associated with the disproportionate representation of African-American students classified as seriously emotionally disturbed.* Unpublished doctoral dissertation, Howard University, Washington, DC.

Skiba, R., & Grizzle, K. (1992). Qualifications v. logic and data: Excluding conduct disorders from the SED definition. *School Psychology Review, 21*(1), 23–28.

Skiba, R. J., Knesting, K., & Bush, L. D. (2002). Culturally competent assessment: More than nonbiased tests. *Journal of Child and Family Studies, 11*(1), 61–78.

Skiba, R. J., Michael R., Nardo, A., & Peterson, R. (2000). *The color of discipline: Gender and racial disparities in school punishment.* Bloomington: Indiana Education Policy Center.

Skrtic, T. (1991). The special education paradox: Equity as the way to excellence. *Harvard Education Review, 61*, 148–206.

Slavin, R. E., Madden, N. A., Dolan, L. J., Wasik, B. A., Ross, S., Smith, L., & Dianda, M. (1996). Success for all: A summary of research. *Journal of Education for Students Placed at Risk, 1*(1), 41–76.

Snyder, H. N., & Sickmund, M. (1999). *Minorities in the juvenile justice system: 1999 national report series, juvenile justice bulletin.* Washington, DC: U.S. Department of Justice, Office of Justice Programs, Office of Juvenile Justice and Delinquency Prevention.

Sprague, J., Walker, H., Golly, A., White, K., Myers, D. R., & Shannon, T. (2001). Translating research into effective practice: The effects of a universal staff and student intervention on indicators of discipline and school safety. *Education and Treatment of Children, 24*, 495–511.

Stein, S., & Merrell, K. W. (1992). Differential perceptions of multidisciplinary team members: Seriously emotionally disturbed vs. socially maladjusted. *Psychology in the Schools, 29*, 320–330.

Teplin, L. A. (2001, November 12). *Psychiatric disorders among jail detainees: Implications for treatment.* Paper presented at the National Conference on Health Care, Albuquerque, NM.

U.S. Department of Education. (1994). *National agenda for achieving better results for children and youth with serious emotional disturbance.* Washington, DC: Author.

U.S. Department of Education. (1999a). *Reducing class size: What do we know?* Washington, DC: Author.

U.S. Department of Education. (1999b). *21st annual report to Congress on the implementation of the Individuals with Disabilities Education Act.* Washington, DC: Author.

U.S. Department of Education. (2000). *22nd Annual Report to Congress on the Implementation of the Individuals with Disabilities Education Act.* Washington, DC: Author.

U.S. Department of Education. (2001). *Prevention research & the IDEA discipline provisions: A guide for school administrators.* Washington, DC: Author.

U.S. Department of Education. (2002). IDEA data tables [On-line]. Available: www. IDEAdata.org/tables24th

U.S. Public Health Service. (1999). *Mental health: A report of the surgeon general.* Washington, DC: Author.

U.S. Public Health Service. (2000a). *Report on the surgeon general's conference on children's mental health.* Washington, DC: Author.

U.S. Public Health Service. (2000b). *Youth violence: A report of the surgeon general.* Washington, DC: Author.

U.S. Public Health Service. (2001). *Mental health: Culture, race, ethnicity. A supplement to the surgeon general's report on mental health.* Washington, DC: Author.

Valdes, K. A., Williamson, C. L., & Wagner, M. M. (1990). *The national longitudinal transition study of special education students, statistical almanac: Vol. 3. Youth categorized as emotionally disturbed.* Menlo Park, CA: SRI International.

Wagner, M. (1995). Outcomes for youths with serious emotional disturbance in secondary school and early adulthood. *Future of Children, 5*(4), 90–112.

Walker, H. M., Colvin, G., & Ramsey, E. (1995). *Antisocial behavior in school: Strategies and best practices.* Pacific Grove, CA: Brooks/Cole.

Wehby, J. H., Symons, F. J., Canale, J. A., & Go, F. J. (1998). Teaching practices in classrooms for students with emotional and behavioral disorders: Discrepancies between recommendations and observations. *Behavioral Disorders, 24*(1), 51–56.

Woodruff, D., Osher, D., Hoffman, C., Gruner, A., King, M., Snow, S., & McIntire, J. (1999). The role of education in a system of care: Effectively serving children with emotional or behavioral disorders. In *Systems of care: Promising practices in children's mental health, 1998 series, vol. 3.* Washington, DC: American Institutes for Research, Center for Effective Collaboration and Practice.

Yeh, M., McCabe, K., Hurlburt, M., Hough, R., Hazen, A., Culver, S., Garland, A., & Landsverk, J. (2002). Referral sources, diagnoses, and service types of youth in public outpatient mental health care: A focus on ethnic minorities. *Journal of Behavioral Health Sciences & Research, 29*(1), 45–60.

Zabel, R. H., & Nigro, F. A. (1999). Juvenile offenders with behavioral disorders, learning disabilities, and no disabilities: Self-reports of personal, family, and school characteristics. *Behavioral Disorders, 25*(1), 2–40.

CHAPTER SIX

English-Language Learner Representation in Special Education in California Urban School Districts

ALFREDO J. ARTILES[1]
ROBERT RUEDA
JESÚS JOSÉ SALAZAR
IGNACIO HIGAREDA

INTRODUCTION

Most studies of inequality in special education focus attention on the over-representation of African American students, particularly boys, in certain categories of special education. In these studies, Latinos are often said to be "under-represented" in special education. There is, of course, great social and economic diversity within the Latino community. This study explores the difference in treatment on the basis of language in a large cluster of urban school districts where Latinos predominate. It finds that there is little difference in the early grades, but that students who are classified as limited English proficient (LEP) or English-language learners (ELLs) are seriously overrepresented in two special education categories in the later grades. The study also finds that ELLs with less primary language support are more likely to experience classroom segregation.

Because the number of Spanish-speaking students is growing rapidly and the knowledge base on the above issues is almost nonexistent, basic research is urgently needed. Even without new research, however, the patterns found in this study suggest a new focus for civil rights compliance offices and for staff development work within school districts. While there are clearly questions related to language development that the schools need to address, overassignment of students to special education seems a poor and possibly destructive answer.

Policies and programs that address the needs of English-language learners have been controversial throughout the history of education in the United

States. Although bilingual programs have existed for English-learner immigrants since the latter part of the nineteenth century, societal attitudes toward English learners have shifted over time, depending on economic, political, and historical forces (Baca & Cervantes, 1989). California is a good example of this swinging pendulum. This state has moved from pioneering programs for English learners in the 1970s to the passing of Proposition 227—which greatly restricted native-language support systems in the schools, such as bilingual education—in the late 1990s.

The intersections of English learners and special education are little understood. In most research that compares Latinos and other groups in special education, Latinos are not overrepresented the way that blacks are in certain categories of special education. When the issue of language is added in, however, the results change and a serious civil rights issue emerges. Urban school districts in California that have high minority immigrant student populations provide an important setting for study of this intersection, especially in the face of Proposition 227. Furthermore, in the political tension between bilingual education proponents and the English-only movement lies huge potential for educational benefit—or harm. English learners already experienced poor educational outcomes before any of the recent changes. What will happen to this group as California significantly reduces the language support these students need to enhance their opportunities to learn? Will assumptions about English learners' "difference" based on language become entangled with assumptions about their ability or learning differences, and thus lead to increased levels of special education placement? What will the impact of English immersion classes versus bilingual classes for English learners be in terms of overrepresentation in special education and/or increased isolation from regular classrooms and schools?

As a first effort to tackle some of these complex questions, we set out to obtain a descriptive profile of English-learner placements in special education in several large urban districts in California. We examined placement patterns according to special education programs and by disability categories. We also compared the restrictiveness of special education service (i.e., more or less segregated) for English learners placed in the new language programs that followed Proposition 227, specifically looking at restrictiveness from the regular classroom as language support was reduced. Given that English learners are expected to make a rapid transition to English-only classes, we also examined placement patterns by grade level.

In summary, in eleven urban school districts in California that have high proportions of English learners, high Latino enrollments, and high poverty levels, we found overrepresentation of English learners in special education emerging by grade five and increasingly visible through grade twelve. At the district level, the English-learner population was overrepresented in the mental retardation (MR) and language and speech impairment (LAS) categories, especially at the secondary level. In terms of odds ratios, English learners were 27 percent more likely than English-proficient students to be placed in special education in elementary grades and almost twice as likely in secondary grades.

Looking at degree of isolation, we found that English learners who were placed in the straight English immersion classes—those with the least home language support—were more likely to be placed in resource specialist classes or the "special day class" option than were English learners in modified English immersion or bilingual classrooms. For example, English learners placed in straight English immersion classrooms were almost three times more likely to be placed in the special education resource specialist program than ELLs from bilingual classrooms.

We based the study on data for the 1998–1999 school year, the first year Proposition 227 was implemented. Although studies based on large databases have limitations, the descriptive profile represents a snapshot of English-learner representation in special education in California at a particular point in time, allowing examination of issues that can get obscured when data are aggregated at the national level. Specifically, most studies of special education placement focus on ethnicity or race, but few focus on English learners. English-learner placement is rarely "unpacked"—that is, variations by disability category, grade level, and type of language support are rarely examined—and few studies focus on older (secondary) students.

The school districts we report on have undergone significant policy changes over the past few years, including policy related to the instruction of English learners. Although it will be important to track these changes over time in a longitudinal fashion, it is also important to document the current situation. We begin by outlining the policy and reform contexts and sketching the evolution of the overrepresentation problem in California.

Contemporary Policies and Reforms for English Learners in California

Immigrants and other linguistic and ethnic minorities lived in California under increasingly adverse circumstances in the 1990s, as a severe economic recession and an unprecedented immigration wave changed the state's educational and political landscapes. These trends were followed by passage of Proposition 227 and its predecessors, Propositions 187 and 209.[2]

Proposition 227, which aimed to abolish bilingual education programs, represents the first time citizens were asked to cast their vote to impose an educational curriculum for schoolchildren. Some of the arguments advanced to justify this proposition included the low efficacy of bilingual programs, as reflected in the persistently poor academic achievement of English learners and their low reclassification rate as fluent English proficient (FEP) (Gándara et al., 2000). Voters approved Proposition 227 in June 1998, even though only one-third of English learners were in bilingual programs at that time, many of them were taught by unqualified teachers, and there was little evidence on the quality of bilingual program implementation (Gándara et al., 2000).

It should be noted that Proposition 227 was approved when school districts were being bombarded with multiple and often contradictory reforms that included class-size reduction, elimination of social promotion, standards and accountability movements, new testing programs, reductionist reading methods reforms, and tougher disciplinary measures. Furthermore, teachers were expected to orchestrate the implementation of these competing reforms simultaneously. At the same time, the state's constructivist-oriented language arts framework had been replaced by a framework that emphasized basic skills, phonics, and direct instruction. These and other changes occurred within a relatively short period of time and in an overlapping fashion, without a great deal of attention to coherence or possible contradictions.

Overview of Minority Representation in Special Education in California

Minority overrepresentation in special education has been contested in California for the last thirty years, and litigation has played a major role. *Diana v. State Board of Education* (1973) and *Larry P. v. Riles* (1979) dealt with issues related to assessment bias, disproportionate placement, and the long-term consequences of special education placement. It has been argued that these cases have had a considerable impact on special education legislation (e.g., nondiscriminatory assessment requirements) and evaluations of the overrepresentation problem (Figueroa & Artiles, 1999).

Diana (1973) was a class action suit filed by nine Mexican American families before the advent of extensive bilingual education. Chief among the families' complaints was linguistic bias in assessment practices, since English learners were tested with English instruments and placement decisions in mild mental retardation (MMR, then called EMR) programs were based on such test results. The families further argued that these tests and the MMR curricula were oblivious to the students' culture. Another complaint in this suit was the overrepresentation of Mexican American students throughout the state's special education programs. In the settlement, California agreed to test students in their first language as well as in English and to use nonverbal intelligence tests.

In sum, Mexican American students were to be reevaluated using nonverbal intelligence tests, districts were required to report on their reevaluation efforts and on plans for transitioning students from MMR programs to general education, and districts had to monitor whether Mexican American students were overrepresented in MMR (*Diana v. State Board of Education*, 1973).

In contrast to *Diana, Larry P.* focused on overrepresentation of African American students in special education and argued that intelligence tests were culturally (rather than linguistically) biased. Coincidentally, this case was tried by the same judge. The California Department of Education refused to settle out of court, and the case went to trial in 1977. Two years later, Judge Peckham ruled that IQ tests were culturally biased against African American students and described special education programs as "dead end," "inferior," and "stigmatizing" (MacMillan & Reschly, 1998, p. 17). He also concluded that reliance on biased assessment instruments was closely related to overrepresentation patterns.

Although considerable efforts have been devoted to understanding African American placement in high-incidence disabilities, we know significantly less about ELL representation in these programs. This study presents preliminary evidence about the contexts of English learner overrepresentation in California's special education programs. The goals of the study are to assess representation of English learners in various disability categories and grade levels, to examine whether English learners in various language programs and grade levels are more likely to be overrepresented and/or more isolated in distinct special education programs.

METHODS

Context Characteristics: The School Districts, Populations, and Programs[3]

We used databases from eleven urban districts in California that are currently undergoing major reforms, including in special education. The districts are heavily populated by English learners, particularly of Latino descent. The student ethnic background for the eleven districts during the 1998–1999 school year was as follows: 69 percent Latino/a, 13.6 percent African American, 10.5 percent white, 4.3 percent Asian, 1.9 percent Filipino, 0.4 percent Pacific Islander, and 0.3 percent American Indian/Alaska Native. The majority of the student population came from low-income families as defined by eligibility for free or reduced-price lunch programs—85 percent of elementary and 71 percent of secondary students in the study were eligible for these programs in the 1998–1999 school year.

English Learner Population   Consistent with national trends, the English learner population has been growing rapidly in these districts. Enrollment data indicate that this population more than doubled between 1981 and 1997. The overwhelming majority is Latino (94% of the elementary population, 91% of the secondary population). The percentages of other groups of English learners for elementary and secondary combined were as follows: American Indian (0.1%), Asian American (3.3%), black (0.3%), white (2.5%), Filipino (0.7%), and Pacific Islander (0.1%). During the 1998–1999 school year, 42 percent of the student population was classified as English learner (53% in elementary and 27% in secondary grades). In the 1996–1997 academic cycle, 19 percent of the population was categorized as fluent English proficient, and 35 percent was designated English only (EO).[4] The redesignation rate from limited to fluent English has been increasing slowly in recent years, though it is still relatively small. For instance, during the four academic years from 1993 to 1997, the percent of English learners who were redesignated grew from 4 percent to 8 percent.

Special Education Population and Programs   The special education systems in these districts provide services to a host of disability categories in a continuum of educational programs that range from special education schools to services in the general education classroom. The districts together reported that in the 1998–1999 school year 7.2 percent of the student population was receiving special education services (5.4% in K–5 and 9.34% in 6–12), and 7.6 percent of the English learner population was identified as having special educational needs (5.3% in K–5 and 14.06% in 6–12). The largest proportion of special education students was in the specific learning disability (SLD) category—about 2.2 percent in K–5 and 7.5 percent in 6–12.

Teaching Force   The teaching force was largely white and a sizable proportion was underqualified. In the 1999–2000 academic year, the majority of teachers were white (49%) and female (68%). Latino and African American teachers represented about 40 percent of the teaching staff (25% and 15%, respectively). Almost 25 percent of the teachers had emergency credentials or waivers.

Language Programs   In response to Proposition 227, new language programs were created; the programs used in elementary grades include straight English immersion, modified English immersion, and primary language instruction (bilingual). District policies stipulate that instruction in straight English immersion programs should be carried out "primarily in English with primary language support provided *by the paraprofessional for clarification purposes.*" The modified English immersion program provides instruction "primarily in English with primary language instructional support *provided by a bi-*

lingual authorized teacher for concept development" (California Department of Education, n.d.). Bilingual education offers core instruction in the primary language with daily (English-language development)[5] instruction. Students transition to English instruction. Placement in bilingual education requires that parents sign an exception waiver.

Language programs in secondary grades include English as a Second Language (ESL) and English-only classes; other language support programs are not available in these grades. English learners with limited English proficiency are placed in classes for students with different proficiency levels. English learners who have not been redesignated as fluent English proficient are placed in English-only classes.

Restrictiveness in Special Education Services   The resource specialist program (RSP) is a more integrated special education option than the special day class (SDC) program by virtue of the time students spend in the general education classroom. In the SDC program, students spend more than 60 percent of the school day restricted from the regular education classroom. In RSP, students are restricted from the regular education classroom between 20 percent and 60 percent of their time in school. Considering that current language programs provide distinct types of language support for English learners, we examined whether placement in a given language program would affect English learners' odds of being placed in more or less segregated special education programs (SDC or RSP, respectively). We report only elementary grades because little language support is available at the secondary level.

Data Analysis Procedures

The district databases contain student demographic, achievement, English proficiency, and program placement data. We used the districts' databases for the academic year 1998–1999. These databases are compiled for internal compliance and administrative purposes. Thus, the ideal level of accuracy and precision that would normally be expected for research purposes does not exist. Nevertheless, the databases provide a window into current practice. The special education data were downloaded from each of the eleven districts' centralized databases. Each district was assured of student anonymity.

We focused on the aggregate of districts as the unit of analysis. We conducted descriptive analyses to discern placement patterns for various student categories (e.g., by language proficiency, special education service, disability category, grade level). We targeted disability categories (MR, LAS) that have been historically affected by overrepresentation.[6] We could not include students with SLD because of technical problems with the database. Although overrepresentation in the ED category has been persistently documented (particularly for African Americans), enrollment data indicated that English learners were rarely placed in this category, thus we did not include it in the study. Two special educational programs (RSP, SDC), as well as two grade levels (elementary, secondary), and three language programs (straight English immersion, modified English immersion, bilingual), were also included in the analyses.

The study objectives focused on disproportionate representation patterns. We defined disproportionate representation as the "extent to which membership in a given group affects the probability of being placed in a specific special education disability category" or service option, such as RSP (adapted from Oswald, Coutinho, Best, & Singh, 1999, p. 198). Consistent with Chinn and Hughes' (1987) definition, "We have reported as disproportionate percentages exceeding plus or minus 10 percent of the percentage expected on the basis on the school-age population (e.g., for blacks in 1978, the percentage of total school enrollment was 15.72 percent. According to the 10 percent criterion a range from 14.15 percent to 17.29 percent would be considered proportionate representation for blacks that year)" (p. 43).

In order to contextualize these analyses, we calculated odds ratios for English learners and English-proficient students in two disability categories (MR, LAS) at the elementary and secondary levels. We also calculated odds ratios for English learners in two special education services (RSP, SDC) in three language programs. The odds ratio is calculated as follows:

> The basic element in the index is the "odds" of being assigned to a particular special education category. For example, a measurement of the odds of [an English learner's] being assigned to an [MR] class is the percentage of [English learners] who are classified as [MR] divided by the percentage of [English learners] who are not in special programs. . . . The odds of [an English-proficient] student's being designated [MR is the percentage of English proficient students classified as MR divided by the percentage of English-proficient students who are not in special programs]. . . . The disproportion index is the ratio of these two odds. (adapted from Finn, 1982, p. 328)

When the odds ratio is equal to one, then English learners and English-proficient students are equally likely to be assigned to a disability category. If the odds ratio is greater than one, then English learners are more likely to be assigned to a disability category, and if the odds ratio is less than one, then English learners are less likely to be assigned to a disability category than are English-proficient students.

RESULTS

Unpacking English-Learner Overrepresentation:
Language Proficiency, Disability Category, and Grade Level

English learners were disproportionately overrepresented in special education when their percentage exceeded "plus or minus 10% of the percentage expected on the basis on the school-age population" (Chinn & Hughes, 1987, p. 43). For example, 42 percent of students in these districts were English learners. This means the thresholds for English learner under- and overrepresentation would be 37.8 percent and 46.2 percent (i.e., 42 – 4.2 and 42 + 4.2). Table 1 presents English-learner enrollment in the target districts and by grade level (elementary, secondary). These data suggest that English-learner overrepresentation at the district level is not a problem; the same pattern is observed in elementary grades. However, English learners are overrepresented in secondary grades; in fact, the percent of English learners in secondary special education programs is 11.3 percent above the overrepresentation threshold (see Table 1).

A different configuration of patterns emerges when the data are disaggregated by grade. Table 2 presents English-learner enrollment in general and special education by grade; under- and overrepresentation thresholds are also reported. These data suggest that, although English learners are not overrepresented in grades K–4, the problem emerges in grade five, and it remains clearly visible until grade twelve. The percentage of English learners placed in special education that is above the overrepresentation threshold in grades 6–12 ranges between 19 percent and 26 percent.

Moreover, the proportion of all English learners enrolled in special education increases consistently from kindergarten until grade six from 2 percent to 16 percent, and it varies from grade seven to grade twelve (between 11% and 16%, rising in the junior and senior years; see Figure 1).

A different set of patterns is observed when the data are examined by disability category. At the district level, the English-learner population is overrepresented in the mental retardation and language and speech impairment categories (see Table 3). In contrast, at the district level the English-proficient group is not overrepresented in special education programs or disability categories. Furthermore, although English-learner representation in elementary grades is not a problem, they are noticeably overrepresented in secondary grades in the MR and LAS categories (see Table 3), as well as in the aggregate special education population (see Table 1). The only instance of English-proficient student overrepresentation is observed in the aggregate special education population in elementary grades, where it is only 1.3 percentage points above the overrepresentation threshold.

TABLE 1

Overrepresentation of English Learners in Special Education at the
District and Grade Levels, 1998–1999

	ELL Percentage of Total Student Population	Percentage in Special Education	Under-/ Overrepresentation Thresholds[a]	Overrepresented? (Yes/No)	Percentage Points above 10% Overrepresentation Threshold
All Districts	42	45	37.8–46.2	No	NA
Elementary Grades (K–5)	53	50	47.7–58.3	No	NA
Secondary Grades (6–12)	27	41	24.3–29.7	Yes	11.3

[a] Minus or plus 10% of the percentage expected on the basis of the general education population.

TABLE 2

Overrepresentation of English Learners in Special Education by Grade,
1998–1999

Grade	ELL Percentage of Total Student Population	Percentage in Special Education	Under-/ Overrepresentation Thresholds[a]	Overrepresented? (Yes/No)	Percentage Points above 10% Overrepresentation Threshold
K	62	58	55.8–68.2	No	NA
1	62	56	55.8–68.2	No	NA
2	60	55	54–66	No	NA
3	54	49	48.6–59.4	No	NA
4	47	48	42.3–51.7	No	NA
5	32	43	28.8–35.2	Yes	7.8
6	18	46	16.2–19.8	Yes	26.2
7	17	45	15.3–18.7	Yes	26.3
8	15	43	13.5–16.5	Yes	26.5
9	21	42	18.9–23.1	Yes	18.9
10	14	35	12.6–15.4	Yes	19.6
11	8	28	7.2–8.8	Yes	19.2
12	8	33	7.2–8.8	Yes	24.2

[a] Minus or plus 10% of the percentage expected on the basis of the general education population.

FIGURE 1
English Learners in Special Education

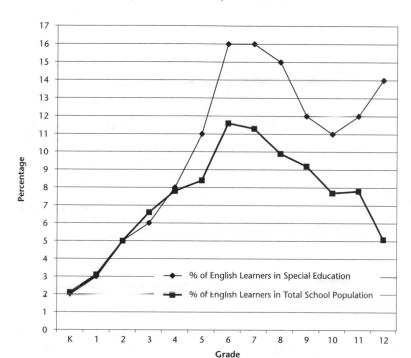

Compared to their English-proficient counterparts, larger proportions of English learners are placed in each disability category. The percentage of all English learners placed in MR was 0.94, whereas it was 1.87 in LAS. In contrast, the percentage of English-proficient students in MR and LAS is 0.29 and 1.39, respectively.

With regard to placement odds, English learners are more likely to be placed in special education than are English-proficient students (see Table 4); specifically, English learners are 27 percent more likely to be placed in elementary grades and almost twice as likely to be placed in secondary grades. For the MR category, the situation in secondary classes is dramatic, as English learners are more than three times as likely to be placed in this program. English learners are less at risk for placement in elementary LAS classes than their English-proficient counterparts (see Table 4), but are 38 percent more likely to be placed in LAS secondary classes

TABLE 3

Overrepresentation of English Learners by Disability Categories at the
District and Grade Levels, 1998–1999

	ELL Percentage of Total Student Population	Percentage in Mental Retardation (MR)	Percentage in Language and Speech Impairment (LAS)	Overrepresented? (Yes/No)	Percentage Points above 10% Overrepresentation Threshold
Districts	42	55	49	Yes in MR and LAS	MR = 8.8 LAS = 2.8
Elementary Grades (K–5)	53	—	51	No	NA
Secondary Grades (6–12)	27	55	34	Yes in MR and LAS	MR = 25.3 LAS = 4.3

RESTRICTIVENESS IN SPECIAL EDUCATION SERVICES BY LANGUAGE PROGRAM IN ELEMENTARY GRADES

We examined whether placement in a given language program would affect English learners' odds of being placed in more (SDC) or fewer (RSP) segregated special education programs. The enrollment in RSP classes is 48 percent English learner (52% English proficient), whereas English learners represent 42 percent of the population in more separate SDC classes (i.e., 58% is English proficient). In turn, 14.5 percent of all elementary English learners are receiving services in RSP and SDC classes (8.7% in RSP and 5.8% in SDC). Of the 8.7 percent of all elementary English learners placed in RSP classes, 4.8 percent is not receiving language support, since the students are placed in English immersion programs, while 2.2 percent is placed in modified English immersion classes and only 1.7 percent in bilingual programs. Similarly, many English learners placed in SDC classes (2.2% of the 5.8%) receive little support, as they are being educated in English immersion classes, whereas 1.7 percent is placed in modified English immersion and 1.9 percent in bilingual classes.

Table 5 suggests that English learners receiving the least language support (i.e., placement in straight English immersion) have a greater chance of being placed in RSP classes. More specifically, elementary English learners in the straight English immersion program are more than twice as likely to receive RSP services than are English learners placed in the modified English immer-

TABLE 4

English Learner Special Education Placement Odds[a] (Odds Ratios)
by Disability and Grade Level, 1998–1999

| | *Special Education Placement Odds[b] of ELLs (Compared to English-Proficient Students)* | |
	Elementary (Grades K–5)	*Secondary (Grades 6–12)*
Special Education	1.27	1.91
Mental Retardation	Data not available	3.25
Language and Speech	0.94	1.38

[a] The comparison group for the calculation of placement odds is English-proficient students. The category "English proficient" includes children and youngsters classified as English-only students (native English speakers), "redesignated fluent-English proficient" students (former English learners who have been redesignated as English proficient); and IFEP students who have a non-English home language but test as English proficient upon enrollment in school.

[b] If odds ratio = 1, then ELLs and English-proficient students are equally likely to be assigned to a disability category. If odds ratio > 1, then ELLs are more likely to be assigned to a disability category than English-proficient learners, and if odds ratio < 1, then ELLs are less likely to be assigned to a disability category than English-proficient students.

sion model, and almost three times more likely than English learners placed in bilingual programs (see Table 5).

The odds for being placed in SDC classes are higher for English learners in straight English immersion programs when compared with English learners in modified English immersion programs and bilingual education programs (32% and 19%, respectively; see Table 5).

DISCUSSION

Several interesting trends were identified through a descriptive analysis of placement data in large urban school districts in California. We highlight three patterns observed in the placement data and discuss the implications of the findings.

Grade Level

A consistent pattern was considerable overrepresentation for English learners in special education in secondary grades. Although problems begin to emerge toward the end of elementary school, significant overrepresentation was observed in grades 6–12, particularly in the last grades of high school. It is not clear whether this pattern is associated with a lack of language support in secondary

TABLE 5

Disproportionate Representation of English Learners in Straight English Compared to Bilingual and Modified English Classes, by Restrictiveness of Special Education Placement, 1998–1999

Type of Special Education Service	ELLs in Straight English Immersion Compared to ELLs Assigned to Modified English Immersion	ELLs in Straight English Immersion Compared to ELLs Assigned to Bilingual Education
Resource Specialist Program (RSP)[a]	2.26	2.95
Special Day Class[b] (SDC)	1.32	1.19

[a] *Resource Specialist Program:* Services are provided outside the general education classroom for at least 21 percent but not more than 60 percent of the school day.

[b] *Special Day Class:* Services are provided outside the general education classroom for more than 60 percent of the school day.

grades or whether these students entered secondary grades with a preexisting label assigned in elementary school. Let us remember that minority dropout rates are exacerbated in secondary grades as well. In addition to the need for advocacy that will bring more language support for this age group, future research ought to assess the dynamics of special education placement in secondary grades and trace the consequences of a preexisting disability label on English learners' high school careers.

Overrepresentation in Disability Categories

Although the district-aggregated data suggested that there is English-learner overrepresentation in the MR and LAS categories, the problem was basically in the secondary grades. It is intriguing that English-learner overrepresentation was found in the LAS category. Unfortunately, we know little about how school psychologists and communication disorders professionals in these districts apply exclusionary linguistic and cultural considerations and eligibility criteria when working with English learners. Future studies must address these trends and should disaggregate student ethnicity, language-proficiency subgroups, and generational differences within the English-learner population to obtain a more complete understanding of how and who gets labeled LAS and the consequences of such labels for student opportunities to learn. Future studies also need to focus on the SLD category, as this is the largest category in the special education field.

Language Support and Special Education Programs

ELLs who were receiving the least support in their primary language (i.e., straight English immersion programs) had a greater chance of being placed in resource specialist programs and special day class programs than ELLs placed in language programs with greater native-language support. There are at least two important differences between straight English immersion and the other language programs. First, language support is provided by adults with notable training differences (paraprofessionals v. certified bilingual teachers), which may translate into meaningful differences in the nature and quality of language support provided to English learners in these programs. Second, the goals of language assistance vary in important ways. Straight English immersion stresses the use of students' first language (e.g., Spanish) for clarification purposes, whereas modified immersion and bilingual programs promote concept development in the primary language. This important difference in goals might translate into uneven opportunities to develop complex conceptual understanding and ultimately more sophisticated cognitive and language skills.

This finding resonates with other research that found that language support makes a difference in the educational experiences of English learners (Baca & Cervantes, 1989; Finn, 1982; Ortiz, 1997; Portes, 1999; Rumbaut, 1998). Unfortunately, California law demanded that English learners achieve native-like English proficiency in a very short time and with less than optimal primary language support. As we know, such an approach contradicts the evidence about the critical importance of language as a key tool that mediates development and learning (Cole, 1996). In fact, a basic premise of bilingual education is that students' primary language must be developed first so that they can use it to learn a second language (August & Hakuta, 1997). On the other hand, we cannot gauge the potential influence of the multiple reforms that are being implemented in these districts, such as Proposition 227 and reading instruction. Future studies must examine the impact of the confluence of many (often contradictory) reforms on English learners' educational experiences.

Placement in more or less segregated special education settings may also have important consequences for English learners, particularly in terms of access to interactions with nondisabled peers and access to programs that can enrich the social and cultural capital of English learners. Moreover, the law requires that all students with disabilities be educated in the least restrictive environment to the maximum appropriate extent. However, we should not assume that the quality of educational experiences in inclusive settings is always better than what is experienced in RSP classes—indeed, schools that have moved hastily to full inclusion programs with little preparation and support could create rather negative experiences for both special education and English learners.

Future studies must document the potential interactions between level of program segregation, type of language support, and opportunities to learn. In the districts we studied, the question about misclassification certainly arises in the LAS category. Are school personnel equating a lack of English proficiency with language and speech impairments? What measures are being taken to discriminate between English learners who have special needs and English learners who only need second-language support? Students should be diagnosed as having LAS when adequate instruments are used to document deficiencies in speech and/or language (e.g., articulation, fluency, voice, expressive or receptive language). In short, a lack of English proficiency should not be interpreted as language impairment.

IMPLICATIONS

Monitor English-Language Learners

It is imperative that federal agencies and districts develop monitoring systems to track English learners and their subgroups, especially in light of the multiple policy changes and reforms being undertaken. At the federal level, for example, annual reports to Congress should include information on English learners— for the population as a whole and its subgroups. While this information has appeared in some reports in the past, the numbers and issues are now significant enough that it should be included in every report. At the district level, especially when problems of overrepresentation are suspected, monitoring efforts should try to "unpack" important factors such as linguistic, cognitive, academic performance, and socioeconomic data.

Conduct Theoretically Grounded Research

We argue that an explicit theoretical framework plays a decisive role in defining what becomes relevant or unimportant in the analysis of minority special education representation. Our approach suggests that such analyses should use a multilevel perspective and pay close attention to contextual, historical, political, and cultural forces. In the work presented here, for example, a focus on context and language, allowed us to unpack intriguing placement patterns related to language programs for English learners. This is important, because if we had used gross measures of special education placement for the whole district we would not have seen English-learner overrepresentation. Although we cannot infer causality, we have a better sense of the association between language support and special education placement. It is an important question, but we do not know whether the patterns reported here were caused by these language policies (e.g., Proposition 227) or by the interaction of the multiple reforms being carried out in the districts.

There is also a need to create comprehensive databases and to coordinate efforts so that researchers have easier access to multiple databases that will allow them to conduct more complex studies. These have been elusive tasks because efforts to create national and state databases tend to exclude students with disabilities (Vanderwood, McGrew, & Ysseldyke, 1998). Therefore, we might run the risk of losing track of English learners if increasing numbers continue to be placed in special education. Another potential obstacle is that existing national datasets do not always allow analyses of sociocultural factors without combining more than one database (e.g., OCR and NCES), a cumbersome task requiring considerable expertise often not available on research teams.

Design and Implement a Research Program

We need to design a comprehensive research program that traces not only the dynamics of special education placement patterns, but also their antecedents (e.g., eligibility decision meetings, assessment practices, prereferral/referral interventions, tracking in general education). Funding for prospective studies is needed to document how dynamic sociocultural forces (e.g., opportunity to learn, instructional practices, beliefs) mediate learning in general education as well as referrals to and placement in special education (Artiles, 2000).

As one example of the interaction of these complex variables, Gutierrez and her colleagues (2000) recently reported achievement data from a school district in California that had implemented an English-only literacy program for the past three years with heavy reliance on phonics instruction. They reported that the proportion of Spanish-speaking children scoring at the 50th percentile on the SAT9 decreased from 32 percent in the first grade to 15 percent by the third grade. It is uncertain what sort of outcomes can be expected for English learners in California as Proposition 227 and other reforms are implemented and as their consequences are felt in placements in the special education system.

We believe it is best to study these complex questions with a variety of methods to map out the multiple facets of overrepresentation. Longitudinal studies with mixed quantitative and qualitative components are also needed to assess the origins, evolution, and consequences of the current wave of conservative reforms on minority representation in special education. Similarly, the inclusion of longitudinal data and both short-term and long-term outcomes will greatly enhance the breadth and sophistication of future analyses, particularly as investigators trace the repercussions of multiple reforms for English-learner representation in special education.

To conclude, as schools become more diverse, it is important to examine how people grapple with notions of difference (Minow, 1990). What are the criteria used to compare these students that lead to judgments about difference? Who defines such norms? What are the views of difference upon which authors of systemic reforms base their positions? What are the bureaucratic and procedural consequences of these assumptions?

These are indeed critical questions educators face as a new wave of English-only initiatives gains momentum. While our data do not allow us to make causal inferences, they suggest that English learners may be adversely impacted by such legislation, as reflected by increased special education placement patterns.

We also suggest, as have others, that English-learner overrepresentation must be tackled beyond the boundaries of special education. Heller, Holtzman, and Messick (1982) conclude that disproportionate representation is a problem "if [children] are unduly exposed to the likelihood of [special education] placement by virtue of receiving poor-quality regular instruction, [and] if the quality and academic relevance of the special instruction programs block students' educational progress, including decreasing the likelihood of their return to the regular classroom" (p. 18). As we examine special education placement evidence twenty years after the publication of Heller et al.'s report, we concur on the imperative to monitor the quality of educational programs offered to English learners in general, bilingual, and special education, as well as the long-term consequences of placement decisions for these students.

NOTES

1. The first author acknowledges the support of the COMRISE Project at the University of Virginia under grant #H029J60006, awarded by the U.S. Department of Education, Office of Special Education Programs.
2. These two initiatives denied basic educational and health services to illegal immigrants and discontinued affirmative action programs in university admissions and employment, respectively.
3. We tend to aggregate the data to describe the characteristics of the participating school districts to ensure anonymity.
4. In these districts, "English learner" is defined as "limited English proficient students acquiring English and speakers of non-mainstream language forms acquiring mainstream English." "FEP" is defined as "students identified through the formal initial assessment process as having sufficient English academic language proficiency to successfully participate in a mainstream English program." In turn, "English-only [EO] students are identified on the basis of parent responses to the Home Language Survey at the time of

enrollment. English-only students speak various language forms, including mainstream and non-mainstream forms" (California Department of Education, n.d.).

5. English-language development (ELD) is the "state-designated term for instructional programs to develop listening, speaking, reading and writing skills in English" (California Department of Education, n.d.).

6. The state definitions of disability categories are available from the California Department of Education.

REFERENCES

Artiles, A. J. (2000, July). *The inclusive education movement and minority representation in special education: Trends, paradoxes, and dilemmas.* Keynote address presented at the International Special Education Conference, Manchester, England.

Artiles, A. J., & Trent, S. C. (2000). Representation of culturally/linguistically diverse students. In C. R. Reynolds & E. Fletcher-Jantzen (Eds.), *Encyclopedia of special education, vol. 1* (2nd ed., pp. 513–517). New York: John Wiley & Sons.

August, D., & Hakuta, K. (Eds.). (1997). *Improving schooling for language-minority children: A research agenda.* Washington, DC: National Academy Press.

Baca, L. M., & Cervantes, H. T. (1989). *The bilingual special education interface* (2nd ed.). Columbus, OH: Merrill.

California Department of Education. (n.d.). Unpublished data on file with the authors.

Chinn, P. C., & Hughes, S. (1987). Representation of minority students in special education classes. *Remedial and Special Education, 8,* 41–46.

Cole, M. (1996). *Cultural psychology.* Cambridge, MA: Harvard University Press.

Diana v. State Board of Education, Civil Action No. C-7037RFP (N. D. Cal. Jan. 7, 1970 & June 18, 1973).

Figueroa, R. A., & Artiles, A. J. (1999). Disproportionate minority placement in special education programs: Old problem, new explanations. In A. Tashakkori & S. H. Ochoa (Eds.), *Education of Hispanics in the U.S.: Politics, policies, and outcomes* (pp. 93–117). New York: AMS Press.

Finn, J. D. (1982). Patterns in special education placement as revealed by the OCR surveys. In K. A. Heller, W. H. Holtzman, & S. Messick (Eds.), *Placing children in special education: A strategy for equity* (pp. 322–381). Washington, DC: National Academy Press.

Gándara, P., Maxwell-Jolly, J., García, E., Asato, J., Gutierrez, K., Stritikus, T., & Curry, J. (2000). *The initial impact of Proposition 227 on the instruction of English learners.* Santa Barbara, CA: Linguistic Minority Research Institute.

Gutierrez, K. D., Asato, J., Santos, M., & Gotanda, N. (2000). *Backlash pedagogy: Language and culture and the politics of reform.* Unpublished manuscript, University of California, Los Angeles.

Heller, K. A., Holtzman, W. H., & Messick, S. (Eds.). (1982). *Placing children in special education: A strategy for equity.* Washington, DC: National Academy Press.

Larry P. v. Riles. (1979). C-71-2270, FRP. Dis. Ct.

Lerner, J. W. (1997). *Learning disabilities: Theories, diagnosis, and teaching strategies* (7th ed.). Boston: Houghton Mifflin.

MacMillan, D. L., & Reschly, D. J. (1998). Overrepresentation of minority students: The case for greater specificity or reconsideration of the variables examined. *Journal of Special Education, 32,* 15–24.

Minow, M. (1990). *Making all the difference: Inclusion, exclusion, and American law.* Ithaca, NY: Cornell University Press.

Ortiz, A. A. (1997). Learning disabilities occurring concomitantly with linguistic differences. *Journal of Learning Disabilities, 30,* 321–332.

Oswald, D. P., Coutinho, M. J., Best, A. M., & Singh, N. N. (1999). Ethnic representation in special education: The influence of school-related economic and demographic variables. *Journal of Special Education, 32,* 194–206.

Portes, P. R. (1999). Social and psychological factors in the academic achievement of children of immigrants: A cultural history puzzle. *American Educational Research Journal, 36,* 489–507.

Reschly, D. J. (1997). *Disproportionate minority representation in general and special education: Patterns, issues, and alternatives.* Des Moines: Iowa Department of Education.

Rumbaut, R. G. (1998, March). *Transformations: The post-immigrant generation in an age of diversity.* Paper presented at the annual meeting of the Eastern Sociological Society, Philadelphia.

Vanderwood, M., McGrew, K. S., & Ysseldyke, J. E. (1998). Why we can't say much about students with disabilities during education reform. *Exceptional Children, 64,* 359–370.

CHAPTER SEVEN

Disability, Race, and High-Stakes Testing of Students[1]

JAY P. HEUBERT

INTRODUCTION

This chapter focuses on tests that have high stakes for individual students. They are "high-stakes" tests because they are used in making decisions about which students will be promoted or retained in grade and which will receive high school diplomas.

Students with disabilities—and the minority students who are often over-represented in programs for students with disabilities—have a lot to gain or lose from the standards movement and from high-stakes testing in particular. On the one hand, students with disabilities and minority students are often the victims of low expectations and weak instruction, and stand to benefit from efforts to provide high-quality instruction for all students (National Research Council [NRC], 1997).

On the other hand, low expectations and weak instruction increase the risk that students with disabilities will fail high-stakes tests and suffer the well-documented negative consequences associated with being retained in grade or denied standard high school diplomas. As discussed more fully below, even as their pass rates improve in some states, students with disabilities are now failing some state graduation tests at rates as high as 70 percent to 95 percent, and nonpass rates would be even higher if they accounted for students with disabilities who drop out before they have taken graduation tests. Heightened pressure to achieve high pass rates among general education students may also fuel inappropriate referrals to special education (Allington & McGill-Franzen, 1992). Moreover, minority students are often overrepresented among those improperly placed in special education (Individuals with Disabilities Education Act [IDEA], 1997), and there is evidence that states with high minority enrollments in special education are also likely to have high-stakes testing policies.[2]

Thus this study, which focuses generally on high-stakes testing of students with disabilities, is particularly relevant to minority students with disabilities.

This paper argues that if states and school districts use test scores in deciding whether individual students will be promoted or given high school diplomas, they should do so only after students have been taught the kinds of subject matter and skill the tests measure. This position is one with two decades of support in the law (*Debra P. v. Turlington*, 1981) and in the standards of the testing profession (American Educational Research Association [AERA], American Psychological Association [APA], & National Council on Measurement in Education [NCME], 1999; AERA, 2000; NRC, 1999). This paper also reports evidence suggesting that many students, and especially many students with disabilities, are not yet being taught the subject matter and skills they need to meet state standards and pass high-stakes tests.

The objective of the "standards" movement in U.S. public education is to enable all students to attain high levels of academic achievement. In principle, standards-based reform has three key elements: 1) state standards that identify what students should know and be able to do, 2) efforts to align teaching and learning with the state standards, and 3) student assessments, also aligned with the state standards, the results of which can be used to measure student progress and to promote accountability for improved teaching and learning (Elmore, 2000).

Accountability provisions can take many forms. High-stakes testing is designed to hold individual students accountable for their own test performance. *System* accountability measures are those aimed at the providers of education, such as states, school districts, and schools. Federal law, for example, now requires states and school districts (a) to include students with disabilities in large-scale testing programs, with appropriate accommodation and, if necessary, alternative assessment; and (b) to report performance data for students with disabilities, publicly and in disaggregated form (IDEA, 1997; Improving America's Schools Act [IASA], 1994). Under federal legislation enacted in 2002 and effective in 2005, most school districts will have to demonstrate on state assessments that students with disabilities, English-language learners, minority students, and low-socioeconomic-status (SES) students have made adequate yearly progress, and that overall graduation rates are rising (No Child Left Behind Act [NCLBA], 2002).[3] Similarly, some states subject school districts or schools to specific rewards or sanctions based on student performance, and it is now common for schools and school districts to receive favorable or adverse publicity based on student test scores (Goertz & Duffy, 2001). It remains the case, however, that far more states sanction individual students for poor test performance than impose sanctions on individual adults, be they teachers, administrators, school board members, legislators, parents, or taxpayers (Goertz & Duffy, 2001).

The section below briefly describes the growth and current scope of graduation testing and promotion testing in the United States. The second section explores current controversies regarding the likely effects of promotion and graduation tests on minority students and on students with disabilities. (As noted throughout this volume, test-score data on minority students in special education are often limited.) The third section describes some important and broadly accepted norms of appropriate test use, which, if observed, would reduce the negative effects of high-stakes testing. The final section describes some elements of a sound testing program.

THE EXTENT OF HIGH-STAKES TESTING
IN THE UNITED STATES

At present, about twenty states require students to pass graduation tests as a condition of getting standard diplomas (Olson, 2001), up from sixteen in 1997 (NRC, 1997) and eighteen in 1998 (NRC, 1999). Of these twenty, more than two-thirds set graduation-test standards at the tenth-grade level or higher (AFT, 1999).

The number of states with exit exams is expected to reach between twenty-six and twenty-nine within the next few years (AFT, 2001; Goertz & Duffy, 2001; NRC, 2001; Shore, Madaus, & Clarke, 2000). Some states, however, facing very high diploma-denial rates, have postponed or are considering postponing the dates by which graduation-test requirements would go into effect; these include Alabama, Alaska, California, Maryland, North Carolina, and Wisconsin (Blair, 2002; Keller, 2001; Olson, 2001). New York has delayed application of its general graduation requirements to students with disabilities, and other states are considering doing so. Graduation testing is thus expanding but its growth has been gradual and somewhat uneven.

In recent years, promotion testing has grown far more rapidly than graduation testing. In response to concerns about "social promotion," a rapidly growing number of states—seventeen in 2001, compared with only six in 1999—require students to pass standardized tests as a condition of grade-to-grade promotion or soon will do so, and thirteen states have both middle school and elementary school promotion-test policies (AFT, 1999, 2001, Table 12). In addition, many school districts, particularly in urban areas, have adopted promotion-test policies even where states have not. For example, New York City has a promotion-test policy although New York State does not, and Boston has a promotion-test policy although Massachusetts does not. This means that large numbers of the nation's minority students—and increasing numbers of all students—are subject to state or local promotion-test programs.

These high-stakes testing policies plainly apply to students of color. How do they apply to students with disabilities? As noted earlier, federal law requires states and school districts to include students with disabilities in large-scale assessments, and to report their scores publicly, in disaggregated form, as a way of determining how well schools are serving these students. This is a matter of system accountability. Federal law is silent, however, on whether states or schools districts should impose *high-stakes consequences on individual students with disabilities* who fail large-scale tests. In other words, while federal law mandates participation in large-scale tests and public reporting of disaggregated scores, it is for states to decide whether large-scale tests will result in individual high-stakes consequences and, if so, for which students.

States have addressed this question in different ways where students with disabilities are concerned. For example, some states authorize Individualized Education Program (IEP) teams to make individual decisions about whether students with disabilities who do not pass a promotion test may nonetheless advance to the next grade (Quenemoen, Lehr, Thurlow, & Thompson, 2000), or to decide whether students with disabilities who do not pass the state exit exam may nonetheless receive standard diplomas if they meet the requirements of their IEPs (Guy, Shin, Lee, & Thurlow, 1999; Thurlow & Thompson, 1999). Other states require students with disabilities (with appropriate accommodation) to pass promotion tests as a condition of advancing to the next grade (Quenemoen et al., 2000) and/or to pass graduation tests as a condition of receiving standard diplomas (Office of Special Education Programs [OSEP], 2000).

In some states, students with disabilities who fail state exit tests are eligible for alternative diplomas or certificates, such as IEP diplomas, certificates of completion, or certificates of attendance (Guy et al., 1999; Thurlow & Thompson, 1999). Unfortunately, there is little research on the value of such certificates and alternate, nonstandard diplomas in terms of a student's future opportunities for education or employment. The only alternative certificate on which there is extensive research is the General Equivalency Diploma, or GED, and evidence suggests that GED holders are more like high school dropouts in terms of future educational and employment opportunities than they are like individuals who hold standard high school diplomas (NRC, 2001). Indeed, the U.S. Department of Education's Office of Special Education Programs treats GED holders as dropouts rather than as high school graduates (OSEP, 2000, Table AD4), and under the Individuals with Disabilities Education Act (IDEA) a student with disabilities who has not received a *standard* high school diploma is entitled to special education and related services until the age of twenty-one or twenty-two (IDEA, 1997). States and school districts should therefore think carefully before they decide to award students alternatives to standard diplomas.

EFFECTS OF HIGH-STAKES TESTING

Many researchers and practitioners believe that standards-based reform will have the greatest impact on students—including many minority students and students with disabilities—who do not now have access to rigorous, high-quality education. There are serious disputes, however, over whether promotion and graduation testing will help such students or hurt them. As discussed below, the story is complex and the evidence incomplete. It seems fair to say, however, that the benefit will be greater, and the harm less, if students are taught the relevant subject matter and skills before they must pass high-stakes tests.

Graduation Tests

Even on graduation tests that measure basic skills, minority students and students with disabilities usually fail at higher rates than other students, especially in the years after such tests are first introduced. For example, in the 1970s, when minimum competency tests gained popularity, 20 percent of black students, compared with 2 percent of white students—a discrepancy of ten to one—initially failed Florida's graduation tests and were denied high school diplomas (*Debra P. v. Turlington*, 1979). And while many students with disabilities were excluded from state graduation-test programs (NRC, 1999), those who did participate failed at rates over 50 percent (McLaughlin, 2000).

For a variety of reasons, failure rates typically decline among all groups in the years after a new graduation test is introduced (Linn, 2000). This was true of "minimum competency" graduation tests that many states adopted in the 1970s and 1980s; after a few years; for example, black failure rates in Florida were far lower than 20 percent. It also appears to be true for graduation tests adopted more recently. Texas, for example, which has a graduation test set at the seventh- or eighth-grade level (Schrag, 2000), reports that pass rates of blacks and Latinos roughly doubled between 1994 and 1998, and that the gap in failure rates between whites, blacks, and Latinos narrowed considerably during that time (Viadero, 2000). More recent research, discussed below, questions whether the achievement gap between whites, blacks, and Latinos has actually narrowed in Texas (Klein, Hamilton, McCaffrey, & Stecher, 2000; Linn, 2001). In any case, 1998 data from the Texas graduation tests show continuing disparities: cumulative failure rates of 17.6 percent for black students, 17.4 percent for Hispanic students, and 6.7 percent for white students (Natriello & Pallas, 2001).

Data for students with disabilities are harder to find, but they show a similar pattern: higher pass rates over time accompanied by continuing, disproportionately high failure rates. For example, New York has reported that the number of students with disabilities who passed the state's new Regents English Exam in 1998–1999 was nearly twice as high as the number who took the exam two years earlier (Keller, 2000). While this suggests dramatic improvement, the data can be interpreted in different ways. New York reports the following pass rates for students with disabilities on the Regents English Exam: 5.1 percent in 1997–1998, 6.1 percent in 1998–1999, and 8.0 percent in 1999–2000 (New York Department of Education, 2000, 2001). This represents a 2.9 *percentage point* increase and a 57 *percent* increase over two years in the proportion of students with disabilities earning Regents Diplomas. At the same time, it suggests that high percentages did *not* pass the Regents Exam during these years: 94.9 percent in 1997–1998, 93.9 percent in 1998–1999, and 92.0 percent in 2000. These "nonpass" rates are particularly high, considering that New York calculates them using only students with disabilities who completed high school (New York Department of Education, 2000, 2001).[4] A recent study (Koretz & Hamilton, 2001) confirms highly disproportionate failure rates among students with disabilities in New York and raises concerns about possibly excessive levels of difficulty of the Regents English Exam for some students with disabilities, which the authors believe could cause very high failure rates or undesirable responses by teachers or students, such as excessive coaching. In June 2001, New York decided to extend from 2004 to 2008 a special safety net under which students with disabilities who fail one or more of the new Regents Exams—by 2004 there will be five such exams—may nonetheless receive standard *local* high school diplomas if they pass the older, less rigorous Regents Competency Test for each subject required. In 1999–2000, 54.1 percent of students with disabilities who completed high school that year received such standard local diplomas (New York Department of Education, 2001).

In Massachusetts, the proportion of students with disabilities who passed both state graduation tests in the tenth grade has risen considerably, from 11 percent in 2000 to 29 percent in 2001, and students will have four additional opportunities to pass any test they have failed. At the same time, disproportions remained high in 2001: 71 percent of enrolled tenth-grade students with disabilities had yet to pass both graduation tests, compared with 24 percent of enrolled students without disabilities, and the rates for black students (63% not passing both tests), Hispanic students (71%), and English-language learners (70%) were two to three times higher than the nonpass rates for white students

(23%) and Asian students (32%) (Massachusetts Department of Education, 2001).[5] These statistics are based on total tenth-grade enrollment of students with disabilities. Thus, they do not account for pre–tenth-grade dropout or retention, even though ninth-grade retention apparently increased statewide in the years before 2001. Pass rates would be lower if the statistics took dropouts and retention into account.

Similar gaps between students with and without disabilities can be found in data from other states. In 2001, Alaska's tenth-grade students with disabilities failed different portions of the state graduation test in the following percentages: reading, 78.9 percent (compared with 34.1% for other students); writing, 95.7 percent (compared with 53.4% for other students); and math, 91.1 percent (compared with 56.0% for other students) (Alaska Department of Education, 2001). In 2001, failure rates for Alaska's eleventh-grade students with disabilities showed even higher failure rates. In both years, failure rates for Alaska Natives, blacks, and Hispanics were higher than those for white students. Unfortunately, the state does not post data indicating how many students have passed all three exams, which is what students must do to receive standard diplomas. The statistics just cited, however, do not bode well for students with disabilities. It is perhaps not surprising, therefore, that Alaska has postponed the date at which its graduation requirement goes into effect (Olson, 2001).

In California, where most special education students are minority students (OSEP, 2000),[6] ninth graders had the option in spring 2001 of taking two state exams that they will have to pass to receive standard diplomas in 2004. Only 10.3 percent of students with disabilities passed both tests, compared with 42.2 percent of all students (Wise et al., 2002, Table 5.1, p. 80). The rate at which English-language learners passed both exams was also quite low (11.9%), and the pass rates for black students (22.8%) and Hispanic students (22.8%) were well below those for white students (61.4%) and Asian students (64.5%) (Wise et al., 2002, Table 5.1, p. 80). Moreover, when one includes the students who chose not to take the exams in 2001, only 6.5 percent of all ninth-grade students with disabilities passed both tests, and only 8.1 percent of all ninth-grade English-language learners did so (Wise et al., 2002, p. 81). Students who failed California's exit exam as ninth graders in spring 2001 will have additional opportunities to pass the new state graduation tests.

In states with higher overall pass rates, the performance gaps between students with and without disabilities are smaller but noteworthy and disproportionate. In April 2001, for example, Alabama reported that 3 percent of all seniors had failed the reading test and 4 percent had failed the math test. Comparable figures for students with disabilities in the twelfth grade were 23 percent and 27 percent, respectively, six to nine times as high as for all Alabama seniors.[7] Moreover, these statistics understate the actual diploma-denial rate for students with disabilities, both because students had to pass *both* tests to receive standard diplomas—which as many as 50 percent of twelfth-grade students with disabilities may not have done—and because it appears that most students with disabilities had dropped out before twelfth grade. Students with disabilities represented only 4.6 percent of twelfth-grade enrollment (Alabama Department of Education, 2001), even though students with disabilities represent a much higher percentage of total enrollments.

It is rare to find test-score data for students with disabilities that have been further disaggregated by race. Where other achievement data have been disaggregated, however, racial disparities within disability categories emerge. For example, David Osher et al. report in this volume that 66 percent of black students with emotional and behavioral disturbance received failing grades, compared with only 38 percent of white students who have this disability. Moreover, as Donald Oswald et al. point out in their chapter, post–high school outcomes for minority students with disabilities are substantially lower than those for white students with disabilities. These studies suggest that it would be valuable to disaggregate test-score data to show the combined effects of disability and race, both in publicly available reports and in test-score data available to researchers.

An important, largely unanswered question concerns the extent to which improved pass rates on graduation tests actually reflect improved teaching and learning. Such improvements are plainly a possible explanation, and the most desirable one. During the 1980s, however, when many states reported sharply improved pass rates on graduation tests, scores on the National Assessment of Educational Progress (NAEP)—a highly regarded nationally administered examination—showed little or no improvement in student learning. Indeed, evidence that minimum competency tests were not producing improved student performance on the NAEP is one reason why the current standards movement emphasizes higher standards, and why some states have been raising graduation-test standards.

More recent fourth- and eighth-grade NAEP scores suggest improvements in student mathematics performance during the period 1990–1996, particularly in some states (including Texas and North Carolina) that pursued certain "systemic reform policies" (Grissmer, Flanigan, Kawata, & Williamson, 2000, p. 58).[8] At the same time, NAEP scores consistently show much less gain in student performance than do the state-test results, and NAEP scores also suggest a widening racial achievement gap among thirteen- and seventeen-year-olds (National Center for Education Statistics [NCES], 2001, pp. 22–23). For example, as noted above, data from the Texas graduation test, the Texas Assessment of Academic Skills (TAAS), suggest that the achievement gap between white and black students and between white and Latino students closed dramatically between 1994 and 1998. More recent research using NAEP data indicates, however, that the achievement gap between white students and other groups in Texas actually *increased* slightly during this period (Klein et al., 2000). For Robert Linn (2001), this evidence "raises serious questions about the trustworthiness of the TAAS result for making inferences about improvements in achievement in Texas or about the relative size of the gains for different segments of the student population" (p. 28). It also raises questions about the factual basis of the decision in *GI Forum v. Texas Education Agency* (2000), in which a federal judge relied heavily on evidence of a narrowing racial achievement gap on the TAAS in upholding the legality of the Texas graduation test. Moreover, as Daniel Losen and Kevin Welner discuss in this volume, the low TAAS participation rates of students with disabilities, most of whom are minority, also suggest that evidence before the court understated the racial achievement gap.

Unfortunately, NAEP does not yet include enough students with disabilities (or English-language learners) in its samples to provide meaningful *state-level* performance scores for these groups (NCES, 2001). Time will tell whether future state NAEP results for students with disabilities confirm the state-test gains that some states have reported for students with disabilities.

What factors other than improved achievement may explain increased pass rates on state tests? First, it is well known that scores on a test can increase as students become familiar with that test's format, "with or without real improvement in the broader achievement constructs that tests and assessments are intended to measure" (Linn, 2000, p. 4). Studies show that improvements on a state's tests may not be confirmed when students take other tests that supposedly measure the same knowledge and skills (Koretz & Barron, 1998; Koretz, Linn, Dunbar, & Shepard, 1991). When teachers "teach to the test," for example, student scores typically rise as students become familiar with particular item formats, whether or not they actually know more about the subjects being tested (Madaus & Clarke, 2001; Mehrens, 1998).

Second, some states may reduce high failure rates, actual or projected, by making the state graduation tests easier or by setting lower cutoff scores that students must achieve to pass. In New York, for example, failure rates on a state test dropped substantially after the state created a temporary "low-pass" category for students who were below the state's original passing score. Similarly, increased pass rates in Texas may be due in part to changes in the test that made it easier for students to pass (Schrag, 2000).

Third, if low-achieving students are not part of the test-taking population, then the pass rates of those who remain will be higher—even if the achievement of those who actually take the test has not improved. Studying an administration of New York's new Regents Exam, for example, Koretz and Hamilton (2001) found that only about 6 percent of actual test takers were students with disabilities, even though students with disabilities represented about 12 percent of the relevant student population; given significantly lower pass rates among students with disabilities, the absence of half of these students would produce increased pass rates for those who did take the test. Sometimes low-performing students with disabilities are encouraged to postpone taking the test until they are likelier to pass;[9] this may be legitimate, but it does boost the pass rate for those who do take the test.

Special education placement practices can also distort pass-rate information. If low-performing general education students are improperly placed in special education, some states or school districts may not count these students' scores in calculating pass rates for general education students, and the pass rates for those who remain in general education will be inflated artificially (Allington & McGill-Franzen, 1992).

Similarly, if a graduation test is administered in tenth grade and large numbers of low achievers were retained in ninth grade the year before, those retained will not be part of the test population and the pass rate for those who were promoted to tenth grade will be higher. Such retention is not uncommon. It is well documented, for example, that ninth-grade retention in Texas has increased dramatically since the mid-1980s (Murnane & Levy, 2001). In Massachusetts, improved pass rates among tenth graders in 2001 followed increased ninth-grade retention in previous years. In California, a 2001 survey of educators indicates that 55 percent of principals and 32 percent of teachers anticipate that the state's new graduation test will have "a strongly negative or negative impact on student retention rates" (Wise et al., 2002, p. 45). As noted above, minority students and English-language learners are often disproportionately represented among those retained in grade. There is also evidence that low-achieving students with disabilities have sometimes been retained in grade when the alternative would have been for them to take state tests (Thurlow & Johnson, 2000).

Last but not least, if low-performing students have dropped out of school before taking a graduation exam, the pass rates will be higher for those who remain in school. There is considerable debate about whether graduation testing causes increased dropout rates. Walt Haney (2001) offers evidence that the Texas graduation test has led to significantly increased dropout rates, especially for minority students. Other scholars (Carnoy, Loeb, & Smith, 2001), while agreeing that ninth-grade retention in Texas has increased dramatically since the mid-1980s (Murnane & Levy, 2001), dispute claims that graduation testing is the cause. Brian Jacob (2001), using a national longitudinal database, finds no general relationship between graduation testing and dropping out but concludes that such tests do increase the probability of dropping out among the lowest achieving students. A 2001 survey of educators in California suggests that 80 percent of principals and 61 percent of teachers believe that the state's new graduation test will have "a strongly negative or negative impact on student dropout rates" (Wise et al., 2002, p. 45).

On the one hand, it appears that many low achievers start to disengage from school well before graduation tests loom (NRC, 2001). On the other hand, failing a graduation test can increase the likelihood that low achievers will leave school (Clarke, Haney, & Madaus, 2000). Also, the current climate of accountability places new pressures on schools to increase student pass rates, which in turn can lead to increased and/or understated dropout rates (Schrag, 2000); for example, an education research group concluded in May 2001 that the Texas dropout rate is more than twice that reported by the state education department (Benton, 2001). Unfortunately, this critical issue is complicated by a lack of uniformity among the states in defining and counting dropouts (NRC, 2001); Texas counts GED holders as high school graduates, for example, while the U.S. Department of Education counts such individuals as high school dropouts (OSEP, 2000, Table AD4). Under the 2002 No Child Left Behind Act, school districts will soon be required to show improved high school graduation rates based on the size of the entering class, a change that should increase uniformity in the counting of dropouts and the calculation of dropout rates.

In sum, reported graduation-test pass rates should be viewed in the context of such factors as (a) improper exemptions, exclusions, or absences of students with disabilities or English-language learners from the test-taking population, which are far higher in some states than in others (Citizens' Commission on Civil Rights, 2001; Robelin, 2001); (b) improper special education placements; (c) grade retention in the years prior to high-stakes testing; (d) dropout rates and the formulas by which they are computed; and (e) improper testing accommodations that may artificially inflate some students' scores (Allington, 2000; Sack, 2000).

Promotion Tests

As noted above, promotion testing has been growing in the elementary and secondary grades (AFT, 2001), and especially in urban school districts. In Chicago, New York, and other cities, tens of thousands of students, the vast majority of them minority students, have been retained in grade. And while the application of such policies to students with disabilities varies, as previous discussion indicates, there are states and school districts in which students with disabilities who fail promotion tests are subject to retention in grade (Quenemoen et al., 2000).

How well do students with disabilities fare on such tests? Two multistate studies conducted by the National Center for Educational Outcomes provide evidence that students with disabilities are much likelier than nondisabled students to fail state achievement tests. One such report (Ysseldyke et al., 1998) examines tests that twelve states administered during 1995–1996 and 1996–1997 in grades six through eleven. It shows that students with disabilities typically failed these tests at rates thirty-five to forty percentage points higher than those for "all" students, and the gap would have been even higher had students with disabilities been compared with nondisabled students rather than with "all" students.[10] Similar gaps are evident in a study of pass rates on tests that seventeen states administered, mostly in grades eight through twelve, in two subsequent years, in 1997–1998 and 1998–1999. This report (Thurlow, Nelson, Teelucksingh, & Ysseldyke, 2000, Tables 4–9, 12) also shows large performance gaps between students with disabilities and "all" students: 23 to 47 percentage points in reading, 19 to 42 percentage points in math, and 25 to 44 percentage points in writing, all of which would have been even higher had the comparison been between students with and without disabilities. While not focusing specifically on tests used for promotion, both these reports provide strong evidence that the overall achievement gap is large at both the elementary and secondary levels. It is possible that some students with disabilities may be more highly motivated to pass promotion tests than they are other state tests (Roderick & Engel, 2001). On the other hand, as discussed above, students with disabilities fail *graduation* tests at highly disproportionate rates. Overall, therefore, these studies suggest that students with disabilities fail promotion tests (and other state achievement tests) at substantially higher rates than nondisabled students.

If students with disabilities and minority students who fail promotion tests are retained in grade, they are at substantially increased risk of dropping out. Students retained in grade even once are much likelier to drop out later than are students not retained, and the effects are even greater for students retained more than once (Hauser, 2001; NRC, 1999; Shepard & Smith, 1989). "[T]here is no dispute that retention in grade is a very strong predictor of who will drop out" (NRC, 2001, p. 41), and some scholars (Lillard & DeCicca, 2001) have concluded that retention is the single strongest predictor of which students will drop out of school.

Promotion testing is thus likely to increase, perhaps significantly, the numbers of students with disabilities and minority students who suffer the serious consequences of dropping out. These consequences include much lower average earnings and substantially reduced opportunities for employment and further education. Congress has already expressed serious concern about the disproportionately high dropout rates of students with disabilities (IDEA, 1997).

Given the relationships between promotion testing, retention in grade, and increased dropout rates, the National Research Council (1999) has described simple retention in grade as "an ineffective intervention" (p. 285). There is thus good reason to question the value of promotion-test policies, even as such policies proliferate.

Promotion and graduation testing may also have unintended consequences for teachers. As noted above, high-stakes testing is intended to raise teacher motivation and effectiveness, and there is evidence that with appropriate professional development, support, resources, and time, teaching effectiveness can improve significantly (Elmore, 2000). There is already evidence, however, that the negative publicity associated with poor test scores can lead experienced teachers to leave urban schools for the suburbs (Lee, 1998). Such trends exacerbate a nationwide teacher shortage that is already most acute in urban schools and that is at least as serious for special education teachers (Gonzalez & Carlson, 2001) as for teachers in general education. Unfortunately, efforts to improve low-performing schools—and to educate all children effectively—will be undermined if those schools lose strong teachers.

On the other hand, testing policies that lead to improved teaching and learning are likely to benefit minority students, English-language learners, and students with disabilities even more than they do other students. New York Education Commissioner Richard Mills defends stringent graduation-test requirements partly because he hopes they will bring an end to low-track classes, in which students—most of them black students, Hispanic students, and/or English-language learners—typically receive poor-quality, low-level instruction. This position is grounded in solid evidence that placement in typical low-track classes is educationally harmful for students (NRC, 1999; Oakes, Gamoran, & Page, 1992), and that students will learn more if they are placed in more demanding classes (NRC, 1999; Weckstein, 1999).

Advocates for minority children and low-SES children hope that high standards will provide the political and legal leverage needed to improve resources and school effectiveness so that all children receive—*beforehand*—the high-quality instruction they need to be able to meet demanding academic standards. Disability-rights groups likewise hope that high standards will provide the political and legal leverage needed to improve resources and school effectiveness so that students with disabilities get the help they need *in time to meet demanding academic standards.* They count on state standards and tests to drive improvements in IEPs so that IEPs reflect more of the knowledge and skills that all students are expected to acquire (NRC, 1997). There is certainly evidence that higher expectations and improved instruction lead to improved achievement (Elmore, 2000; IDEA, 1997; Thurlow & Johnson, 2000).

STANDARDS OF APPROPRIATE TEST USE

Whether high-stakes testing helps or hurts depends largely on whether such tests are used to promote high-quality education for all children—the stated objective of standards-based reform—or to penalize students for not having the subject matter and skills that they have not been taught in school.

This is the principal theme that former U.S. Education Secretary Richard Riley, a strong proponent of standards-based reform, emphasized in his February 22, 2000, State of American Education address. Riley called for a "midcourse review" of the standards movement, a step he said was needed "because there is a gap between what we know we should be doing and what we are doing" (Riley, 2000, p. 6).

The sections that follow focus chiefly on two issues of appropriate test use: the principle that promotion tests and graduation tests should measure only the knowledge and skills that schools have afforded students the opportunity to acquire and the principle that high-stakes decisions should be based on multiple measures of student achievement, rather than on a single test score.

Teaching Students the Necessary Subject Matter and Skills before Using Test Results to Make High-Stakes Decisions about Individual Students

In former secretary Riley's call for a "midcourse review," he said that state standards should be "challenging but realistic. . . . [Y]ou have to help students and teachers prepare for these [high-stakes] tests—they need the preparation time and resources to succeed, and the test must be on matters that they have been taught" (Riley, 2000, p. 7).

Not coincidentally, these concerns are also reflected in norms of appropriate test use that the testing profession, the National Research Council, and American Educational Research Association (AERA) have articulated. The *Standards for Educational and Psychological Testing,* issued in December 1999 by the AERA, the APA, and the NCME (and referred to here as the *Joint Standards*), assert that promotion and graduation tests should cover only the "content and skills that students have had an opportunity to learn" (AERA et al.,

1999, Standard 13.5, p. 146). The congressionally mandated NRC study, *High Stakes: Testing for Tracking, Promotion, and Graduation,* reached a similar conclusion in 1999: "Tests should be used for high-stakes decisions . . . only after schools have implemented changes in teaching and curriculum that ensure that students have been taught the knowledge and skills on which they will be tested" (NRC, 1999). So does the AERA, which, in its July 2000 *Position Statement Concerning High-Stakes Testing in Pre-K–12 Education,* recommends the following "condition[] essential to sound implementation of high-stakes educational testing programs. . . . When content standards and associated tests are introduced as a reform to . . . improve current practice, opportunities to access appropriate materials and retraining consistent with the intended changes should be provided before . . . students are sanctioned for failing to meet the new standards" (p. 2).

Moreover, a committee of the National Research Council expressly recommended that this principle be applied individually to each student with disabilities:

> If a student with disabilities is subject to an assessment used for promotion or graduation decisions, the IEP team should ensure that the curriculum and instruction received by the student through the individual education program is aligned with test content and that the student has had adequate opportunity to learn the material covered by the test. (NRC, 1999, p. 295)

Are students being taught or given "adequate opportunity to learn" the requisite subject matter and skills *before* individual high-stakes consequences such as grade retention and diploma denial take effect? Researchers, advocacy organizations, educators, and federal and state governments are trying in different ways to answer this question, for students generally and/or for students with disabilities. Some focus on indicators of student achievement, such as test scores, on the assumption that *"the best evidence that a school system is providing its students adequate opportunity to learn the required material is whether most students do, in fact, learn the material"* (Wise et al., 2002, p. 93, emphasis in original). Others (Citizens' Commission on Civil Rights, 2001; Cohen, 2001) are looking at whether states and school districts have met system accountability standards that are intended to gauge how well schools are serving different groups of students. Some (Porter & Smithson, 2000, 2001) are conducting surveys that ask teachers and administrators how much alignment they see between standards, curriculum, instruction, and tests, and developing techniques for expressing the amount of alignment. Others are examining written documents—state standards, the state curriculum, the tests that are administered, the actual lesson plans from which teachers teach—to determine how well they are all aligned.

By these measures, there is evidence of progress. As discussed earlier, increasing proportions of students—all students, minority students, students with disabilities—appear to be passing state tests over time.[11] More states meet current federal system accountability requirements than did so two years ago (Citizens' Commission on Civil Rights, 2001; Cohen, 2001; Robelin, 2001).

At the same time, there are plainly many students who are not yet being taught the subject matter and skills that state standards reflect and that students need if they are to pass state tests. Several different types of evidence support this conclusion.

One kind of evidence consists of recent graduation–test score data showing failure rates of 60 percent to 90 percent for students with disabilities, minority students, and English-language learners. If "all children can learn," as the standards movement and at least three federal statutes assert (IASA, 1994; IDEA, 1997; NCLBA, 2002), these failure rates must be due at least in part to poor-quality instruction for the groups whose failure rates are so high.[12]

Other kinds of evidence tend to reinforce the view that many educational systems are not yet at the point where they offer all students instruction that enables them to meet state standards. For example, many states do not yet meet federal system accountability standards that require them to include all their students in large-scale assessment programs and to report disaggregated scores for students with disabilities, English-language learners, and different racial groups (Citizens' Commission on Civil Rights, 2001; Cohen, 2001; Goertz & Duffy, 2001; Robelin, 2001; Thompson & Thurlow, 2001). States not meeting these standards lack basic information without which it is difficult even to *know* how well low-achieving groups are performing, much less to improve instruction so as to *address* any problems that the data might reveal. In other words, some important preconditions to systemic improvement, designed to identify and help address the needs of low achievers, have yet to be met in a number of states.

Studies call particular attention to the need for improved standards-based education for students with disabilities. For example, Don Dailey, Kathy Zantal-Wiener, and Virginia Roach (2000), in a three-state, OSEP-funded study of standards-based reform and students with disabilities, found that special education teachers "lacked guidance about how to align IEPs with the standards," that they were "by and large . . . not involved in school-wide discussions about standards," that special education teachers "tended to use the IEPs rather than the standards as a guide for instruction," and that "most IEPs were not

aligned with the standards" (pp. 8–9). They also found that many special education and general education teachers did not know how to link pedagogy,
standards, and content, "lacked the knowledge and skills to co-teach in a classroom," and "tended to have a 'wait and see' attitude about exposing students
with disabilities to and engaging them in standards-based instruction" (pp. 8–
9). The authors did not identify which three states they studied, and it is therefore unclear whether these states administer high-stakes graduation or promotion tests. It is also unclear how generalizable these findings are. In these states
and many others like them, however, it does not appear that IEP teams "ensure
that the curriculum and instruction received by the student through the individual education program is aligned with test content and that the student has
had adequate opportunity to learn the material covered by the test" (NRC,
1999, p. 295). This is also a concern for minority students, who are overrepresented among students with disabilities.

Similarly, while there are not many published empirical studies that explore actual alignment within states between standards, assessments, curriculum, and instruction, research indicates that there remain discrepancies
between what high-stakes tests measure and what students have been taught.
Preliminary results of a ten-state study by Andrew Porter and John Smithson
(2000) suggest that there is little overlap between a state's standards and what
fourth- and eighth-grade teachers in the state say they teach students. The overlap teachers reported between state tests and instruction ranged from a low of
from 5 percent to a high of 46 percent, depending on the subject, grade level,
and state (Boser, 2000; Porter & Smithson, 2000). However, these results are
preliminary, the teacher samples are small, and the study is limited to the fourth
and eighth grades. More recent studies by Porter, Smithson, and their colleagues offer a few more examples of the overlap between teaching and tests
within particular states; while it is not clear how representative the examples
are, the overlap is small in each case.[13]

All these statistics and findings have their limitations, and research suggests
that alignment will increase as teachers increasingly focus instruction on the
subjects that state tests measure (Madaus & Clarke, 2001). Taken together,
however, they suggest that many teachers are not yet teaching students the full
range of subject matter and skills that state tests measure, and that the gap is
probably greatest for students with disabilities, minority students, and English-
language learners. Where this is the case, it would be inappropriate to use results of these tests in making promotion or graduation decisions for individual
students. It seems problematic, therefore, that so many states and school districts are moving forward with high-stakes graduation and/or promotion tests.

Using Multiple Measures to Make High-Stakes Decisions about Individual Students

As noted above, increasing numbers of states and school districts automatically deny grade promotion or high school diplomas to students who fail state or local tests, regardless of how well the students have performed on other measures of achievement, such as course grades. Former secretary Riley is not alone in believing that states and school districts should "incorporate multiple ways of measuring learning" (Riley, 2000, p. 6), particularly in making high-stakes decisions about promotion and graduation.

The National Research Council (1999) emphasizes that educators should always buttress test-score information with "other relevant information about the student's knowledge and skills, such as grades, teacher recommendations, and extenuating circumstances" (p. 279) when making high-stakes decisions about individual students. This is consistent with the testing profession's *Joint Standards*, which state that "in elementary or secondary education, a decision or characterization that will have a major impact on a test taker should not automatically be made on the basis of a single test score. Other relevant information . . . should be taken into account if it will enhance the overall validity of the decision" (AERA et al., 1999, Standard 13.7, p. 146). Similarly, the AERA *Position Statement* (2000) provides that "[d]ecisions that affect individual students' life chances or educational opportunities should not be made on the basis of test scores alone. Other relevant information should be taken into account to enhance the overall validity of such decisions" (p. 2).

Why is it so important to use multiple measures in making such critical decisions about individuals? One reason is that decisions based on grades may have less disproportionate racial impact than test scores; this is the conclusion of a recent study examining student grades and scores on the Massachusetts graduation exam (Brennan, Kim, Wenz-Gross, & Siperstein, 2001).

More broadly, the answer is that *any* single measure is inevitably imprecise and limited as to the information it provides. Proponents of high-stakes testing sometimes point out problems often associated with exclusive reliance on student grades in making promotion and graduation decisions: that there has been grade inflation during the last three decades, for example, and that there is variation among teachers, schools, and school districts in what particular grades mean.

The evidence on K–12 grade inflation is less clear than many people seem to assume. Daniel Koretz and Mark Berends (2001), using national databases to explore possible math grade inflation between 1982 and 1992, concluded that high school math grades increased slightly during this period but that grades actually *declined* slightly after taking into account modest improvements in math achievement during this time. Even assuming that there are valid concerns about grades, however, it does not follow that grades should be ignored altogether.

Standardized tests, like grades, are limited in what they measure. It is well known, for example, that standardized-test scores are no better than high school grades in predicting first-year college achievement, and that grades and test scores together provide a better prediction of freshman grades than either measure alone. Grade-point averages are also better indicators than standardized tests of student motivation over time, a factor strongly related to later success in school and the workplace. Moreover, as the following examples illustrate, even the best standardized tests are typically less precise than most people think:

- What are the chances that two students with identical "real achievement" will score more than ten percentile points apart on the same Stanford 9 test? For two ninth graders who are really at the 45th percentile in math, the answer is 57 percent of the time. In fourth-grade reading, the probability is 42 percent.
- How often will a student who really belongs at the 50th percentile according to national test norms actually score within 5 percentile points of that ranking on a test? The answer is only about 30 percent of the time in mathematics and 42 percent in reading. (Rogosa, 1999, cited in Viadero, 1999, p. 3)

Unfortunately, as former secretary Riley noted, "There is a gap between what we know we should be doing and what we are doing" (2000, p. 7). This is the case in the many states and school districts that make promotion or graduation decisions relying solely on student test scores. Such practices, though widespread, do not seem consistent with norms of appropriate test use.

To complicate matters, there is at present no satisfactory mechanism for ensuring that states and school districts respect even widely accepted norms of appropriate, nondiscriminatory test use. The two existing mechanisms—professional discipline through the associations that produce the *Joint Standards* or legal enforcement through the courts or administrative agencies—have complementary shortcomings. Professional associations such as the AERA, APA, and NCME have detailed standards but lack mechanisms for monitoring or enforcing compliance with those standards. For courts and federal civil rights agencies, the reverse is true; they have complaint procedures and enforcement power, but lack specific, legally enforceable standards on the appropriate use of high-stakes tests. Recognizing the problem, the U.S. Department of Education's Office for Civil Rights (OCR, 2000) has released a carefully crafted resource guide that, while not legally binding, aims to promote the appropriate use of tests used in promotion and graduation decisions. In 2001, the new Bush administration "embargoed" this resource guide, leaving its status uncertain; it remains available, however, and is helpful on a wide range of issues associated with promotion and graduation testing, assessment of students with disabilities and English-language learners, and other civil rights issues.

ELEMENTS OF A SOUND TESTING POLICY

Given these concerns, what are some elements of a sound high-stakes testing policy within the larger context of standards-based reform? First, states should adopt standards for what students should know and be able to do. And while such standards continually evolve, this is something virtually all the states have done (AFT, 2001). Second, policymakers and educators should strive to align each of the following with state standards: (a) state and local large-scale assessments; (b) state and local curricula; and, perhaps most important, (c) actual instruction. This objective is a challenging one, and there is evidence of major gaps. Often, graduation testing and promotion testing precede the alignment of curriculum and instruction with state standards (Elmore, 2000), and in many cases the tests are not well aligned with state standards: "There is little evidence to suggest that exit exams in current use have been validated properly against the defined curriculum and actual instruction; rather, it appears that many states may not have taken adequate steps to validate their assessment instruments, and that proper studies would reveal important weaknesses" (Stake, 1998, cited in NRC, 1999, p. 179).

The steps mentioned thus far do not include high-stakes testing. Even before alignment is complete, states and school districts can use large-scale assessments to help drive improvements in curriculum and instruction, and virtually all do. But the *Joint Standards*, the 1999 NRC study, and the July 2000 AERA *Position Statement* all assume that alignment will occur *before* such instruments become high-stakes tests for students. As noted above, all three say that tests should be used to decide whether individual students will be promoted or given high school diplomas only *after* students have been taught the kinds of subject matter and skill the tests measure.

The *Joint Standards* (1999), the NRC study (1999), and the AERA *Position Statement* (2000) describe measures a state or school district should take if it elects to use tests for high-stakes purposes. One, just noted, is not to use tests for high-stakes purposes until schools are actually teaching students the relevant subject matter and skills. Second, test users should make sure that a high-stakes test is valid for its intended purpose. This may sounds obvious, but it is not something every test user does. Chicago, for example, received national publicity for its use of the Iowa Test of Basic Skills (ITBS) in making promotion decisions, even though the district's chief accountability officer acknowledged that the ITBS is not valid as a measure of which students should be promoted or held back (NRC, 1999).

Third, a test use is inappropriate unless it leads to the best available treatment or placement for students (NRC, 1999). This means that states and school districts should refrain from using test scores (or other information) to justify educational decisions that are demonstrably harmful to students. Based on the weight of research evidence, two placements or treatments that typically harm students are retention in grade and placement in typical low-track classes (Hauser, 2001; NRC, 1999; Oakes et al., 1992). Retention and low-track placements are inimical to the goal of helping all students reach high levels of achievement. Both are inconsistent with principles of appropriate test use.

Fourth, test developers should take students with disabilities, English-language learners, minority students, and other groups into account beginning with initial test development, and should take steps to ensure that the test is equally valid for all major student populations that will take it (AERA, 2000; AERA et al., 1999; NRC, 1999).

Fifth, test users should not rely solely on test-score information in making promotion and graduation decisions (AERA, 2000; AERA et al., 1999; NRC, 1999). Instead, as colleges do, states and school districts should look at multiple measures of student achievement and readiness, and allow high achievement on one measure to balance lower performance on another.

Further, some states measure not only absolute achievement in the form of a percentage of students passing a test but also improvement over time (i.e., higher percentages of students passing a test). And some states measure whether school districts or schools are succeeding in closing the gap between high-achieving and low-achieving students. Each of these measures adds something important. An absolute standard signals that schools set high expectations for all students rather than lower expectations for some. A standard based on improvement recognizes that different students, schools, and school districts start out at different places and rewards progress. A standard based on whether schools are closing the achievement gap—between white students and minority students, between nondisabled students and students with disabilities, between native English speakers and English-language learners—encourages schools to pay more attention to these very important goals. This is the theory behind the new federal yearly progress requirements for Title I recipients. The baseline for these improvements will be established in 2002–2003 (NCLBA, 2002).

Sixth, the debate over high-stakes testing is often framed in terms of either-or choices: whether a student who does not seem ready for the next grade should be retained or promoted, or whether a student who has not mastered the necessary knowledge and skill should receive a diploma. In each case, the choice is between unattractive alternatives. Though often unacknowledged, there is almost always a preferable third option: Any information schools can use to make a promotion or graduation decision can be used years earlier—before students reach a "gatepost"—to determine which children are performing poorly and to help get them the support they will need to be able to meet high standards. Teachers typically know, long before a promotion or graduation test, which students will need help if they are to pass. Effective early intervention is critical, as recent research shows (Grissmer et al., 2000).

Seventh, tests by themselves do not improve learning, any more than a thermometer reduces fever. At best, good tests provide information that can be used to improve instruction. It is important that this information, along with information from other sources, be available—in an understandable form—to policymakers, educators, parents, and students. And it is equally important for all concerned to know which policies and practices are likeliest to produce improved teaching and learning (Elmore, 2000; Grissmer et al., 2000). Educators and parents also need access to the resources that it takes to make the necessary changes in teaching and learning. Unfortunately, it is well known that many school districts and schools lack the resources they need to enable all children to reach high levels of achievement (National Academy of Education, 1995; NRC, 1999).

Finally, these questions all call for additional research: on what interventions work, on how treatments effective in some settings can be implemented widely, and, not least, on how high-stakes testing policies affect student learning and dropout rates, for students generally and for such important groups as students of color, English-language learners, and students with disabilities.[14] There is also a need for improved special education data broken out by race so researchers, policymakers, and practitioners can better understand the status and needs of minority students with disabilities.

In conclusion, the standards movement and high-stakes testing present both opportunities and risks to students with disabilities, minority students, English-language learners, and minority students with disabilities. These students are among those who stand to benefit most if all students receive high-quality instruction. Such students are also at great risk, however, especially in states that administer high-stakes promotion and graduation tests before having made the improvements in instruction that will enable all students to meet the standards. Even failure rates well below 70–95 percent are plainly unacceptable, for these students and for society at large.

Educators and policymakers are right to be concerned about educating all students to high levels, and reaching this objective is obviously no simple matter. Promotion and graduation tests are one part of this picture, and debates over the necessity and desirability of such testing will continue even as it becomes more widespread. One thing is clear, however: If states and school districts are going to use high-stakes testing, then it is important that such testing be done properly. The basic principles of appropriate test use are relatively clear and enjoy broad support among researchers and practitioners. States and school districts that disregard these principles put their students—and themselves—at risk. The prospect of high failure rates has already produced a political backlash against some states' high-stakes testing programs. Lawsuits are also likely, if only because no reliable alternatives exist by which to ensure appropriate use of tests that affect students' life chances in such important ways. The stakes are high indeed.

NOTES

1. This paper was written with support from the Carnegie Scholars Program of the Carnegie Corporation of New York, and from the National Center on Accessing the General Curriculum (NCAC), pursuant to cooperative agreement #H324H990004 under CFDA 84.324H between the Center for Applied Special Technologies (CAST) and the U.S. Department of Education, Office of Special Education Programs (OSEP). The opinions expressed herein are the author's; they do not necessarily reflect the position or policy of the Carnegie Corporation or of OSEP, and no endorsement should be inferred. The author holds the copyright for this paper and all rights pertaining thereto.

2. For example, of the seven states in which data for 1998 show that minority students outnumber white students in special education—Hawaii, California, Louisiana, Mississippi, New Mexico, South Carolina, and Texas (Office of Special Education Programs [OSEP], 2000, Table AA3)—all but California had exit exams in 1997–1998 (NRC, 1999), and California has since decided to administer exit tests as well. In the nine states where OSEP data for 1998 show that minority students represent 40 percent to 50 percent of special education enrollments—Alabama, Alaska, Arizona, Delaware, Florida, Georgia, Maryland, New York, and North Carolina (OSEP, 2000, Table AA3)—five (Alabama, Florida, Georgia, New York, and North Carolina) had exit exams in 1998 (NRC, 1999) and the remaining four have since decided to adopt them (American Federation of Teachers [AFT], 2001).

3. The new federal statute defines graduation rates in terms of the percentage of secondary school students who earn standard diplomas in the customary amount of time (No Child Left Behind Act, 2002).

4. Pass rates for each year would be lower if New York's calculations included all students with disabilities who enrolled that year, rather than only those who completed high school that year, and if the calculations included students with disabilities who had once been part of that year's graduating class but had dropped out or been retained in grade and thus had not completed high school that year. In either case the same numerator would be divided by a larger denominator and the resulting pass rate would be lower.

5. The data on students with disabilities were furnished upon request by Jeffrey Nellhaus, Associate Commissioner for Student Testing, Massachusetts Department of Education, by email dated November 16, 2001. I am grateful to Mr. Nellhaus. Similar data by race and ethnicity are publicly available in the report cited above (Massachusetts Department of Education, 2001); a student who has passed both tests is referred to as one "earning a competency determination."

6. See note 2 for further information about the source of data on minority representation among special education students in California.

7. Since "all seniors" includes students with disabilities, who in effect are counted as part of both groups, the actual difference between students with disabilities and *nondisabled* students is even higher than Alabama's figures suggest.

8. These include "state standards by grade, assessment tests linked to these standards, good systems for providing feedback to teachers and principals, some accountability measures, and deregulation of the teaching environment" (Grissmer et al., 2000, p. 58). The same study found that after controlling for family characteristics, results on the 1996 fourth-grade NAEP test showed black students in Texas outscoring black students in the other forty-nine states; white students in Texas outscoring white students in the other forty-nine states; and Latino students outscoring Latino students in forty-five of the other forty-nine states (Grissmer et al., 2000, p. 72).

9. This appears to be the case in New York. Personal conversation with James Kadamus, Deputy Commissioner of Education, New York, June 2000.

10. Ysseldyke et al. (1998) compare the performance of students with disabilities with that of "all" students, which means that students with disabilities are being counted in each group. Since students with disabilities have lower pass rates than nondisabled students, the 35–40 percentage point difference is smaller than what one would have found by comparing students with disabilities and students without disabilities. The gap between students with disabilities and students without disabilities, had it been calculated, would thus have been even higher than the 35–40 percentage points reported.

11. The previous section also notes, however, that pass rates on state tests are often not confirmed by scores on other tests, such as NAEP, that supposedly measure much of the same knowledge and skills as state tests, and that state-test pass rates would be lower if states accounted more fully for dropouts, retained students, and other students who are sometimes not included when pass rates are calculated.

12. That some of these data come from ninth-, tenth-, or eleventh-grade students, who still have time to acquire the requisite knowledge and skills, reduces only partially the seriousness of such high failure rates.

13. The examples offered in one study (Council of Chief State School Officers [CCSSO], 2001, pp. 24–25) show a .37 overlap in one state between instruction and the state fourth-grade math test, and a .33 overlap in one state between instruction and the state eighth-grade science test. The other recent report, while providing specific information on overlap in only one unnamed state, notes that in that state "instructional content was

not very well aligned with either the state test or the NAEP test for Grade 8 science (.17 for the state test, and .18 for the NAEP test)" (Blank, Porter, & Smithson, 2001, p. 26).

14. As the NRC study (1999) notes, "High-stakes testing programs should routinely include a well-designed evaluation component. Policymakers should monitor both the intended and unintended consequences of high stakes assessments on all students and on significant subgroups of students, including minorities, English-language learners, and students with disabilities" (p. 281).

REFERENCES

Alabama Department of Education. (2001, April 25). *Alabama high schools exceed expectations on new higher standards graduation exam.* Montgomery: Author.

Alaska Department of Education. (2001). *Statewide spring 2001 HSGQE student test results.* Juneau: Author.

Allington, R. (2000, May 10). Letters: On special education accommodations. *Education Week,* p. 48.

Allington, R., & McGill-Franzen, A. (1992). Unintended effects of reform in New York. *Educational Policy, 6,* 397–414.

American Educational Research Association. (2000). *AERA position statement concerning high-stakes testing in pre-K–12 education* [On-line]. Available: http//www.aera.net. about/policy/stakes.htm

American Educational Research Association, American Psychological Association, & National Council on Measurement in Education. (1999). *Standards for educational and psychological testing.* Washington, DC: American Psychological Association.

American Federation of Teachers. (1999). *Making standards matter 1999.* Washington, DC: Author.

American Federation of Teachers. (2001). *Making standards matter 2001: A fifty-state report on efforts to implement a standards-system.* Washington, DC: Author.

Benton, J. (2001, May 20–24). Falling through the cracks: Dropout figures vary with formula. *Dallas Morning News,* p. 1.

Blair, J. (2002, February 13). Citing deficit, governor now proposes Wis. delay exam. *Education Week,* p. 23.

Blank, R., Porter, A., & Smithson, J. (2001). *New tools for analyzing teaching, curriculum and standards in mathematics and science: Results from survey of enacted curriculum project final report.* Washington, DC: Council of Chief State School Officers.

Boser, U. (2000, June 7). Teaching to the test? *Education Week,* pp. 1, 10.

Brennan, R., Kim, J., Wenz-Gross, M., & Siperstein, G. (2001). The relative equitability of high-stakes testing versus teacher-assigned grades: An analysis of the Massachusetts Comprehensive Assessment System (MCAS). *Harvard Educational Review, 71,* 173–216.

Carnoy, M., Loeb, S., & Smith, T. (2001, January 13). *Do higher test scores in Texas make for better high school outcomes?* Paper prepared for the forum of The Civil Rights Project at Harvard University and Achieve, Inc., Dropouts in America: How severe is the problem? What do we know about intervention and prevention? Harvard University, Cambridge, MA.

Citizens' Commission on Civil Rights. (2001). *Closing the deal: A preliminary report on state compliance with final assessment and accountability requirements under the Improving America's Schools Act of 1994.* Washington, DC: Author.

Clarke, M., Haney, W., & Madaus, G. (2000). High-stakes testing and high school completion. *National Board on Educational Testing and Public Policy, 1*(3), 1–11.

Cohen, M. (2001, January 19). *Review of state assessment systems for Title 1.* Memorandum to Chief State School Officers from the Assistant Secretary for Elementary and Secondary Education, U.S. Department of Education. Available at http://www.ed.gov/offices/OESE

Council of Chief State School Officers. (2001). *Using data on enacted curriculum in mathematics and science: Sample results from a study of classroom practices and subject content* (Summary Report from Survey of Enacted Curriculum Project). Washington, DC: Author.

Dailey, D., Zantal-Wiener, K., & Roach, V. (2000). *Reforming high school learning: The effect of the standards movement on secondary students with disabilities.* Alexandria, VA: Center for Policy Research on the Impact of General and Special Education Reform.

Debra P. v. Turlington, 474 F. Supp. 244 (M.D. Fla. 1979); aff'd in part and rev'd in part, 644 F.2d 397 (5th Cir. 1981); rem'd, 564 F. Supp. 177 (M.D. Fla. 1983); aff'd, 730 F.2d 1405 (11th Cir. 1984).

Elmore, R. (2000). *Building a new structure school leadership.* Washington, DC: Albert Shanker Institute.

GI Forum v. Texas Education Agency, 87 F. Supp. 2d 667 (W.D. Tex. 2000).

Goertz, M., & Duffy, M. (2001). *Assessment and accountability systems in the 50 states: 1999–2000.* Philadelphia: Consortium for Policy Research in Education.

Gonzalez, P., & Carlson, E. (2001, April 30). *Preliminary results from the study of personnel needs in special education (SPeNSE).* Paper presented at the annual meeting of CSPD, Washington, DC. Available at www.spense.org

Grissmer, D., Flanigan, A., Kawata, J., & Williamson, S. (2000). *Improving student achievement: What state NAEP scores tell us.* Santa Monica, CA: Rand.

Guy, B., Shin, H., Lee, S., & Thurlow, M. (1999). *State graduation requirements for students with disabilities* (Technical Report No. 24). Minneapolis: University of Minnesota, National Center on Educational Outcomes.

Haney, W. (2001, January 13). *Revisiting the myth of the Texas miracle in education: Lessons about dropout research and dropout prevention.* Paper prepared for the forum of The Civil Rights Project of Harvard University and Achieve, Inc., Dropouts in America: How severe is the problem? What do we know about intervention and prevention? Harvard University, Cambridge, MA.

Hauser, R. (2001). Should we end social promotion? Truth and consequences. In G. Orfield & M. Kornhaber (Eds.), *Raising standards or raising barriers? Inequality and high-stakes testing in education* (pp. 151–178). New York: Century Foundation Press.

Improving America's Schools Act of 1994, 20 U.S.C. sections 6301 et seq.

Individuals with Disabilities Education Act, 20 U.S.C. section 1401 et seq. (1997).

Jacob, B. (2001). Getting tough? The impact of high school graduation exams. *Educational Evaluation and Policy Analysis, 23,* 99–122.

Keller, B. (2000, April 12). More N.Y. special education students passing state tests. *Education Week,* p. 33.

Keller, B. (2001, October 3). Calif. to study whether graduation test should be delayed. *Education Week,* p. 24.

Klein, S., Hamilton, L., McCaffrey, D., & Stecher, B. (2000). *What do tests scores in Texas tell us?* Santa Monica, CA: Rand.

Koretz, D., & Barron, S. (1998). *The validity of gains on the Kentucky Instructional Results Information Systems (KIRIS).* Santa Monica, CA: Rand.

Koretz, D., & Berends, M. (2001). *Changes in high school grading standards in mathematics, 1982–1992.* Los Angeles, CA: Rand.

Koretz, D., & Hamilton L. (2001). *The performance of students with disabilities on New York's revised Regents Examination in English.* Los Angeles: National Center for Research on Evaluation, Standards, and Student Testing.

Koretz, D., Linn, R., Dunbar, S., & Shepard, L. (1991, April). *The effects of high-stakes testing on achievement: Preliminary findings about generalization across tests.* Paper presented at the annual meeting of the American Educational Research Association, Chicago.

Lee, J. (1998, December 4). *Using high-stakes test results to give disadvantaged kids access to outstanding responsive teachers.* Paper presented at The Harvard Civil Rights Project/ Teachers College conference on high-stakes testing and civil rights, New York.

Lillard, D., & DeCicca, P. (2001). Higher standards, more dropouts? Evidence within and across time. *Economics of Education Review, 20,* 459–474.

Linn, R. (2000). Assessments and accountability. *Educational Researcher 29*(2), 4–16.

Linn, R. (2001). *The design and evaluation of educational assessment and accountability systems.* Los Angeles: National Center for Research on Evaluation, Standards, and Student Testing.

Madaus, G., & Clarke, M. (2001). The adverse impact of high-stakes testing on minority students: Evidence from one hundred years of test data. In G. Orfield & M. Kornhaber (Eds.), *Raising standards or raising barriers? Inequality and high stakes testing in education* (pp. 85–106). New York: Century Fund.

Massachusetts Department of Education. (2001). *Spring 2001 MCAS tests: State results by race/ethnicity and student status.* Boston: Author

McLaughlin, M. (2000, June 30). *High-stakes testing and students with disabilities.* Paper presented at the National Research Council conference on the role of the law in achieving high standards for all, Washington, DC.

Mehrens, W. A. (1998, April). *Consequences of assessment: What is the evidence?* Paper presented at the annual meeting of the American Educational Research Association, San Diego.

Murnane, R., & Levy, F. (2001). Will standards-based reforms improve the education of children of color? *National Tax Journal, 54,* 401–416.

National Academy of Education. (1995). *Improving education through standards-based reform* (M. McLaughlin, L. Shepard, & J. O'Day, Eds.). Washington, DC: Author.

National Center for Education Statistics. (2001). *The condition of education 2001.* Washington, DC: U.S. Government Printing Office.

National Research Council. (1997). *Educating one and all: Students with disabilities and standards-based reform* (L. M. McDonnell, M. J. McLaughlin, & P. Morison, Eds.). Washington, DC: National Academy Press.

National Research Council. (1999). *High stakes: Testing for tracking, promotion, and graduation* (J. Heubert & R. Hauser, Eds.). Committee on Appropriate Test Use. Washington, DC: National Academy Press.

National Research Council. (2001). *Understanding dropouts: Statistics, strategies, and high-stakes testing* (A. Beatty, U. Neisser, W. Trent, & J. Heubert, Eds.). Washington, DC: National Academy Press.

Natriello, G., & Pallas A. (2001). The development and impact of high stakes testing. In G. Orfield & M. Kornhaber (Eds.), *Raising standards or raising barriers: Inequality and high-stakes testing in public education* (pp. 19–38). New York: Century Foundation Press.

New York Department of Education, Office of Vocational and Educational Services for Students with Disabilities. (2000). *2000 pocket book of goals and results for individuals with disabilities.* Albany: New York Department of Education.

New York Department of Education, Office of Vocational and Educational Services for Students with Disabilities. (2001). *2001 pocket book of goals and results for individuals with disabilities.* Albany: New York Department of Education.

No Child Left Behind Act, Public Law 107-110 (January 8, 2002).

Oakes, J., Gamoran, A., & Page, R. (1992). Curriculum differentiation: Opportunities, outcomes, and meanings. In P. Jackson (Ed.), *Handbook of research on curriculum* (pp. 570–608). New York: Macmillan.

Office for Civil Rights. (2000). *The use of tests when making high-stakes decisions for students: A resource guide for educators and policymakers.* Washington, DC: U.S. Department of Education.

Office of Special Education Programs. (2000). *To assure the free appropriate public education of all children with disabilities: Twenty-second annual report to Congress on the implementation of the Individuals with Disabilities Education Act.* Washington, DC: U.S. Department of Education.

Olson, L. (2001, January 24). States adjust high-stakes testing plans. *Education Week*, pp. 1, 18–19.

Porter, A., & Smithson, J. (2000, April). *Alignment of state testing programs, NAEP, and reports of teacher practice in grades 4 and 8.* Paper presented at the annual meeting of the American Educational Research Association, New Orleans.

Porter, A., & Smithson, J. (2001). *Defining, developing, and using curriculum indicators.* Philadelphia: Consortium for Policy Research in Education.

Quenemoen, R., Lehr, C., Thurlow, M., & Thompson, S. (2000). *Social promotion and students with disabilities: Issues and challenges in developing state policies* (NCEO Synthesis Report No. 34). Minneapolis: University of Minnesota, National Center on Educational Outcomes.

Riley, R. W. (2000, February 22). *Setting new expectations* (annual State of American Education address). Paper presented at Southern High School, Durham, NC.

Robelin, E. (2001, November 28). States sluggish on execution of 1994 ESEA. *Education Week*, pp. 1, 26–27.

Roderick, M., & Engel, M. (2001). The grasshopper and the ant: Motivational responses of low-achieving students to high-stakes testing. *Educational Evaluation and Policy Analysis, 23*, 197–228.

Sack, J. (2000, April 19). Researchers warn of possible pitfalls in spec. ed. testing. *Education Week*, p. 12.

Schrag, P. (2000). Too good to be true. *American Prospect, 4*(11), 46.

Shepard, L. A., & Smith, M. L. (Eds.). (1989). *Flunking grades: Research and policies on retention.* London: Falmer Press.

Shore, A., Madaus, G., & Clarke, M. (2000). Guidelines for policy research on educational testing. *National Board on Educational Testing and Public Policy, 1*(4), 1–7.

Stake, R. (1998, July). Some comments on assessment in U.S. education. *Educational Policy Analysis Archives* [Online] *6*(14). Available: http://epaa.asa.edu/epaa/v6n14.htm

Thompson, S., & Thurlow, M. (2001, June). *2001 state special education outcomes: A report on state activities at the beginning of a new decade.* Minneapolis: University of Minnesota, National Center on Educational Outcomes.

Thurlow, M., & Johnson, D. (2000). High-stakes testing of students with disabilities. *Journal of Teacher Education, 51,* 305–314.

Thurlow, M., Nelson, J., Teelucksingh, E., & Ysseldyke, J. (2000). *Where's Waldo? A third search for students with disabilities in state accountability reports* (Technical Report No. 25). Minneapolis: University of Minnesota, National Center on Educational Outcomes.

Thurlow, M., & Thompson, S. (1999). *Diploma options and graduation policies for students with disabilities.* Minneapolis: University of Minnesota, National Center on Educational Outcomes.

Viadero, D. (1999, October 6). Stanford report questions accuracy of tests. *Education Week,* p. 3.

Viadero, D. (2000, May 31). Testing system in Texas yet to get final grade. *Education Week,* p. 1.

Weckstein, P. (1999). School reform and enforceable rights to an adequate education. In J. Heubert (Ed.), *Law and school reform: Six strategies for promoting educational equity* (pp. 306–389). New Haven, CT: Yale University Press.

Wise, L., Sipes, D. E., Harris, C., George, C., Ford J., & Sun, S. (2002). *Independent evaluation of the California High School Exit Examination (CAHSEE): Analysis of the 2001 administration.* Sacramento: California Department of Education. Available at http://www.cde.ca.gov/statetests/cahsee/2001humrroreport.html

Ysseldyke, J., Thurlow, M., Langenfeld, M., Nelson, J., Teelucksingh, E., & Seyfarth, A. (1998). *Educational results for students with disabilities: What do the data tell us?* (Technical Report No. 23). Minneapolis: University of Minnesota, National Center on Educational Outcomes.

CHAPTER EIGHT

Legal Challenges to Inappropriate and Inadequate Special Education for Minority Children[1]

DANIEL J. LOSEN

KEVIN G. WELNER

INTRODUCTION

Special education can provide vital benefits to children who need supports and services. For some children reality may approach this ideal, but many students who are deemed eligible to receive special education services are unnecessarily isolated, stigmatized, and confronted with fear and prejudice, regardless of race. In addition, for minority children, special education is far too often a vehicle for segregation and degradation that results from misdiagnosis and inappropriate labeling.[2]

For these minority students, the civil rights movement brought about critical legal protections. Among the most important was Title VI of the Civil Rights Act of 1964, which provides that "[n]o person in the United States shall, on the ground of race, color or national origin, be excluded from participation in, be denied benefits of, or be subjected to discrimination under any program or activity receiving Federal financial assistance."[3] Inspired by such achievements, grassroots activists and lawyers embarked upon a successful campaign on behalf of students with disabilities,[4] culminating in the passage, in 1975, of the legislation now known as the Individuals with Disabilities Education Act (IDEA).[5]

Despite important legislative and judicial progress over the last thirty-seven years, minority students remain doubly vulnerable to discrimination. First, they tend to receive inequitable treatment in segregated and unequal schools.[6] Second, they are put disproportionately at risk of receiving inadequate or inappropriate special education services because of systemic problems with special education identification and placement.[7] While we focus in this chapter on the latter issue, we are mindful of the former.

The following exploration of legal issues emphasizes systemic challenges, in part because of our broader concerns about inequality of educational opportunity and in part because of our awareness that poor and minority parents are reliant on systemic change due to their limited resources for pursuing independent individual legal challenges. Discrimination based on disability and race/ ethnicity has been targeted by powerful laws, but civil rights litigants have seldom used these laws in concert. This chapter describes the relative strengths of Title VI and disability law, as well as the added benefits of combining these two sources of protection to bring systemic challenges.

This chapter is divided into two parts. The first part reviews legal challenges to overrepresentation and to inadequate or inappropriate special education services for minority students and explores past challenges under disability law and under Title VI. The second part examines new ways of combining Title VI with disability law and the possible advantages of a combined approach. Part two also considers how the new standards-based reform movement can be leveraged to achieve greater equality of educational opportunity for minority students deemed eligible for special education services.

This chapter highlights the strengths of various legal challenges and reaches three main conclusions, all of which are grounded in the fact that special education identification and placement is a long process that begins in the regular education classroom and involves many interconnected factors and subjective decisions. The first conclusion is that, given the relative strength of disability law, complaints on behalf of minorities harmed in the process of identification or placement are generally strongest when built on a combination of disability law and Title VI. In reaching this conclusion we acknowledge that the U.S. Supreme Court's opinion in *Alexander v. Sandoval,* handed down in 2001, may limit this combined approach to the realm of administrative complaints.[8] The Court in *Sandoval* held that private litigants may not directly rely on Title VI's implementing regulations to file a discrimination claim in a formal court of law. This highly technical ruling forecloses the possibility of directly adding a Title VI discriminatory impact claim to a court challenge rooted in disability law, but it would not limit the ability to do so when filing a claim with the U.S. Department of Education's Office for Civil Rights (OCR).[9]

Further, the holding in *Sandoval* leaves open one possible legal avenue for private enforcement of rights set forth in the Title VI regulations. Another civil rights statute enables private parties to sue state actors responsible for the "deprivation of any rights, privileges, or immunities secured by the Constitution and laws."[10] In the words of Justice Stevens (dissenting in *Sandoval*), "[T]his case is something of a sport. Litigants who in the future wish to enforce the Title VI regulations against state actors in all likelihood must only reference § 1983 to obtain relief."[11] In fact, one court has, since *Sandoval*, allowed plaintiffs to use §1983 to invoke the Title VI regulations.[12] Because of this alternative approach to enforcing Title VI rights, the Court's *Sandoval* decision presently has an uncertain impact on the combined litigation we suggesth. This chapter's discussion of legal actions should therefore be read as concerning actions enforcing Title VI regulations via § 1983. That said, advocates must be wary of this legal avenue, since it is highly susceptible to an eventual Supreme Court decision foreclosing this possibility and perhaps striking down the "disparate impact" cause of action altogether.[13]

The second conclusion is that isolating one particular step in the identification and placement process as the cause of a racially identifiable harm may limit plaintiffs to ineffective, marginal remedies. Therefore, legal challenges will generate the best remedies when they redress the system of inseparable factors that drive overrepresentation of minority students.

The third conclusion is that standards-based education reforms, as embraced by almost every state, provide officially adopted benchmarks for progress and set (in some states, at least) high expectations for all schools and students.[14] These benchmarks offer courts persuasive and specific evidence of educational adequacy. Consequently, standards-based reforms provide a compelling new means for advocates to strengthen the entitlement claims of minority students and leverage comprehensive, outcomes-based remedies for all students subjected to discriminatory school practices. For example, successful plaintiffs could use standards benchmarks to set concrete compensatory goals, monitor settlements, and ensure that agreed-upon input remedies yield actual benefits for children.

LEGAL CHALLENGES TO MINORITY OVERREPRESENTATION

In the late 1960s and throughout the 1970s and early 1980s, successful lawsuits such as *Hobson v. Hansen*,[15] *Diana v. State Board of Education*,[16] and *Larry P. v. Riles*[17] emphasized the discriminatory treatment of overrepresented Latino and African American students in racially isolated special education classes. The past few decades have witnessed a scaling back of legal avenues for challenging racially discriminatory practices. For instance, courts have expressed reluctance to side with Title VI plaintiffs where remedies entail intervening in the "local control" of public schools.[18] However, coinciding with this narrowing of available Title VI causes of action has been the growing strength of disability law. While this chapter argues that Title VI challenges are still worth pursuing and expanding, especially with respect to administrative complaints, it begins with a review of challenges to disability law violations, which in some cases are easier to prove.

DISABILITY LAW

Three laws—Section 504 of the Rehabilitation Act of 1973, Title II of the Americans with Disabilities Act, and the Individuals with Disabilities in Education Act—provide procedural and substantive protection for students who have been misclassified and/or placed in overly restrictive settings. Section 504[19] and Title II of the Americans with Disabilities Act[20] are federal antidiscrimination laws that prohibit discrimination based on disability and are applicable in public schools. To simplify the analyses here, all further references in this chapter to Section 504 can be assumed to cover Title II as well, due to parallel language and interpretations of the laws.

IDEA includes provisions that grant funds for special education implementation and ensure that all states provide entitlements and procedural rights to eligible individuals and their parents or guardians. IDEA also includes detailed requirements regarding reporting and monitoring of its provisions by state governments. Among the IDEA requirements are those requiring states to intervene by revising policies, procedures, and practices where significant racial disproportionality exists in special education identification and placement.[21]

The 1997 IDEA amendments reemphasized the act's preference that students with disabilities be taught in general education classrooms.[22] Further, the act's congressional findings noted that IDEA's successful implementation "has been impeded by low expectations" and acknowledged substantial concerns about students with cognitive and emotional/behavioral disabilities who are taught in restrictive, segregated classrooms.[23]

FREE AND APPROPRIATE PUBLIC EDUCATION
UNDER IDEA AND SECTION 504

By law, all students with disabilities are entitled to be educated with their regular education peers to the maximum extent appropriate given each student's special education needs.[24] This ensures exposure to the same curriculum, the same high academic standards, and the same opportunities for socialization. The shorthand version of this concept is taken from language in the IDEA: a Free and Appropriate Public Education (FAPE) in the Least Restrictive Environment (LRE). The concept of LRE is subsumed under the definition of "appropriate" in FAPE.

Individually, some students clearly benefit from educational settings separate from the regular classroom. Accordingly, IDEA authorizes student placements based on individual needs, rather than on disability type (such as "educationally mentally retarded"). The right to an individual eligibility determination and subsequent Individualized Education Program (IEP), along with the right to be educated with regular education peers to the "maximum extent appropriate," lie at the heart of IDEA.

The U.S. Department of Education (DOE) Office for Special Education Programs (OSEP) is charged with ensuring that states properly enforce the provisions of IDEA. Furthermore, the DOE's Office for Civil Rights regards the failure to provide FAPE as a form of disability discrimination under Section 504.[25]

APPROPRIATE AND MEANINGFUL ACCESS

IDEA also emphasizes that special education is not a place—rather, it consists of supports and services.[26] The services provided should ensure, not diminish, access to the general curriculum to the maximum extent appropriate. Therefore, a decision to place any student in an educational setting that is more restrictive than the regular education classroom can only be justified in terms of individual benefits to the student, not in terms of administrative convenience to the school.[27] However, it is also true that, without needed aids and services in the classroom, or without regular education teachers who can deliver instruction in ways that meet individual students' needs, schools cannot be considered to be providing "meaningful" access.

Minority students deemed eligible for special education are significantly more likely than their white counterparts to wind up in substantially separate settings with a watered-down curriculum. They are in double jeopardy of experiencing a denial of educational opportunity, first on account of racial discrimination and again on account of their disability status. Not surprisingly, overrepresentation data for black students in special education mirror overrepresentation in such undesirable categories as dropping out,[28] suspension and expulsion,[29] low-track placement,[30] involvement with juvenile justice,[31] and underrepresentation in Advanced Placement (AP) and gifted classes.[32] The consistency of this pattern of denial and restriction suggests that underlying political and social forces connect these phenomena.[33]

Moreover, minority students tend to be overrepresented in certain categories of disability while underrepresented in others. As a general rule, classifications that carry greater stigma and entail more restrictive placements, such as "emotionally disturbed" and "mild mental retardation," have disproportionately been the preserve of students of color.

There are important differences between the legal requirements of Sections 504 and IDEA relevant to concern about overrepresentation and underservicing. For instance, the assurance of a FAPE under IDEA applies only to students who, because of their disability, need special education and related services.[34] Section 504's protections, on the other hand, include all students covered by IDEA, as well as students whose disabilities substantially impair one or more major life activities, or have a record of a disability, or are regarded as having a disability.[35] A student in need of counseling only outside of the classroom might not be covered under IDEA but would likely be covered under Section 504.[36] Most individuals protected under Section 504 are entitled to a free appropriate public education in much the same way that students with qualifying disabilities are entitled to FAPE under IDEA.[37]

If a minority student were identified as educationally mentally retarded but did not, in fact, have a disability, that student would not need special education services. Although under a strict interpretation such a student might not be entitled to a FAPE under the IDEA, he or she, particularly if harmed by the wrongful placement, should be eligible for FAPE under Section 504.

At a minimum, misidentified students are protected from discrimination that results from "having a record of" or "being regarded as having" a disability. The Section 504 regulations, for example, explain the coverage for a nondisabled individual as follows: "*[H]as a record of* such an impairment means *has a history of,* or *has been misclassified as having,* a mental or physical impairment that substantially limits one or more major life activities."[38] Accordingly, nondisabled students who were treated by a school as if they were disabled fall under Section 504's definition of "qualified handicapped person."[39]

Overrepresentation directly concerns the inadequacy of special education and indirectly implicates the inadequacy of general education, especially where that general education leads to wholesale misidentification. In this regard, Section 504 has two litigation advantages over IDEA. It affords substantive compensatory remedies to misidentified nondisabled minority students pursuant to its discrimination protections, and it entitles some misidentified students to be eligible for FAPE under its broader definition of "handicapped."[40]

Because of their more expansive reach, the Section 504 regulations provide an important vehicle for systemic challenges seeking comprehensive remedies for minority students who have been underserved and misidentified. Many students wrongfully identified as having a disability can seek compensatory remedies under Section 504 (and sometimes Title VI), which enables them to make up for time lost and other harm incurred as a result of the school's misidentification. In related contexts, court-imposed solutions have embodied the notion that victims of misidentification are entitled to much more than the right to return to the regular education classroom.[41]

Another advantage to Section 504 claims is that, in defining "appropriate" in Free Appropriate Public Education, the regulations promulgated under Section 504 include regular or special education and related aides and services that are "designed to meet individual educational needs of handicapped persons as adequately as the needs of non-handicapped persons are met."[42] Misidentified and underserved minority plaintiffs seeking regular education reform thus have a foothold in the Section 504 regulations.

PRIVATE ENFORCEMENT OF IDEA

According to the National Council on Disabilities, no state is even close to full compliance with IDEA.[43] This federally funded organization also notes that the practical burden of IDEA enforcement rests heavily on the shoulders of individual parents and children.[44] For instance, IDEA gives parents the legal right to refuse to consent to an evaluation of their child, thereby preventing special education identification. Parents acting on behalf of their children may also enforce IDEA through private litigation. They can bring individual actions against their school districts, as well as against their states, if their children are not being provided with beneficial services. In addition, given the evidence suggesting that many minority students are denied FAPE or LRE because of misclassification or denial of entitlements, advocates would likely be on steady ground should they decide to file both individual and systemic challenges.

Private individual lawsuits, however, can often take years to resolve. Given the pragmatic constraints on court challenges, poor and minority children with disabilities and their families often find that the legal services needed to avail themselves of such IDEA protections are far beyond their financial reach, and that they are "frequently not represented as players in the process."[45] Private litigants, consequently, are more likely to be wealthier white parents who have the resources to sue. Although any parent can raise systemic issues, plaintiffs more commonly challenge specific failures and seek remedies that primarily impact their own children.

Moreover, individual challenges seeking individual remedies generally must exhaust state administrative processes before a lawsuit can be filed in state or federal court—even when the action alleges that an individual failure is rooted in a systemic violation.[46] For example, individuals seeking to remedy a specific disciplinary decision directed at a special education child must exhaust the administrative remedies spelled out under IDEA and under the state laws and regulations implementing IDEA.[47] On the other hand, challenges seeking systemic remedies are not necessarily required to exhaust administrative procedures. Courts have allowed such actions against a school, district, or state based on their failure to provide IDEA's unique procedural rights.[48]

This difference in exhaustion requirements, as well as the lack of practical options for aggrieved parents with minimal resources, helps to explain why systemic class action challenges under IDEA are especially important to poor and minority students with disabilities. Such challenges may be combined with allegations of discrimination pursuant to different treatment and disparate impact theory. But challenges pertaining to exclusion from participation and/or denial of benefits may still offer unique opportunities for driving IDEA and Section 504 compliance.

OVERREPRESENTATION ISSUES IN DESEGREGATION CASES

Despite diminishing opportunities to raise challenges pursuant to desegregation orders, several cases do confront overrepresentation issues in the context of dual (racially segregated) systems. This approach is more than a historical curiosity; hundreds of school districts remain under court supervision[49] or remain party to administrative agreements to desegregate with the U.S. Department of Education.

Once desegregation began in earnest—following enactment of the 1964 Civil Rights Act, the 1965 Elementary and Secondary Education Act, and cases such as *Swann*[50]—schools exhibited a wave of within-school race discrimination, which took the form of tracking, abuse of expulsions and suspensions, and special education placements in substantially separate classrooms.[51] Early desegregation opinions reported widespread abuses involving minority students with average and above-average IQ scores being relegated to isolated classes for mentally retarded students.[52] This use of racially discriminatory special education placement to circumvent *Brown*'s mandate was built on at least two pervasive normative beliefs: the stereotypical belief of white intellectual superiority, and a well-grooved pattern of paternalism and animus toward people with disabilities. The predictable consequence of these beliefs was that many special education programs existed as segregated ghettos within public schools.[53]

Present-day minority overrepresentation in special education in a given school district may evidence the continuing impact of a prior dual system in that district as well as a veiled continuation of that system. Courts have ruled that school districts that carried out an intentionally segregative policy in one area of operation are presumed to have acted intentionally with regard to all other areas resulting in segregation.[54] Courts presume intent when significant disparities exist and (at least in theory) order remedies designed to dismantle formerly dual systems "root and branch."[55] Based on these precedents, challenges to minority overrepresentation in special education may take advantage of a presumed intent framework if the district is under a desegregation order.[56] Legal claims linking overrepresentation in special education to a school district's previous operation of a segregated system have successfully prompted courts to require school districts to remedy racial disparities in special education.[57] However, given that courts have also refused to recognize connections to the prior de jure system, plaintiffs taking this approach will be expected to provide strong evidence establishing the link.

The overrepresentation issue now often arises as an aspect of judicial review of desegregation consent decrees. In one recent example, Alabama District Court Judge Myron Thompson, in *Lee v. Macon County*, consolidated the issue of unitary status and reviewed eleven school districts.[58] On August 30, 2000, the district court issued revised consent decrees in all eleven cases, addressing the state's persistent problem of minority student overrepresentation in special education. The decrees are comprehensive, including remedies to overrepresentation in the categories of "emotionally conflicted, specific learning disability, and mental retardation." Alabama, which has had one of the worst track records of any state in terms of statistical overrepresentation of African Americans,[59] agreed to extensive corrective measures. The Alabama consent decree included the following reforms:

A. *To conduct awareness and prereferral training.* Teachers will be made aware of the tendency to refer minority students disproportionately, and receive training in how to use certain teaching and behavior management techniques that will improve learning for all students and diminish overreliance on special education to reach children that may pose challenges in the classroom.

B. *To monitor the agreement, including yearly status conferences.* The state will collect data for its own evaluation and report these data to the parties.

C. *To make certain changes to the Alabama Code.* The IDEA encourages, but does not require, prereferral intervention. The Alabama Code will go much further and require prereferral intervention for six weeks, in most cases, before a child can be referred for special education.

D. *To revamp the assessment.* The new code also revises criteria for determining specific learning disabilities, emotionally conflicted as well as mentally retarded (MR). It also requires that home behavior assessments be attempted for students suspected of MR. Other contextual factors must be considered for all three categories to rule out other causes of low achievement that are not actually rooted in a disability.

E.   *To provide culturally sensitive psychometrics and training.* New measures of aptitude that are culturally sensitive will be used in determining eligibility for minority students. Psychologists and school personnel will be trained in their proper administration.

F.   *To allocate funds to accomplish the decree's goals using a state improvement grant.* The funds are not for the changes in the decree except for the piloting of a mentoring program. Many of the changes in the decree will be funded through a state improvement grant.

G.   *To require reevaluation of all borderline MR students.* Minority students who were borderline MR (IQ of 65 or above, or not assessed with an adaptive behavior measure) will be retested and others will be given the option. Students who were wholly misidentified will be provided with supports and services to aid them in their transition back into regular education classrooms. Students who no longer meet the new code's criteria for MR or are deemed no longer eligible under the terms of the new agreement would be evaluated for possible placement if they were subsequently deemed eligible in another disability category.

Plaintiffs have not always prevailed when bringing such claims in the desegregation context. In *Vaughns v. Board of Education of Prince George's County,* for instance, the plaintiffs unsuccessfully alleged, among other things, that the disproportionate number of African American students in special education programs should be redressed as a vestige of the prior intentional discrimination.[60] Although the court acknowledged a disturbing statistical overrepresentation of black children among those classified as educationally mentally retarded, or EMR (African Americans comprised 47.4% of the student population and 67.7% of EMR students), that court found no violation of the desegregation order.

These desegregation cases taken together offer important lessons for advocates. On the one hand, the holding in *Vaughns* offers a reminder that many judges are extraordinarily reluctant to intervene in educational policy decisions, preferring to defer to the discretion of local decisionmakers. On the other hand, some cases[61] point to the systemic nature of discrimination, while *Lee* offers the promise of systemic, meaningful remedies to such discrimination. The following two sections continue building the argument for comprehensive challenges to overrepresentation.

DISPARATE IMPACT ANALYSIS IN EDUCATION CASES

Plaintiffs challenging racially discriminatory special education overrepresentation can also bring a § 1983 action invoking regulations promulgated by the U.S. Department of Education under Title VI. Such actions allow plaintiffs to rely on statistical evidence of discrimination; plaintiffs are not required to either allege or prove that the defendant intentionally discriminated.

Specifically, the Title VI regulations describe an "effects test" prohibiting the use of "criteria or methods of administration which have the effect of subjecting individuals to discrimination or have the purpose or effect of defeating or substantially impairing accomplishment of the objectives of the educational program."[62] Similar effects-test regulations exist with regard to discrimination on the basis of disability (Section 504)[63] and gender (Title IX).[64] These gender and disability protections may also be germane to a minority overrepresentation case under "disparate impact" legal theory.

PRIVATE ACTIONS

Courts conduct the following three-pronged analysis to determine whether the effects of a school district's policy or program violate the Title VI regulations.[65] First, the plaintiff must establish that a criteria or method of administration has both a negative and disparate impact on a protected class.[66] In legal parlance, this is referred to as establishing a *prima facie* case. If the *prima facie* case is established, the defendant district must demonstrate that the policy or practice at issue is an educational necessity. Upon such proof, the burden then shifts again to the plaintiff to demonstrate a less discriminatory alternative that can reasonably meet the defendant's "educationally necessary" goals.[67] Although a plaintiff is not required to prove that the defendant intended to discriminate, evidence of such intent can bolster the plaintiff's disparate impact claim.

It is important to note that, even before the recent *Alexander v. Sandoval* decision, private Title VI litigants encountered judges with some reluctance to apply the law as set forth above. For instance, in *Georgia State Conference of Branches of NAACP v. State of Georgia*, the court relied heavily on employment case law and theory to insist on a difficult particularity requirement.[68] Specifically, the court of appeals rejected a Title VI disparate impact challenge to the overrepresentation of minority students in EMR classes. The plaintiffs had claimed that nondisabled black students were misidentified as a result of improper procedures and test use. For evidence, the plaintiffs relied on the disparity between the number of black students in the general population and the number of black students identified as EMR and placed in separate classes.[69]

The court overruled the lower court finding that the plaintiffs had established a *prima facie* case, reasoning that the statistical analyses of plaintiffs' experts failed to establish the causal link between the particular code violations (and misinterpretations), the misidentification of black students, and the statistical racial disparity. The court suggested that the plaintiffs might have prevailed had they reviewed the files of similarly situated white students for the purpose of racial comparisons.

The *Georgia State Conference* decision suggests that advocates should present disproportionality arguments with as much particularity as possible whenever they attempt to tie causation to a given identifiable element in a process. However, requiring such a high degree of particularity may be inappropriate in special education overrepresentation cases. For a contrasting approach, consider *Larry P. v. Riles*, wherein the court found a disparity by comparing the percentage of black students in general education and in EMR placement.[70]

Further, studies have identified many interconnected and often highly subjective factors that contribute to minority overrepresentation.[71] IQ test disparity reliance, testing biases of school psychologists, school politics, dynamics of the special education team, failure to communicate to parents in the dominant language of the home, lack of adequate counseling services, poor behavior management skills on the part of teachers, inadequate reading programs, lack of prereferral interventions, stereotypes, animus, overuse of retention, funding mechanisms, and resource inequalities are just some of the many, often race-linked, factors under the school's control that contribute to minority overrepresentation.[72] Many of these factors are interdependent and confound one another for the purposes of statistical analysis.

Tying together the relationship between regular and special education classrooms, a trial court judge in New York noted that adequacy arguments under state constitutions and statutes may bolster comprehensive remedies in bringing combined legal challenges to inappropriate or inadequate special education services. Specifically, Justice Leland Degrasse Jr., in *Campaign for Fiscal Equity v. New York*,[73] highlighted as evidence of inadequacy in the regular education program the fact that far greater proportions of students in New York City were assigned to special education classrooms in restrictive settings than were their suburban counterparts.[74] While the decision did not challenge the overrepresentation of minorities in special education directly, it did take the important step of equating overrepresentation in special education with regular education inadequacy.[75] Moreover, the plaintiffs prevailed on their disparate impact Title VI claim. Although this case was reversed on June 25, 2002, New York's Supreme Court of the Appelate Division stated that improper identification and restrictive placements for special education "is a problem of the educational system. . . ."[76] Thus, both decisions described minority overrepresentation and isolation in special education as a problem rooted in the inadequacies of regular education, although the lower court's interpretation of New York's adequacy requirements was overruled.

OCR ENFORCEMENT POLICY AND PRACTICE

Outside the desegregation context, legal challenges to overrepresentation are most often raised in the form of OCR-initiated compliance reviews and resolution agreements, as well as through private complaints investigated by OCR. OCR has an affirmative legal duty to intervene and remedy potentially discriminatory methods of special education administration. This duty includes an obligation to consider whether less discriminatory alternatives exist whenever a district defends a policy causing a disparity as educationally necessary.[77] While the agency responds to private complaints, its interventions in special education practices are usually based on indices of significant disproportionality that it derives from an annual sampling of school districts. Its investigations typically emphasize either different treatment or disparate impact analysis under Title VI, but the agency sometimes exercises its jurisdiction to combine this with a Section 504 analysis.

As a matter of policy, OCR seeks to resolve disputes through a "partnership process" without issuing a letter of violation against the school district.[78] Consequently, the agency rarely issues findings of violation, instead reaching negotiated agreements with the districts. There are clear benefits to this approach, especially considering that effective long-term change is most likely when school district personnel are convinced to take the lead. However, to date this approach has failed to provide the sort of clear, widely circulated guidelines that would be provided by more direct and public enforcement efforts. Instead, the agency's lack of clarity has apparently resulted in a high degree of enforcement inconsistency, and both school officials and advocates are left guessing as to OCR's interpretation of its own regulations.

Another concern is that OCR is subject to bureaucratic and political pressures that limit the effectiveness of its enforcement activities. The impact of these pressures can be seen in a July 6, 1995, internal memorandum from then Assistant Secretary for Civil Rights Norma Cantú to all staff, entitled, "Minority Students and Special Education."[79] This memo offers a detailed outline of how to investigate possible violations under disparate treatment and disparate impact theory. Interestingly, it discusses a number of legal frameworks that combine Title VI with Section 504. These combined approaches would, as a general rule, involve more intensive investigations and more comprehensive remedies. After introducing this prospect, however, the memorandum cautiously recommends that the "approach . . . should be used only in selected cases" where preliminary data do not permit the investigation to be narrowed.[80] Accordingly, OCR has stated that when it receives complaints concerning minority issues in special education, the agency rarely investigates beyond the specific issues raised by the complainant.[81] The memo suggests an agency preference for limiting investigations when possible because "extensive data would [otherwise] likely need to be collected."[82]

However, a review of OCR resolution agreements, in addition to discussions with attorneys who have pursued complaints with the agency, suggests three types of troubling inconsistencies in agency agreements. First, OCR enforcement varies in terms of the depth of the investigation. Second, and related to the first, there is inconsistency in terms of the comprehensiveness of the remedy sought by the OCR. Third, OCR's rigor in subsequent monitoring appears to vary considerably.

Most important, if public dissemination of enforcement activity happens at all, the evidence suggests it is on a very small scale. Therefore, OCR's preferences for negotiated resolution agreements, combined with its failure to proactively disseminate those agreements and other information about outcomes, monitoring, and enforcement policy to the public, severely mitigates any ripple effect from its usually narrow investigations and agreements. The preference for investigation and identification of particular violations over more systemic ones, combined with the preference for negotiated settlements rather than issuing letters of violation, has important practical implications. Furthermore, OCR presently has no system for reporting and recording minority special education cases within the agency.[83] This makes agency evaluation especially difficult for outsiders as well as agency officials. Such a low level of information access is particularly troubling, given the national dimension of the problem, the readily available case-tracking technology, and the fact that the agency has been aware of the problem for years.

COMBINING DISABILITY LAW WITH TITLE VI
TO DRIVE SYSTEMIC CHALLENGES

When Claims Might Be Linked

In cases that first establish a FAPE/LRE-based disability law violation, a Title VI claim—that is, an action grounded in § 1983 and the Title VI implementing regulations—can be added where minority children are overrepresented among those harmed by the disability violation. This is because once the FAPE violation is established for all disabled students, overrepresentation will mean that minority students are in the class disproportionately harmed by the violation. One advantage to this approach is that the violation is readily identifiable as a particular administrative method or practice causing disproportionate harm. A second advantage is that there can be no effective response of educational necessity proffered in defense of a systemic violation of FAPE.

A combined approach could, for instance, be forceful in challenging the overrepresentation of minority students in alternative schools ostensibly created to address discipline concerns. Special education students and minority students are overrepresented among students suspended and expelled from school.[84] Thus, minority children are doubly at risk of discrimination in discipline, first by race/ethnicity and again by disability. Because alternative schools sometimes fail to provide disabled students with any special education services whatsoever, disproportionate disciplinary placements of minority students in such settings are ripe for legal challenge.[85]

Based in part on such disciplinary concerns, the Florida Department of Education ordered a withholding or reduction of Palm Beach County's state and federal funding for students with disabilities.[86] Responding to a complaint on behalf of students with disabilities, filed March 3, 1999, the department found serious and systemic noncompliance with state and federal requirements for students with disabilities in the district's Alternative Education Programs.[87] The superintendent of the district later entered into a resolution agreement with OCR regarding a related race- and disability-based complaint. With regard to race, the OCR agreement paraphrased the complaint as follows: "[T]he District discriminates, on the basis of race, in the areas of discipline, general treatment, and the provision of educational opportunities. . . . [T]he District discriminates against students at [the alternative school], on the basis of disability because students are not provided an appropriate education."[88] In a letter to the complainant, OCR described finding "significant disproportion" by race in the number of African American students involved in incidents where law enforcement became involved, and significant disparities in the rate of referrals and the meting out of discipline to African American students for a wide range of offenses.[89]

Although some may welcome the growing number of alternative schools to educate students with problematic behavior, these substantially separate programs raise serious new concerns. To the extent that states often fail to monitor alternative education programs for IDEA compliance, systemic challenges sounding in both Title VI and disability law may be effective in curtailing the inappropriate use of these programs.

As a general matter, combined challenges could be useful where minority students are disparately harmed by systemic state and/or district disability law violations such as the following: a state's funding mechanism that creates incentives for restrictive placements; a state's or district's system of classification and placement that fails to consider for inclusion broad groups of students with disabilities, as in Illinois;[90] a district that routinely fails to meet time lines for writing and implementing IEPs for students it has deemed eligible for special education, as in Baltimore;[91] a state or district that fails to ensure that students' IEPs explain why the chosen placement is the least restrictive environment and to design steps for students' progress toward a lesser restrictive placement; a state that fails to ensure that all students with disabilities are included in statewide assessments and their scores reported publicly; a state or district, as in Palm Beach County, that places students in alternative schools with no certified special educators on staff; or a district that consistently fails to identify students with disabilities until after they have failed a promotion test and/or repeated a grade.

ADVANTAGES OF INCLUDING A DISPARATE IMPACT CLAIM

As demonstrated by the earlier survey of disability law challenges to inadequate services, misidentification, and minority overrepresentation, individuals who incurred harm within the special education system can seek direct remedies for that harm. However, this remedial approach focuses on only the most superficial symptoms of what may be serious, endemic problems. An approach that supplements disability law with Title VI's implementing regulations has greater potential—to focus inquiry and remediation at deeper layers of these problems, in particular racial inequities in regular and special education. That is to say, inclusion of a Title VI claim holds the potential to expand the litigation's scope beyond the particular disability law violation to the whole process that caused minority students to suffer the harm in disproportionate numbers.

Plaintiffs in such a comprehensive action would be better situated to seek outcome goals, such as reductions in dropout rates and improved academic achievement—goals that are crucial to overrepresented minority groups. Additionally, these plaintiffs could demand that the data used for monitoring compliance (or lack thereof) be disaggregated by race and ethnicity along with disability classification. This race and ethnicity data might also help plaintiffs monitor the efficacy of Title VI input remedies that seek to reduce rates of minority special education referrals, such as training in multicultural education for both regular and special education teachers.

Another benefit of combined Title VI/disability law litigation lies in its potential ripple effect—forcing nonparty states and districts to address their own

problems with racial disproportionality. Because of the visibility and seriousness of such litigation, observing states and districts might take proactive steps
to diminish all three problems—misidentification, misclassification, and inadequate services for minority students. Otherwise, given the many nonracial compliance issues facing states, and despite IDEA's new provisions, there is little incentive for states to focus on racial inequities in special education.

Combined approaches also hold an advantage with regard to the vital issue
of resources. As a practical matter, states or districts found liable for violating
disability law face politically difficult resource-distribution choices. Adding a
Title VI claim ensures that the needs of minority students, who are at greater
risk of suffering the harm, receive high priority in the remedy stage. More generally, adding the Title VI claim to a disability claim could result in important
priority-setting with regard to how and where the disability violations' remedies
are provided.

A final advantage to adding a Title VI claim is unique to challenges made
under Section 504. Remedies in such a combined action can include interventions in the regular education classroom, as well as changes to special education
practices and policy. To the extent that minority students are disproportionately subjected to inadequate reading and math instruction, and that such instructional resource inequities are among the causes of overrepresentation,[92]
remedies pursuant to Section 504 and Title VI on behalf of minority misclassified students could seek to require significant improvements in curriculum and teacher quality in those subject areas, targeted to classrooms serving
minority students.

ADDING DISABILITY CHALLENGES TO TITLE VI:
RETHINKING *GI FORUM*

The above discussion largely assumes disability law as the starting point. That
is, it examines the addition of Title VI claims to an action otherwise grounded
in disability law. However, the reverse should also be considered. To investigate
this possibility, this section uses *GI Forum v. Texas Education Agency*, a recent
Title VI case involving the high-stakes testing system in Texas.[93] The Texas
court was called on to determine the legality of the state's use of the Texas Assessment of Academic Skills (TAAS) as an exit exam in light of high dropout
rates, as well as racially disparate and high failure rates for minority test-takers.
Foundationally, the plaintiffs attempted to present their case in terms of the in-
justice of the state's denying a diploma to minority students who had already
been given passing grades by the state's teachers. The defendants prevailed, in
part because they were able to shift the court's attention from the disparate im-

pact to the general appropriateness and wisdom of the state's standards and testing regime.

The *GI Forum* defendants buttressed their argument by showing a dramatic increase in minority passage rate on the TAAS and a lesser but still significant increase in scores on national standardized tests of reading and math (the National Assessment of Educational Progress, or NAEP). Yet between 1994 (a year after full implementation of the TAAS as a graduation requirement) and 1998, the percentage of tested students in grade ten who were excluded from the summary of pass rates on the TAAS because they were in special education rose from 3.9 to 6.3.[94] Moreover, large percentages of students with disabilities did not participate in the test, suggesting that overall pass rates would be substantially lower if most students with disabilities took the test *and* had their scores reported. Specifically, the National Center for Educational Outcomes reported in 1999 that 42 percent or *fewer* students with disabilities participated in the TAAS.[95] Moreover, during the period from 1993–1994 to 1999–2000 the percentage of students enrolled in special education grew tremendously.[96]

These data were not considered by the *GI Forum* court because special education was not directly implicated by the complaint's allegations. In contrast, combined challenges to high-stakes tests, based on disability law as well as Title VI, would allow a close examination of how the introduction of tests correlates with prior demographics concerning enrollment in special education, with resulting test exemptions, and with the dropout rates for students with disabilities. Texas apparently benefitted from special education and nonparticipation in testing exemptions of questionable legality to bolster its argument and undermine the Title VI claim brought by nondisabled minorities. A fuller exploration of how TAAS impacted identification and possibly drove the overrepresentation of minorities may have helped the plaintiffs' case by shedding doubt on the apparent achievement gains. The *GI Forum* court also disregarded disturbingly high dropout and retention rates, concluding that they were merely correlational. However, under IDEA, states *must* consider dropout rates along with scores on state assessments to determine whether students are benefiting from special education.

IDEA AND HIGH STANDARDS

The Supreme Court, back in 1982, first addressed the issue of the level of educational opportunity ensured by IDEA's mandate of a FAPE for each special education student. In *Board of Education v. Rowley*, the Court held that, while an

IEP need not maximize the potential of a disabled student, it must provide "meaningful" access to education.[97] The placement must also confer "some educational benefit" upon the child for whom it is designed.[98] In determining the degree of educational benefit necessary to satisfy IDEA, the Court explicitly rejected a bright-line rule, noting that children of different abilities are capable of greatly different levels of achievement. Accordingly, the Court adopted an approach that requires each lower court to consider the potential of the particular disabled student before it.

Important for the purposes of this chapter is the fact that the *Rowley* Court offered some helpful guidelines concerning what, at that time, constituted meaningful educational opportunity:

> Such instruction and services must be provided at public expense, *must meet the State's educational standards,* must approximate the grade levels used in the State's regular education, and must comport with the child's IEP. . . . [I]f the child is being educated in the regular classrooms of the public education system, [the placement] should be *reasonably calculated to enable the child to achieve passing marks and advance from grade to grade.*[99]

But the Court in *Rowley* was interpreting IDEA before the 1997 amendments. The "State's educational standards" are now higher and, more important, a new crucial hurdle has been placed in front of students. No longer is it sufficient for students "to achieve passing marks and advance from grade to grade." In 1982, this statement from the Supreme Court may have summarized well what students like Amy Rowley had to do to graduate. Now, however, they must also clear hurdles linked to meeting high standards as assessed by high-stakes tests. In fact, 20 U.S.C. § 1401(c)(8)(B) expressly defines "Free Appropriate Public Education" as "special education and related services that . . . meet the standards of the State educational agency."

Accordingly, the placement should now—in school districts and states where students' promotion and/or graduation are tied to high-stakes tests—be *reasonably calculated to enable the child to achieve passing marks, achieve passing scores on high-stakes exams, and advance from grade to grade, eventually meeting state and district graduation requirements.* The nature of the benefit to which minority students eligible for special education services are now entitled appears to have increased in many states operating within standards-based regimes. If this assumption is correct, minority students who challenge FAPE violations could be individually entitled to meaningful opportunities to meet the states' high standards—not just "some benefit."[100]

CONCLUSION:
SYSTEMIC REMEDIES FOR SYSTEMIC FAILURES

This chapter has examined persistent inequalities affecting minority students and surveyed various legal challenges to overrepresentation, misidentification, and underservicing in special education. The most straightforward challenges focus on overrepresentation and FAPE/LRE violations and are well grounded in disability law precedent. Judge Thompson's decree issued in the consolidated desegregation cases in Alabama offers one important example of comprehensive systemic remedies. Another is the recently settled *Corey H.* case in Illinois.[101]

U.S. public schools are justifiably praised for their noteworthy accomplishments and for pursuing a bold vision of high standards for all students. Unfortunately, many complex problems remain, and policymakers favor superficial quick fixes.[102] Systemic legal challenges play a critical role in bringing about more comprehensive remedies and carry the potential to leverage meaningful long-term improvements for minority children. Both the legal action of advocates and government-initiated intervention at the state or federal level are needed.

In general, the persistent and disturbing patterns of overrepresentation and underservicing cry out for stepped-up enforcement and oversight activity by both state and federal government enforcement agents. On the federal level, OSEP should make use of new enforcement options, especially the partial withholding of funds to target specific compliance.[103] Likewise, OCR needs to exercise a wider range of enforcement measures, including seeking broader remedies and issuing letters of violations for obstinate noncompliant school districts. Further, OCR should aggressively disseminate information on its enforcement activities and maintain an easily accessible database documenting its activities. The Office for Civil Rights, the Department of Justice, and the Office of Special Education Programs would each benefit from greater exchange of information regarding minority overrepresentation in special education and related enforcement activity. All these federal agencies should bring intensive pressure to bear on states for failure to monitor and intervene in the face of persistent and significant overrepresentation.

Similarly, states must take seriously their new duty to monitor for disproportionality, intervene where appropriate, and make information about both disproportionality and state interventions readily available to the public. To this end, states must not focus solely on district data, since disproportionality at the school level may be masked by districtwide data, and disproportionality at the state level may not be reflected in data from school districts that are highly segregated.

The need for comprehensive and systemic intervention suggests a concomitant need for technical assistance and supports that consider the needs of students and teachers in regular education classrooms alongside potential problems in the process of evaluation and placement. Shining more light on the numerical disparities by collecting information from every school and district and publicly reporting these data is an important first step designed to generate public sentiment for meaningful reform. To meet their new obligations under federal law, states will need to collect and analyze data that look at race and the restrictiveness of placement, not just identification. These data should also be used at the district and school levels to help track the effectiveness of interventions.

State and federal enforcement agents responding to disproportionality should take a hard look at the numbers and not be swayed from intervention simply because school districts appear to rely on so-called objective testing and are in procedural compliance with the IDEA. But if remedies *only* seek to correct numerical disparities they will be short-sighted. Reducing the paper disparity without improving the quality of both regular and special education classrooms could result in further underservicing of students with academic and special education needs. Specifically, OCR and OSEP can carefully observe the comprehensive court-ordered remedies in places like Alabama and Illinois to help states that are out of compliance to adopt and adapt the most effective of these measures. Furthermore, the No Child Left Behind Act of 2001 requires that schools be held accountable if they fail to improve educational performance of either minority children or students with disabilities.[104] These new accountability requirements, if properly enforced, could provide important disincentives against inappropriately labeling students as having disabilities and either removing them from general education classrooms, or leaving them there but with inadequate supports and services.

Advocates must resist overemphasizing inputs and persist in demanding remedies that consider outcomes for children as well as inputs to the system, and then monitor remedies to adjust them accordingly. The most effective remedies will go beyond the special education evaluation process and entail regular education reforms. As Thomas Hehir points out, "Simply focusing on special education may not only be ineffective, but may also inadvertently promote continued segregation [of students with disabilities]."[105]

In light of the above, we endorse both "input" and "outcome" remedies. On the input side, advocates should seek remedies that improve both regular and special education. These include higher-quality, experienced teachers; more teacher training in what is popularly called "classroom management"; training for special and regular education teachers in the provision of challenging academic curriculum through multiple modes of instruction; smaller class size; the use of programs of instruction that are proven effective;[106] more inclusive, heterogeneous classrooms; teacher practica in inclusive settings; certification requirements that reflect IDEA mandates; time for regular and special education teacher collaboration and problem-solving; more pervasive and effective student supports and services (and corresponding additional resources); incentive programs to attract and keep talented, multilingual special educators and regular education teachers; and requirements that racial data are collected, reported, and used in the evaluation process.

Beneficial combinations of inputs, such as those outlined above, should drive worthwhile outcomes. But in recent years, educational policymakers have put a great deal of faith in the additional idea that the process of measuring those outcomes and holding schools accountable for meeting certain outcome objectives will itself drive better practices. In the context of the issues addressed in this chapter, we agree that remedies should include incentives to improve outcome measures that focus on achievement and graduation rates (with diplomas) of students with disabilities and those who have been misidentified and need to be transitioned back into regular education classrooms. This will ensure that the inputs listed above are evaluated, that adjustments will be made to maximize effectiveness, and that schools will have concrete incentives to make other changes voluntarily.

In addition, remedies should recognize that preventing misidentification and providing for more inclusion will necessarily entail improvements in general and special education. But state special education funds are often linked to identification (Parrish, this volume). Therefore, reductions in racial disparities in special education, which would also likely result in fewer students being identified, should not cause states to reduce total education expenditures in a successful district. To the contrary, state and federal law should contain rewards for reducing racial disparities while improving educational outcomes for all subgroups of students.

Advocates seeking remedies can anchor measures of effectiveness by using the states' own Title I mechanisms for determining adequate progress. As in *Corey H.*, advocates and school officials can sit down together and hammer out realistic numeric goals and create multiyear plans to ensure that the necessary inputs are employed and outcomes measured accurately.[107] Researchers can play a vital role in helping attorneys and school officials learn which inputs are most effective in improving regular and special education.

In line with our enforcement recommendations, collaboration with knowledgeable researchers is critical to shaping remedies with a lasting positive impact. To the extent that the best solutions may still need to be discovered, advocates armed with the call for higher expectations for all can play a central role in setting up evaluative frameworks and demanding disaggregated data that can shed light on what works and what doesn't.

The legal challenges recommended above are ultimately intended to instigate meaningful education reforms as well as better federal enforcement. By moving the litigation ball forward, advocates can create incentives for educators to endorse systemic reform and collaborate with researchers and the community to find meaningful solutions. Given that the overrepresentation of minority students in unnecessarily restrictive programs has continued at high levels for over fifty years, additional litigation, especially systemic challenges combining disability law with Title VI, is sorely needed.

NOTES

1. Kevin Welner's work on this chapter was supported by a postdoctoral fellowship granted by the Spencer Foundation and the National Academy of Education. The authors would also like to thank Sam Bagenstos, Gary Orfield, Kathleen Boundy, Sharon Soltman, Dennis Parker, Martha Minow, and Janette Klingner for their insightful comments on earlier drafts of this chapter and Delia Spencer and Vanessa Yolles for their research assistance. However, the opinions and ideas expressed herein are solely the responsibility of the authors. For a more extensively cited and detailed version of this chapter, see Daniel J. Losen and Kevin G. Welner, *Disabling Discrimination in Our Public Schools: Comprehensive Legal Challenges to Inappropriate and Inadequate Special Education Services for Minority Children*, 36 HARV. C.R.-C.L. L. REV. 407 (2001).
2. According to Assistant Secretary of Education Judy Heumann, Director of the Office for Special Education and Rehabilitative Services under President Clinton, the system of both regular and private education is racially discriminatory because "[m]inority children are more likely not to receive the kinds of services they need in the regular ed[ucation] system and the special ed. system. . . . And special education is used as a place to move kids from a regular classroom out into a separate setting." *The Merrow Report: What's So Special About Special Education?* (PBS television broadcast, May 10, 1996) [hereinafter *The Merrow Report*], *transcript available at* http://www.pbs.org/merrow/tv/transcript/index.html (last visited July 8, 2002).
3. 42 U.S.C. § 2000(d) (1994).
4. *See* Mills v. Bd. of Educ., 348 F. Supp. 866 (D.D.C. 1972); Pa. Ass'n. for Retarded Children v. Commonwealth, 343 F. Supp. 279 (E.D. Pa. 1972).
5. The Individuals with Disabilities Education Act Amendments of 1997 (IDEA), 20 U.S.C. §§ 1400-87 (1997) (1994 & Supp. V 1999) (originally enacted as the Education for All Handicapped Children Act of 1975, Pub. L. No. 94-142, 89 Stat. 773); for a general description of the federal funding scheme under IDEA, see 147 CONG. REC. S1889 (2001) (statement of Sen. Jeffords); *see also* 143 CONG. REC. S4401 (1997) (statement of Sen. Gregg) (emphasizing that "the Federal Government has failed to live up to its obligation to fund 40 percent of the cost of special education").

6. *See* JEAN ANYON, GHETTO SCHOOLING: A POLITICAL ECONOMY OF URBAN EDUCATIONAL REFORM (1997); JEANNIE OAKES, KEEPING TRACK: HOW SCHOOLS STRUCTURE INEQUALITY (1985); Linda Darling-Hammond, *Inequality and Access to Knowledge, in* HANDBOOK OF RESEARCH ON MULTICULTURAL EDUCATION 465, 465–83 (James A. Banks and Cherry A. McGee Banks, eds. 1995).

7. The Individuals with Disabilities Education Act Amendments of 1997 (IDEA) state in the congressional findings that, "Greater efforts are needed to prevent the intensification of problems connected with mislabeling and high dropout rates among minority children with Disabilities." 20 U.S.C. § 1400(c)(8)(A); *see also* Theresa Glennon, *Race, Education and the Construction of a Disabled Class,* 1995 WIS. L. REV. 1237 (1995).

8. 532 U.S. 275 (2001).

9. Alexander v. Sandoval, 532 U.S. at 281-82. These regulations are described in some detail later in this chapter. *See infra* p. 177.

10. 42 U.S.C. § 1983 (1994).

11. *Sandoval,* 532 U.S. at 300 (Stevens, J., dissenting); *see also* Bradford C. Mank, *Using § 1983 to Enforce Title VI's Section 602 Regulations,* 49 U. KAN. L. REV. 321 (2001); Powell v. Ridge, 189 F.3d 387, 400-03 (3d Cir. 1999).

12. *See* Lucero v. Detroit Public Schs., 160 F. Supp. 2d 767, 783 (E.D. Mich. 2001) (relying, in part, on 6th Circuit precedent, the court permitted plaintiffs to use disparate impact Title VI regulations with § 1983 to challenge opening of an elementary school on allegedly contaminated site). *But see* S. Camden Citizens in Action v. N.J. Dep't. of Envtl. Prot., 274 F.3d 771, 788 (3d Cir. 2001) (rejecting the use of § 1983 to ground a private action based on Title VI regulations).

13. Readers should also note that the Office for Civil Rights (OCR) administrative complaint mechanism allows organizations, not just aggrieved individuals, to pursue both disparate impact arguments and combined disability/Title VI arguments. Technically speaking, OCR cannot order injunctive relief, only the withdrawal of federal funds. But as discussed later in this chapter, OCR can use this leverage for settlement purposes and through negotiated resolution agreements can seek the equivalent of court-ordered injunctive and declaratory relief.

14. *See* 20 U.S.C. § 6311(b)(1994).

15. 269 F. Supp. 401 (D.D.C. 1967), *aff'd sub nom.* Smuck v. Hobbson, 408 F.2d 175 (D.C. Cir. 1969).

16. Consent decree entered in C-70-37 RFP (N.D. Cal. 1973).

17. 793 F.2d 969 (9th Cir. 1984).

18. *See* Tuttle v. Arlington County School Board, 195 F.3d 698 (4th Cir. 1999); Eisenberg v. Montgomery County Public Schools, 197 F.3d 123 (4th Cir. 1999); GI Forum v. Texas Education Agency, 87 F. Supp. 2d 667 (W.D. Tex. 2000). As part of this same trend, school systems throughout the nation are being released from desegregation obligations. *See* Missouri v. Jenkins, 515 U.S. 70 (1995); Freeman v. Pitts, 503 U.S. 467 (1992); and Board of Education v. Dowell, 498 U.S. 237 (1991).

19. 29 U.S.C. § 794 (1994).

20. 42 U.S.C. §§ 12101-213 (1994).

21. 20 U.S.C. 1418(c) (Supp. IV 1998); 34 C.F.R. § 300.755; 34 C.F.R. § 300.519; 20 U.S.C. 1415(k) (Supp. IV 1998).

22. 20 U.S.C. § 1412(a)(5) (Supp. IV 1998).

23. 20 U.S.C. § 1401(c)(4) (Supp. IV 1998).

24. 20 U.S.C. § 1412 (Supp. V 1999).

25. Memorandum from Norma Cantú, Assistant Secretary for the Office of Civil Rights, U.S. Department of Education, *Minority Students and Special Education* (July 6, 1995) (on file with author). The authors are mindful that the George W. Bush administration may arrive at different interpretations of disability law.

26. 20 U.S.C. § 1411(b)(2)(C) (Supp. V 1999).

27. 20 U.S.C. § 1412(a)(5) (Supp. V 1999).

28. MICHELLE FINE, FRAMING DROPOUTS: NOTES ON THE POLITICS OF AN URBAN PUBLIC HIGH SCHOOL (1991).

29. OFFICE FOR CIVIL RIGHTS, U.S. DEP'T OF EDUC., ELEMENTARY AND SECONDARY SCHOOL CIVIL RIGHTS COMPLIANCE REPORTS (1998) (Table on Suspensions and Expulsions per Racial/ Ethnic group for 1997-1998).

30. For a full description of legal challenges to tracking, *see also* Daniel J. Losen, Note, *Silent Segregation in Our Nation's Schools*, 34 HARV. C.R.-C.L.L.REV. 517 (1999); Kevin G. Welner and Jeannie Oakes, *(Li)ability Grouping: The New Susceptibility of School Tracking Systems to Legal Challenges*, 66 HARV. EDUC. REV. 451 (1996).

31. BUILDING BLOCKS FOR YOUTH, AND JUSTICE FOR SOME (2000); *see also* Parrish, this volume.

32. MARA SAPON-SHEVIN, PLAYING FAVORITES: GIFTED EDUCATION AND THE DISRUPTION OF COMMUNITY (1994).

33. For a discussion of such forces, see KEVIN G. WELNER, LEGAL RIGHTS, LOCAL WRONGS: WHEN COMMUNITY CONTROL COLLIDES WITH EDUCATIONAL EQUITY (2001).

34. Individuals with Disabilities Education Act (IDEA) Amendments of 1997 § 602(3)(A)-(B), 20 U.S.C. § 1401(3)(A)-(B) (Supp. V 1999) (listing eligible categories of disability).

35. *See* 42 Fed. Reg. 22, 685 (1977).

36. 29 U.S.C. §§ 705(20)(B), 794 (1994); 34 C.F.R. § 104.3 (j) (2000).

37. 29 U.S.C. § 794.

38. *See* 34 C.F.R. 104.3(j)(2)(iii) (emphasis added).

39. 34 C.F.R. § 104.3(j).

40. 29 U.S.C. § 706(8).

41. 20 U.S.C. § 1412(a)(16) (Supp. V 1999). See, for example, the recent consent decree in Alabama described below.

42. 34 C.F.R. § 104.33 (b) (2000).

43. *See* NAT'L COUNCIL ON DISABILITY, BACK TO SCHOOL ON CIVIL RIGHTS: ADVANCING THE FEDERAL COMMITMENT TO LEAVE NO CHILD BEHIND (2000), *available at* http://www.ncd.gov/ newsroom/publications/backtoschool_2.html (last visited July 8, 2002).

44. *Id.* at 70.

45. *See id.* at 12.

46. 20 U.S.C. § 1415(f), (g), and (l) (Supp. V 1999).

47. *See* Smith v. Robinson, 468 U.S. 992, 1021 (1984).

48. For example, in *Doe v. Rockingham County School Board,* the district court held that the student was not required to exhaust administrative proceedings because the district had failed to provide a prompt hearing and notice and had sought to maintain the disciplinary suspension during the pendency of the hearing. Doe v. Rockingham County Sch. Bd., 658 F. Supp. 403 (W.D. Va. 1987); *see also* M. v. Bridgeport Bd. of Educ., 96 F. Supp. 2d 124 (D. Conn. 2000) (distinguishing between substantive and structural claims as to whether administrative processes should be exhausted).

49. Wendy Parker, *The Future of School Desegregation*, 94 NW. U. L. REV. 1157, 1159 (2000).

50. Swann v. Charlotte-Mecklenburg Board of Education, 402 U.S. 1 (1971).

51. *See* MARTHA MINOW, MAKING ALL THE DIFFERENCE: INCLUSION, EXCLUSION AND AMERICAN LAW 24 (1990) (noting attempts to circumvent *Brown* as particularly prevalent in the southern states); KENNETH J. MEIER ET AL., RACE, CLASS, AND EDUCATION: THE POLITICS OF SECOND-GENERATION DISCRIMINATION (1989).

52. Dayton Board of Education v. Brinkman, 443 U.S. 526 (1979), as discussed in Georgia State Conference of Branches of NAACP v. Georgia, 570 F. Supp. 314 (S.D. Ga. 1983); Hobsen v. Hansen, 269 F. Supp. 401 (D.D.C. 1967); United States v. Yonkers Bd. of Educ., 624 F. Supp. 1276, 1453-62 (S.D.N.Y. 1985).

53. MEIER ET AL., *supra* note 51.

54. *See, e.g.*, Keyes v. Denver School District No. 1, 413 U.S. 189 (1973).

55. *See, e.g.*, Green v. County School Board of New Kent County, 391 U.S. 430 (1968).

56. *Keyes*, 413 U.S. at 208.

57. *See, e.g.*, United States v. Yonkers Bd. of Educ., 624 F. Supp. 1276 (S.D.N.Y. 1985).

58. Lee v. Phoenix City Bd. of Educ., C.A. No. 70-T-854 (M.D. Ala. 2000). The consent decrees consist of two documents in each case: an order approving the consent decree on statewide special education issues, and the consent decree itself, *Lee v. Macon County Bd. of Educ.*, 267 F. Supp. 458 (M.D. Ala. 1967).

59. Jeremy D. Finn, *Patterns in Special Education Placement as Revealed by the OCR Surveys, in* PLACING CHILDREN IN SPECIAL EDUCATION: A STRATEGY FOR EQUITY 358 (Kirby A. Heller et al., eds. 1982).

60. 574 F. Supp. 1280 (D. Md. 1983).

61. *See, e.g.*, United States v. Yonkers Bd. of Educ., 624 F. Supp. 1276 (S.D.N.Y. 1985).

62. 34 C.F.R. § 100.3(b)(2) (2000). Title VI, section 602, "authorize[s] and direct[s]" federal departments and agencies that extend federal financial assistance to particular programs or activities "to effectuate the provisions of section 2000d [section 601] . . . by issuing rules, regulations, or orders of general applicability." 42 U.S.C. § 2000d-1 (1994).

63. 34 C.F.R. 104.4(b)(4).

64. 34 C.F.R. 106.1 et seq.

65. *See, e.g.*, Powell v. Ridge, 189 F.3d 387 (3d Cir. 1999); Elston v. Talladega County Bd. of Educ., 997 F.2d 1394, 1407 (11th Cir.), *rehearing denied*, 7 F.3d 242 (11th Cir. 1993).

66. *E.g., Elston*, 997 F.2d at 1407.

67. *See, e.g.*, GI Forum v. Tex. Educ. Agency, 87 F. Supp. 2d 667, 677 (W.D. Tex. 2000).

68. Georgia State Conference of Branches of NAACP v. Georgia, 775 F.2d 1403, 1422 (11th Cir. 1985).

69. *Id.*, 775 F.2d at 1421-22.

70. 793 F.2d 969 (9th Cir. 1984).

71. For a complete analysis of the many inextricable factors that cause overrepresentation, see Harry et al., this volume.

72. On the issue of poverty, see the discussion in Marshalyn Yeargin-Allsopp et al., *Mild Mental Retardation in Black and White Children in Metropolitan Atlanta: A Case-Control Study*, 85 AM. J. PUB. HEALTH 324, 324-28 (1995). For a discussion of issues affecting second-language learners, see Artiles et al., this volume; *see also* PATRICIA T. CEGELKA ET AL., EDUCATIONAL SERVICES TO HANDICAPPED STUDENTS WITH LIMITED ENGLISH PROFICIENCY: A

CALIFORNIA STATEWIDE STUDY (1986) (noting that teachers unfamiliar with the effect of language development on student achievement may refer students for special education assessment); Richard A. Figueroa, *Psychological Testing of Linguistic-Minority Students: Knowledge Gaps and Regulations*, 56 EXCEPTIONAL CHILD 145 (1989) (finding that diagnostic testing of limited English proficient students is often performed primarily in English). For a discussion of cultural issues (bias) in IQ testing, see JIM CUMMINS, BILINGUALISM AND SPECIAL EDUCATION: ISSUES IN ASSESSMENT AND PEDAGOGY (1984); Asa G. Hilliard, III, *Behavioral Style, Culture, and Teaching and Learning*, 61 J. NEGRO EDUC. 370 (1992). For an examination of resource and funding issues and their impact on schooling opportunities, see DAVID C. BERLINER AND BRUCE J. BIDDLE, THE MANUFACTURED CRISIS: MYTHS, FRAUD, AND THE ATTACK ON AMERICA'S PUBLIC SCHOOLS (1995); and JONATHAN KOZOL, SAVAGE INEQUALITIES: CHILDREN IN AMERICA'S SCHOOLS (1991). For a study linking lower parent education levels to late identification, see Judith Palfrey et al., *Early Identification of Children's Special Needs: A Study in Five Metropolitan Communities*, 111 J. PEDIATRICS 651 (1987). Concerning the lack of prereferral interventions and behavioral issues, see Osher et al., this volume; *see also*, NAT'L ASSOCIATION OF BLACK SCHOOL EDUCATORS AND ILLIAD PROJECT, ADDRESSING OVER-REPRESENTATION OF AFRICAN AMERICAN STUDENTS IN SPECIAL EDUCATION: THE PREREFERRAL INTERVENTION PROCESS, COUNCIL FOR EXCEPTIONAL CHILDREN (2002) (recommending a focus on prereferral intervention to reduce over-representation); THE NAT'L RESEARCH COUNCIL, MINORITY STUDENTS IN SPECIAL AND GIFTED EDUCATION, ES-3, 4 (2002) [hereinafter MINORITY STUDENTS] (specifically concluding that behavior management issues, inadequate regular education instruction, and resource inequalities are likely contributing factors to racial disparities in special education). Finally, for a more general discussion of many of these factors and how they all drive achievement, *see* THE BLACK-WHITE TEST SCORE GAP (Christopher Jencks and Meredith Philips, eds. 1998).

73. *See* Campaign for Fiscal Equity v. New York, 719 N.Y.S. 2d 475, 484-88 (2001) (holding that the "sound basic education" provision of the State Constitution requires that students need to be capable of civic engagement and sustaining competitive employment, rather than merely prepared to serve on a jury or vote).

74. *Id.* at 537-8.

75. "The evidence demonstrates that the primary causes of New York City's overreferral and overplacement in restrictive settings are a lack of support services in general education . . ." *Id.* at 538.

76. Campaign for Fiscal Equity v. New York, 2002 WL 1369966, at *11; 2002 N.Y. Slip Op. 05327 (June 25, 2002).

77. *See generally*, U.S. DEP'T OF EDUC., OFFICE FOR CIVIL RIGHTS, CASE RESOLUTION MANUAL, *available at* www.ed.gov/offices/OCR/docs/ocrcm.html (last visited, July 8, 2002).

78. U.S. COMM'N ON CIVIL RIGHTS, EQUAL EDUCATIONAL OPPORTUNITY PROJECT SERIES 209-13 (1996).

79. Memorandum from Norma Cantú, *supra* note 25, at 19.

80. *Id.*

81. Telephone interview with Timothy Blanchard, Senior Attorney at the U.S. Department of Education, Office for Civil Rights (Sept. 25, 2000).

82. Memorandum from Norma Cantú, *supra* note 25, at 19.

83. *See, e.g.,* Glennon, this volume.

84. *See* Osher et al., this volume.
85. *See* Kevin G. Welner and Kenneth R. Howe, *Steering Toward Separation: The Evidence and Implications of Special Education Students' Exclusion from Choice Schools, in* SCHOOL CHOICE AND DIVERSITY (Janelle Scott, ed. 2002).
86. Sch. Bd. of Palm Beach County, Order No. DOE-99-440-FOF (Fla. Dep't of Educ. Sept. 27, 1999).
87. *Id.*
88. Letter from Gary S. Walker, Director, Atlanta Office, Southern Division, Office for Civil Rights, Department of Education, to Dr. Joan Kowal, Superintendent, Palm Beach County School District (Aug. 13, 1999) (on file with authors).
89. Letter from Gary S. Walker, Director, Atlanta Office, Southern Division, Office for Civil Rights, Department of Education, to Barbara Burch, Esq. (Sept. 7, 2000) (on file with authors).
90. *See Corey H.*, discussed in Soltman & Moore, this volume.
91. Vaughn G. v. Mayor of Balt., Civil Action No. 84-1911 (MJG) (D. Md. May 1, 2000) (monitoring to reduce achievement disparity includes an annual school report regarding "significant progress" defined in terms of specific narrowing of the test score gap, increases in the rates of high school completion, and increases in the percentage of students receiving diplomas).
92. *See* MINORITY STUDENTS, *supra* note 72, at ES-3-4.
93. GI Forum v. Texas Education Agency, 87 F. Supp. 2d 667 (W.D.Tex. 2000).
94. Walt Haney, *The Myth of the Texas Miracle in Education*, 8 EDUC. POL'Y ANALYSIS ARCHIVES (2000), *available at* http://epau.asa.edu/epaa/v8n41 (last visited July 8, 2002).
95. National Center on Educational Outcomes, *1999 State Special Education Outcomes: A Report on State Activities at the End of the Century* (Dec. 1999). Available at http://www.coled.unm.edu/nceo/OnlinePubs/99StateReport.html (last visited Dec. 8, 2001)
96. According to data available on the website of the Texas Education Agency (TEA), more than 12 percent of all Texas children are eligible for special education services. Based on a review of data from previous years, this percentage represents a significant increase of nearly 100,000 students between 1993–1994 and 1999–2000—a change from 10.7 percent of those enrolled to 12.1 percent. *See* Tex. Educ. Agency, Texas Public School Statistics, *available at* http://www.tea.state.tex.us/perfreport/pocked (last visited June 28, 2001).
97. Bd. of Educ. v. Rowley, 458 U.S. 176, 192 (1982).
98. *Id.* at 200.
99. *Id.* at 203 (emphasis added and footnote omitted).
100. *Id.* at 214 (White, J., dissenting).
101. *See* Corey H. v. Bd. of Educ., 27 Individuals with Disabilities Educ. L. Rptr. 688 (N.D. Ill. 1998). *See also* Soltman and Moore, this volume.
102. *See* David Tyack and Larry Cuban, TINKERING TOWARD UTOPIA: A CENTURY OF PUBLIC SCHOOL REFORM (1995).
103. *See* Hehir, this volume.
104. Pub. L. No. 107-10, 115 Stat 1425 § 1111 (2002).
105. *See* Hehir, this volume.
106. *See generally*, HARD WORK FOR GOOD SCHOOLS: FACTS NOT FADS IN TITLE I REFORM (Gary Orfield and Elizabeth H. DeBray, eds. 1999).
107. *See* Soltman and Moore, this volume.

CHAPTER NINE

Evaluating the Office for Civil Rights' Minority and Special Education Project

THERESA GLENNON

INTRODUCTION

This chapter is an initial effort to evaluate the enforcement activities of the U.S. Department of Education Office for Civil Rights (OCR) related to the disproportionate representation of minority students in special education from 1994 through 2000. I review OCR's history and activities related to this problem and then evaluate its performance. Finally, I suggest improvements in OCR's protection of the civil rights of minority children pertaining to special education, including 1) increasing activities in the areas of development and dissemination of guidelines, public education, and community outreach; 2) improving the effectiveness of compliance reviews and complaint investigations through evaluation and staff training; and 3) employing a broader range of enforcement tools and eliminating administrative barriers.

Early in her tenure, Norma Cantú, the assistant secretary for civil rights at the U.S. Department of Education (DOE) in the Clinton administration, identified the disproportionate placement of minority students in special education as one of her office's three top priority areas for civil rights enforcement.[1] She acknowledged that OCR's failure "to find effective ways to address [this issue] has generated serious criticism of OCR's effectiveness in carrying out its responsibilities under Title VI [of the Civil Rights Act of 1964], which prohibits discrimination on the basis of race, color or national origin."[2]

OCR's effective enforcement of Title VI on behalf of minority students has become more urgent in light of the U.S. Supreme Court's recent ruling in *Sandoval v. Alexander*, which denies private plaintiffs a private right of action under the Title VI disparate impact regulations.[3] Federal Title VI regulations, issued under Section 602 of Title VI, are not limited to situations in which there is proof of intentional discrimination. The regulations also prevent recipients of federal funds from using any apparently neutral methods or criteria that have an adverse and disparate impact on racial or ethnic groups.[4] OCR's effective administrative enforcement of the Title VI regulations is essential in order to establish clear guidelines, collect and evaluate data, and monitor the actions of the nation's 15,000 school districts.[5] This analysis is designed to encourage OCR to continue its focus on the rights of minority students regarding special education and to increase the impact of its work.

ENFORCEMENT HISTORY OF THE OFFICE FOR CIVIL RIGHTS

OCR was originally established to enforce Title VI, which states that "no person in the United States shall, on the basis of race, color, or national origin, be excluded from participation in, be denied the benefits of, or be subjected to discrimination under, any program or activity receiving federal financial assistance."[6] This statute empowered federal agencies to issue rules and regulations to give effect to Title VI and to terminate federal funds to recipients that refused to correct discriminatory practices.[7]

In 1979, OCR became part of the newly created U.S. Department of Education.[8] OCR is directed by an assistant secretary for civil rights, and about 20 percent of its employees staff the Washington, DC, headquarters.[9] The other 80 percent of OCR's staff is located at twelve regional enforcement offices across the country, which handle all complaints, pursue compliance reviews, and conduct public education, outreach, and technical assistance activities.[10]

In accordance with federal regulations, OCR can request compliance reports from all education entities that receive federal assistance; investigate and resolve complaints of racial discrimination by recipients; initiate compliance reviews of recipients to ensure that they are fulfilling their obligations under Title VI law and regulations; and inform recipients and beneficiaries of Title VI's protections against discrimination.[11]

OCR is credited with achieving the integration of numerous southern school districts that had failed to desegregate their schools in response to *Brown v. Board of Education* and the passage of Title VI.[12] In 1964, more than 98 percent of black students in the South were still attending segregated schools. By 1972, only about 8.7 percent of black students were attending completely segregated schools. Although some of this integration came about through litigation by private parties and the U.S. Department of Justice, the overwhelming majority of southern school districts were integrated due to OCR's enforcement efforts, which involved hundreds of consent agreements and some with-holding of federal funds.[13]

Despite this achievement, OCR was subject to criticism by civil rights advocates, who sued OCR in 1970 for failing to enforce Title VI against re-calcitrant school districts. In 1977, a federal district court ordered OCR to investigate all complaints that fell within its jurisdiction and to conduct agency-initiated compliance reviews according to specific time frames and procedures.[14]

At the same time, OCR's jurisdiction was greatly broadened by the addition of Title IX,[15] which prohibits discrimination on the basis of gender by educational institutions receiving federal funds, and Section 504,[16] which prohibits discrimination on the basis of disability.[17] Already struggling to fulfill its mission under Title VI, a combination of political pressures and administrative inadequacies prevented the agency from redesigning its enforcement activities to meet this dramatic expansion of its mission.[18]

According to some commentators, OCR's efficacy began to be further undermined in 1981 by the political beliefs of those appointed to responsible positions within the Reagan administration.[19] Soon thereafter, OCR's enforcement was severely limited by the U.S. Supreme Court decision in *Grove City v. Bell*, which found that Title IX's impact was restricted to the specific program or activity within an educational institution that actually received the federal funds.[20] OCR strictly interpreted *Grove City* to require a determination that the specific program or activity complained about actually received federal funds prior to proceeding with an investigation under any of its antidiscrimination statutes, and the agency dropped numerous discrimination charges and terminated more than eight hundred investigations.[21] Until *Grove City* was reversed by congressional action expanding coverage to entire institutions in 1988,[22] this complex preliminary jurisdiction determination undermined OCR's ability to conduct complete investigations within the Court-ordered time limits, leading to severely limited investigations, vague remedial agreements, and pressure on complainants to withdraw complaints.[23]

These various factors led OCR to give little attention to attacking the widespread existence of so-called second-generation racial discrimination in school discipline, ability grouping, and placement in special education and gifted programs during four different administrations between 1972 and 1993. Congressional investigators were told by some OCR staff in 1988 that they had received the message that they were not to vigorously pursue claims regarding these forms of second-generation racial discrimination under Title VI.[24]

OCR neglected the overrepresentation of minority students in special education despite major lawsuits and reports that raised the profile of this issue.[25]

For example, one highly publicized lawsuit, *Larry P. v. Riles*, resulted in an important plaintiffs' verdict in 1979 that affected students throughout California.[26] Other suits successfully challenged the disproportionate representation of minority students in lower track and special education classes in recently desegregated school districts.[27] In addition, a blue-ribbon committee issued a national report in 1982 that analyzed and condemned this overrepresentation.[28]

THE DEVELOPMENT OF OCR'S MINORITIES AND SPECIAL EDUCATION PROJECT

In 1994, the assistant secretary for civil rights designated minority overrepresentation in special education as a priority for agency enforcement and established an OCR task force to study the issue, which was given the acronym MINSPED. As a first step, the task force prepared two important memoranda. A 1995 memorandum, authored by the assistant secretary and circulated to all regional enforcement offices, described the ways in which inappropriate placement in special education harmed minority students: limiting their access to the core curriculum, stigmatizing them, and creating significant racial separation.[29] The memo outlined the legal theories available to investigators, including Title VI, which prevents minority students from being disproportionately denied the opportunity to participate in the regular education program,[30] and Section 504, which requires schools to use validated evaluation tools to prevent misclassification, to place students in the least restrictive educational settings, and to ensure disabled students meaningful access to the benefits of the educational program.[31]

OCR also issued an "Investigative Guide" to data collection and analysis for MINSPED investigators.[32] This report identified proactive compliance reviews and complaint resolution as the primary enforcement tools.[33] The memo advised investigators to focus on three phases of the special education process: referral, evaluation and placement, and the actual provision of special education services. The "Investigative Guide" contained detailed forms to be completed for each student file reviewed during an investigation. These forms were designed to help investigators identify racial disparities at a number of points in the special education process, including the availability and use of prereferral interventions, the procedures and reasons for referrals for special education evaluations, application of evaluation criteria, and the educational benefits received by students in special education.

Enforcement offices experienced difficulties with the forms, which were time consuming yet yielded highly inconsistent and limited information.[34] Investigators who used the "Investigative Guide" forms faced lengthy delays and inaction on requested data analyses from OCR statisticians at headquarters. These difficulties posed significant barriers to the development of a disparate impact case. As investigators in each enforcement office developed their own data collection forms, the investigative practices of the enforcement offices diverged in important ways.

Over time, a MINSPED National Network emerged, including at least one member from each enforcement office actively involved in MINSPED compliance reviews. The network was sustained through periodic telephone calls[35] in which network members shared difficulties regarding data collection in compliance reviews and evaluation of the efficacy of the MINSPED agreements staff entered into with state and local education agencies.[36]

Enforcement offices retained the discretion, subject to approval by the assistant secretary, to select MINSPED activities. The staff created a proposed "docket" of enforcement activities in all areas for the upcoming year. In the MINSPED area, enforcement dockets focused almost exclusively on compliance reviews and rarely contained public education or project evaluation activities. Staff selected sites for compliance reviews based on statistics in the 1994 report, "Elementary and Secondary School Compliance Report: Projected Values," and other information obtained through their own research.[37]

The initiation of the MINSPED project was accompanied by an important change in all OCR case resolution procedures. Under prior administrations, every complaint and compliance review had to result in an official Letter of Finding that detailed the evidence OCR had obtained and its conclusions as to whether a recipient of federal funds had violated federal law. As part of an effort to eliminate a serious backlog in OCR's complaint caseload and accelerate the implementation of remedies, OCR began to employ a "partnership" approach in complaint resolution and compliance review activities.[38] Under this approach, OCR encourages states and local school districts to enter into cooperative agreements to implement measures to reduce the disproportionate placement of minority students in special education.[39] The partnership approach has reduced the amount of time investigators spend collecting evidence and increased the amount of time they spent talking to school personnel, community groups, and parents.[40] The agency also hoped that this less confrontational approach would lead school personnel to undertake the agreed-upon measures in a more positive fashion, trying to approach state and local education agencies with the recognition that they "share a common goal of providing equal opportunity and access to high-quality education for all students."[41]

Almost all compliance reviews ended with voluntary agreements by the local school district under review to put in place a range of measures designed to reduce the misuse of special education for students of color.[42] While some investigators described being shown agreements to use as samples, OCR has stated that there are no template or model MINSPED agreements.[43] Although the contents of the agreements vary, many agreements include provisions regarding 1) development and implementation of prereferral strategies for all students experiencing learning or behavior problems prior to referral for special education evaluations; 2) in-service training of all staff members concerning teacher expectations and effective education for a diverse student population; 3) standardization of prereferral, referral, and evaluation procedures, including the use of validated testing and assurances that identification is based on a wide range of factors, not just performance on IQ tests; and 4) tracking and reporting to OCR on prereferral interventions, evaluations for need for special education, identification as disabled, and restrictiveness of placement of all special education students by race.[44] The agreements vary widely in the level of detail they contain, particularly with regard to required school district remedial actions and information to be provided to OCR.

Many agreements covered only MINSPED issues, although some included issues such as minority student underrepresentation in gifted and talented classes or overrepresentation in the lower tracks of ability-grouping programs. Some of the agreements clearly led local education agencies to initiate new activities, such as teacher training on diversity or prereferral strategies for struggling students. In other cases, school districts appear to have complied by primarily reporting on existing programs or by increasing the level of uniformity in their interventions.[45]

None of the agreements set requirements for numerical changes. OCR staff reported that the political environment has been so hostile to "quotas" that the inclusion of *any* numerical goals has been completely discouraged. Thus, in some cases, OCR informed school districts that they had successfully completed their monitoring periods and terminated monitoring, even though the districts did not show any significant decrease in the disproportionate numbers of minority students placed in special education.[46]

OCR initiated only two MINSPED compliance reviews in Fiscal Year 1993,[47] but it greatly increased the number of proactive MINSPED compliance reviews beginning in fiscal year 1994. Between July 1, 1993, and June 30, 2001, OCR initiated approximately 168 MINSPED compliance reviews.[48] During that same time period, OCR entered into approximately 147 agreements with individual school districts and five agreements with state departments of education based on these compliance reviews. As demonstrated in Figure 1, the initiation of compliance reviews peaked in fiscal year 1996 and has dropped off sharply since then.[49] OCR initiated only six MINSPED compliance reviews in fiscal year 2001.[50]

FIGURE 1

Compliance Reviews Initiated in Fiscal Years 1994–2001

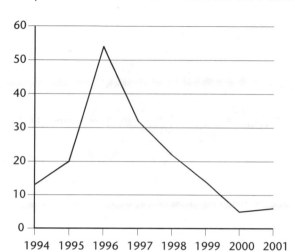

The enforcement offices varied dramatically in the number of MINSPED compliance reviews they initiated between July 1, 1993, and June 30, 2001, as depicted in Figure 2.[51]

While some of these differences can be explained by regional variations in demographics and priorities, these inconsistencies raise the concern that MINSPED did not receive the same level of attention across the various offices. In addition to agency-initiated compliance reviews, OCR responded to 190 complaints that raised MINSPED issues between July 1, 1993, and June 30, 2001, and "facilitated change" in approximately forty-nine cases.[52]

EVALUATING THE EFFECTIVENESS OF OCR'S MINSPED ENFORCEMENT EFFORTS

OCR's enforcement efforts raised the awareness of more than two hundred local school districts and five state education departments about the ongoing overrepresentation of minority students in special education. While this issue has received the continuing attention of scholars, some school districts informed OCR officials that they had never noticed that their minority students were overrepresented in their special education programs.[53] Unfortunately, OCR has not gathered the information necessary to permit an adequate assessment of the impact of its MINSPED enforcement efforts on the experiences of

FIGURE 2

MINSPED Compliance Reviews Initiated in Fiscal Years 1994–2001

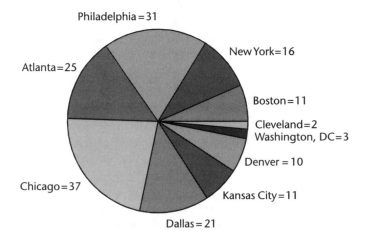

minority students in the jurisdictions where it intervened.[54] However, OCR's enforcement experiences over the last eight years, if properly reviewed and evaluated, could be invaluable in effecting change in this challenging area. Based on the limited information available, such an evaluation should include questions regarding structural barriers, tactical choices, and administrative obstacles that may have prevented the agency from having a greater impact, both within and beyond the jurisdictions subject to compliance reviews. It is hoped that OCR's commitment to the civil rights of minority students in special education can be reinvigorated and its approach honed through such self-evaluation and attention to these issues.

STRUCTURAL BARRIERS

OCR's MINSPED project faced three major structural barriers. One important barrier is the sheer breadth of OCR's mission. OCR's jurisdiction includes race, national origin, gender, disability, and age discrimination involving sixty million students attending 109,000 elementary and secondary schools in 15,000 public school districts and 10,000 postsecondary institutions.[55] These educational entities vary greatly in size, demographics, finances, curriculum, and political and social environments, in part due to this nation's commitment to state and local control of public education and independence of private educational entities. The issues concerning public school districts are often quite different from those facing postsecondary educational institutions. Achieving uniform enforcement of civil rights across this diverse, highly decentralized educational system is an extraordinary challenge.

A second structural barrier involves the limited enforcement powers OCR has under Section 602 of Title VI. OCR seeks to resolve complaints and compliance reviews by agreement, and these agreements can incorporate a variety of measures to remedy the violations found. However, where an educational entity refuses to enter into a resolution agreement, the only penalty OCR can impose is to deny *all* federal financial assistance to the recalcitrant state or school district.[56] Sometimes referred to as an "atomic bomb," a funding cutoff penalizes needy students along with education officials. Because this extreme penalty is politically difficult to impose, OCR's leverage in negotiations with state and local educational agencies may be lessened.[57] In contrast, Congress recently granted OCR greater discretion to tailor penalties for violations of the IDEA, permitting the secretary to withhold partial payments for substantial violations.[58] Because the IDEA now requires state education agencies to evaluate and revise its policies and practices where there is racial disproportionality in special education, DOE may be able to create a process by which OCR can request that the secretary investigate a recalcitrant school district for violations of the IDEA related to MINSPED issues, and use the new discretion to withhold partial funding to address IDEA violations in this context.[59]

OCR's ability to focus on the proactive MINSPED project has also been hampered by inadequate resources to proactively enforce civil rights laws and investigate every complaint received. In fiscal year 2000, OCR received 4,897 complaints and resolved 6,364 complaints.[60] Every complaint is initially reviewed to determine if it falls within OCR's jurisdiction. If it does, an OCR team develops a case plan and initiates case resolution and investigation procedures.[61] Some complaints require on-site investigations, and some are extremely complex, requiring lengthy and time-consuming investigations. In addition, many complaint resolution agreements require ongoing monitoring. In fiscal year 2000, OCR conducted monitoring activities involving 2,049 complaints.[62] Given current staffing levels, the requirement to respond to all complaints significantly reduces OCR's ability to conduct proactive enforcement activities.

QUESTIONING TACTICAL DECISIONS

Once OCR identified the disproportionate representation of minority students in special education as a priority area for enforcement, it had to select strategies for achieving its enforcement goals. As an office that has traditionally viewed itself as a law enforcement agency, OCR has often focused on identifying the minimum legal duties of educational entities under the various civil rights statutes it must enforce. Achieving real reductions in the overrepresentation of minority students in special education, however, requires changes in educational practices and a commitment by public schools to create equal educational opportunity, not merely avoid legal violations.[63] This goal requires educational leadership at all levels, including the federal government. OCR initially planned to pursue a multifaceted strategy of public education, compliance reviews, and complaint reviews. In practice the agency focused on typical law enforcement activities—compliance reviews and complaint resolution—and public education measures have been minimal.

Because OCR cannot hope to reach all relevant state and local education agencies through compliance and complaint reviews, a public education strategy is also necessary. While OCR developed some informational resources for its staff, it did not produce any public documents to educate educational agencies or the public about the issue of disproportionate representation or its MINSPED project.[64] OCR has posted on its website extensive policy guidance on other priority areas, such as racial and sexual harassment and the use of high-stakes testing, yet it has not posted policy guidelines about minorities and special education, and its MINSPED project is only mentioned briefly in OCR annual reports.[65] OCR's planned report on promising educational practices to prevent disproportionate representation has never been issued.[66] OCR has done little to target those on the front lines in our nation's schools—teachers and school administrators—to inform them about the rights of students to be protected from misidentification and misplacement in special education and programmatic strategies that have been shown to be effective in reducing the disproportionate placement of minority students in special education.[67]

OCR has not made strong efforts to reach out to nongovernmental organizations, such as the NAACP or National Association for Protection and Advocacy Systems, on MINSPED issues. These organizations would be able to conduct outreach and education activities for their own constituents, or to collaborate on public education activities with other related federal offices, such as the Office of Special Education and Rehabilitative Services (OSERS) or the federally funded Equity Assistance Centers, which provide technical assistance to state and local education agencies on educational strategies that promote equal educational opportunity.[68]

In addition, OCR has done little to publicize its compliance reviews and the agreements it has reached with state and local education agencies. Thus, much of the time and effort OCR invested in its MINSPED project has remained hidden from view beyond those school districts or state educational agencies it investigated. Although the existence of the reviews is mentioned in OCR's annual reports, the names of the educational entities reviewed and the existence and contents of individual agreements are only available through a Freedom of Information Act request. This means that other school districts and states cannot easily examine agreements and use them as guidance to voluntarily adopt the measures OCR has required of other state and local educational agencies.[69]

Another potentially effective strategy that has received little attention is action by the Department of Justice (DOJ) to seek judicial enforcement of the rights of minority students regarding special education. This strategy would require extensive cooperation from both OCR and DOJ. School districts often respond to high-profile litigation by initiating changes in their policies and practices. For example, the Third Circuit Court of Appeals' well-publicized decision mandating the provision of special education in the least restrictive environment[70] led to a massive inclusion effort by school districts within the circuit. Similarly, the Supreme Court's recent holdings that school districts can be liable for damages for sexual harassment has spurred great activity by school districts nationwide to develop and implement policies and practices to respond more effectively to allegations of sexual harassment.[71] Disproportionate representation in special education has been raised in the context of school desegregation cases, and OCR should work closely with DOJ to identify other desegregation cases in which this strategy deserves consideration.[72] While OCR's enforcement options may be limited, well-targeted litigation by DOJ would increase national awareness of this issue.

The narrow focus of most compliance reviews may also have limited OCR's effectiveness in reducing the disproportionate representation of minority students in special education. Compliance reviews usually focused only on the referral, evaluation, and placement of minority students in special education. They often did not include other issues, such as the racially disproportionate use of discipline, resource inequalities, significant racial gaps in performance on achievement tests, and underrepresentation in gifted and talented programs. This single-issue focus may be helpful in some instances, but it could also undermine OCR's ability to direct school districts toward more comprehensive reforms in both general and special education—reforms that may be necessary to resolve the overrepresentation problem, given the evidence that multiple factors contribute to this problem.

OCR statistics demonstrate the pervasive, negative effects of race in the educational environment. For example, OCR data show that while African American students comprise 17 percent of students in public schools, they represent 33 percent of the students who were suspended, 31 percent of the students who were expelled, and only 8 percent of the students in gifted and talented programs.[73] The average scale score for math of African American fourth graders on the National Assessment of Education Performance was thirty-one points lower than the score of white fourth graders,[74] and thirty-three points lower for reading.[75]

While a broader focus in compliance reviews may increase the amount of time OCR staff spend on any one review and could discourage school districts from entering into agreements with OCR without extensive investigation, research shows that the treatment of racial minority groups in special education *and* general education are interrelated, and that a more comprehensive approach may be necessary to protect minority students from shifting forms of discrimination.[76] It benefits minority students little to gain protection from mistaken special education identification and/or overly restrictive placements but find their educational needs unaddressed in general education, or to be subjected to excessive discipline. For example, as the Chicago OCR office staff recognized in their 1999 report evaluating the effectiveness of their MINSPED compliance reviews, OCR's intervention was more effective when it included an emphasis on improving the ability of a school district's reading programs to serve its diverse student population.[77]

ADMINISTRATIVE OBSTACLES

OCR's MINSPED project has encountered several administrative difficulties. These obstacles include inadequate staff resources to accomplish its mission; failure to balance staff time among different types of enforcement activities; insufficient guidance in the development of compliance agreements; inadequate research and statistical information to support OCR's enforcement and education efforts; inadequate staff development and training; and barriers to sharing essential information within OCR.

Enforcement of civil rights is extremely labor intensive. OCR receives close to five thousand complaints each year, and OCR's regulations require resolution of every timely complaint within its jurisdiction, which consumes at least 60 percent of its staff time.[78] For every complaint, OCR must at least make contact with the complainant and the complained-against educational entity, and in most cases OCR seeks a negotiated resolution to the complaint even if it does not pursue further investigation. In addition to its unpredictable and rising complaint caseload, OCR monitors numerous complaint resolution agreements. At the behest of headquarters, OCR enforcement offices place great weight on timely processing of complaints.

At best, only 40 percent of staff time is devoted to proactive work on priority areas such as the MINSPED project. Congress should provide OCR with adequate resources to fulfill its mission. If such funds are not available, Congress should grant OCR greater discretion in its complaint response process. Certainly, greater agency discretion to refuse resolution procedures to complainants raises many concerns that such discretion will not be wisely utilized. If such a change is determined to be desirable, it must be accompanied by procedures to make the complaint review process more transparent, allowing those outside the agency to evaluate the basis for agency decisions to refuse to pursue certain complaints.

Regional enforcement offices outline their planned proactive enforcement activities in proposed enforcement dockets submitted to headquarters each fall. These dockets explain the proactive enforcement activities each office plans to undertake in the coming year concerning each of OCR's priority areas.[79] Once approved, the performance of the regional offices is judged by their completion of the activities described on the dockets.[80]

Because of the limited staff time available for proactive enforcement activities, any activities not listed on the dockets receive little attention.[81] During the period studied, the MINSPED portions of these dockets was reported by staff to have focused almost exclusively on proposals for compliance reviews. This left staff with little time for public education, community outreach, or improvement of OCR's ability to monitor and improve the outcomes of its enforcement efforts.[82] OCR staff did not recall receiving any direction from the assistant secretary's office to redirect the regional offices to a more balanced approach to their MINSPED docket development.[83] Many of the potential strategies that OCR did not employ in the MINSPED context, discussed above, require a great deal of time and attention from well-trained and experienced staff. Given dockets replete with compliance reviews and a rising complaint caseload, OCR staff report that they did not have time to attempt many of these other strategies.[84]

OCR staff also report receiving little guidance on the conduct of MINSPED compliance reviews, and in particular on the negotiation and agreement phase of the review process.[85] As a result, many compliance review agreements contain vague phrases and limit OCR's ability to review the quality of a school district's compliance or to seek further action from school districts when their performance of the terms of the agreement produce little effect on the school performance and special education placement of minority students.

While OCR uses statistics to help select its targets for MINSPED compliance reviews, its enforcement efforts have been hampered by a lack of coordination and adequate collection and analysis of essential statistical information. Until 2000, the agency employed a sampling method rather than collecting data from every single school district. While sampling data identified national and state trends, it did not provide regular information over time about individual school districts. OCR now gathers data from every school district and has developed a unified data collection system for special education with other agency offices. Because of the importance of effective data collection to the analysis of the MINSPED and other issues, this new data collection procedure should receive outside review to ensure that it is meeting the informational needs of the agency, state and local school officials, and student advocates.

Data collection problems have also impeded any national evaluation of the effect of OCR's MINSPED activities, and OCR has devoted few resources to such an evaluation. In 1999, OCR's MINSPED national network acknowledged that the lack of a usable, coordinated data collection system prevented an adequate assessment of the effectiveness of the agency's proactive compliance review strategy.[86] It recommended that the agency employ the same data collection instruments in all regional offices and produced suggested forms for this purpose.[87] To date, this recommendation has not received formal action, although some enforcement offices have voluntarily adopted the suggested forms. Only one office, the Chicago office, conducted an evaluation of the results of its MINSPED compliance reviews.[88] That report suggested that the focus of compliance reviews should be shifted from special education referral, evaluation, and placement procedures to elementary school reading programs and regular education intervention programs. OCR's failure to conduct regular self-evaluations prevents the agency from making the most effective use of its limited resources or from gathering information from the compliance review process about what works to reduce disproportion and disseminate that information to state and local education agencies.

The lack of organized self-evaluation regarding the impact of one of the agency's top priorities points to another administrative problem within OCR: lack of adequate mandatory opportunities for staff professional development. To be effective, OCR staff need to receive substantive and skills-oriented training on a regular basis. They need to understand the legal context of the enforcement efforts and stay up-to-date on research evaluating the effectiveness of educational strategies designed to increase educational opportunity. They also need professional-level training in essential skills involved in investigations, negotiations, public education, and outreach, and efficient use of computer technology. They should also be able and encouraged to participate in conferences held by other stakeholders in education.[89]

OCR staff is also faced with barriers to accessing helpful information. While OCR maintains a Case Information System (CIS II), it contains very limited information.[90] Thus, a staff member who wanted to evaluate the contents of MINSPED compliance review agreements would not be able to search the CIS II, or any other computerized system, for such information. These documents, along with all other crucial case documents, are available only in the hard-copy files and personal computers of individual investigators in the twelve enforcement offices.[91] OCR reports that it is working to develop a new computerized case management system that would increase the data and documentation available to its staff.[92] Public access to documentation also needs to be increased. For example, while OCR has created an electronic library that contains letters of findings, policy documents, and other helpful materials, this electronic library is not available to the public.[93]

RECOMMENDATIONS

OCR deserves commendation for turning its attention to this form of discrimination, which so limits educational opportunities for many minority students. It is essential that OCR receive the strong support and political commitment of the federal executive and legislative branches to continue and improve its enforcement concerning the overrepresentation of minority students in special education. The following recommendations should be considered to increase the agency's effectiveness.

1. Retain enforcement of the civil rights of minority students regarding special education as a top priority.

2. Increase OCR MINSPED activities to develop and disseminate MINSPED guidelines and data to the public and conduct public education and community outreach on this critical issue.

    a. Develop and widely publicize clear legal requirements and policy guidelines for states and school districts.

    b. Make information on preventive educational strategies and relevant MINSPED data easily accessible on OCR's website, along with links to other sources of information on the topic.

    c. Conduct outreach and education activities targeting education professionals and national and community advocacy organizations.

    d. Share information about MINSPED compliance review investigations and agreements with state and local education agencies across the nation and the public, and encourage state and local officials to use the information to conduct self-evaluations and voluntarily adopt nondiscriminatory and preventive educational practices.

e. Collaborate with other DOE offices, Equity Assistance Centers, and related nongovernmental organizations to increase public and professional knowledge about this issue.

f. Develop internal policies to ensure that OCR staff time is allocated to MINSPED public education and project evaluation activities in addition to compliance reviews and complaint resolution.

3. Increase active enforcement by improving the effectiveness of compliance reviews and complaint investigations.

a. Increase OCR initiation of MINSPED compliance reviews, which by FY 2000 had dropped to only five per year nationwide.

b. Expand the focus of compliance reviews to evaluate and remedy the multiple factors that lead to disproportionate representation in special education, by including, for example, evaluation of discriminatory practices in elementary school reading programs.

c. Improve and coordinate data collection activities at the national level and improve the collection of and dissemination of data with regard to evaluating the effectiveness of complaint resolution and compliance review agreements in reducing the disproportionate representation of minority students in special education.

d. Evaluate the compliance review process and resulting agreements to provide staff with clear guidelines for maximizing the results of this effort and to increase the consistency of MINSPED activities across the enforcement offices.

e. Organize staff professional development and training opportunities, including substantive knowledge about the MINSPED issue and investigation, negotiation, and agreement-drafting skills; maintain the MINSPED network.

4. Employ the full range of enforcement tools.

a. Seek authority for partial withholding of funds or develop a protocol for referring matters, where appropriate, to OSERS for investigation and enforcement through partial withholding under the IDEA.

b. Collaborate with the DOJ to pursue MINSPED issues in desegregation cases. Where states and school districts refuse to change their practices to reduce disproportionality, refer those matters to DOJ for legal action.

CONCLUSION

OCR's admirable efforts to reduce minority overrepresentation in special education have been hampered by structural, tactical, and administrative barriers. OCR's early success with desegregation shows that, given clear legal standards and the political will to enforce those standards, dramatic change is possible. The ongoing and dramatic overrepresentation of minority students in special education described throughout this volume demands that OCR, with the support of the executive and legislative branches, give this issue top priority. In so doing, it should emphasize public education and collaboration with other stakeholders, increase the effectiveness of its compliance and complaint reviews, remove administrative barriers to pursuing its civil rights goals, and employ the full range of available enforcement tools. Title VI "makes serious civil rights enforcement possible in American education, but it only works when the executive branch is committed to full implementation and when this standard is supported by the courts."[94] OCR can and must be effective in remedying the circumstances that lead to this serious misuse of special education.

NOTES

1. Memorandum from Norma V. Cantú to All Staff of the Office for Civil Rights, U.S. Department of Education 1 (July 6, 1995) [1995 Cantú Memo] (on file with author). Disproportionate representation can also violate Section 504 of the Rehabilitation Act of 1973, 29 U.S.C. § 794 (West, 1999).
2. 1995 Cantú Memo, *supra* note 1, at 1.
3. 121 S.Ct. 1511 (2001). For a discussion of the implications of *Sandoval v. Alexander*, see Daniel J. Losen and Kevin G. Welner, this volume.
4. *See, e.g.*, 28 C.F.R. § 42.104(b)(2)(2000); 34 C.F.R. § 100.3(b)(2)(2000).
5. STEPHEN C. HALPERN, ON THE LIMITS OF THE LAW: THE IRONIC LEGACY OF TITLE VI OF THE 1964 CIVIL RIGHTS ACT 304-05 (1995).
6. 42 U.S.C. § 2000d (West 1994). While Title VI enforcement was initially conducted by staff scattered among a variety of offices at the Department of Health, Education and Welfare, in 1965 the agency established OCR, giving it enforcement authority, involving it in the development of all relevant regulations, and giving it full responsibility for interpretive guidelines. GARY ORFIELD, THE RECONSTRUCTION OF SOUTHERN EDUCATION 324, 328 (1969).
7. 42 U.S.C. § 2000d-1. In this chapter, "recipient" refers to any educational entity that receives federal funds.
8. Department of Education Organization Act of 1979, Pub. L. No. 96-88, 20 U.S.C. § 3401 et seq. (West 2000).
9. UNITED STATES COMMISSION ON CIVIL RIGHTS, EQUAL EDUCATIONAL OPPORTUNITY PROJECT SERIES, VOL. I, at 187-90 (December, 1996) [CCR 1996 Report].
10. *Id.* at 188-89. The twelve Enforcement Offices are located in Boston, New York, Philadelphia, Atlanta, Chicago, Dallas, Kansas City, Denver, San Francisco, Seattle, Cleve-

land, and Washington, DC. They are grouped into four "Enforcement Divisions" by region.

11. 34 C.F.R. §§ 100.6, 100.7 (2000).

12. Jeremy Rabkin, *Office for Civil Rights*, in THE POLITICS OF REGULATION 338 (James Q. Wilson, ed. 1980).

13. *Id.*

14. Adams v. Califano, No 70-3095 (D.C.D.C. Dec. 29, 1977). This consent order covered three actions then pending in the district court: *Adams v. Califano*, No. 70-3095 (brought by representatives of racial minorities in seventeen southern and border states; representatives of national origin minorities, women, and handicapped persons intervened); *Women's Equity Action League v. Califano*, No. 74-1720 (brought by representatives of women); and *Brown v. Califano*, No. 75-1068 (brought by representatives of racial minorities in the thirty-three other states).

15. Education Amendments of 1972, 20 U.S.C. §§ 1681-1688 (West 2000)

16. Rehabilitation Act of 1973, 29 U.S.C. § 794.

17. In addition, OCR has enforcement responsibility for The Age Discrimination Act of 1975, 42 U.S.C. §§ 6101-6107 (West 1995) and Title II of the Americans with Disabilities Act, 42 U.S.C. §§ 12, 131-12, 134 (West 1991 & Supp.). OCR also helps implement civil rights provisions in Title V, part A, of the Elementary and Secondary Education Act, the magnet schools assistance program. 20 U.S.C. §§ 7201-13 (West 2000).

18. HALPERN, *supra* note 5, at 84-91, 106-07, 287-88; Rabkin, *supra* note 12, at 344-45.

19. HALPERN, *supra* note 5, at 194-200.

20. 104 S. Ct. 1211 (1984)(holding that Title XI applied only to particular college programs that received federal financial assistance; in this case, the financial aid office).

21. HALPERN, *supra* note 5, at 198-200.

22. Civil Rights Restoration Act, 102 Stat. 28 (1988). The Act was passed over a veto by President Reagan. HALPERN, *supra* note 5, at 202.

23. Committee on Education and Labor, U.S. House of Representatives, A Report on the Investigation of the Civil Rights Enforcement Activities of the Office for Civil Rights U.S. Department of Education 28 (December 1988)[1988 House Report].

24. *Id.* at 35.

25. While this chapter focuses on the efforts of OCR, it should be noted that the Office of Special Education and Rehabilitative Services [OSERS] of DOE also failed to provide school districts with guidance and incentives to reduce the overrepresentation of minority students in special education prior to 1994.

26. Larry P. v. Riles, 495 F. Supp. 926, 989-90 (N.D. Cal. 1979), *aff'd in part and rev'd in part*, 793 F.2d 969 (9th Cir. 1984). For discussion of *Larry P. v. Riles* and other litigation challenging the disproportionate representation of minority students in special education, *see* Theresa Glennon, *Race, Education, and the Construction of a Disabled Class*, 1995 WISC. L. REV. 1237, 1263-86.

27. *See, e.g.,* Little Rock Sch. Dist. v. Pulaski City Special Sch., 778 F.2d 404, 410, 422, 427-28 (8th Cir. 1985); McNeal v. Tate County Sch. Bd., 508 F.2d 1017, 1020 (5th Cir. 1975); Anderson v. Banks, 520 F. Supp. 472, 500-01(S.D. Ga. 1981); *cf.* Quarles v. Oxford Mun. Separate Sch. Dist., 868 F.2d 750, 753-54 (5th Cir. 1989).

28. PLACING CHILDREN IN SPECIAL EDUCATION: A STRATEGY FOR EQUITY (Kirby A. Heller et al., eds. 1982).

29. 1995 Cantú Memo, *supra* note 1, at 1-3.

30. *Id.* at 1.

31. *Id.* For a more detailed discussion of the legal theories related to this issue, *see* Losen and Welner, this volume.

32. Statistical/Analytic Investigative Procedures, Over-Representation of Minorities in Special Education Placement, Investigative Guide, Office for Civil Rights, Surveys and Statistical Support Branch, April 1994 [Investigative Guide].

33. Compliance reviews are investigations of state or local education agencies relating to one or more issues that OCR has identified to be of concern. They are described as proactive because OCR selects the issues and educational entities that will be the subject of compliance reviews. "Complaint resolution" describes OCR's efforts to resolve complaints concerning alleged discriminatory practices that have been filed with the agency, and OCR's complaint resolution activities are thus primarily reactive in nature. CCR 1996 REPORT, *supra* note 9, at 206-07.

34. This and other information cited in this chapter were gathered through interviews with OCR staff and Megan Whiteside Shafer, a former member of the OCR staff.

35. OCR staff reported that there was no regular schedule, but that these telephone calls occurred approximately every month or two.

36. While members of the MINSPED Network reported that it was difficult to specifically assess the benefits of the network, they expressed the belief that this rather informal sharing of information assisted staff in improving the specificity of the monitoring requirements in their agreements, learning about educational strategies to reduce disproportion and overall special education placement rates, and developing a list of available educational consultants to recommend to local school districts.

37. The biennial Elementary and Secondary School Civil Rights Compliance Reports, which report data from a sample of U.S. school districts, are the best (and often only) available source of racial, ethnic, and gender information on rates of corporal punishment, suspension and expulsion, identification in the categories of mental retardation, serious emotional disturbance, and specific learning disability, receipt of high school diploma, English Language Learners, Gifted and Talented, and AP Math and Science in public schools. This major data collection effort has had its own difficulties. The 1996 data proved unusable, and the report on the 1998 data was not made available until August 2000. For the first time in 2000, OCR collected data from all local school districts. It also developed an electronic data submission program and worked with other agency offices to develop a single, unified data collection system regarding students with disabilities. These are important steps toward improving the quality of the data available to OCR and the public. Accessibility of the data continues to be a problem. The 1994 and 1998 Civil Rights Compliance Data have not been posted on the agency's website; they are only available from the Office for Civil Rights by written request. As of January 2002, the 2000 data have not been made available.

38. CCR 1996 REPORT, *supra* note 9, at 209-12.

39. *Id.* at 209. This approach is outlined in U.S. Department of Education, Office for Civil Rights, Case Resolution Manual, *available at* http://www.ed.gov/offices/OCR/doc/ocrcrm.html (last visited Jan. 16, 2002).

40. *Id.* at 211.

41. *Id.* at 210 (quoting Norma Cantú).

42. *See supra* note 34.
43. Letter from Rebekah Tosado, Attorney, Office of the Assistant Secretary, to Theresa Glennon, p. 2 (October 11, 2000) (on file with author).
44. This description is based on a review of more than fifty compliance-review agreements between OCR and state or local education agencies furnished to the author in response to a Freedom of Information Act ("FOIA") Request, Letter from Theresa Glennon to Nicole Huggins, Attorney, Office for Civil Rights, July 21, 2000[FOIA Request](on file with author).
45. *Id.*
46. *See, e.g.,* Memo from Megan Whiteside to Brenda Wolf and Monitoring Letters received through FOIA Request, which show such results in several school districts, including Laurel Public School District, MS; Montgomery County, MD, and Appoquinimink, VA.
47. U.S. CIVIL RIGHTS COMMISSION, EQUAL EDUCATIONAL OPPORTUNITY AND NONDISCRIMINATION FOR STUDENTS WITH DISABILITIES: FEDERAL ENFORCEMENT OF SECTION 504, Table 3.11, p. 75 [CCR 1997 Report].
48. These data are based on documentation provided in response to Freedom of Information Act Requests. This documentation lists all complaints raising MINSPED issues filed with OCR between July 1, 1993, and June 30, 2001, and all compliance reviews concerning MINSPED issues initiated by the agency in that same time period [Complaint Summary and Compliance Review Summary](on file with the author).
49. Compliance Review Summary, *supra* note 48.
50. *Id.*
51. *Id.*
52. Complaint Summary, *supra* note 48.
53. These statements were made by local school district officials to Megan Whiteside Shafer in the course of her work on compliance reviews. In 1997, Congress required state education agencies to collect and examine "data to determine if significant disproportionality based on race is occurring in the State" regarding the identification and/or placement in particular educational settings, and if such a disproportionality is found, the State must review and revise its policies, practices, and procedures to ensure that they comply with statutory requirements. Individuals with Disabilities Education Act Amendments of 1997, Pub. L. 105-17, § 618 (c); 20 U.S.C. § 1418(c) (West 2000).
54. For a discussion of the efforts OCR has made to evaluate its enforcement efforts, *see infra* text. While the author requested all compliance reviews concerning MINSPED issues, it is possible that some compliance reviews that affected minority students in special education, such as reviews concerning compliance with the least restrictive education requirement in predominantly minority school districts, were not listed on its data collection system under MINSPED and therefore were not available for this analysis.
55. CCR 1996 REPORT, supra note 9, at 164.
56. 34 C.F.R. § 100.8. Complex procedures, including express findings on the record, thirty days notice to Congress, opportunity for an administrative hearing and judicial review, must be followed for every funding termination. *Id.* at §§ 100.9-100.11. OCR can also make a recommendation to the Department of Justice that it bring an action against a noncompliant educational entity. *Id.* at § 100.8(a).
57. Rabkin, *supra* note 12, at 342-43; HALPERN, *supra* note 5, at 294-95.

58. The 1997 Amendments to the Individuals with Disabilities Education Act permit the secretary of education to "withhold, in whole or in part, any further payments to the State, for substantial violations of the IDEA. 20 U.S.C. § 1416(a)(West 2000).

59. Individuals with Disabilities Education Act Amendments of 1997; Pub. L. 105-17, 20 U.S.C. § 1408 (West 2000).

60. Office for Civil Rights, Fiscal Year 2000 Annual Report to Congress [2000 OCR Annual Report].

61. *Id.*

62. *Id.* The majority of complaints filed with OCR, 55 percent in fiscal year 2000, involved allegations of discrimination on the basis of disability. *Id.*

63. HALPERN, *supra* note 5, at 304.

64. For example, OCR's Investigative Guide and 1995 Cantú Memo have not been easily available to the public. Nor have OCR's Title VI handbook, which included a section on MINSPED, or a comprehensive report on the issue prepared by Project FORUM of the National Association of State Directors of Special Education (NASDE) for OCR and the Office of Special Education Programs (OSEP) at DOE, been made easily available to the public. The Project FORUM report, one of five reports NASDE has conducted on the disproportionate representation of minority students in special education, is available for sale on the NASDE website, but that information is not prominently displayed on the OCR website.

65. *See, e.g.,* The Use of Tests as Part of High-Stakes Decision-Making for Students: A Resource Guide for Educators and Policy-Makers (December, 2000)(archival file) and Revised Sexual Harassment Guidance: Harassment of Students by School Employees, Other Students, or Third Parties, January 2001 (*available at* http://www.ed.gov/offices/OCR). The OCR 2000 Annual Report, *supra* note 60, does not even mention minorities in special education as a priority area.

66. The National Academy of Sciences has just completed a two-year study of the disproportionate number of students from minority backgrounds placed in special education. The publication of this study provides OCR with an excellent opportunity to step up its public education efforts. NATIONAL RESEARCH COUNCIL, MINORITY STUDENTS IN SPECIAL AND GIFTED EDUCATION (M. Suzanne Donovan and Christopher T. Cross, eds. 2002) National Academy Press, Washington, DC.

67. In 2000, OCR staff with whom the author spoke could only recall one conference OCR sponsored for educational professionals and advocates for students. Held in New Orleans, it targeted the southern tier of the country and included several workshops on legal issues and best practices related to disproportionate representation. The Access to a Quality Education conference, September 20–22, 2000, held in New Orleans, Louisiana, was sponsored by the Southern Division of the Office for Civil Rights and the U.S. Department of Education–funded Equity Assistance Centers. This conference, which was attended by numerous education professionals and the author, provided participants with excellent resources on disproportionate representation and other educational equity issues.

68. Information about the federally funded Equity Assistance Centers, which were originally funded to assist school districts in their desegregation efforts but now focus on other educational equity issues as well, can be found at http://www.ed.gov/EdRes/EdFed/equity.html.

69. The need for greater public dissemination of information regarding OCR enforcement was identified by the Civil Rights Commission as well. CCR 1996 REPORT, supra note 9, at 205.

70. Oberti v. Board of Educ., 995 F.2d 1204 (3d Cir. 1993).

71. Davis v. Monroe Country Bd. of Educ., 119 S. Ct. 1661 (1999).

72. *See* Losen and Welner, this volume.

73. OFFICE FOR CIVIL RIGHTS, U.S. DEPARTMENT OF EDUCATION, 1998 ELEMENTARY AND SECOND-ARY SCHOOL CIVIL RIGHTS COMPLIANCE REPORT, PROJECTED VALUES FOR THE NATION at 1 (2000) (available on request from the Office for Civil Rights; data on file with author).

74. National Center for Education Statistics, The Nation's Report Card: Mathematics 2000 at 59 (2001).

75. National Center for Education Statistics, The Nation's Report Card: Fourth-Grade Reading Highlights 2000 at 6 (2001).

76. *See* Beth Harry et al., this volume. African American boys may be especially vulnerable to discrimination across a wide range of educational practices. *See*, Theresa Glennon, *Knocking Against the Rocks: Evaluating Institutional Practices and the African-American Boy*, 5 J. HEALTH CARE L. & POL'Y 601 (2002).

77. Increasing OCR's Impact: Draft Report of the Chicago Office Minorities and Special Education Team 37-42, 45-6 (June 30, 1999)(on file with author).

78. Office for Civil Rights, Fiscal Year 1999 Annual Report to Congress, [1999 OCR Annual Report].

79. CCR 1996 REPORT, supra note 9, at 207-08.

80. This performance review process was explained to the author by Megan Whiteside Shafer.

81. The 1999 OCR Annual Report, *supra* note 78, describes the goal of 40 percent allocation of staff time to proactive enforcement activities. Some staff reported that complaint investigations and monitoring often consumed closer to 80 percent of the time of regional enforcement staff. In addition, some staff complained that there was simply too much work given the number of staff available. Certainly, OCR increased its handling of complaints and conducting of compliance reviews between fiscal years 1993 and 1999. In fiscal year 1993, OCR had 854 full-time equivalent employees in action. Those employees received approximately 5,090 complaints, resolving 4,484 of those complaints, and initiated approximately eighty-nine compliance reviews during that fiscal year. By fiscal year 1999, OCR staff had diminished to 737 full-time equivalent employees. They received 6,628 complaints, resolved 5,369, and initiated seventy-six compliance reviews. *Id.* Because OCR does not provide further information about the degree of staff time required for its various activities, it is difficult to determine whether staff shortages unduly restrict the agency's ability to pursue a more effective approach to protecting minority students from misuse of the special education system, but the adequacy of its staffing levels requires careful scrutiny.

82. The limitations on public education and outreach were reported in CCR 1996 REPORT, *supra* note 9, at 213-14.

83. Some of the information in this section is based on conversations with Megan Whiteside Shafer and current OCR staff who wished to remain anonymous.

84. *See also*, CCR 1996 REPORT, *supra* note 9, at 213-15.

85. *Id.* at 214-15.

86. Minorities and Special Education, Measuring Impact of OCR Compliance Reviews: A Recommended Approach developed by OCR's Minorities and Special Education National Network 1 (undated memorandum)(on file with author).

87. *Id.* at 2-3.

88. Increasing OCR's Impact, *supra* note 77.

89. For example, some of the OCR staff who wanted to attend the Civil Rights Project Conference on Minority Issues in Special Education, a topic clearly relevant to their work, informed me that they were unable to receive the funding to attend.

90. The information available through the CIS II is described in the CCR 1996 REPORT, *supra* note 9, at 215.

91. Telephone call with Nicole Huggins, July 21, 2000.

92. 2000 OCR Annual Report, *supra* note 60.

93. CCR 1996 REPORT, *supra* note 9, at 215.

94. Gary Orfield, *The 1964 Civil Rights Act and American Education, in* LEGACIES OF THE 1964 CIVIL RIGHTS ACT 89, 128 (Bernard Grofman, ed. 2000)

I am especially grateful to Megan Whiteside Shafer for her significant assistance in conducting this analysis of OCR's enforcement activities regarding minorities in special education. Ms. Shafer was on the staff of the OCR Enforcement Office in Philadelphia for five years. She personally conducted compliance reviews concerning minorities in special education and participated in the OCR national network related to the issue and generously shared her expertise and experiences with me.

CHAPTER TEN

IDEA and Disproportionality: Federal Enforcement, Effective Advocacy, and Strategies for Change

THOMAS HEHIR

Overrepresentation and inappropriate placement of minorities have been historic problems within special education—persisting even after the passage of Public Law 94-142, the nation's special education law. Researchers have debated the extent to which some overrepresentation may result from poverty, but most acknowledge that poverty alone cannot fully account for this phenomenon, particularly in categories such as mild mental retardation (Harry & Anderson, 1995; Hehir & Gamm, 1997). In addition, students with disabilities who are served in urban settings in which minorities predominate have a higher likelihood of being placed in segregated settings than their white suburban counterparts, and a lower likelihood of accessing challenging curricula (Harry & Anderson, 1995; Patton, 1998; U.S. Department of Education, 1996). Not until the 1997 reauthorization of the Individuals with Disabilities Education Act (IDEA 97), which required that states collect and monitor data from schools for overidentification and restrictiveness by race and intervene when appropriate, did the nation's special education legislation directly address racial disproportionality.

Federal enforcement under IDEA has been criticized as weak overall (National Council on Disability, 1996); therefore, it is not surprising that federal enforcement of what IDEA requires of states in terms of racial disproportionality has been minimal or indirect. Despite this disappointing record, the law as amended in 1997 does contain promising options for enforcement, which could improve compliance on this issue if well applied. Moreover, advocates for the disabled and leaders from both political parties are calling for greater federal oversight and better outcomes for the children targeted as beneficiaries of our education expenditures. These demands for greater accountability hold promise for better enforcement.

In addition to trying to improve implementation through federal oversight, there are a number of situations in which effective advocacy can improve implementation through state and local activity. This chapter reviews the relevant federal enforcement structure and the federally protected rights under disability law most pertinent to concerns of minority overidentification and restrictiveness. It further examines the role of the federal government as it influences and is influenced by political pressures and advocacy efforts at these different levels. Finally, the chapter explores ideas for advocacy strategy and suggests comprehensive approaches that pursue change on the local, state, and federal levels. In each section the focus is on the enforcement of IDEA through the Office of Special Education Programs (OSEP), the federal office within the U.S Department of Education (DOE) that has statutory responsibility for implementing the act.

Specifically, this chapter will provide 1) a firsthand description of the political dynamic of federal enforcement in IDEA; 2) an overview of important relevant changes to IDEA, including the relatively new enforcement options; and 3) a proposed strategy for enforcement that could reduce overrepresentation and promote the effective implementation of IDEA for minorities who have disabilities. The ideas presented here were developed over my six years as director of OSEP during the Clinton administration and my previous fifteen-plus years of experience in urban education. I state this not simply to reinforce my credibility to speak on the issue, but also so the reader may take into account my biases.

THE ENFORCEMENT STRUCTURE

Concerns about minority overrepresentation in special education could potentially trigger intervention by any one of three federal agencies. Enforcement of the federal antidiscrimination provisions that protect the civil rights of students with disabilities and students who are racial minorities is conducted by the Office for Civil Rights (OCR) of the U.S. Department of Education and by the U.S. Department of Justice (DOJ). The Office for Civil Rights has jurisdiction to review complaints on matters such as racial overrepresentation and may intervene in a variety of ways. It can also initiate its own investigation, called a compliance review. Ultimately, OCR can withhold all federal education funding from a district if necessary, but it usually brokers a resolution agreement with the district that is in violation. The agency can also refer cases to the Department of Justice for further adjudication. OCR has jurisdiction to enforce antidiscrimination laws, including disability-based claims under Section 504 of the Rehabilitation Act of 1973 and claims of racial discrimination under Title VI of the Civil Rights Act of 1964. But it is not charged with federal oversight of the IDEA. A critical difference is that IDEA is a grants-to-states program. Unlike Section 504, enforcement and oversight of IDEA by OSEP focuses primarily on proper implementation of the act by states, not on whether students experience discrimination.

Therefore, it is OSEP, the grant administrator, and not OCR that is charged with the proper implementation of IDEA. In the course of giving grants to states and school districts to provide special education, the IDEA also specifies what kinds of students must be served in what kind of educational setting, how such services should be provided, and includes extensive due-process rights for parents and children to ensure that students with disabilities receive a free appropriate education. The law also contains "child find provisions," which require that school districts identify for services all students with qualifying disabilities. Part of the grant package is that states must provide parents with a broad array of rights, including clear notice of the right to challenge identification, placement, and the specific nature of the educational services the school offers to the student.

OSEP enforces IDEA through state departments of education for Part B (preK–12) and through lead agencies for Part C (infants to age three). The provisions regarding racial disproportionality are found in Part B (students age 3–21). It is important to note, however, that OSEP oversees the implementation and enforcement by the states. By law, each state has its own administrative hearing process to handle complaints and is supposed to perform other oversight and enforcement functions vis à vis schools and districts. OSEP reviews state implementation and ensures that state enforcement efforts are meeting IDEA's requirements. Where states are not complying with the law, OSEP may act to bring about compliance, including withholding of IDEA funds in whole or in part.

Both OSEP and OCR can refer cases to the U.S. Department of Justice for further legal proceedings, but this rarely happens. DOJ's involvement in addressing racial disproportionality in special education is primarily limited to desegregation cases in which DOJ has been a party and special education disparities have been raised as an indicator of unlawful segregation (see Losen & Welner, this volume).

IDEA: OVERREPRESENTATION AND ENFORCEMENT

The lack of attention to the problem of minority overrepresentation needs to be understood against the backdrop of weak federal enforcement of IDEA. In 1996, the National Council on Disability convened 350 disability leaders from throughout the country. These leaders summarized enforcement of IDEA and other relevant laws as follows:

> Despite progress in the last decade in educating students with disabilities, current federal and state laws have failed to ensure the delivery of a free appropriate public education for too many students with disabilities. . . . Lack of accountability, poor enforcement, and systemic barriers have robbed too many students of their educational rights and opportunities and have produced a separate system of education for students with disabilities rather than one unified system that ensures full and equal physical, programmatic, and communication access for all students. (National Council on Disability, 1996, p. 53)

In a subsequent comprehensive report on IDEA enforcement, the National Council on Disability noted, "Although Department of Education Secretary Richard W. Riley has been more aggressive in his efforts to monitor compliance and take more formal enforcement action involving sanctions than all of his predecessors combined, formal enforcement of IDEA has been very limited" (National Council on Disability, 2001, p. 7).

Although problems with racial disparities persist, OSEP did work on the problem of racial disparities in identification and placement through funding research, technical assistance, and personnel preparation. Moreover, before collecting data on race was required by IDEA in 1997, OSEP's largest study of the implementation of the act, the National Longitudinal Transition Study, included race in its entire design (Wagner, Blackorby, Cameto, & Newman, 1993). This study collected a large amount of data that shed light on the issue and was used by proponents of many of the changes included in IDEA 97. Further, OSEP funded a research center on minorities in special education to provide fellowships for promising minority researchers. The National Institute on Urban School Improvement was funded in 1998 to promote inclusive education in urban settings. These activities not only increased our understanding in this area, but also helped develop important infrastructures needed for the work of researching and developing solutions.

The Department of Education has also been active in its legislative role. The changes to IDEA adopted in 1997 that addressed minority overrepresentation were largely proposed to Congress by the Clinton administration.

The 1997 amendments to IDEA addressed both the discretionary grant programs and the Part B program. The findings section of the statute expressed congressional intent that "greater efforts [be made] to prevent the intensification of problems connected with mislabeling and high dropout rates among minority children with disabilities" (IDEA, 1997).

These findings were supported by statutory requirements. States now have an affirmative responsibility to monitor and intervene where overrepresentation occurs. If a state does not do this, it runs the risk of losing its eligibility to receive funds under IDEA.

Finally, the political leadership of the department has used its "bully pulpit" function frequently to draw attention to this issue. During the Clinton administration, Secretary Riley directly addressed this issue in speeches, and Assistant Secretary Judy Heumann promoted inclusive education and racial equity in countless speeches throughout her tenure. The Eighteenth Annual Report to Congress on the Implementation of IDEA devoted a good deal of analysis by the administration to the issue of special education in urban areas (U.S. Department of Education, 1996).

OSEP's monitoring and enforcement of IDEA with regard to reducing racial disproportionality have been indirect, in that they have addressed problems and sought legal remedies in areas that particularly impact minorities. For example, minorities are disproportionately placed in more restrictive settings. OSEP's monitoring activity has routinely reviewed whether students were being educated in the least restrictive environment (LRE), and therefore this federal oversight has likely benefited a large percentage of minority children with disabilities. Likewise, because minority children with disabilities are disproportionately subjected to school expulsion, OSEP's enforcement activities involving the prohibition of ceasing services for students expelled from school likely had particularly important benefits for minority children, as would OSEP's enforcement of ensuring the provision of education to students in correctional facilities.

The provision of services in the LRE—that is, the statutory preference for providing education as much as appropriate within mainstream settings—received much attention from the political leadership in both the Reagan and Clinton administrations. The law requires that educational settings be determined based on each student's individual need. However, based on research showing that students with disabilities progress faster academically and socially when educated with nondisabled peers (see p. 235, National Longitudinal Transition Study), the law also requires that students with disabilities be educated with nondisabled peers to the maximum extent appropriate. OSEP's monitoring process has reflected an emphasis on this legal requirement.

Although enforcement involving sanctions and the threat of withholding funds has been infrequent, this activity may have arguably produced demonstrable change. From the 1986–1987 school year to the 1996–1997 school year, the number of students receiving special education services primarily in general education classrooms increased significantly, from 27 percent to 44 percent (Hehir & Gamm, 1997). It is likely that minority students benefited from this activity, given the high rate of minorities within special education and the well-documented tendency to educate minority students who have disabilities in more restrictive settings than white students who are similarly challenged.

THE POLITICAL DYNAMICS OF FEDERAL ENFORCEMENT OF IDEA

During the Clinton years, enforcement of IDEA that involved the threat of withholding funds and which had an impact on minority students was initiated twice. Both examples illustrate the political dynamic of federal enforcement of IDEA. One involved the movement to withhold funds from the state of Virginia for failing to provide services to students expelled from school. The other involved the state of California's refusal to provide services to students with disabilities incarcerated in state prisons. In Virginia, the affected students were disproportionately African American. California prisons, like those elsewhere, have disproportionate numbers of inmates who are minorities (Bilchik, 1999; Males & Macallair, 2000). Both of these actions involved the DOE's historic pre–IDEA 97 *interpretation* of the statute's requirement that Free Appropriate Public Education (FAPE) be provided to all eligible students (those determined disabled under IDEA), regardless of school expulsion or incarceration (personal communication, R. Davila to F. New, 1989).

Both actions brought intense political reaction and statutory changes in IDEA, and both have become recurring legislative flashpoints in Congress. During congressional consideration of the No Child Left Behind Act, two proposals to limit the FAPE entitlement for certain violations of school discipline failed to win approval.

Virginia's Refusal to Provide FAPE to Expelled Students with Disabilities

In 1994 the DOE was informed by disability advocates in Virginia that the state was not providing services for students with disabilities who were expelled from school for behavior not deemed to be a manifestation of their disability. (See IDEA 97 for definition of manifestation and for legal requirements for determination.) The DOE informed Virginia that if it would not ensure that these students would receive FAPE, then the department would move to with-hold the state's IDEA grant. A period of intense negotiation and political opposition ensued. Although the DOE assured the chief state school officer for Virginia that the state could legally expel students from school as long as they continued to provide services, Virginia refused to serve those students. The Republican governor, George Allen, publicly criticized the Clinton administration's action as being soft on school discipline.

While directing OSEP, I received a call from a DOE official, who had been informed by the White House that the president had read the governor's criticism in the press clips and wanted to know what the DOE was doing. She warned, "You're going to have to explain this one, Tom." As we had done with Secretary Riley prior to the enforcement action, we explained to the White House that we were enforcing the previous administration's interpretation of IDEA, which stated that all special education students were entitled to FAPE, even those expelled. Further, we explained that this interpretation was central to the statute's requirement that "all students" meant *all* students, a principle that was reinforced by a U.S. Supreme Court decision, *Rochester School Dist. v. Timothy W.* (1989). In the midst of our attempts to persuade the White House, I received another call from the Democratic senator from Virginia, Chuck Robb, who implored us to seek a compromise. In the end, the White House supported our action, regarding it as legally correct yet politically risky.

The disability advocacy community, which strongly supported the administration's action, saw Virginia's action as undermining the fundamental principle of IDEA—that all disabled students were entitled to FAPE and that any compromise on that principle could bring about more widespread exclusion. In a meeting with leading advocates from the disability community shortly after the action, the advocates unanimously urged the secretary to hold firm on the issue.

The State of Virginia ultimately brought suit in federal court (Fourth Circuit) against the DOE's action and won. The court agreed with Virginia that the DOE's interpretation of the statute was faulty and that IDEA did not contain language that meant that the act protected students expelled from school. However, Virginia's victory was temporary. When IDEA was reauthorized, both the Clinton administration and the disability community insisted that the "Virginia problem" be corrected statutorily by insisting on language that prohibited ceasing services for students expelled from school. This was not an easy sell, and the behind-the-scenes discussions were intense.

Specifically, I recall an incident when the administration was sent a Statement of the Administration's Position (SOP) on a draft version of the IDEA that did not include the sought-after language. The draft of the SOP from the

White House that Assistant Secretary Judy Heumann and I were reviewing did not address the issue either. The Department of Education's assistant secretary for legislation, Kay Cassteavens, met with us and informed Judy that we were not going to prevail on this position. She believed that the only way this could be saved was if Judy would personally meet with the president's senior staff. That day Judy wheeled (she uses a wheelchair) up to the White House with Kay, met with the president's senior staff, and prevailed. Kay informed me afterward that Judy had won the issue single-handedly. Her argument that the disability community was solidly behind this position was undoubtedly not lost on the White House political operatives. (See Shapiro, 1993, for discussion of the political strength of the disability community.) As a result, IDEA 97 added strong language prohibiting the cessation of services for students with disabilities who were suspended and/or expelled from school.

In 2001, Congress agreed to take up the issue again in 2002, when it is expected to reauthorize the IDEA. On April 25, 2002, the Senate held hearings on behavioral issues and IDEA, and concerns about discipline were in the forefront of those discussions.

California and FAPE for Incarcerated Youth

OSEP monitoring of California in 1994 identified the fact that the state was not serving students with disabilities incarcerated in its prisons (Office of Special Education Policy, 1994). OSEP sought "corrective action"—an assurance from California that by a certain date the students would be served—and warned that IDEA funds would be put on hold if it did not comply. California refused, and eventually then-governor Republican Pete Wilson became involved. The gist of his opposition was that these inmates didn't deserve special education services because of their crimes ("Phonics for Felons," 1996). As was the case in Virginia, the governor accused the Clinton administration of overstepping its bounds by threatening to withhold funds (Edds, 1994). I attended a meeting with congressional staff at which the governor's lobbyists made it clear that they intended to use his influence to change the statute during the upcoming reauthorization.

Unlike the case in Virginia, there was little advocacy at the state level for the DOE's position. Some California disability advocates told me this issue was "a loser." When I related this conversation to the assistant secretary, she replied, "Tom, I've been to those [prisons] in California and they are filled with African Americans and Chicanos. I will not sell them down the river."

The issue was addressed with mixed results when the reauthorization finally occurred. The statute made it clear that students who were identified as disabled under IDEA, who had not received a high school diploma, and who were incarcerated in adult correctional facilities must be served. However, inmates over eighteen who had not been previously identified as disabled under IDEA were not eligible. Further, the DOE could only withhold funds proportional to the number of students in those facilities. Arguably, the changes in IDEA related to this issue represented a weakening of the law. On the other hand, the new statute codified important legal rights that would have otherwise continued to be susceptible to legal challenge and differing judicial interpretations of the statute.

Before IDEA 97, there was neither explicit statutory nor regulatory language, making enforcement of the administration's interpretation open to a reversal in federal court. However, the amendments clearly relieved states from serving a population, albeit small, of prison inmates over eighteen who had not been previously identified. Further, the codification also rescinded important enforcement leverage, the potential to withhold all IDEA funds for a state. The diminished power specific to incarcerated youth was counterbalanced by the addition of important enforcement tools, increasing OSEP's power overall.

For those who seek greater DOE involvement in IDEA enforcement as it relates to minority populations, the lesson is clear—increasing federal enforcement is a highly political endeavor, and one that never ends. These examples also show how federal enforcement can lead to demonstrable change. The ultimate result of the Virginia action was that no school district in the country can legally expel a student with a disability without providing for continuing educational services.

Second, political forces heavily influence federal enforcement. This dynamic can result in turning an important issue into a political football, as happened in Virginia. Depending on the political landscape, something may be lost in order to preserve what was once regarded as a right, as was the case in California.

Third, and possibly most important, IDEA can be changed by Congress. Although IDEA is viewed properly by many as a civil rights bill, technically it is a voluntary "grants to the states program." States are required to do more for students with disabilities under IDEA than under the civil rights provisions of Section 504 of the Rehabilitation Act or the Americans with Disabilities Act (ADA). States can refuse to accept funds under IDEA (as New Mexico did for several years) and are, therefore, relieved of the requirements that go beyond Section 504 or ADA.

During my time at OSEP, three states, Connecticut, Illinois, and Pennsylvania, considered withdrawing from the infant and toddler program, Part C of IDEA. New Hampshire considered withdrawing from the school-age program, Part B of IDEA. All these actions were turned back by strong advocacy at the state level. However, in my opinion, this aspect of IDEA—that it is a voluntary state program—has had an inappropriate chilling effect on compliance monitoring and enforcement.

Further, the federal financial commitment to the program, estimated at approximately 13 percent of the additional cost of educating students with disabilities necessary to comply with Part B of IDEA—a cost that is in excess of a states' general education per pupil expenditures (President's Budget Request for FY 2000)—is relatively small and falls short of the original promise to fund 40 percent of the excess cost. Awareness of this federal funding shortfall adds to the reluctance by federal agents to strictly enforce the law. As a matter of fact, on-site monitoring of Part C did not begin until 1997 and was opposed by some in OSEP as risky and potentially threatening to state participation in the program.

I offer these cautions not to discourage advocates from seeking increased federal monitoring of overrepresentation and improved implementation of IDEA for minorities with disabilities, but to encourage effective, thoughtful, multilevel strategies.

OSEP AND COMPLIANCE

In addition to withholding funds, OSEP employs a number of other less dramatic strategies to leverage compliance. These strategies broadly involve activities concerning state eligibility to receive funds under IDEA, the legal basis for OSEP's monitoring activity. Essentially, states must assure OSEP that they are implementing the statute consistent with its dictates. Although each state must assure this annually in order to receive funds, no state is fully in compliance with the program (National Council on Disability, 1996). OSEP engages in two major activities to ensure that, although noncompliance exists, the states are moving to correct noncompliance: on-site monitoring, and determining whether states are eligible to receive funds under the act.

Every three or four years, and more frequently in problematic states, OSEP conducts on-site monitoring visits to the states to ascertain their level of compliance with IDEA. These visits typically result in a monitoring report that details noncompliance, and the state must develop a corrective action plan in response to the findings. Any state that fails to do this may be deemed ineligible to receive funds, thus triggering a withholding action. Therefore, states always respond by developing a plan, which must be approved by OSEP. It is important to influence both the monitoring and corrective action plans that result. Advocates must be vigilant and communicate with OSEP about the status of a state's effort, as the states will present their efforts to OSEP in the best light. Grassroots advocates can influence OSEP's view of the states' efforts. The Virginia enforcement action is an example of how advocacy complaints that OSEP received translated into enforcement.

OSEP also monitors state eligibility to receive funds on an ongoing basis. For instance, states must have their special education regulations approved by OSEP as being consistent with IDEA. Changes in state regulations or ongoing policies that violate IDEA can threaten a state's eligibility status. This is essentially what happened in Virginia. In less extreme cases, OSEP routinely requires changes in state law or regulations to comply with IDEA and, at times, has slowed the release of funds for a state's failure to respond. Advocates have been effective in using this process to push through changes at the state level.

Finally, if states have been ineffective with their corrective actions over time, OSEP may either seek a compliance agreement or designate a state a high-risk grantee. These actions heighten the level of federal scrutiny and may be precursors to withholding funds. Even in the face of political backlash, advocates at the state level have reported to me that OSEP's actions have improved implementation.

NEW ENFORCEMENT OPTIONS

Although Congress limited some of OSEP's withholding options where juvenile justice is at issue, it added important enforcement options to IDEA 97. The Senate report that accompanied the bill summarized these changes and emphasized the importance of enforcement:

> The bill authorizes the Secretary to withhold part B funds, in whole or in part, from States that are not in compliance with part B [grants to states for students ages 3 to 21]. . . . Thus, based on the nature and degree of noncompliance, the Secretary may determine the level of funding to be withheld and the type of funding to withhold (e.g., the entire State set-aside or the set-aside for administrative purposes). . . . In addition, the Secretary may initiate other actions to ensure enforcement, such as requiring the State to submit a detailed plan for achieving compliance, imposing special considerations on the State's part B grant, referring the matter to the Department of Justice for appropriate enforcement action, and other enforcement actions authorized by law. The committee has included in express reference "referral to the Department of Justice" in section 616(a)(1)(B) to the authority now in current law of the Department of Education to refer instances of noncompliance to other agencies. (PL 105-17, Section 616)

The potential importance of these changes to those interested in enforcement in this area are significant. Specifically, the potential to partially withhold funds may be the most important feature. In the past, the withholding option applied to the entire state grant. Therefore, every school district and every child with a disability in a program receiving federal IDEA funds would be affected. Even some advocates have been cautious in recommending withholding because it has the potential to hurt students. Also, withholding a full state grant is likely to invoke an intense political reaction, as was the case in California and Virginia. Conceivably, a future enforcement action in the area of overrepresentation could involve a few school districts within a state, thus focusing the sanction more closely on the problem. Another option that could be employed in extreme cases is a referral to the Justice Department. Given the relationship between IDEA and other statutes, particularly the Americans with Disabilities Act, this type of action may promote a more powerful intervention.

Other amendments to IDEA, although not directly involving overrepresentation, have the potential to address some of the historic problems in this area. One by-product of overrepresentation has been the fact that assignment to special education classes has frequently meant removal from the general education curriculum and a watered-down curriculum. The 1997 amendments address this issue directly, pointing out the denial of equal educational opportunity. The same can also sometimes be said for those appropriately identified; whether a child is disabled or not, they should have access to the general education curriculum (McDonnell, McLaughlin, & Morison, 1997). Disability advocates have long fought against assumptions of low expectations that frequently undergird the systems that served them (Shapiro, 1993). In IDEA 97 debates, disability advocates successfully impressed upon Congress the need to have strong provisions in the bill that emphasized access to the curriculum. All Individualized Education Programs (IEPs) must now address this issue, and following the recently enacted No Child Left Behind Act of 2001, there is no question that students with disabilities must be included in district and state accountability systems.

In addition to the requirement that IEPs address the issue of access, states must establish performance goals for their IDEA programs. At a minimum, these goals must address students' progress in achieving general curriculum standards while also addressing the need to reduce dropout rates. These provisions are potentially important to minority students served in special education programs because the students have higher dropout rates and perform less well on statewide assessments. Further, the requirement that states address the issue of dropout rates is particularly important in states that are employing high-stakes assessment programs—that is, they deny promotion or graduation based on the performance assessments. Research in this area strongly suggests that, when these policies are implemented, dropout rates increase (Heubert &

Hauser, 1999). It is hoped that the affirmative obligation of states to address this issue will provide an important counterbalance to those policies. The existence of this requirement may also provide an importance enforcement lever.

The 1997 amendments strengthened the role of parents in the special education process. Of particular importance is the new requirement that parents must be involved in decisions about the placement of their children. It has been my experience that African American parents have frequently objected to the placement of their children in special classes. They now have a clear and legally guaranteed opportunity to voice such objections.

Finally, IDEA 97 created Community Parent Training Centers, which are designed for underserved and minority populations. There are currently over thirty centers funded to serve diverse populations, from rural Indian reservations to South Central Los Angeles. These centers should provide a valuable source of information on implementation of IDEA for minority populations, as well as a foundation for grassroots advocacy.

TOWARD AN EFFECTIVE ENFORCEMENT STRATEGY

This chapter has thus far dealt primarily with federal law and federal enforcement. The following conclusions can be drawn from this discussion:

1. The history of federal enforcement of IDEA reveals a federal government that is reluctant to be aggressive, particularly as it relates to the imposition of sanctions.
2. Aggressive enforcement can result in political backlash and statutory changes.
3. Effective enforcement is enhanced by activism at the local level.
4. There are other less volatile federal enforcement mechanisms that advocates can use to promote change.
5. IDEA 97 adds important statutory requirements relevant to this issue.
6. The increased range of enforcement options in IDEA 97 may increase federal enforcement.

A proper understanding of the potential for increased IDEA enforcement must go beyond federal enforcement. Indeed, IDEA's enforcement and compliance scheme has always been constructed to be multileveled—including state government enforcement as well as judicial and due process enforcement. This multilevel approach was created to address both systemic and individual compliance problems: "In the first arena, the federal government initiates action; in the second arena it is the state government; and in the third area it is the parents of students with disabilities" (National Council on Disability, 1996, p. 36). A thorough understanding of the enforcement of IDEA must take into account all three arenas.

It should be clear from the discussion that state implementation is influenced heavily by federal behavior. However, the impact of individual judicial/due process action should not be ignored. Individuals bringing claims against school districts can have an impact that goes far beyond the student involved. Successful use of due process has caused some school districts to change entire programs to ward off similar future claims by other parents (Hehir, 1990). Class action suits, such as *Pennsylvania Association for Retarded Children v. Pennsylvania* in 1971, in which the state agreed to educate all previously excluded disabled students, arguably led to the passage of PL 94-142 in the first place (Hehir & Gamm, 1997).

Further, both the states and the federal government have used these types of suits to reinforce their enforcement goals. Massachusetts filed as a plaintiff intervenor in a class action suit brought on behalf of students with disabilities in the Boston Public Schools. (*Allen v. McDonough*, 1982) The federal government has filed *amicus* briefs in a number of cases on the side of the plaintiffs. A notable example involved a student with various medically oriented related services, *Cedar Rapids Community School District v. Garrett Frey* (1999). In this case the Department of Education, through the solicitor general, argued that IDEA requires the school system to provide the supports the child needed to access FAPE. The Supreme Court agreed in a 7 to 2 decision. This case will affect decisions involving thousands of students for years to come.

Given the history of federal enforcement (or lack thereof), an advocacy strategy is most likely to be effective if it considers activities involving all three prongs of the compliance scheme contained in IDEA. Given the changes to IDEA and the nature of IDEA enforcement, I believe an effective enforcement strategy is possible. I recommend the following:

Seek to influence OSEP's monitoring activities with the state.   Know the contents of existing monitoring reports and corrective action plans. These are public documents that are often posted on OSEP's website (www.ed.gov/offices/OSERS/OSEP). If advocates' concerns have not been addressed by OSEP, let the advocates know. Each state has a contact person assigned to be responsive to the concerns of the public. Individuals at the state level are valuable sources of data. If the contact isn't responsive, write. All federal correspondence is tracked and the person responsible cannot ignore a letter. Although I recognize that federal government agencies often act slowly, there are examples where OSEP's monitoring of states has been heavily influenced by local advocates, as was the case in Virginia. Further, OSEP holds public meetings when it does on-site monitoring. The input from these meetings often directs the agency's inquiry.

Make states defendants.   If advocates feel a class action suit is necessary, then states, regardless of their previous action, should be made defendants. The *Corey H.* case (see Soltman & Moore, this volume) is an excellent example of the use of multiple prongs to promote change. This action has yielded positive results. The Illinois State Board of Education (ISBE) was forced to provide Chicago with more resources to train staff for working with students with disabilities in inclusive settings at the school level. Further, the deposition filed by the former chief state school officer in which he denied his responsibility to ensure compliance was subject to inquiries between OSEP and ISBE concerning the state's eligibility to receive funds under IDEA. Under *Corey H.,* Chicago has moved toward higher levels of compliance with demonstrable change in student placements. (See Soltman and Moore, this volume, for a comprehensive description of the changes resulting from the *Corey H.* litigation.)

It should be noted, however, that not all class action suits have joined states as defendants (*Allen v. McDonough* [Boston Public Schools], *Chandra Smith v. Los Angeles Unified School District*). I believe this has been a serious mistake in that states have both the resources and the statutory responsibility to deal with noncompliance. Large urban school districts may not be capable of effectively addressing these issues without strong state involvement.

Develop a long-range comprehensive plan and be persistent in pursuing it.   A favorable court ruling or administrative review should be regarded as only the beginning of a protracted struggle. Given the element of risk that Congress can change the IDEA, I believe it is also appropriate to bring most of these cases under Section 504 of the Rehabilitation Act and the Americans with Disabilities Act as well as IDEA. Having findings derived from these broader civil rights statutes may ultimately serve to protect actions that are less likely to seek and gain political support. In addition, filing under federal antidiscrimination law may reduce the threat to IDEA from weakening amendments. Generally, I recommend that advocates avoid the prospect of political involvement in enforcement by using enforcement mechanisms less likely to evoke the reaction. For example, an enforcement action in which advocates, OSEP, and a state join in seeking change within a local education agency (LEA) through a corrective action plan is not likely to involve intense political reaction at a national level. Of course, these may ultimately not be effective and advocates will need to seek stronger action through the courts. When this is the case, the use of multi-pronged approaches is recommended to minimize political interference.

1. *Use a multiprong approach.*   The use of more than one prong of enforcement increases the likelihood of success and decreases the likelihood of unanticipated negative consequences, such as weakening of the law. If OSEP and the state are already involved in seeking corrective action in an LEA or group of LEAs, those opposing the enforcement to file due process claims or class action suits may spur action (Hehir, 1990). Finally, it has been my experience that politicians are less likely to intervene in matters involving the courts. Obviously, as the Virginia and California actions have shown, politicians seem free to exercise influence over administrative reviews.

2. *Seek school-level remedies.*   Advocates seeking true reform of instructional practice need to move beyond systemwide remedies and seek school-level remedies. School principals, teachers, and individual schools must become deeply involved in any effort to promote greater racial equity in special education. School principals are at the heart of the process of finding solutions to the emerging challenges of special education reform. Although early litigation has been successful in gaining access to schools for students with disabilities, a second generation of problems has emerged (Hehir & Gamm, 1997). Chief among these issues, argues Jay Heubert of Columbia University, are the fragmentation and balkanization of educational programs and instructional staff (Heubert, 1997). He points to many schools and districts that have separate staff and administrators for general education, special education, vocational education, bilingual education, and Title I programs. Too often these programs exist in isolation, with little communication among staff members. If students with disabilities are to be educated effectively in their local schools and integrated appropriately in regular classrooms with nondisabled peers, the staffs of these fragmented programs will have to collaborate with one another in new and innovative ways. Federal law now allows for this to occur.

Once the appropriate administrators are involved, intervenors need to focus on improving the teachers' ability to address the needs of disabled students. Inadequate preservice and in-service training, scheduling conflicts, and lack of administrative support all contribute to the problem. The solution, again, lies with the active intervention and advocacy of school administrators. Only they can establish the institutional expectation of inclusiveness and sense of mission that are necessary if progress is to occur. With clear expectations established, the need for significant, high-quality staff development will undoubtedly be necessary to move systems forward. Intervenors should seek remedies that require such opportunities for staff development; Part B funds can be used for this purpose.

3. *Have a clear vision of the change you want to see.*   This last piece of advice is probably the most important. Enforcement action brought about by advocates through litigation or government monitoring can have a positive impact on the education of children but might also bring negative unintended consequences. Although the education of children with disabilities has been greatly improved by such intervention, court interventions in large cities may have had mixed results (Heubert & Hauser, 1999; Tatel, 1993). In special education, such interventions may have encouraged centralized bureaucratic approaches that have discouraged school-level accountability for the education of students with disabilities, thus inadvertently encouraging segregated placements. New York, Boston, and Baltimore, which have long-standing special education lawsuits, have at the same time been faulted for high levels of disability segregation (New York State Department of Education, 2000). In the Baltimore case, a "remedy" for noncompliance for some students was placement in segregated private special education schools. All three districts serve a majority of minority students.

4. *Include numeric goals, but avoid overreliance on numbers.*   Intervenors need to be clear about the goals they seek to achieve. In the area of overrepresentation, this is critical. Although numeric analysis of disproportionality is important, some higher incidence of disability can be expected as a result of poverty. Therefore, in high-poverty districts, strict numeric proportionality may mean that some children in need are not receiving services.

Once advocates have been successful in securing an action against a district or state, the selection of remedies must be done with care to ensure greatest positive impact and minimal unintended results. Some lawsuits and government monitoring efforts, triggered by numerical findings of overrepresentation, have relied on "input" remedies such as changing referral and assessment procedures of the district. While these input remedies have been important and may have prevented some inappropriate referrals to special education, they may not have promoted significant reform in how students of color fare in the special education system. A critical question remains: What happens to students once they are identified as having a disability? Do they receive services that truly benefit them? State-reported data and the National Longitudinal Transition Study (NLTS) show that disabled students in cities are almost three times more likely to be segregated in separate schools and far more likely to be kept out of challenging academic programs than their suburban counterparts (Wagner et al., 1993). Almost 11 percent of urban youth with disabilities go to special schools, compared with about 3 percent of disabled suburban youth. Adding the figures for those in special schools with those served in regular schools but not in regular classes, the NLTS found that over 26 percent of disabled urban students were segregated, compared to 13 percent of suburban youngsters. The same study found that only 38 percent of urban students had the option of integration into some or all regular academic classes, compared to 59 percent of suburban students with disabilities. The NLTS also found that, for students with disabilities who graduate from high school, integration was associated with better educational results. LRE thus provides an important perspective from which to examine these cases (Wagner et al., 1993)

Those who seek to improve special education in large urban systems must go beyond a simple numerical analysis of evaluation and referral practices and move to a more sophisticated kind of "benefit" analysis (Hehir & Gamm, 1997). The goal should not simply be to reduce the numbers of students identified as needing special education, but to ensure that all who need appropriate services receive them. The focus should not only be on preventing inappropriate referrals but also on ensuring that those eligible for services under IDEA receive valuable benefits.

IDEA 97 has made it clear that, for most students with disabilities, special education should be seen not as a place where students receive services, but as a vehicle by which students access a challenging, appropriate curriculum. The problem of overrepresentation, therefore, must be viewed through a wider lens that considers not only the determination of eligibility but also the results of that identification. Indeed, this kind of benefit analysis would serve every child covered by IDEA.

As advocates work to address issues of disproportionality, it is important to emphasize that many of the innovations associated with promoting better, more inclusive education for students with disabilities can be beneficial for all students. In-class support for students with disabilities can also be used for other students who may be having difficulty. The availability of such support may also decrease referrals to special education and improve performance of all students in the class (Snow, 1998). Effective approaches for supporting students experiencing difficulty learning to read in the early grades may not only help students with disabilities get off to the right start but also prevent later inappropriate referrals. Schoolwide approaches to managing inappropriate behavior in school have been shown not only to increase the capacity of schools to meet the needs of students with behavioral disabilities but also to markedly reduce school suspensions (Sugai, Sprague, Horner, & Walker, 2000). Intervenors should be seeking the adoption of such practices. The greater the degree to which the remedies sought in these cases employ strategies that benefit all students, the higher the likelihood that roots of inequity both for students who have disabilities and those inappropriately identified will be effectively addressed.

In conclusion, there is much that advocates can do to address the issues of racial inequity in special education. Effective strategic advocacy in special education has been shown to promote substantive change. Further, IDEA 97 creates new opportunities for change. Well-informed strategic action on the part of advocates is needed to end the legacy of inequity for minorities in special education, which has gone on for far too long.

REFERENCES

Allen v. McDonough. 386 Mass. 103, 434 N.E.2d 1224 (1982).

Bilchik, S. (1999). Minorities in the juvenile justice system. Juvenile justice: A century of change. In *1999 National report series: Juvenile justice bulletin*. Washington, DC: U.S. Department of Justice, Office of Justice Programs, Office of Juvenile Justice and Delinquency Prevention.

Cedar Rapids Community School District v. Garrett F. 526 U.S. 66 (1999).

Chandra Smith v. Los Angeles Unified School Dist. CV 93-7044 RSWL (C.D. CA. 2001).

Corey H. v. City of Chicago, F. Supp., 1998 U.S. Dist. LEXIS 2485, Slip Opinion at 2 (E.D. Ill. February 18, 1998).

Edds, M. (1994, May 14). Allen declares victory in school funding dispute but some officials say the battle over disciplinary policy is far from over. *Virginian-Pilot*, p. D3.

Education for All Handicapped Children Act of 1975, PL 94-142, 20 U.S.C. sec. 1400 et seq.

Harry, B., & Anderson, M. G. (1995). The disproportionate placement of African American males in special education programs: A critique of the process. *Journal of Negro Education, 63*, 602–619.

Hehir, T. (1990). *The impact of due process on the programmatic decisions of special education directors.* Unpublished doctoral dissertation, Harvard Graduate School of Education, Cambridge, MA.

Hehir, T., & Gamm S. (1997). Special education: From legalism to collaboration. In J. Heubert (Ed.), *Law and school reform* (pp. 205–227). New Haven, CT: Yale University Press.

Heubert, J. (1997). The more we get together: Improving collaboration between educators and their lawyers. *Harvard Educational Review, 67*, 531–582.

Heubert, J. P., & Hauser, R. M. (Eds.). (1999). *High stakes: Testing for tracking, promotion, and graduation.* Washington, DC: National Academy Press.

Individuals with Disabilities Education Act Amendments of 1997, Pub L. No. 105-17, §1400, 37 Stat. 111 (1997).

Males, M., & Macallair, D. (2000). *The color of justice: An analysis of juvenile adult court transfers in California.* Washington, DC: Building Blocks for Youth.

McDonnell, L. M., McLaughlin, M. J., & Morison, P. (1997). *Educating one and all: Students with disabilities and standards-based reform.* Washington, DC: National Academy Press.

National Council on Disability. (1996). *Achieving independence: The challenge for the 21st century. A decade of progress in disability policy setting an agenda for the future.* Washington, DC: Author.

National Council on Disability (2001). *Back to school on civil rights.* Washington, DC: Author.

New York State Department of Education. (2000). *Reforming education for students with disabilities.* Albany: New York State Education Department, Office of Vocational and Educational Services for Individuals with Disabilities

Office of Special Education Policy. (1994). *Monitoring report: California.* Washington, DC: Author.

Patton, J. M. (1998). The disproportionate representation of African Americans in special education: Looking behind the curtain for understanding and solutions. *Journal of Special Education, 32,* 25–31.

Pennsylvania Association for Retarded Citizens v. Pennsylvania, 334 F.Supp 1257 (E.D. Pa. 1971); 343 F.Supp. 279 (E.D. Pa. 1972).

Phonics for felons: California may seek IDEA exemption for state prison inmates. (1996). *California Special Education Alert, 3*(4), 2–3.

Rochester School Dist. v. Timothy W. 493 U.S. 983 (1989).

Shapiro, J. P. (1993). *No pity: People with disabilities forging a new civil rights movement.* New York: Random House.

Snow, C. (Ed.). (1998). *Preventing reading difficulties in young children.* Washington, DC: National Research Council.

Sugai, G., Sprague, J. R., Horner, R. H., & Walker, H. M. (2000). Preventing school violence: The use of office discipline referrals to assess and monitor school-wide discipline interventions. *Journal of Emotional and Behavioral Disorder, 8,* 94–101.

Tatel, D. (1993). Desegregation versus school reform: Resolving the conflict. *Stanford Law and Policy Review, 4,* 61–72.

U.S. Department of Education. (1996*). To assure the free and appropriate public education of all children with disabilities* (Eighteenth annual report to Congress on implementation of the Individuals with Disabilities Education Act). Washington, DC: Author. [www.ed.gov/pubs/OSEP(96AnlRpt/chap4b.html]

Wagner, M., Blackorby, J., Cameto, R., & Newman, L., (1993). *What makes a difference? Influences on post school outcomes of youth with disabilities* (Third Comprehensive Report from the National Longitudinal Transition Study of Special Education Students). Washington, DC: U.S. Department of Education.

CHAPTER ELEVEN

Ending Segregation of Chicago's Students with Disabilities: Implications of the *Corey H.* Lawsuit

SHARON WEITZMAN SOLTMAN
DONALD R. MOORE

In May 1992, attorneys from Designs for Change (DFC), a Chicago-based school reform organization, and Northwestern University Legal Clinic[1] filed a federal class action lawsuit charging that Chicago and Illinois officials had illegally segregated students with disabilities in schools. The lawsuit, called *Corey H. et al. v. Chicago Board of Education and Illinois State Board of Education*[2] was brought on behalf of the more than 40,000 students with disabilities then enrolled in the Chicago Public Schools.[3] The lawsuit alleged violations of the least restrictive environment (LRE) provisions of the federal Individuals with Disabilities Education Act (IDEA).[4]

The *Corey H.* lawsuit reflects lessons learned from many years of research and advocacy efforts by DFC, much of which specifically focused on remedying racial disparities in special education. For example, DFC research in the 1980s revealed that 13,000 Chicago students were classified as mildly mentally retarded (Educable Mentally Handicapped, or EMH) and were overwhelmingly enrolled in separate classes or schools. Chicago had by far the largest enrollment of students in EMH classes of any urban school system in the nation, and more than 10,500 of these 13,000 students were African American. These data (coupled with direct experience in assisting parents of students with disabilities) indicated that, while many Chicago students who needed special education services were not receiving them, thousands of Chicago's African American students were misclassified in segregated classes for the mentally retarded.[5] DFC's reform efforts seeking to remedy the problem of misclassification of African American students as EMH had mixed results, in part due to the narrow focus on one disability label. *Corey H.* is much broader in scope and remedy than prior efforts, as it encompasses the unwarranted segregation of all students with disabilities.

Under the IDEA, all children with disabilities are entitled to a "free, appropriate, public education" (FAPE)[6] based on their individual needs,[7] including being educated in the least restrictive environment. The IDEA's LRE mandate requires that "to the maximum extent appropriate, children with disabilities . . . are educated with children who are not disabled, and special classes, separate schooling, or other removal of children with disabilities from the regular educational environment occurs only when the nature or severity of the disability of a child is such that education in regular classes with the use of supplementary aids and services cannot be achieved satisfactorily."[8] Research since the LRE requirement became part of federal law in 1975[9] has documented the positive educational and social effects of educating children with and without disabilities together in the regular education classroom.[10]

This chapter analyzes DFC's previous research and reform strategies, the litigation strategy through the *Corey H.* settlements, and initial implementation of the settlement agreements. The authors emphasize both the multimethod advocacy effort employed and the view of schools and school districts as complex "human systems." Carrying out litigation intended to benefit students with disabilities within this broader framework dramatically enhances the prospects for achieving major improvements in students' educational experiences and academic achievement.

The advocacy strategy supporting *Corey H.* was research based and combined several advocacy methods, such as community organizing, media exposure, and lobbying. Strategies in the lawsuit were based on a view of schools and school districts as human systems whose organizational and political dynamics must be carefully analyzed if litigation is going to contribute to concrete improvements in educational quality, not just paper victories. For example, the school principal has been shown to be vital in initiating school-level changes; therefore, any school-level remedy for implementing the LRE mandate must take into account the critical leadership role of the principal.[11] This theoretical focus also shaped the decision to define the *Corey H.* class as all children with disabilities so that the remedies could encompass the organizational changes necessary to educate them in the least restrictive environment.

The court approved the settlement agreements with the Chicago Board on January 16, 1998, and with the State Board on June 19, 1999, both of which are being overseen by the court through at least January 2006. The Chicago Board agreed to settle prior to the trial, and the State Board settled after the trial. These settlement agreements commit the defendants to a significant re-structuring of a wide range of policies and practices that affect the education of the 55,000 students with disabilities currently enrolled in the Chicago Public Schools.[12]

In February 1998, after a trial that focused on the Illinois State Board of Education's liability, Judge Robert Gettleman entered a finding for the *Corey H.* plaintiffs. The court ruled that students with disabilities in the Chicago Public Schools were being illegally segregated and were not being educated in compliance with the LRE mandate; that teachers in the Chicago Public Schools were not adequately prepared to teach Chicago's students in the LRE; that the State Board had failed to identify and correct LRE violations in the Chicago Public Schools over a period of years, ignoring its legal obligation to do so; and that the Illinois system of special education teacher certification based on specific disability classifications was contributing to noncompliance with the LRE mandate.

These settlement agreements reflect the view that the school is the essential unit of change for improving educational quality. Individual Chicago public schools will develop schoolwide plans for making basic changes and will receive professional development and support in implementing these plans. Schools are then held accountable through state and local oversight for this implementation, both during and after the restructuring process at each school. The State Board and the Chicago Board have together allocated more than $43 million dollars to support this school-driven change process. Also central to the settlement agreements are changes in policies and practices to ensure student placement decisions based on individual needs, rather than on disability labels and comprehensive state monitoring and enforcement of the LRE mandate in Chicago. A court-appointed monitor is charged with overseeing all aspects of implementation and assisting the parties in settling disputes, if possible, before taking them to the court.[13]

The plaintiffs' attorneys continue to negotiate specific procedures for implementing various aspects of the settlement agreements and to monitor the Chicago Board and the State Board to determine whether initial changes that were promised are in fact occurring. At the same time, the Policy Reform Team at Designs for Change, as well as other advocacy groups, are active outside of the litigation process in pressing for the settlement agreements to be implemented—for example, by organizing families of students with disabilities to press for implementation in their individual schools, seeking media coverage for progress resulting from the settlement agreements, and lobbying to prevent action by the state legislature intended by opponents of the *Corey H.* decision to thwart the implementation of the settlement agreements.

The initial settlement agreement with the Chicago Board was reached more than five years after the case was filed, while the agreement with the State Board was reached seven years after filing. Thus, the implementation of the agreement with the Chicago Board was in progress for about four years and implementation of the State Board agreement was in progress for thirty months when this was written. The agreements will be in force at least until 2006.

PREVIOUS RESEARCH AND REFORM

Northwestern University Legal Clinic's Special Education Reform Initiatives

In 1988, the Northwestern University Legal Clinic initiated a Special Education Project to train law students by having them represent students with disabilities in an effort to secure an appropriate education consistent with state and federal law.[14] As of 1992, when *Corey H.* was filed, Northwestern attorneys had represented over one hundred students with disabilities in due process hearings, in litigation, and in school-level meetings to determine student evaluation and placement. This experience led the Legal Clinic's attorneys to conclude that, even when skilled advocates were available to assist families of students with disabilities on an individual basis, the potential for securing appropriate educational experiences was limited. One issue on which a case-by-case approach to advocacy was particularly ineffective was least restrictive environment, given deeply entrenched school system procedures and practices that placed a substantial portion of students with disabilities in segregated classrooms or schools. Thus, the Legal Clinic's attorneys were open to considering class action litigation to address the LRE issue.

The Northwestern legal team had a detailed understanding of special education law and of the Chicago Board and the State Board, as well as extensive experience in litigating complex class action lawsuits. Further, the Legal Clinic was able to draw on the capabilities of law students to conduct extensive legal research and of law school faculty members to advise the team on specialized legal issues.

DFC Early Strategy and Reform Initiatives

Designs for Change is an educational research, advocacy, and assistance organization focused on improving the quality of education in major U.S. school systems, with a particular focus on Chicago. DFC concentrates especially on improving the quality of education for low-income students, minority students, and students with disabilities. It is committed to linking applied research and policy analysis with advocacy for systemic reform.

Early DFC Research and Resulting Conceptual Frameworks

After its founding in 1977, DFC carried out a number of multicity educational research projects to identify promising urban education reform strategies. Based on these investigations, in 1983 DFC identified twenty-one practices employed in effective advocacy efforts,[15] which have formed the basis for DFC's educational advocacy (see Table 1).

DFC also refined an analytical model for understanding the educational process that has guided its reform efforts. For example, the research on school effectiveness indicates that the quality of classroom instruction is critically important in determining student achievement: however, the nature of classroom instruction is shaped decisively, for instance, by the extent to which teachers collaborate, trust one another, and believe that they are encouraged to innovate.[16] Therefore, improving instructional practice must be viewed in part as an effort to change such key aspects of the school community as teachers' beliefs, deeply rooted organizational routines, and existing political bargains (in other words, to restructure the school community as a "human system").[17]

Further, the school community must be viewed as existing within the context of a nested set of larger human systems that include the local school district, the state government, and the federal government. A key challenge for advocates is to determine what changes in policy, customary practice, and resource allocation at the various levels of this complex human system will have a positive impact on the practices of school communities, and thus on students' educational experiences and learning outcomes.

DFC began to carry out the practices of effective advocacy in Chicago in the early 1980s in order to catalyze fundamental improvements in Chicago's public schools. These advocacy efforts focused on improving the overall quality of education on a schoolwide basis for all students—especially teaching students to read—and improving the quality of education for students with disabilities. DFC's advocacy efforts during the 1980s had a significant impact on subsequent efforts to ensure that the LRE mandate was carried out.

Improving Schoolwide Educational Quality

DFC's efforts resulted in a successful campaign to restructure the Chicago school system through a change in Illinois state law that applies only to Chicago—the Chicago School Reform Act of 1988. This law shifted significant

TABLE I

Practices Employed in Effective Advocacy Efforts

Area 1. Maintaining a Strong Organization

1. Provide project leadership
2. Have staff dedicated to improving services for substantial numbers of children at risk
3. Make a commitment to improve the group's maintenance activities (e.g., clear definition of responsibilities, accurate internal communication, clear decisionmaking)
4. Sustain needed funds

Area 2. Developing a School Improvement Strategy That Shapes Action

5. Carry out a cycle of analysis and intervention
6. Develop a clear advocacy strategy for improving services for substantial numbers of children at risk
7. Focus on a subsystem of the education system that shapes services to a particular group of children at risk
8. Focus on central issues determining the quality of services to children
9. Envision a clear solution
10. Bring about or capitalize on a major policy change
11. Focus on implementation

Area 3. Gathering Comprehensive Accurate Information

12. Document problems and solutions
13. Gather comprehensive accurate information about the educational system

Area 4. Building Support

14. Use media effectively
15. Develop a support network
16. Build a committed constituency

Area 5. Intervening to Improve the Schools

17. Intervene at multiple levels
18. Use multiple tactics
19. Carry out specific intervention tactics competently
20. Use bargaining orientation
21. Be persistent

decisionmaking authority to elected local school councils and to principals at each of Chicago's schools (which at present number more than 550); abolished principal tenure and placed principals on four-year contracts with their local school councils; established a school-level improvement planning process; gave principals increased control over curriculum and teacher selection; and granted an average of $500,000 in new discretionary funding to each school.

From this and other schoolwide improvement efforts, DFC honed its skills in carrying out activities such as the preparation of research reports, media advocacy, and lobbying to support the adoption and implementation of a major public policy change, and gained extensive firsthand knowledge of key institutions and actors in the educational and public policy arenas in Chicago and Illinois. Further, DFC's research about Chicago schools and its direct efforts to assist specific schools clarified how organizational change strategies can be carried out in light of the complex organizational dynamics of specific urban schools. Finally, the experience clarified common school-level barriers to the education of students with disabilities in the least restrictive environment, and barriers to collaboration between special education and regular education staff.

Initial DFC Systemic Efforts to Improve the Quality of Education for Students with Disabilities

Beginning in 1981, DFC organized parents of children with disabilities to work both to improve the quality of education for individual students and to help press for systemic changes. DFC served as a federally funded Parent Training and Information Center (PTIC) from 1982 to the present. Through understanding student evaluation, placement, and Individualized Education Program (IEP) development processes, DFC gained detailed insight into how Chicago special education was shaped at the school community, school district, and state levels. During the same period in the 1980s, DFC pursued a series of advocacy efforts to restructure the special education system in Chicago and statewide. These efforts laid critical groundwork for the *Corey H.* lawsuit and served as lessons to the plaintiffs' attorneys that helped them structure the lawsuit and the settlement agreements.

Attacking the Misclassification of Chicago Students into Classes for the Mentally Retarded   Initially, DFC gathered extensive information about the misclassification problem, including data about patterns of placement by race in Chicago special education. These data, coupled with direct experience in assisting parents of students with disabilities, indicated that, while many Chicago students who needed special education services were not receiving them, thousands of Chicago students (primarily African Americans) were misclassified in segregated classes for the mentally retarded. DFC found that 13,000 Chicago students were classified as mildly mentally retarded, and that EMH students were overwhelmingly enrolled in separate classes or schools. Chicago had by far the largest enrollment of students in EMH classes of any urban school system in the nation, and labeled African American students as EMH at more than twice the rate for white students (3.8% of Chicago's African American students were labeled EMH, compared with 1.7% of white students). Experts on the assessment of mental retardation advised DFC that, if proper student assessment procedures were employed, no more than 1.25 percent of any ethnic group should be classified as EMH.[18]

Once students were labeled EMH in Chicago, they were nearly always placed in segregated EMH classrooms in "cluster programs," which serve a number of neighborhood schools. EMH students were typically bused away from their siblings and friends to schools that did not view the EMH students "housed in" their school as "their children." These EMH classes frequently were characterized by extremely low expectations for student achievement, and it was virtually impossible for these students to escape the EMH label and segregated classrooms for the duration of their elementary and secondary education experience.[19]

Thus, DFC launched an advocacy campaign aimed at securing a fundamental restructuring of Chicago's EMH program. To do so, DFC pressed for the adoption of specific standards, for the reassessment of all students currently enrolled in the program, and for consistent, high-quality transition assistance for all misclassified students.

One strategy centered on a consent degree between the Chicago Board and U.S. government, which settled a lawsuit charging the Chicago Board with illegal racial segregation.[20] DFC sought to have specific commitments for restructuring Chicago's EMH program incorporated into the court-ordered plans for implementing the desegregation consent decree to which the Chicago Board had agreed. This effort met with modest success. The implementation plans contained a general commitment to restructure the EMH program in order to resolve a previous lawsuit on the EMH issue.[21] After DFC submitted detailed recommendations to the court to make the EMH restructuring plan much more specific, the federal judge presiding in the case required the Chicago Board to meet with DFC, hear DFC's concerns, and then to report to the court about what actions they would take to address these concerns. However, the court never specifically required the Chicago Board to incorporate any of DFC's detailed recommendations into their plans.

To bring public attention to the issue, DFC released a report on the short-comings of Chicago's EMH program, titled *Caught in the Web: Misplaced Children in Chicago's Classes for the Mentally Retarded.*[22] Along with extensive media coverage for the release of this report, follow-up media stories documented the experiences of individual misclassified students. Additionally, DFC organized a citywide EMH coalition of parent, school reform, and civil rights groups to press for the changes spelled out in *Caught in the Web*, aggressively monitored the Chicago Board's implementation of its massive reassessment of the 13,000 EMH students, pointed out how Chicago's reassessment efforts failed to meet accepted legal and professional standards, and filed related complaints with the State Board.

These advocacy efforts produced a mixture of successes and failures. DFC forced the Chicago Board to reevaluate all students in EMH classes on a specific timetable. As a result, about 3,500 students formerly classified as EMH were either returned to regular classrooms or diagnosed as having some other disability. However, DFC was unable to get the Chicago Board to carry out student reevaluation procedures recommended by national experts, who estimated that an additional 3,500 students still remained misclassified in Chicago's EMH classes. Nor was DFC able to secure consistent transition help for misclassified students who were returned to regular education classrooms.

These efforts contributed to a marked decline in the placement of additional students in EMH classes in subsequent years. The statewide enrollment in EMH classes for African American students fell by half—from 14,821 in 1981 to 7,381 in 1989. However, the overall placement rates in Chicago and in Illinois in separate special education classrooms and schools did not decline significantly during the 1980s. In 1986, 26 percent of all Illinois students with disabilities were enrolled full-time in separate classrooms and schools, while in 1989 this percentage stood at 24 percent—a marginal drop. Further, the comparable percentages of African American students in Illinois fell only slightly during the 1980s; they were 36 percent in 1986 and 34 percent in 1989.[23]

Thus, one major lesson of the campaign to restructure Chicago's EMH program was that Designs for Change had to extend its concerns beyond a specific disability label to focus more broadly on the issue of least restrictive environment. A second lesson was that in advocating for students to be placed in less restrictive settings, strong guarantees were needed that these students would receive proper aids and supports, rather than simply being "dumped" into the regular classroom.

Challenging Delays in Evaluation and Placement in Chicago   One persistent problem that DFC's parent education and organizing effort constantly confronted in the early 1980s was delay in the evaluation and placement of students with disabilities. In 1986, the federal Office for Civil Rights (OCR) issued a letter of findings against the Chicago Board[24] stating that 78 percent of students referred for special education evaluation had not been evaluated within the 60-day time limit mandated by state law. Further, 41 percent of those judged to need special education services did not receive them within the legal time lines. A substantial number of students waited two or more years to be evaluated and provided with services, and delays were particularly severe for Hispanic students. After the OCR letter of findings was issued, the Chicago Board failed to negotiate a satisfactory settlement of the complaint, and OCR moved toward a trial before an administrative law judge in 1987.[25]

Designs for Change gained friend of the court status in the OCR proceeding, submitted extensive pretrial and posttrial briefs, and secured substantial media coverage about these problems. After the administrative law judge ruled in 1988 that Chicago was indeed violating requirements for timely evaluation and placement, DFC offered detailed recommendations to OCR as to what would constitute an adequate remedy.

The time-lines initiative resulted in a mixture of successes and failures. In 1989, the Chicago Board was only completing 42 percent of student evaluations within sixty days. By 1994 this percentage had risen to 75 percent and continued to climb. Major improvement had taken place,[26] but DFC was unable to persuade OCR to press for specific requirements in its corrective action plan that addressed critical defects in the Chicago Board's compliance plan. DFC urged OCR not only to insist on numerical targets for the percentage of evaluations completed within sixty days, but also to require that Chicago be found in compliance only if a review of a sample of completed evaluations indicated that all evaluation components had been appropriately carried out, and only if a review of a sample of placements indicated that all services promised by students' IEPs were actually being provided. Further, DFC urged OCR to determine whether the Chicago Board was improving its compliance rate for student evaluations by shifting staff (such as counselors and social workers) from providing direct services to students with disabilities to completing evaluations.

OCR refused to negotiate a corrective action plan that dealt with these questions. This allowed the Chicago Board in many cases to come into compliance with numerical time lines while still failing to meet basic quality standards, and thus to continue violating the rights of many special education students to appropriate evaluation and educational services. A major lesson of this experience that the attorneys applied in the *Corey H.* litigation was the need to seek specific guarantees that address quality issues, beyond numerical targets.

Challenging Ineffective State Monitoring and Enforcement   Compared with other state education agencies, the Illinois State Board was particularly reluctant to aggressively monitor and enforce state and federal education law. This reluctance was even more pronounced in relation to the Chicago Public Schools. DFC sought in the mid-1980s to press for meaningful monitoring and enforcement by the State Board of laws on the misclassification of minority students in special education, timely evaluation and placement, and the provision of adequate services to limited English proficient students with disabilities. DFC conducted an analysis of all written communications (obtained through a Freedom of Information Act request) between the State Board and five urban school districts (including Chicago) about the State Board's monitoring and evaluation of special education compliance. This analysis revealed the State Board's failure to address racial disparities in special education placement, lack of specific standards for judging compliance, and repeated citing of school districts for the same problems year after year with no follow-up enforcement action taken.

To remedy these problems, DFC lodged complaints with the State Board, the Senate Education Committee of the Illinois General Assembly, and the federal Office of Special Education Programs. The bottom line near the end of the 1980s was that changes in the State Board's monitoring and enforcement initiatives were primarily cosmetic. The bureaucracy blunted efforts to initiate more aggressive enforcement, even when the board's leadership took steps in that direction. A lesson from this experience that the attorneys applied to the *Corey H.* lawsuit was that only long-term, aggressive, and independent oversight of any changes in enforcement practices promised by the State Board would result in meaningful improvements.

Analyzing the Implementation of the LRE Mandate in Chicago and Illinois   DFC consistently advocated that students with disabilities must be educated in the least restrictive environment. As noted earlier, the campaign to decrease the number of African American students in separate EMH classes was successful, but ten years later the overall percentage of African American students in separate special education classes and schools (when students with all special education labels were analyzed) had not diminished significantly. Thus, DFC concluded that a major change in Chicago's implementation of the LRE mandate was the best strategy for ensuring that students with disabilities, particularly minority and low-income students, would be exposed to more challenging educational programs, would gain social competence needed to function in life, and would achieve better educational outcomes.

At the same time, implementing the LRE mandate was the single special education reform issue that generated the strongest opposition to change. Historically, Illinois was one of the first states to require the education of students with disabilities as a matter of state law. However, Illinois established a special education delivery system tightly organized around specific disability categories based on the view that disabilities could be identified with precision and that each disability could best be "treated" by a specialist in that disability working solely with students who "had" that particular disability.

Advocates for carrying out the LRE mandate in Illinois were opposed not only by many special educators committed to the state's segregated special education system, but also by some disability advocates and parents who viewed mainstreaming as a threat to the system of separate specialized treatment that they believed was best. Some also feared that school districts would "dump" students with disabilities into regular education programs where they would be ridiculed, would not receive promised support, and would fail academically. To counter such opposition, DFC analyzed the current status of LRE implementation in Illinois, as well as best practices for implementing LRE across the nation, and summarized both in a draft position paper of December 1991, *Caught in the Web II: The Segregation of Children with Disabilities in Chicago and Illinois*.[27] This research report summarized the benefits of educating students with disabilities in the least restrictive environment, the extreme degree of segregation and isolation of students with disabilities in Chicago and Illinois, and some of the underlying dynamics that led to this segregation.

Caught in the Web II revealed the striking degree and scope of segregation to which Illinois students with disabilities were subjected compared with those in other states, based on annual reports of the federal Office of Special Education Programs.[28] Each annual report provides state-by-state data by disability about the number and percentage of students with disabilities educated in different educational environments along the LRE continuum: regular class, resource room, separate class, separate facility, and residential facility. In Illinois for the 1988–1989 school year:

- Only slightly more than 3 percent of Illinois students with cognitive disabilities were educated in regular classrooms or part-time resource settings; Illinois ranked 49th among the states in integrating students with cognitive disabilities.
- Only 20 percent of Illinois children with physical disabilities were educated in regular classes or part-time resource room settings; Illinois ranked 48th among the states in integrating students with physical disabilities.

- Illinois ranked 46th among the states in terms of educating children with disabilities in regular education classrooms or part-time resource placements, considering all disabilities.
- Illinois' pattern of segregating students with cognitive and emotional disabilities had worsened during the 1980s. In 1983–1984, about 7 percent of Illinois students with cognitive disabilities were educated for most of the day in regular or resource classes; by 1988–1989, that percentage decreased to just over 3 percent. Similarly, the percentage of children with emotional disabilities in these less restrictive learning environments decreased from 31 percent in 1983–1984 to 23 percent in 1988–1989.[29]

Further analysis indicated that the segregation that characterized special education statewide was also a reality in Chicago.[30]

Underlying these statistics was a pattern of practice in Chicago and many other Illinois school districts in which the disability label assigned to a student usually dictated the nature of that student's placement (contrary to federal law). An EMH label in Illinois almost always meant a segregated classroom in a cluster program, usually at a school outside the student's neighborhood to which the student was bused.[31] A physical disability label in Chicago meant assignment to a handful of accessible schools in which most other students enrolled had physical disabilities. A Trainable Mentally Handicapped (TMH) label (moderate to severe cognitive disability) almost always meant that a child was placed in a separate, segregated school.

Further causes of this segregation included problematic state policies, such as financial reimbursement policies that rewarded placement of students in private segregated settings outside of the public schools, and a special education teacher certification system based on a set of narrow categorical disability labels.

The extent of segregation prompted attorneys from the Northwestern University Legal Clinic and DFC to undertake a systematic review as to whether the types of problems being encountered by students with disabilities that the Legal Clinic was then representing could be addressed effectively by a class action lawsuit focused on enforcing the LRE mandate. After the attorneys determined that it was advisable to proceed with the lawsuit, the first public step in carrying out DFC's commitment to a multimethod advocacy strategy was to hold a press conference to highlight the findings about the extreme segregation of students with disabilities in Chicago and Illinois and to enable the plaintiffs' attorneys to publicly communicate the focus and rationale for the *Corey H.* lawsuit.[32]

THE *COREY H.* LAWSUIT

Initial Strategy Decisions

Lessons from Previous Experience

The *Corey H.* attorneys understood that it would require a costly multi-year commitment to carry out a class action lawsuit focused on enforcing the LRE mandate. As they undertook their representation of the plaintiffs, they drew on lessons from past experiences, including the following:

- Seeking changes in such specific disability categories as "mildly mentally retarded" had had a limited impact on securing improvements in the quality of education for students with disabilities, particularly minority and low-income students.
- Seeing the school community as the essential unit of change meant that the improvement of special education and regular education should be seen as inextricably linked.
- A meaningful remedy should draw on the lessons of research about unusually effective urban schools.
- An effective remedy should both build commitment at the school community level to bring about appropriate changes and bring school district–, state-, and federal-level enforcement to bear in those school communities that fail to improve.
- An effective remedy for improving the quality of education for students in the LRE must entail clear obligations to provide adequate staffing, aids, and supports, as well as professional development for special education and regular education staff.
- An effective remedy must address the State Board's crucial role in monitoring and enforcing state and federal law in local districts. Further, there must be ongoing independent monitoring of settlement agreements or court orders, with the possibility of sanctions, to ensure that promised changes in monitoring and enforcement are actually carried out.

Defining the Class

A key prefiling decision concerned whether to define the plaintiff class as including all students with disabilities in Chicago or to limit the plaintiff class to those subcategories of students with disabilities who were the most segregated, such as students labeled mildly mentally handicapped and emotionally handicapped. The attorneys decided to include all students with disabilities in the class, since there was evidence of unjustified segregation compared to other states and cities with respect to students in all disability categories, and since the remedy envisioned would have been unworkable if illegal segregation had been established only with respect to particular subcategories of disabled students.

The Defendants

The attorneys decided that, in addition to the State Board, Chicago should be the sole district defendant because Chicago was the largest school district in the state and because the plaintiffs' attorneys already had a commitment to improve Chicago's schools, as well as familiarity with the Chicago school system as a whole and its special education program in particular. Nevertheless, the attorneys believed that a legal victory would also have an impact on the State Board's statewide policies and practices, both because some statewide remedies would be deemed necessary to correct specific violations established by the litigation and because changes resulting from the lawsuit would stimulate advocates in other local districts to press for similar reforms.

Pressing for Settlement Based on the Likelihood of Prevailing

The plaintiffs' attorneys pursued one overriding strategy throughout the litigation. Because the plaintiffs' attorneys had already amassed substantial data about Chicago's special education program and about the State Board's policies and practices (especially special education monitoring and enforcement), the attorneys were optimistic that they could further buttress their case through focused discovery and could prevail in establishing the defendants' liability. At the same time, the plaintiffs' attorneys believed that it was preferable to reach settlement agreements with the defendants, if possible, rather than to carry out an extended trial and then have remedies imposed by the court. Settlements would have the maximum potential to result in coherent remedies likely to improve educational quality. Thus, the plaintiffs' attorneys sought to demonstrate to the defendants that the plaintiffs would prevail if the case went to trial and, at the same time, that the plaintiffs were open to serious settlement discussions.

The plaintiffs' attorneys hoped that they could reach a rapid settlement with at least one of the defendants. Subsequent to the 1988 Chicago School Reform Act, the new general superintendent of schools appointed an outsider with a commitment to the LRE mandate, Thomas Hehir, to head Chicago's special education program. Although Hehir initiated reforms within the school system that were supportive of the LRE mandate, no immediate settlement negotiations ensued after the lawsuit was filed. For the first two years after filing, the litigation followed a traditional path. After nine months of discovery and related briefing concerning the defendants' motions to dismiss and the plaintiffs' motion for class certification, the court ruled for the plaintiffs on both issues. The plaintiffs then began both depositions and extensive document discovery.

Joint Expert Agreement and Extended Settlement Discussions

An important break from tradition occurred late in 1993 when the plaintiffs suggested that the parties engage a panel of joint experts with diverse backgrounds, experience, and perspectives to investigate and draw conclusions about the plaintiffs' claims. Plaintiffs made this suggestion because they hoped to avoid a battle of the experts if the case went to trial and to facilitate settlement discussions. Finally, based on the plaintiffs' extensive knowledge of the Chicago school system, the plaintiffs were confident that the experts' findings would verify the plaintiffs' allegations.

After nine months of negotiations, the parties arrived at a set of key agreements that allowed an investigation by the joint experts to go forward. Plaintiffs and defendants agreed on 1) a set of questions that would be the subject of the joint experts' investigation, 2) a set of rules for the conduct of the joint experts' investigation,[33] 3) a set of documents that would be shared with the experts,[34] and 4) a panel of three joint experts with collective backgrounds at the university, state department, and local district levels to carry out the investigation.

During the last six months of 1994, the joint experts conducted their investigation and analysis employing qualitative and quantitative methods to assess how well the LRE mandate was being implemented in Chicago. Their analysis was based on data collected through document reviews, interviews with Chicago Schools central office personnel, interviews with State Board staff, analysis of quantitative data from national sources, and a structured qualitative study of fifty-five Chicago schools.[35]

The agreement provided that the parties would receive a written report from the joint experts upon completion of their investigation. Although the joint experts were prepared to submit their written report, the defendants requested that the parties instead be given an oral report, with the promise that, if warranted, the defendants would begin settlement discussions thereafter. Within two weeks after the joint experts' oral report in 1995, the parties began settlement discussions that would last for nearly two years. During this period, the plaintiffs' attorneys sought the advice of dozens of individuals and organizations throughout the country. The joint experts subsequently prepared a written report of their findings as trial preparations proceeded in 1997.

Despite the settlement with the Chicago schools, the case against the state did proceed to trial. Although the report was never publicly released, Brian McNulty, one of the joint experts, testified at trial regarding the documentation of continuing systemic violations of the LRE mandate in Chicago and Illinois.[36] Further, Alice Udvari-Solner testified at trial to the following key findings:

- There was an overwhelming pattern in which the categorical label given a student through the evaluation process automatically determined the nature of the student's placement.
- Individualized education programs consistently failed to justify the placement of students in segregated settings rather than in less restrictive settings.
- Regular classroom educators and school administrators did not have a clear understanding of what the LRE meant or how it should be implemented.
- Regular classroom educators believed that students with disabilities who participated in their classes were obliged to master the regular education curriculum with few modifications, and that it was up to special educators to enable students with disabilities to keep up in the regular classroom.
- Regular education and special education teachers almost never collaborated.
- Adaptations made for students with disabilities in the regular classroom were "very simple or low tech."[37]

Overall, the experts concluded at trial that Chicago's special education program was in stark violation of the LRE mandate.

Preparations for Trial and Settlement with Chicago

With no settlement having been reached, a trial date was set for October 1997. In August 1997, the Chicago Board attorneys and the plaintiffs reopened settlement negotiations and quickly reached a tentative settlement agreement. This agreement was preliminarily approved by the court[38] a week before the scheduled trial and, with minor modification, was formally approved by the court in January 1998 after a fairness hearing. Key provisions of the agreement illustrate the top-down, bottom-up nature of the change strategy.

The Chicago Board was required under the agreement to carry out a school-by-school restructuring process to implement the LRE mandate through what has become the Education Connection program. The Chicago Board committed more than $24 million for local school systemic change over the seven-year course of the agreement. Each year, thirty schools are slated to begin a three-year process to design and implement a plan for educating students with disabilities in the LRE. These schools are given $110,000 to support this educational restructuring process ($10,000 for planning and professional development in Year 1 and $50,000 for implementation in both Years 2 and 3). Each school's plan must be approved by the court-appointed monitor to ensure that the plan is appropriately focused on the LRE objectives of the settlement agreement and that funds are allocated for proper purposes.[39]

The agreement requires that all Chicago Board policies "promote" the education of children with disabilities in the LRE. In addition, it requires changes in some specific policies, such as a change in the way standardized tests are administered and reported to the public to include children with disabilities.[40]

Another provision requires Chicago elementary schools to implement an informal curriculum-based, problem-solving assessment process for students who are at risk of failure or who are having behavior difficulties.[41] The Chicago Board must provide sufficient staff to provide students with disabilities an appropriate education in the LRE and carry out other required services for students with disabilities.

In addition, a key provision of the agreement required the Chicago Board to fund a court-appointed monitor to collect information about the implementation of the agreement and to take any reasonable steps necessary to ensure compliance.

Trial and Finding of Liability against the Illinois State Board of Education

With the Chicago settlement preliminarily approved, preparations for the October 1997 trial focused on State Board liability. The plaintiffs' attorneys presented two types of evidence at trial. First, they presented evidence that students with disabilities in the Chicago Public Schools had been unnecessarily segregated in restrictive settings. Second, they proffered evidence that the State Board had failed to ensure that students in the Chicago Public Schools were educated in the LRE. The plaintiffs documented, for example, that it was the State Board's policy until 1990 that placement decisions were made prior to writing an individualized education program and immediately after a student's disability label had been determined; that the Board's system for monitoring and correcting LRE problems in Chicago was ineffective; that the State Board's system of preparing and certifying special education teachers based on narrow disability categories contributed to student segregation; and that the Illinois special education reimbursement system created incentives for segregated placements.

Among the key witnesses for the plaintiffs was Brian McNulty, who concluded that continuing systemic violations of the LRE mandate in Chicago and Illinois were "persistent and pervasive." His testimony cited analysis carried out by the joint experts that compared rates of placement in federal LRE categories for Illinois for the 1993–1994 school year to the placement rates for other states and to the national average rate. Evidence included investigations or evaluations carried out by the Office for Civil Rights, the Office of Special Education Programs (OSEP), and the Illinois State Board between 1990 and 1996, which confirmed Chicago's systematic LRE violations. McNulty cited a "self-monitoring project" involving ninety-five schools that was carried out in 1995–1996 and 1996–1997 by the Chicago Public Schools, which confirmed fundamental problems in IEP decisionmaking and service delivery, such as failure to include modifications in IEPs to enable students to participate in the LRE, lack of collaboration and consultation among special educators and regular educators in the implementation of IEPs, and lack of knowledge among regular educators about how to adapt instruction for students with disabilities. McNulty also concluded that the State Board's monitoring and enforcement efforts were fundamentally inadequate.

In response to substantial evidence about pervasive LRE violations in Chicago and lack of meaningful state enforcement, the State Board offered no evidence justifying the ineffectiveness of its monitoring and enforcement efforts. Their core defense was that oversight of the state's monitoring must be left to the federal officials charged with that responsibility, not the courts. The State Board also argued that repeated approvals of their plans for carrying out their obligations under federal law indicated that the State Board's monitoring and enforcement were adequate. Further, the State Board argued that it was responsible for the "general supervision" of special education in local school districts, rather than for "ensuring" that students with disabilities were educated in the LRE.

Rejecting these defenses in a February 19, 1998, decision, the court found the State Board in violation of the IDEA for its continuing failure to ensure that 1) placement decisions are based on each student's individual needs as determined by his or her IEP; 2) LRE violations are identified and corrected; 3) teachers and administrators are fully informed about their responsibilities for implementing the LRE mandate and are provided with the technical assistance and training necessary to implement the mandate; 4) teacher certification standards comply with the LRE mandate; and 5) state funding formulas that reimburse local agencies for educating students with disabilities support the LRE mandate.

The court offered the State Board the opportunity to submit a comprehensive compliance plan within two months that aimed to remedy the violations, but rejected the State Board's plan in June 1998. Subsequently, the court engaged its own expert to make recommendations regarding remedy. In December 1998, the court held an evidentiary hearing on remedies. After enlisting settlement assistance from the court in February 1999, the parties agreed to a remedial settlement agreement,[42] key provisions of which include the following:

- The State Board must completely overhaul its process for monitoring and enforcing the LRE mandate in Chicago, with numerous specific requirements as to the content of the State Board's procedures—such as whether numerical targets for individual schools and for the entire school district are met; whether students with disabilities have access to and support in specialized schools (including vocational, magnet, and charter schools); whether students in various educational environments are making appropriate progress from year to year; whether IEPs are implemented; whether adequate special education personnel are provided; and whether regular and special educators are adequately trained to carry out the LRE mandate.
- The State Board must provide $19.25 million to be used at the local school level to carry out two- to three-year corrective action plans to remedy any problems identified through its monitoring.
- The State Board must modify specific state policies that have an impact on educating children with disabilities in the LRE, such as state-funded preschool programs, state-sponsored testing, state funding policies, and the statewide system for certifying special education and regular education teachers.
- A court-appointed monitor would exercise essentially the same oversight responsibilities as those spelled out in the Chicago settlement agreement.

COREY H.: INITIAL IMPLEMENTATION AND IMPACT

At the time that this chapter is being completed, implementation of the settlement agreement with the Chicago Board had been in progress for four years and with the State Board for thirty months. Each will run until at least January 2006. Much of the plaintiff attorneys' time to date has been dominated by further negotiations and legal advocacy aimed at turning general commitments from the two settlement agreements into more detailed plans that would lead to significant school-level improvements.

Advocacy Concerning the Specifics of Implementation

Each settlement agreement included a commitment for the State Board and the Chicago Board to develop a major implementation plan.[43] The settlement agreements also called for the development of additional plans (besides the two major implementation plans) to address such specific issues such as districtwide and school-level targets and benchmarks for progress. Further, the agreements provided for studies to inform future decisions about specific issues, and the procedures for carrying out these studies are the focus of ongoing debate among the parties. From the early stages of implementation to the present, aggressive participation and oversight by the plaintiffs' attorneys and the court monitor have been critical to move from general commitments to meaningful specifics.

By early 2002, many key aspects of implementation were still being put into place. For example, the State Board's newly developed procedures for monitoring LRE compliance in individual Chicago schools, required by the settlement agreement to be completed in July 1999, had not yet received final approval from the monitor. Further, the first State Board monitoring cycle involving twenty-five Chicago schools was not yet completed, so the new procedures' effectiveness is still unknown. Likewise, even though the agreement with the Chicago Board was nearly at the halfway mark, the systematic assessment of the impact of Education Connection (school-based restructuring) for the nearly fifty schools that have completed the three-year cycle was just getting under way.

To implement the settlement agreement, one of the defendants typically develops a required document (an implementation plan or a monitoring instrument) and the plaintiffs are then given the opportunity to comment on this document. If resolution of disagreements through discussion is not possible, the court monitor then makes a determination. Any party is then free to appeal to the court for relief. Given these dynamics, the plaintiffs' attorneys have spent much of their time for the past several years commenting on the defendants' plans, discussing these plans with the defendants and with the monitor, commenting on rulings proposed by the monitor, and, in some cases, appealing to the court.

Such issues have included details of the State Board monitoring process; local school- and districtwide targets for improvement; a new teacher certification system in Illinois that complies with the IDEA's LRE mandate; the allocation of the $19.25 million committed by the State Board under the settlement agreement to carry out corrective action plans; and the satisfaction of the State Board's obligation to determine whether policies and practices for the allocation of state and federal categorical funds support the LRE mandate.

As such issues arise on a daily basis, the importance of executing the methods of effective advocacy is constantly underscored. Attorneys need to have a clear understanding of how schools work as human systems and how changes in public policy at one level of the system are likely to have an impact on the implementation of the LRE mandate in individual schools.

Multiple Advocacy Methods at Work

DFC's research indicates the need to employ multiple methods in a successful advocacy campaign, and that litigation can be supported by the consistent use of these adjuncts. We offer two examples of the multiple methods employed by DFC to press for changes that support the implementation of the settlement agreements.

Defining a "Regular Classroom"

The first example concerns the definition of a "regular classroom." The definition is critical for judging progress in the *Corey H.* lawsuit, since one of the major targets for progress hinges on the percentage of students being educated in the regular classroom,[44] and for establishing a standard to guide schools in providing meaningful inclusion of children with disabilities in less restrictive settings. After receiving comments from all parties, the monitor defined a regular classroom as a classroom in which fewer than 50 percent of students had disabilities, that taught the regular education curriculum, and that was not remedial.[45] The plaintiffs had advocated unsuccessfully in an appeal to the court that a classroom should be considered a regular classroom only if fewer than 30 percent of enrolled students had disabilities. The monitor had ruled that there was no justification in law or regulation for adopting this more stringent standard.

Shortly before he issued his definition of a regular classroom, however, the monitor provided comments to the State Board regarding newly proposed Illinois special education rules to implement the 1997 amendments to the Individuals with Disabilities Education Act. In his comments, the monitor urged that the board provide an operational definition of the regular classroom, a term that it had employed throughout its proposed rules.[46] At the same time, DFC commented on these proposed regulations and urged that any definition of a regular classroom limit the percentage of students with disabilities in a regular classroom to 30 percent. Subsequently, the board incorporated into its final rules a definition of a regular classroom nearly identical to the monitor's definition, except that the board adopted the 30 percent limitation proposed by Designs for Change as part of its definition. The monitor subsequently agreed to adopt a definition consistent with the one that had been adopted by the State Board. Thus, DFC was able to advocate through the State Board rule-making process to influence a key standard that will now be employed in the *Corey H.* case to evaluate Chicago's systemwide compliance.

Lobbying against Legislative Opposition

A second illustration of this multimethod approach is DFC's advocacy effort for statewide changes in special education teacher certification. From the time that the initial settlement agreement with the Chicago Board was announced, DFC and other advocacy groups that support the *Corey H.* decision have sought to secure positive media coverage and support among elected officials for the process of change mandated by *Corey H.* DFC was aware that pro-inclusion decisions elsewhere have sometimes resulted in a media backlash, in which defenders of categorical methods have attacked inclusion as a hare-brained scheme that will destroy the effectiveness of special education. DFC was well aware that an Illinois coalition of special education parents, special education teachers, and private schools were mobilizing to oppose the implementation of *Corey H.*

Thus, when the initial settlement agreement with the Chicago Board was preliminarily approved by the court in October 1997, DFC and other advocates supportive of implementation of the LRE mandate held a press conference stressing the extent of current segregation in Illinois and Chicago, the benefits of education in the LRE, and the opportunities that would be provided through implementation of the agreement.[47] As each major new development occurred in the case, DFC sought additional media coverage.

Even before the State Board agreement requiring a redesign of the Illinois certification system was approved by the court in June 1999, those opposing aspects of the *Corey H.* decision launched a campaign against any move to a less categorical system of special education teacher certification. Opponents targeted the Illinois General Assembly in April and May 2000, seeking legislation that would prohibit the State Board from mandating any special education teacher certification system that was not based on existing disability classifications, arguing that students with disabilities were best served by experts trained to deal with their particular disability and that the State Board's proposal would dilute the quality of students' education by leaving their education to inadequately prepared "generalists."

DFC lobbyists worked with parent organizations and groups representing special education professionals to oppose this legislation. Ultimately, over continued DFC opposition, the Illinois House and Senate passed nonbinding resolutions urging the State Board not to implement any new teacher certification program before the General Assembly had an opportunity to examine this issue through public hearings. After this resolution was passed, Judge Gettleman stated on the record that he would not be swayed by these legislative actions. Nevertheless, DFC's Policy Reform Team was extremely concerned that if legislators were not convinced of the merits of restructuring special education teacher certification, legislative opposition could embolden a reluctant State Board to further drag its feet in enforcing the LRE mandate and could set the stage for subsequent legislative action to undermine the LRE mandate, both in Chicago and statewide.

Thus, DFC's Policy Reform Team carried out a campaign to organize public support for the LRE mandate, including mobilization for the hearing mandated by the legislature on changes in teacher certification, scheduled for July 2000. DFC countered arguments about the virtues of the current segregated special education system by analyzing and releasing the first achievement test data that showed extremely low academic performance by the state's students with disabilities. DFC advocates spoke repeatedly with the major legislative sponsors of the call for hearings, who backtracked from their opposition to the new teacher certification system when they further understood the history of the *Corey H.* litigation. A coalition of thirty organizations representing parents of students with disabilities, adults with disabilities, and special educators endorsed the restructured special education teacher certification system and substantially outnumbered opponents when testimony was heard.

Notwithstanding these efforts, six months later the opponents of less categorical certification were able to effectively lobby legislators to support the suspension of the new certification changes. As a result, the court was forced to order the State Board to implement the rules that have been in effect for fifteen months at this writing. Public debate over the move toward less categorical special education certification continues, even in the face of implementation of the new system. At the same time that the attorneys vigorously argue through formal legal channels for continued implementation of an LRE-compliant certification system, there will clearly be a need for Designs for Change and other university-based, parent, and school advocates to actively promote policies and practices supporting teacher certification that better prepares teachers to educate children with disabilities in the LRE.

Early School-Level Implementation

Central to the *Corey H.* settlement agreements are two school-by-school restructuring initiatives. The Chicago initiative (Education Connection) has been under way for more than three years, while the State Board's school-by-school monitoring (which will lead to school-level corrective action plans and financial resources for professional development and technical assistance) has not yet completed a first cycle.

Education Connection Schools

In the first year of implementation, twenty-eight schools began their participation in Education Connection. Over an eight-year period a total of 238 schools will be involved for one to three years. Of the first group of twenty-eight schools, which were scheduled to complete their three-year cycle at the end of the 1999–2000 school year, most did not keep on schedule (in part because these schools comprised the trial group), a few have barely gotten under way, and only a handful have been evaluated by the Chicago Board or the monitor's staff as of the time this chapter is going to press. Monitoring of approximately fifty of these Education Connection schools that have completed the three-year cycle is expected to be carried out during 2002.

One of the plaintiffs' goals is that those Education Connection schools that carry out exemplary plans for serving students in the LRE can become resources to help other schools make changes, either through structured visits to these exemplary schools, or through staff from these exemplary schools who provide technical assistance to the schools just getting started.

Schools Targeted for State Board Compliance Reviews

As described above, the State Board's settlement agreement requires it to develop a new school monitoring system that effectively identifies and corrects problems that contribute to students with disabilities not being educated in the LRE. The implementation plan approved in January 2001 required the State Board to visit twenty-five schools in March 2000 and fifty schools in each of the next six years to determine their level of compliance with the LRE mandate. Further, the plan called for those schools to receive an average of $57,000 in funding to develop and carry out corrective action plans to remedy deficiencies in implementing the LRE mandate. Thus, over a seven-year period of court supervision, if the plan is followed as approved, 325 schools will participate in this process for from one to three years. As noted earlier, the State Board has committed $19.25 million to support technical assistance efforts for these schools, which are to be provided primarily by independent resource groups.

The first two years of the State Board's monitoring, however, did not go according to plan. In July 2001, the court monitor issued a letter finding serious deficiencies in both the quality and timeliness of the State Board's first seventy-five monitoring reports, most of which were produced in May through July 2001. In addition, most of the corrective action plans were not yet developed and approved because the staffs at most of the schools were just finishing the school year or on vacation when the reports were finally issued. To try to get State Board monitoring back on track, adjustments were agreed to by the parties (by amending the implementation plan) for the 2001–2002 school year. The number of schools newly monitored during the year was reduced to thirty-five (instead of fifty), and the State Board was required to reissue monitoring reports and/or corrective action plans for up to sixteen schools that were monitored during the 1999–2000 or 2000–2001 school years. Since schools targeted for state compliance reviews will typically not be Education Connection schools, a total of about 550 Chicago schools will receive assistance in meeting the LRE mandate through either the Education Connection or the State Board's compliance process.

Initial Implementation of the Education Connection Process

As the plaintiffs' attorneys have reviewed plans submitted by Education Connection schools and obtained scattered initial reports about changes in the participating schools, there is evidence of a wide range of individual school responses. At the negative extreme, some schools have sought to use Education Connection as a source of additional operating revenue, have delayed developing plans, or have implemented plans that completely ignore the segregation of an entire group of children identified by disability label. At the positive extreme, a number of schools have fundamentally restructured the way in which they educate students with disabilities. Because the first comprehensive assessment of the schools completing the Education Connection program was not completed at the time of this writing, and because the parties and the monitor have been attempting to incorporate lessons from the experience with this first cohort of schools into the process being carried out with the subsequent cohorts, it is impossible to offer empirically based conclusions about the overall impact at this point.

Based on anecdotal information, it is possible to speculate that the more successful experiences involve assistance from a skilled consultant at the school site (e.g., as opposed to a centralized trainer); plans that have focused projects with measurable outcomes (e.g., increasing the involvement of children with disabilities in grades K–2 in the regular classroom, or redesigning the math curriculum to take more of a "real-world" approach that would be beneficial to students with disabilities); training that is linked to a specific LRE initiative (training staff to implement a team-teaching model to provide flexible options for students in a high school); and the presence of a school principal and a core of staff that are committed to educating children with disabilities in the least restrictive environment.

One critical barrier to the success of the Education Connection at the high schools stems from the fact that, during the past several years, the Chicago

Board has placed the vast majority of high schools in Chicago on probation based on their poor academic performance. This dramatic reform has undermined compliance. Being on probation means that a school has relinquished its autonomy to an outside consultant who directs "reforms" in the school and faces the possibility that a significant part of the professional staff will be replaced. Recent reports have concluded that the probation process in Chicago has had the opposite effect of what was intended. Test scores and dropout rates have not dramatically changed, and school staff has become demoralized and cynical about new initiatives, including the Education Connection.[48]

Penn Elementary School: A Promise of Change

Penn Elementary School is located on Chicago's West Side in an extremely poor neighborhood. Ninety-six percent of Penn students are African American, and 90 percent are low income. Safety is a continuing concern and source of stress at the school; in one instance during the 1999–2000 school year, students had to stay at school for three extra hours before it was safe to go home because of gunfire in the neighborhood. Third graders score extremely low on standardized tests; only about 13 percent of them scored at or above the national average in reading and math on the Iowa Tests in spring 2000. However, scores have improved steadily at higher grade levels; by eighth grade, nearly 50 percent of Penn students scored at or above the national average in reading and math. The Penn staff's initial focus in the Education Connection program has been on including in the regular classroom and the regular curriculum elementary students who had previously been educated in separate classrooms. School staff accomplished much of this inclusion through effective use of classes cotaught by regular education and special education teachers.

Working with a strong consultant, the staff agreed that they should have much higher expectations for students with disabilities. Students in the primary grades who are labeled EMH have been moved into the regular education curriculum with support, and students labeled trainable mentally retarded, or TMH (moderate to severe cognitive disability) are being educated with students with mild disabilities. Based on a 1999 visit (after Year 2 of Penn's involvement in the Education Connection program), the monitor's staff noted that "very impressive" units had been developed cooperatively by the regular and special education teachers (based on the city and state learning standards) with titles such as The Solar System, The Community, Classification of Animals, Life Cycles, and Matter and Energy.[49] From the first to the second year of Penn's Education Connection participation, more than one hundred students with disabilities moved into increased involvement in the regular classroom activities. The monitor's staff noted that in some instances students who had been in self-contained classes exclusively were spending ninety minutes a day in the regular classroom and that this time was focused on core academic subjects.

The monitor's staff attributed the progress at Penn to the principal's strong support for implementing the LRE mandate and ongoing direct assistance from a skilled consultant who helped teams of teachers to develop cooperative relationships and new curricula. The monitor's staff found "universal enthusiasm" among teachers, with one teacher stating that her students who had historically been segregated were energized by participation in regular classrooms and were making significant educational progress.

The next challenge for Penn will be to expand the inclusion process that has begun in the primary grades into the school's upper grades.

Gauging Outcomes for Students

The success of the *Corey H.* agreements must ultimately be judged by their impact on the quality of students' educational experiences and on their academic achievement and school completion. At present, we lack reliable data to judge the extent to which such improvements are occurring. However, systemwide monitoring efforts by the State Board and studies by the Chicago Board that are required by the settlement agreements, as well as analyses by the court monitor's staff, should provide reliable information over the next several years.

Annual progress toward meeting the districtwide numerical targets will be one measure of progress. However, data that are currently available illustrate the issues entailed in accurately gauging benefits for students. As reported by the Chicago Board, the percentage of Chicago students attending school in regular classrooms and resource rooms combined has increased from approximately 53 percent in 1994 to approximately 61 percent in January 2000, an 8 percent improvement. These data still leave many questions unanswered. For example, given the strong incentive that Chicago Public Schools staff now have to show improvements in inclusion, what percentage of students with disabilities listed as participating in a regular classroom are, in fact, participating in classrooms that enroll less than 30 percent students with disabilities, teach the regular curriculum, and are not remedial classrooms?

Further, even if there is improvement in such numerical indicators of students' placements in less restrictive settings on a citywide or school level, it is important to be sure that this improvement does not simply represent the "dumping" of students with disabilities into regular education classes without adequate staffing and other aids and supports, contrary to a series of guarantees in the settlement agreements. The State Board is obligated to collect districtwide data annually to clarify such issues as the following, which will illuminate the quality of efforts to implement the LRE mandate:

- whether individualized education program decisions regarding LRE are individualized and justified and provide for sufficient staff and other supports necessary for appropriate participation in the LRE
- whether IEPs provide students with access to the regular education curriculum and the supports necessary to master the regular education curriculum
- whether IEPs specify the methods by which progress toward meeting annual goals will be monitored and assessed
- whether IEPs of students in more restrictive settings document consideration of less restrictive options and justify the rejection of those options
- whether lack of adequate personnel or administrative convenience bar students from less restrictive options
- whether students in various educational environments are making appropriate progress from year to year[50]

Beyond these data about the nature of students' educational experiences, it will also be informative to track data over time about the achievement levels and dropout rates for students with disabilities. Another research focus of major interest to the plaintiffs is to pinpoint those schools that are doing an exemplary job of improving educational quality and student achievement for students with disabilities, and then to analyze the practices of these exemplary schools and the process of change that took place.

SOME IMPLICATIONS AND RECOMMENDATIONS

The resources available for litigation and other advocacy efforts to improve the quality of special education for minority and low-income students are extremely limited, and the organizational resistance to significant improvement in the educational systems that these students with disabilities attend is potent.

The *Corey H.* settlement agreements are in an early stage of implementation, and systematic data about their impact on students' educational experiences and student outcomes will not be available for several years. Nevertheless, the plaintiffs have been successful in winning extremely detailed and coherent settlement agreements. Further, one can conclude that, at the very least, significant changes in policy, customary practice, and resource allocations are beginning to occur with respect to both the Chicago Board of Education and the Illinois State Board of Education. Further, the plaintiffs' strategy for catalyzing school-level initiatives to improve the quality of education in the LRE has, at the very least, resulted in substantial improvements in a number of schools.

Key features of this strategy merit serious consideration by other advocates. Features that we conclude will dramatically enhance the prospects for achieving significant improvements in the educational experiences and academic achievement of minority and low-income students with disabilities include the following: a multimethod advocacy strategy in which litigation is viewed as one among a number of change levers; a focus on the school community as the essential unit of change; an analytical approach that views the school community as a human system with complex organizational and political dynamics; a research-based educational and legal reform strategy; and, last, an understanding that the school community is nested in a series of other human systems (the school district, state government, and federal government) and that a key task for effective reform advocates is to determine what changes in policies, characteristic practices, and resource allocations at various levels of the educational system will improve educational practices in school communities and thus the quality of students' educational experiences and educational outcomes.

NOTES

1. Northwestern University Legal Clinic is part of Northwestern University School of Law. Designs for Change's special education policy reform initiatives in Chicago and Illinois are the responsibility of DFC's executive director and coauthor Donald R. Moore. All *Corey H.* litigation decisions are made by the plaintiffs and their attorneys. Coauthor Sharon Weitzman Soltman, a DFC attorney and one of the *Corey H.* plaintiffs' attorneys, is responsible for those portions of this article dealing directly with the litigation. An expanded version of this chapter can be found on the DFC website at www.designsforchange.org.

2. *Corey H. et al. v. Board of Education of the City of Chicago et al. and the Illinois State Board of Education et al.*, No. 92 C 3409 (N.D. Ill. 1992). Hereafter the Chicago Board of Education and the Chicago Public Schools are referred to as the "Chicago Board," and the Illinois State Board of Education is referred to as the "State Board."

3. There are now more than 55,000 children with disabilities in the Chicago Public Schools.

4. Individuals with Disabilities Education Act, 20 U.S.C. §§ 1400 *et seq.* The Complaint also alleged violations of Section 504 of the Rehabilitation Act of 1973, 29 U.S.C. § 794, and the Americans with Disabilities Act, 42 U.S.C. §§ 12101 *et seq.*

5. In current terminology, the EMH label indicated a "mild cognitive disability."

6. Individuals with Disabilities Education Act, 20 U.S.C. § 1412(a)(1).

7. The IDEA requires that, for each child with a disability, knowledgeable school personnel develop and implement an Individualized Education Program (IEP), which specifies goals for that child's educational program, educational and other support services to be

provided to the child, the extent to which the child should participate in the regular classroom, and how progress toward meeting the goals will be measured. See Individuals with Disabilities Education Act, 20 U.S.C. § 1414(d). The statute further establishes a series of procedural safeguards to ensure that the IEP is both correctly crafted and implemented for each child, including, *inter alia*, notice and consent requirements, a requirement that the parents be involved in developing the IEP, and the opportunity for an impartial hearing on a complaint from a parent regarding the identification, evaluation, placement or provision of FAPE to his or her child. See Individuals with Disabilities Education Act, 20 U.S.C. § 1414(d)(1)(B), § 1415.

8. Individuals with Disabilities Education Act, 20 U.S.C. § 1412(a)(5)(A).

9. The Education for All Handicapped Children Education Act, P.L. 94-142 (1975).

10. See, for example, Gail McGregor and R. Timm Vogelsberg, *Inclusive Schooling Practices: Pedagogical and Research Foundations: A Synthesis of the Literature That Informs Best Practices about Inclusive Schooling* (Towson, MD: Paul H. Brookes, 1999).

11. Daniel Levine and Larry Lezotte, *Unusually Effective Schools: A Review and Analysis of Research and Practice* (Madison, WI: National Center for Effective Schools Research and Development, 1999); Designs for Change, *What Makes These Schools Stand Out: Chicago Elementary Schools with a Seven-Year Trend of Improved Reading Achievement* (Chicago: Author, 1998).

12. The settlement agreement with the State Board was developed pursuant to a process overseen by the court to fashion a remedy for the violations found in the court's February 19, 1998, opinion *Corey, H., et al. v. Board of Education of the City of Chicago, et al.*, 945 F. Supp. 900 (N.D. Ill. 1998).

13. The Honorable Joseph Schneider serves as the *Corey H.* court-appointed monitor. Judge Schneider is a retired presiding judge of County Division of the Circuit Court of Cook County. From 1992 to 1995, he served as a court-appointed monitor in a federal class action involving the failure of the Illinois Department of Children and Family Services to fulfill their responsibilities to children in the care of the state. *See B.H., et al., v. MacDonald, et al.*, No. 88 C 5588 (N.D. Ill.). In addition to Judge Schneider, the *Corey H.* monitor's office now includes three full-time staff persons, and the monitor occasionally uses consultants as well.

14. The Legal Clinic's Special Education Project was headed by attorney John Elson and staffed by attorneys Laura Miller and Nancy Gibson, along with Northwestern University law students.

15. Donald R. Moore, Sharon Weitzman Soltman et al., *Child Advocacy and the Schools: Past Impact and Potential for the 1980s*—a report to the Carnegie corporation of New York (Chicago: Author, 1998); Donald R. Moore, Sharon Weitzman Soltman et al., *Standing Up for Children: Effective Child Advocacy in the Schools* (Chicago: Author, 1983).

16. Designs for Change, *What Makes These Schools;* Penny B. Sebring, Anthony S. Bryk, Melissa Roderick, and Eric Camburn, *Charting Reform in Chicago: The Students Speak* (Chicago: Consortium on Chicago School Research, 1996).

17. See, for example, Richard F. Elmore, "Organizational Models of Social Program Implementation," *Public Policy, 26* (Spring 1978), 185–227.

18. Designs for Change, *Caught in the Web: Misplaced Children in Chicago's Classes for the Mentally Retarded* (Chicago: Author, 1982).

19. Designs for Change, *Caught in the Web.*

20. See Educational Components in *United States of America v. Board of Education of the City of Chicago,* No. 80 C 5124 (N.D. Ill.).

21. *Parents in Action on Special Education (PASE) v. Hannon,* 506 F.Supp. 831 (N.D. Ill. 1980). The *PASE* plaintiffs decided not to appeal the decision when the Chicago Board included in the educational components a commitment to discontinue the use of standardized individual tests of intelligence as the sole or primary source of information in special education screening and evaluation of African American and Hispanic students. *United States of America v. Board of Education of the City of Chicago,* No. 80 C 5124, *Desegregation Educational Components,* p. 46.

22. Designs for Change, *Caught in the Web.*

23. Illinois State Board of Education, *The Role of Ethnicity in Special Education Identification and Educational Setting Placement in Illinois* (Springfield: Author, 1991).

24. Office for Civil Rights, U.S. Department of Education, Letter of Findings re. 05-85-5001 (March 28, 1986).

25. *In the Matter of U.S. Department of Education v. Chicago Board of Education and Illinois State Board of Education,* No. 87-504-2.

26. Chicago Public Schools, *Special Report: Special Education Media and Informational Services* (Chicago: Author, 1994), Tables 2, 13.

27. The final version of the report was released ten months later: Designs for Change, *Caught in the Web II: The Segregation of Children with Disabilities in Chicago and Illinois* (Chicago: Author, 1992).

28. U.S. Department of Education, *To Assure the Free Appropriate Public Education of All Children with Disabilities: Thirteenth Annual Report to Congress on the Implementation of the Individuals with Disabilities Education Act* (Washington, DC: Author, 1991).

29. Designs for Change, *Caught in the Web II,* pp. 21–23a.

30. Designs for Change, *Caught in the Web II,* pp. 24–26.

31. Essentially no change had been made in Chicago since DFC had raised this issue in 1985.

32. David Jackson, "Suit seeks to mix disabled kids into school mainstream," *Chicago Tribune,* Chicagoland Section, May 22, 1992, p. 1.

33. The rules covered such issues as communications with the joint experts by the parties, time frames for the investigation, and the experts' latitude to hire individuals to gather data for the investigation.

34. The documents initially supplied to the experts included data analyses that the parties agreed reflected the most recent, most accurate data available showing the LRE placements of all students in the Chicago Public Schools in the spring of 1994. This Chicago database was much more detailed than the data that were customarily reported to the state and federal governments.

35. These fifty-five schools were, for the most part, chosen at random, although some schools were identified by Chicago Board administrators because, in Chicago's view, these schools represented extremes in terms of effectively educating children in the LRE.

36. Trial Tr. at 454 and 451 (McNulty).

37. Trial Tr. at 290-298 (Udvari-Solner).

38. Order Preliminarily Approving Settlement Agreement (October 23, 1997).

39. See Chicago Settlement Agreement, pars. 41 and 42. During the course of implementation, these requirements have been made more specific.

40. Prior to the settlement, Chicago Board policy required exclusion of most categories of students with disabilities from schoolwide or districtwide test results. Since a number of Chicago Board's policies are based on the average schoolwide test scores (e.g., a policy to determine whether a school should be placed on "probation" because it is not adequately serving its students), it is important that students with disabilities be included in the relevant test results. Thus, the agreement requires that Chicago not only administer standardized tests to students with disabilities as determined by each student's IEP, but also include the test results of such students as part of the public reporting of school-by-school and systemwide test results.

41. To implement this process systemwide, the Chicago Board is required to provide training (in curriculum-based assessment, assessment of classroom learning environment, and behavior management and assessment) to approximately one-sixth of all elementary schools each year over a six-year period.

42. The State Board Settlement Agreement was approved by the Court after a fairness hearing on June 19, 1999.

43. The court approved the Chicago Implementation Plan in September 1998. The State Board Implementation Plan, which was supposed to be completed by November 1999, was partially approved in January 2001, but those portions implementing the certification and professional development provisions of the agreement (par. 29-33) are still awaiting approval.

44. *Monitor's Targets and Benchmark Decision* at 34-35.

45. See *Board of Education of LaGrange v. ISBE and Ryan B.*, No. 98-4077 (7th Cir. July 29, 1999).

46. Comments by Joseph Schneider, Court-Appointed Monitor on the Proposed Illinois State Board of Education Rules: Title 23: Part 226 Special Education.

47. See Janita Poe and Michael Martinez (1997, November 4). Agreement reached on special ed lawsuit. *Chicago Tribune*, Chicagoland Section, p. 1.

48. Mario G. Ortiz, "Amid dismal first year results, CPS plans for year two," *Catalyst, 12,* No. 9 (June 1, 2001), 22–23.

49. The monitor's staff's visit took place in May 1999. All references to that visit come from a letter dated June 4, 1999, to Chicago Public School personnel from Rodney E. Estvan of the monitor's staff.

50. New state requirements to report state achievement-test results for students with disabilities (that respond to the Individuals with Disabilities Education Act), coupled with detailed requirements that are part of the *Corey H.* settlement agreement for the reporting of Chicago's Iowa Test results for students with disabilities, will facilitate the tracking of student achievement over time. See Chicago Settlement Agreement, par. 20.

About the Contributors

ALFREDO J. ARTILES is an Associate Professor at Peabody College, Vanderbilt University. His work concentrates on the nature, evolution, and prevention of the overrepresentation of minority students in special education. He currently serves as an advisor to the National Institute for Urban School Improvement, the Joseph P. Kennedy, Jr., Foundation, and the Inter-American Children's Institute on issues related to cultural diversity in special education and international/comparative special education.

AL M. BEST is an Associate Professor at the Medical College of Virginia Campus of Virginia Commonwealth University. His professional interests include collaboration with medical researchers in the analysis and presentation of data. He is coauthor of "The Impact of Socio-Demographic Characteristics on the Identification Rates of Minority Students as Mentally Retarded" in *Mental Retardation* (with D. P. Oswald, M. J. Coutinho, and N. Nguyen, 2001).

JAMES W. CONROY is President of the Center for Outcome Analysis. His research interests are deinstitutionalization, self-determination, and special education. He is coauthor of "Community Placements for Persons with Significant Cognitive Challenges: An Outcome Analysis" in the *Journal of the Association for Persons with Severe Handicaps* (with S. Spreat, in press).

MARTHA J. COUTINHO is a Professor of Special Education at East Tennessee State University. Her professional interests are the education of children with emotional and behavioral disorders, and the role of companion animals in child development. She is coauthor of "Classroom Factors Linked with Academic Gains among Students with Emotional and Behavioral Problems" in *Preventing School Failure* (with P. L. Gunter and T. Cade, 2002).

EDWARD GARCIA FIERROS is an Assistant Professor in the Department of Education and Human Services at Villanova University. His areas of study are aimed at providing equitable opportunities for all learners. Recent projects include minority needs placement patterns and teacher testing preparation strategies. He is coauthor of *Thoughtful Approaches to Implementing Multiple Intelligences: Ideas from Practice and Harvard Project Zero* (with M. Kornhaber and S. Veenema, in press).

THERESA GLENNON is an Associate Professor at the James E. Beasley School of Law at Temple University, where she teaches education law, family law, and legal ethics. Her primary research interests are in the areas of equal educational opportunity and children and families. She is author of "Knocking against the Rocks: Institutional Practices and the African-American Boy" in the *Journal of Health Care Law and Policy* (2002).

BETH HARRY is a Professor of Special Education in the Department of Teaching and Learning at the University of Miami School of Education. Her teaching focuses on the impact of cultural diversity in regular education, on working with families of children with disabilities, and on instructional methods for students with handicaps. She is author of *A Teacher's Handbook for Cultural Diversity, Families, and the Special Education System: Communication and Empowerment* (1997).

THOMAS HEHIR is a Lecturer on Education and Director of the School Leadership Program at the Harvard Graduate School of Education. During the Clinton administration he served as Director of the U.S. Department of Education's Office of Special Education Programs, where he was instrumental in the 1997 reauthorization and implementation of the Individuals with Disabilities Education Act. His other areas of interest include special education in the reform movement and least restrictive environment issues. He is coeditor of *Special Education at the Century's End* (with T. Latus, 1992).

JAY P. HEUBERT is an Associate Professor of Education at Teachers College, Columbia University, and an Adjunct Associate Professor of Law at Columbia Law School. His research interests include high-stakes testing and civil rights issues in education. He is editor of *Law and School Reform: Six Strategies for Promoting Educational Equity* (1999).

IGNACIO HIGAREDA is a doctoral candidate in education at the University of Southern California. His research centers on sociocultural influences on academic achievement for English learners. He has worked on research projects involving hearing and deaf preschoolers' collaborative play, and the impact of paraeducators on language minority students.

JAMES M. JEFFORDS is a U.S. Senator (*Independent*) for Vermont. Currently in his third term, he is Chairman of the Environment and Public Works Committee and a member of several others, including Finance and Veterans' Affairs. Jeffords is former Chairman of the Health, Education, Labor, and Pensions Committee. While a member of the House of Representatives, he cofounded the Congressional Arts Caucus and the Congressional Solar Coalition.

JANETTE K. KLINGNER is an Associate Professor of Bilingual Special Education at the University of Colorado at Boulder. Her research interests include the disproportionate representation of culturally and linguistically diverse students in special education, and outcomes for culturally and linguistically diverse students with disabilities in inclusive classrooms. She is coauthor of "The Changing Roles and Responsibilities of an LD Specialist" in *Learning Disability Quarterly* (with S. Vaughn, 2002).

DANIEL J. LOSEN is a Legal and Policy Research Associate with The Civil Rights Project at Harvard University (CRP). His work concerns the impact of federal, state, and local education law and policy on communities of color. He is engaged in transforming CRP's research into policy guidance for members of Congress and community advocates. He is coauthor of "Disabling Discrimination in Our Public Schools: Comprehensive Legal Challenges to Inappropriate and Inadequate Special Education Services for Minority Children" in the *Harvard Civil Rights-Civil Liberties Law Review* (with K. G. Welner, 2001).

DONALD R. MOORE is Executive Director of Designs for Change, a Chicago-based educational research and advocacy group. His major professional focus has been on finding ways to improve the quality of education for low-income children, minority children, and children with disabilities. He is coauthor of *The Bottom Line: Chicago's Failing Schools and How to Save Them* (with S. W. Soltman, 1985).

ROBERT F. MOORE is an Associate Professor in the Department of Teaching and Learning at the University of Miami. He also serves as coordinator of the undergraduate Special Education Program. His professional interests are strategies and interventions for students at risk for learning and behavioral problems.

GARY ORFIELD is a Professor of Education and Social Policy and Codirector of The Civil Rights Project at Harvard University. He is also Director of the Harvard Project on School Desegregation. Orfield's central interest has been the development and implementation of social policy, with a central focus on the impact of policy on equal opportunity for success in U.S. society. He has been a court-appointed expert in school desegregation cases and been called to give testimony in civil rights suits by the U.S. Department of Justice and others. He is editor of *Diversity Challenged: Evidence on the Impact of Affirmative Action* (2001).

DAVID OSHER is a Managing Research Scientist at the American Institutes for Research. His studies center on knowledge use and interventions for individuals with mental health problems and disorders. He is particularly interested in organizational change, family-driven services, prevention, and reducing disproportionate outcomes. His recent publications include *Addressing Invisible Barriers: Improving Outcomes for Youth with Disabilities in the Juvenile Justice System* (2002).

DONALD P. OSWALD is an Associate Professor in the Department of Psychiatry at Virginia Commonwealth University. He is interested in the system of care for children with disabilities and racial and gender differences in access to services. He is coauthor of "Gender and Socio-Demographic Factors and the Disproportionate Identification of Minority Students as Emotionally Disturbed" in *Behavioral Disorders* (with M. J. Coutinho, A. M. Best, and S. R. Forness, 2002).

THOMAS PARRISH is Deputy Director of the Education Program at the American Institutes for Research, where he also directs the Center for Special Education Finance. His work is in the areas of education reform, evaluation, cost analysis, and finance. His recent publications include *State Special Education Finance Systems and Expenditures, 1999–00* (coauthored with J. J. Anthony, 2002).

ROBERT RUEDA is a Professor at the University of Southern California Rossier School of Education. His research centers on the sociocultural basis of learning as mediated by instruction. He is coauthor of "Apprenticeship for Teaching: Professional Development Issues Surrounding the Collaborative Relationship between Teachers and Paraeducators" in *Teaching and Teacher Education* (with L. Monzo, in press).

JESÚS JOSÉ SALAZAR is a doctoral student at the University of Southern California Rossier School of Education. He conducts program evaluation studies for urban school districts in California. He is author of "A Longitudinal Model for Interpreting Thirty Years of Bilingual Education Research" in *Journal of Bilingual Research* (1999).

ANTHONY E. SIMS is Manager of Specialized Support Programs and State Director of Special Education for the Illinois State Board of Education. His primary area of interest is education and children's mental health, with a focus on cultural competence as an integral component of systemic reform to enhance social and educational opportunities for culturally diverse children. He is author of *A Process for Establishing and Implementing Wraparound Services in the District of Columbia: Preliminary Findings* (1999).

SHARON WEITZMAN SOLTMAN is a Consulting Attorney with Designs for Change (DFC), an educational research and advocacy organization. Her work focuses on urban educational reform, with a particular emphasis on issues affecting children who are poor, minority, or disabled. As a DFC attorney she has represented children with disabilities in two class action lawsuits. She is coauthor of *The Bottom Line: Chicago's Failing Schools and How to Save Them* (with D. R. Moore, 1985).

KEITH M. STURGES is a Qualitative Research Associate at AEL, Inc.'s Regional Education Laboratory in Charleston, West Virginia. He currently conducts applied research on directed school change, special and alternative education, and ethnic disparities in service access and use. His recent publications include "Conducting Ethnographic Classroom Observations of Literacy Instruction," coauthored with J. K. Klingner and B. Harry, in *Reading in the Classroom: Systems for Observing Teaching and Learning* (edited by S. Vaughn and K. Briggs, in press).

KEVIN G. WELNER is an Assistant Professor at the University of Colorado at Boulder School of Education. He specializes in educational policy, law, and program evaluation. His present research examines the intersection of education rights litigation and educational opportunity scholarship. He is author of *Legal Rights, Local Wrongs: When Community Control Collides with Educational Equity* (2001).

DARREN WOODRUFF is a Senior Research Analyst with the American Institutes for Research. He consults with state and local school districts and provides training to educators on such topics as disproportionality, student behavior, and violence prevention. He has also conducted research on issues in comprehensive school reform and children's mental health. His recent publications include "Support for Effective Teaching: Two Child Development–Based Approaches" in the *Journal of Negro Education* (1999).

Name Index

Subject Index

285